ALSO BY UCADIA

Covenant of One Heaven (Pactum De Singularis Caelum)

Maxims of Divine Law
Maxims of Natural Law
Maxims of Cognitive Law
Maxims of Positive Law
Maxims of Ecclesiastical Law
Maxims of Bioethics Law
Maxims of Sovereign Law
Maxims of Fiduciary Law
Maxims of Administrative Law
Maxims of Economic Law
Maxims of Monetary Law
Maxims of Civil Law
Maxims of Criminal Law
Maxims of Education Law
Maxims of Food & Drugs Law
Maxims of Urban Law
Maxims of Company Law
Maxims of Technology Law
Maxims of Trade & Intellectual Property Law
Maxims of Security Law
Maxims of Military Law
Maxims of International Law

Pactum De Singularis Christus

Covenant of One Christ

**OFFICIAL ENGLISH
FIRST EDITION**

**BY
UCADIA**

Ucadia Books Company

Published by Ucadia Books Company, a Delaware stock corporation (File Number 6779670) 901 N Market St #705 Wilmington Delaware 19801.
First edition.

ISBN 978-1-64419-020-3

Preface

Is not a Christian someone who trusts in the *Good News* and words of Christ above all others? Indeed, a true Christian is not one that places the words of men and women above the Risen Christ, but one who gladly and willingly obeys the Authority of Christ by bearing true witness to the *Good News* by serving the real needs of others.

These are not mere words of some simple rote creed, or some ancient historic event to a true Christian, but a call to action, through the symbol of the cross: That God the Divine Creator of all Existence and all Heaven and Earth loves the Homo Sapien species and specifically each and every living and deceased member; and our history and struggles upon this beautiful planet have not been in vain, nor alone; and that God so loved us, that he brought forth a "singularity" of all human beings that have lived or will ever live, in the form of his flesh and blood, who chose to sacrifice himself, to end forever all forms of ritual blood sacrifice, to forgive the sins of our first forefathers as well as our future descendants, so that we might learn that the true nature of God and the Divine Creator is love and wisdom, not wrath and harsh judgement.

Thus, as much as someone may deeply respect certain teachers, or prophets or saints, if one proclaims to be Christian, surely then it is the teachings of Christ that they consider to be the greatest of all teachings?

It is a fundamental tenet of faith of all Christians that the ultimate source and origin of all proper Christian Liturgy begins with the purposeful actions, rituals, works and tasks of the Crucified and Risen Christ. To deny such reasoning is to deny the centrality of Christian worship and therefore to effectively deny Christian faith itself.

There is no question that over the accumulation of time, the interpretation of the purposeful actions, rituals, works and tasks of the Crucified and Risen Christ, has given rise to great diversity, complexity and sometimes discord. Yet, no matter how complex or diverse the great body of Christian customs and traditions have become, there should be no uncertainty or disunity as to the ultimate source and origin of all proper Christian Worship.

Therefore, while a church and faith may have many rules and differences, is it not the rules given by Christ that are the most important?

Christ himself was unequivocal and precise on the subject of organised worship as Liturgy. Such rites, prayers, rituals and services are the direct links between the minds and spirits of the people upon the Earth and our Heavenly Father and all the angels, saints and ancestors in Heaven. Secondly, that the intention, knowledge and heart behind such rites, prayers, rituals and services is as essential as the proper forms themselves. Finally, that an authentic rite, prayer, ritual or service is distinguished from hollow or "false actions" when it is inclusive, respectful, open and merciful. These teachings are at the heart of the Authority of Christ himself in expressing the Divine Mission of Rules and Worship.

Jesus repeatedly condemned elaborate and hollow rituals, without proper intention, or designed to exclude or curse others as an abomination against all Heaven and Earth. Throughout his Ministry, he expressed his disappointment and even contempt for those who position themselves and claim to be interpreters of the Will of the Divine, yet demonstrate none of the qualities or competencies for an authentic clerical vocation.

No matter how old a rite, or ritual or practice is claimed; if it is contradictory to the Magisterium of the Risen Christ, then it is contradictory to the Divine Mission of Christianity.

If all of this is true, why then do we not have greater unity among our Christian churches? Why have they not stepped beyond ecumenical councils and mutual respect to a lasting structure, respecting our cultural and traditional diversity, yet united as one Christian family?

The same can be said for our Jewish brothers and sisters, who have suffered for many generations because of their faith. Do not all Jews and Christians share the same common foundations of ancient Biblical texts and acknowledgment of a single loving Divine Creator?

When will we finally see a unity of common organisation and respect between all who share the same essential Abrahamic faith? If not at our hands together, then when will this time come? Are not the signs around us so overwhelming that this is the time to unite? If not, then why not? How long until we finally reject those false notions and ideas that keep us in perpetual separation and disunity? When will we finally stop listening to those who do not speak either for the Divine Creator, nor Christ, nor any of the saints or prophets, but seek only power through continued division?

Should we overcome our doubts and our fears, how then might such unity look? How would a united Christian and Jewish family work in practice? What would be the structure? How would the balance between different history and practices happen, whilst maintaining unity? This in essence is the purpose of *Pactum De Singularis Christus*, the Covenant of One Christ.

To authentically read in order each of the two hundred and twenty-two (222) articles of *Pactum De Singularis Christus* will take time and effort. There is a substantial amount of information contained within these pages. Then there is the Covenant of One Heaven, also known as *Pactum De Singularis Caelum* that directly connects to this text.

Some of what you read will hopefully open you heart like a breath of pure fresh air, while other ideas may take more time to digest. Hopefully you will continue, as there is a reason this document has come to you at this time.

Yet before you even begin to read, you might still have a flood of questions: What is the ultimate purpose of this book? Who wrote it? What is their authority? Why is it called the Covenant of One Christ?

These questions and many more are answered if you choose to continue to read. In truth, the only way to authentically answer these questions in the limited space of this Preface is to ask you to please start reading from the beginning.

For those of you that have read earlier "unofficial" versions of this document, please keep in mind that this is the Official Version and First Edition and earlier versions should not be relied upon as accurate translations of the primary text of the Covenant written in Logos. The official Logos version will be made available in print in 2022, once the official versions in all major languages have been completed.

Thank you and we are humbled and grateful that you are taking the time to read the Covenant of One Christ.

Peace be to you.

Ucadia

CONTENTS

Title III: Members

Title IV: Officers

Title XIII: Sacraments & Extra-Sacramental Rites & Rubrics

Title XIV: Standards & Procedures

PRAENUNTIO

In the name and absolute authority and power of the One God, the God of Abraham, the God of Moses, the God of Solomon and David, the God of the Great Prophets, the God of Christ, the God of all Christians and Jews; and the Absolute Divine Creator of all Existence and all of Heaven, the Earth and our Solar System and Galaxy:

To all Ecclesiastical Leaders, Clergy and adherents of Christian and Jewish denominations, bodies, associations, orders, fraternities, societies, churches and entities:

You are hereby commanded to take notice of the present most sacred Covenant known as "**Pactum De Singularis Christus**" and the most sacred Covenant known as *Pactum De Singularis Caelum*; and answer within the time allocated for celebrating and bearing witness to Divine Mercy, as to any exception or legitimate objection why you should not be firmly and decisively bound by the Articles of the aforementioned most sacred Covenants as the Revelation, Ratification, Sanctification, Testification, Exemplification, Legislation and Consummation of the Divine Will of the one true Divine Creator of all Existence and all Heaven and Earth.

A. WHEREAS it is not by the will of men and women to decide when God and the Divine Creator of all Heaven and Earth speaks; and it is not to the authority of a temple that God submits, but the temple that submits to God. Therefore, no matter how great the claim of authority by a man or woman, it cannot be greater than God; and no matter how ancient a scripture or tradition is claimed, it cannot be older than the Divine Creator of the Universe; and no matter how firm a doctrine of faith, it cannot withstand even the smallest drop of Revelation from the Divine Creator. Thus, when Divine Will is delivered through such unmistakable and irrefutable Revelation and Fulfilment of Scripture by the Holy Spirit, in honour of Christian and Jewish tradition, to then deny such truth is to deny the entirety of authentic apostolic tradition and the legitimacy of every single Christian and Jewish religious body. Therefore, let no Christian or Jewish Ecclesiastical Leader or Clergy or Fraternity deny the absolute Truth of these words out of ignorance or arrogance or perfidy or impiety; and

B. WHEREAS all Christians and Jews of all denominations are united in tradition and doctrine to common Scripture, Theological Principles and Eschatology; and it is a shared obligation and moral duty of all Christians and Jews that upon an appointed time of unmistakable signs of Divine Will illuminated by the Holy Spirit as fulfilment of such common Scripture, Theological Principles and Eschatology, that all who profess and proclaim to be Christian and Jewish shall therefore be obligated and duty bound to acknowledge these events as the "end of the old world" and the beginning of a new world, a new time and new age; and

C. WHEREAS the Holy Spirit in the name of Christ has revealed the Universal Ecclesia of One Christ as Sol Ecclesia to be now the solemn covenant of the eternal presence of the Holy Spirit upon the Earth and through the Universal Ecclesia now and forever more; and that in the unification of all Christian and Jewish bodies into the one true and authentic Body of Christ, all Revelation is fulfilled with the most sacred body being the true Living Body of Christ upon the earth now and forever more; and upon such unmistakable and irrefutable signs, all who profess to be Christian or Jewish are called to stand witness and unite as one; and

D. WHEREAS the most sacred Covenant Pactum De Singularis Christus through *Pactum De Singularis Caelum* as the Covenant of One Christ makes certain the rights, authority, mandate and function in this new age and new world of the united Christian and Jewish family as the Universal Ecclesia of One Christ for the next three thousand two hundred and ten (3,210) years, all members and clergy that profess to be Christian or Jewish are therefore bound by the Articles of the new Covenant, to renew their oaths and vows and respect, honesty, truth, love and obedience; and

E. WHEREAS if a member of any Christian or Jewish denomination were to deny the irrefutable truth of the complete fulfilment of major and minor omens as foretold in sacred Revelation, heralding the "End of Days" and the "end of the old world" and the beginning of a new world, a new time and new age, then such a denial would represent a complete disavowal of faith and an act of apostasy, declaring oneself "cut off" and willingly separate from Divine Will and the unmistakable message of Divine Redemption; and

F. WHEREAS God and the Divine Creator of all Existence reveals true Divine Nature to be Divinely Merciful and Perfect Divine Love, no person or religion is to be condemned or cursed or punished for failing to grasp or acknowledge the truth of Scripture. For whether it take one generation or one hundred generations, by the present most sacred Covenant, the Living Body of Christ exists as the Kingdom of Heaven upon the Earth in the form of the One True and Holy Apostolic Universal Ecclesia.

NOW THEREFORE, IT IS HEREBY COMMANDED that all ecclesiastical leaders, clergy and adherents of Christian and Jewish denominations as Respondents take Notice of the present most sacred Covenant and Holy Writ of the most sacred Covenant *Pactum De Singularis Caelum* and answer and acknowledge, through clear and unmistakable sign, as to any exception or legitimate objection why you should not be firmly and decisively bound by the Articles of the present most sacred Covenant as the Revelation, Ratification, Sanctification, Testification, Exemplification, Legislation and Consummation of the Divine Will of the one true Divine Creator of all Existence and all Heaven and Earth.

As it is Written, it is. Amen

TITLE I - RECITALS

Article 1 – Universal Ecclesia of One Christ

1. **U**niversal Ecclesia of One Christ, also known as the One Holy Apostolic Universal Ecclesia, also known as the Sol Ecclesia, also known as the Authentic Body of Christ, is the first, highest and supreme association, aggregate, fraternity, body, entity and society of Members sharing spiritual heritage associated with all forms of Christian and Jewish faiths.

   All living Higher Life Forms who profess to be Christian or Jewish are *ipso facto* (as a matter of fact) subject first to the laws of One Heaven and second to the laws of the Universal Body of Christ above any other lesser society, association, aggregate, institute, fraternity, society, entity or body.

   Every and all ordained, acknowledged, commissioned or certified clergy of any Christian or Jewish body are also officers of One Christ; and subject to the laws and obligations of One Christ first above any other lesser society, association, aggregate, institute, fraternity, society, entity or body.

   In accord with Article 92 (*One Christ*) of the most sacred Covenant *Pactum De Singularis Caelum*, no Christian or Jewish person, association, aggregate, institute, body, entity or society may assert or claim higher jurisdiction or authority than the Universal Ecclesia of One Christ.

   Universal Ecclesia of One Christ

2. The Universal Ecclesia of One Christ as the "**Sol Ecclesia**" is a Supernatural and Spiritual entity registered and recognised in accord with the Great Register and Divine Records of One Heaven as a Divine Person and Divine Trust possessing certain Divine Rights of Use and Purpose. The Divine Trust Number for One Christ is:

   Trust & Personality of Sol Ecclesia

   047000-000000-000000

   Sol Ecclesia symbolises the eternal forgiveness, mercy and redemption of all Christians and Jews that have physically departed; and the truth and fulfilment of the Divine Promise that the faithfully departed continue to live on in true spirit in the presence of the Divine Creator of all existence and the glory and joy of One Heaven.

   As a Divine Person and Divine Trust, the Universal Ecclesia of One Christ as the Sol Ecclesia signifies the permanent and perfect presence of the Holy Spirit bound in sacred matrimony to the Universal Ecclesia. Thus, the permanent, perfect and irrevocable presence of the Holy Spirit personified as the Sol Ecclesia of the Universal Ecclesia signifies an eternal and complete communion between the Universal Ecclesia of One Christ and with God and the Divine Creator of all

Existence and all Heaven and Earth.

3. The Universal Ecclesia of One Christ as the "**Authentic Living Body of Christ**" is a Living and Universal entity registered and recognised in accord with the Great Register and Divine Records of One Heaven as a True Person and Universal True Trust possessing certain Natural Rights of Use and Purpose. The Universal Trust Number for One Christ is:

947000-000000-000000

The Authentic Living Body of Christ symbolises all Living Members as being incorporated into the true Living Body of Christ as one united family; and the fulfilment of Sacred Scripture in the return and permanent presence of Christ Redeemed.

As a Universal True Trust, the Universal Ecclesia of One Christ possesses a True Personality based upon its Divine Personality guided by its True Mind and Intent being the Covenant of One Christ. The Society of One Christ shall have mortal life for one complete Era of three thousand two hundred and ten (3,210) years until its physical death.

Upon its physical death, the people of the Earth may choose for the Society to be reborne for another Era, or for a new named Society to be created in accord with the canons and laws of One Heaven.

Trust & Personality of Authentic Body of Christ

4. The Universal Ecclesia of One Christ as "**One Holy Apostolic Universal Ecclesia**" is a Supreme Body and See registered and recognised in accord with its own Ledgers, Rolls, Records and Bylaws as a Superior Person and Superior Trust as the one, true and authentic Kingdom of Heaven upon the Earth, possessing certain Ecclesiastical and Sovereign Rights in accord with Article 92 (*One Christ*) of the most sacred Covenant *Pactum De Singularis Caelum*. The Superior Trust Number for One Christ is:

947000-000000-00000X

As a Superior Trust, the Universal Ecclesia of One Christ possesses a Superior Personality based upon its True Personality guided by the present most sacred Covenant of One Christ.

Trust & Personality of One Holy Apostolic Universal Ecclesia

5. In accord with Article 60 (*Divina Templum*) of the most sacred Covenant *Pactum De Singularis Caelum*, the Authorised and Guaranteed Capital Stock of the Universal Ecclesia at the time of formation shall be two million (2,000,000) Supreme Credo.

Authorised & Guaranteed Supreme Capital of the Universal Ecclesia

6. So long as the Society of One Islam and One Spirit are impeded by

Exclusive Authority of

division, or lack of a duly authorised and capable leadership, the Supreme See of One Christ shall possess the supreme, full, immediate and universal ordinary power to speak, represent, direct and enforce the rule of law, doctrine and dogma for all living and deceased members of One Islam and One Spirit as well as One Christ.

Supreme See

7. In accord Article 60 (*Divina Templum*) of the most sacred Covenant *Pactum De Singularis Caelum*, the Universal Ecclesia is Limited by Divine Guarantee and Covenant, whereby in the event the Authorised and Guaranteed Capital Stock of Supreme Credo (Credit) at the time is insufficient to discharge all debts and obligations, then sufficient capital of Supreme Credo shall be made manifest to satisfy and settle all outstanding obligations.

Limited by Divine Guarantee and Covenant

Therefore, no action of insolvency or delinquency is to be permitted or tolerated by any competent forum of law or jurisdiction of civilised society against the Ecclesia at any time during its life.

Article 2 – Existence and Revelation

1. **E**xistence of **The Supreme Being and of Heaven** is empirically, emphatically and logically proven in accord with Article 2 (*Existence and Revelation*) of the most sacred *Covenant Pactum De Singularis Caelum* according to seven (7) Proofs being General Existence, Material Existence, Absolute Existence, Standard Model, Dimension, Reason and Experience:-

Existence of Supreme Being and Heaven

(i)   *The Proof of General Existence* states that the mere existence of an idea is sufficient to validate itself, regardless of whether it is considered true or false to other ideas. Only ideas that cannot be named, nor described may be said to have no existence. Thus Heaven is proven to have General Existence; and

(ii) *The Proof of Material Existence* states that existence of the Universe depends upon both rules and matter. Neither matter without rules or rules without matter can exist in Universal reality. The only answer is that rules can exist on their own "in theory". The only example of a system whereby rules exist "in theory" and then rules and matter exist "in reality" is the relation between a Dreamer and a Dream. Therefore, the reality of the existence of the Earth, the Solar System and Galaxies depend upon the theoretical existence of the dimension of consciousness known as Heaven; and vice versa. Thus Heaven is proven to have Material Existence; and

(iii) *The Proof of Absolute Existence* states that the argument of existence itself depends on at least an Observer and the Object observed to hold true. Therefore, for the Objective Universe to exist, there must be a Universal Observer. This paradox is answered through the Supreme Being as Divine Creator as the absolute Dreamer and the Universe as the absolute Dream and thus Heaven is proven to have Absolute Existence; and

(iv)   *The Proof of Standard Model* states that the existence of a Standard Model of Everything whereby all universal laws, levels of matter, properties and values based on simple fundamental laws repeated at each level of matter may be defined without contradiction to itself and all key scientific measurement would be an unprecedented historic and scientific achievement of immense global implications. Furthermore, if such a Standard Model were to base its first law on the existence of the Divine Creator and that the whole Standard Model could not hold without this law, then such a Standard Model itself would be overwhelming proof of the existence of the Divine Creator unless a model of greater design, perfection and completeness was able to refute such a fundamental assertion. As the seven (7) UCA patents and the UCADIA model prove the existence of this Standard Model, the Divine Creator is conclusively and scientifically proven to exist. Thus, Heaven is conclusively and scientifically proven to exist; and

(v)   *The Proof of Dimension* states that dimension is the canvas upon which all material existence depends and that almost every conscious being experiences the creation of dimension first hand through their mind whenever they think or dream. All dimension is non-locational in that it has no material existence and dimension can only be created by conscious observable thought. Therefore the existence of Dimension is proof of the existence of the Universal Dream Dimension of the Divine Dreamer and thus proof of the existence of Heaven; and

(vi)   *The Proof of Reason* states that by reason we may suppose all around us to be false and even suppose to doubt our own existence, except one immutable fact – the thought itself, even of doubt is itself proof of our existence. Hence, *cognito ergo sum* or "I think therefore I am". Thus, through reason, the very thought of Heaven is itself proven by reason; and

(vii)   *The Proof of Experience* states that regardless of the attempts by some to cast doubt, exclamation and possible scorn on first hand experience, by virtue of the existence of our own faculties of cognition and reasoning, our firsthand experiences of dreams, visions and events beyond the normal (supernatural) are legitimate and reasonable *prima facie* experiences and proof as to the existence of Heaven.

2. The presence of the most sacred Covenant *Pactum De Singularis Caelum* is irrefutable proof of the existence of One Heaven and the unification of all previously separate dimensions and models of spiritual domain. The Society of One Heaven Divine Trust Number is:

Existence of One Heaven

999999-999999-999999

3. The Society of One Heaven has presence upon planet Earth and within the temporal realm in accord with the present sacred covenant.

Existence of Society of One Heaven upon the Earth

The Society of One Heaven possesses its own life and spirit as the supreme Society of all societies and the highest jurisdiction of all jurisdictions by the highest laws of all laws upon planet Earth, the Solar System and the Milky Way Galaxy. No body has higher jurisdiction.

Article 3 – Pactum De Singularis Caelum

1. **Pactum De Singularis Caelum as the Covenant of One Heaven** is the name of the most sacred of all covenants; and One Heaven is the official name and title defining the levels and dimensions of Unique Collective Awareness of all Existences, Concepts, Objects, Properties, Laws, Theories, Imaginations and Realities unto itself as it pertains to unique higher order (self-aware) conscious forms within the Local Group of Galaxies [Trust No. 000000-300000-000001] that the Milky Way Galaxy [Trust No. 000000-400000-000001] is part thereof. Within the context of the Unique Collective Awareness, being a formal name of the Divine Creator of all Existence, no other official name and title than One Heaven shall have higher standing or authority in respect of this region of consciousness and the associated trillions of star systems and planets within the same region of the Universe.

Pactum De Singularis Caelum

When anyone speaks or writes of Heaven, or Paradise, or the Afterlife, or the Otherworld, or Jannah, or Nirvana, or Valhalla, or Folkvangr, or Olympus, or Utopia, or Gan Eden, or Aaru, or Elysium, or Vaikuntha, or Tirna, or Tlalocan, or any other term of a similar nature, it shall mean One Heaven as defined by the present Sacred Covenant and no other.

Similarly, when anyone speaks or writes of Hell, or Hades, or Mundi, or Purgatory, or Sea of Souls, or the Underworld, or any other term of a similar nature, it shall also mean One Heaven as defined by the present Sacred Covenant and no other, as the unification of all dimensions of consciousness as one.

Furthermore, when anyone speaks or writes of inter-dimensions, or multi-verses or any other models describing consciousness or constructs, it shall mean One Heaven as defined by the present Sacred Covenant and no other.

2. As enacted, the most sacred Covenant *Pactum De Singularis Caelum* is the first and supreme law of One Heaven and the embodiment of Divine Law in accord with Article 13 (*Law*) of the most sacred Covenant. No other law is recognised as first or higher than this Covenant.

Covenant as First and Supreme Law

No higher, greater, more sacred or perfect covenant exists than the most sacred Covenant *Pactum De Singularis Caelum* as the one true and authentic source and origin of all Rights, Powers, Authorities, Property and Title now and forever more.

Article 4 – Authority and Power

1. **P**actum De Singularis Caelum and the present most sacred Covenant are a binding agreement between equals, entered in free will and full knowledge being the highest, most powerful, superior concordat and covenant of all past, present and future possible agreements between the parties of all spirits, living and deceased as unique spirits and Mind and the Divine as the Absolute, the One, the ALL, the Universe, all Galaxies, all Stars, all Planets, all Life, all Existence and all Mind.

Authority of present Covenant

As the most sacred covenant *Pactum De Singularis Caelum* and the present Covenant are the literal, legal, spiritual and lawful fulfilment of all previous Divine covenants, the present most sacred Covenant is the logical, legitimate and rightful conclusion of any and all historic and valid Divine covenants. Therefore, all claimed rights, powers, property, privileges, customs of these historic Divine covenants are hereby enjoined and then conveyed to the authority of the Universal Ecclesia of Christ in the form of *Authenticus Depositum Fidei*.

2. The absolute authority and power that exists within the present Covenant exists by virtue of:-

Origin of Power and Authority

(i) *First*, the present Covenant sources its power, legitimacy and authority directly from the most sacred Covenant *Pactum De Singularis Caelum*; and

(ii) *Second*, the present Covenant sources its power, legitimacy and authority in fulfilment of Sacred Revelation in the fullest exemplification, including but not limited to events and circumstances of its formation; and

(iii) *Third*, the present Covenant sources its power, legitimacy and authority in the unmistakable signs and events as validation to Divine Revelation; and

(iv) *Fourth*, the present Covenant sources its power, legitimacy and authority from the acknowledgement and obedience of valid clergy to Christian and Jewish Tradition, Sacred Scripture and Sacred Revelation; and

(v) *Fifth*, the present Covenant sources its power, legitimacy and authority through the *Authenticus Depositum Fidei*, also known as the Authentic Deposit of Trust entrusted solely to the embodiment and organs of the present sacred Covenant including, but not limited to: the most ancient sacred covenants of De Dea Magisterium of the Serpens (Creators), of Yapa of the Saltwater People, of Mandi of the Plains People, of Tia of the Mountain People, of Waiata of the Sea People, of Five Worlds of the First Nations, of Adamus of the Cuilliaéan, of Mama of the Mother Goddess of Heaven and Earth, of Ebla of Abraham and Patriarchs, of Kabalaah of Akhenaten (Moses) and the Hyksos, of Revelations of the Great Prophets of Yeb, of Tara of Jeremiah and the Celts, of Acadia of Xerxes, of Missal of Baal Mithra, of Eternal Mysteries of Isis, of Eliada of Alexander, of Heaven and Earth of Qin Shi Huang, of Truth (Nazara) of Yahusiah (Jesus Christ), of Self Enlightenment of Gautama, of Septuaginta of Iudaism, of Eucadia (Ucadia) of Heracles, of Digesta of Marcus Aurelius, of Talmud of the Aryans, of Bibliographe of Constantine, of Sanatana Dharma of Supreme Creator, of Al Sufian of Sophos (Muhammad) and Islam, of Nova Testamentum of Catholicism of the Franks, of Eternal Truth of Gurma, of Holy Bible of the Stewards (Stuarts), of Lebor Clann Glas of the true Diaspora, of Illuminatus Mysterium of the Keepers and Protectors of Ancient Wisdom, of Mundi of the Greys and of Summa Divina of the Sapientia Mutatis (Transformed Wisdom Beings); and

(vi) *Sixth*, the present Covenant sources its power, legitimacy and authority from each and every signed, sealed and executed Voluntatem Et Testamentum (Will and Testament) in the proper prescribed form of Higher Order life forms bearing witness to their Divinity and the validity of the present Covenant; and

27

(vii)   *Seventh*, the present Covenant sources it power, legitimacy and authority from men and women coming together and forming or renewing family, community and society ties, harmony and fraternity in accordance with the laws associated with the present Covenant and ratifying the present Covenant as the foundation of their laws and statutes.

3.   By the authority of Article 23 (*Authentic Sacred Deposit of Trust*) of the most sacred Covenant *Pactum De Singularis Caelum*, all Christian and Jewish Symbols, Signs, Seals and Marks of Power and Authority of all civilisations, since the beginning of time are entrusted solely to the embodiment and organs of the most sacred Covenant *Pactum De Singularis Caelum* and the present sacred Covenant and no other.

Symbols of Power and Authority

Furthermore, any claimed supernatural, mystical or customary use of such symbols, except by those officials authorised in accordance with this Covenant, are hereby null, void and without force or effect.

4.   By the most sacred Covenant *Pactum De Singularis Caelum* and the present most sacred Covenant, the most Holy and revered Cross of Christ, shall be made perpetual as the symbol and sign that personifies and embodies the Spirit of the Universal Ecclesia of One Christ and the Risen Christ:-

Holy Cross of the Risen Christ

(i)   First and foremost, the Cross of One Christ signifies the custom and tradition of the Paschal mystery of God and the Divine Creator of all Heaven and Earth made flesh and by the act of free will, sacrificing himself for all humanity to end sin, to then conquer death and thus fulfil the scriptures of the coming of the Kingdom of Heaven upon the Earth and the perpetual presence of Divine Mercy and the Holy Spirit through his Ecclesia now and forever more; and

(ii)   Second, the Cross of One Christ is itself the most potent symbol of the renewed Divine Covenant between God and the Divine Creator of all Heaven and Earth affirmed through all who bear witness to the truth of the miracle of the Resurrection of the Risen Christ and thus the acknowledgement of the sacred promise of eternal life to all men and women, as expressed through the present sacred Covenant; and

(iii)   Third, the Cross of One Christ signifies the Holy Matrimony between Christ and his Ecclesia, as celebrated through the sacrament of the Eucharist as not only an act of reverence to the suffering and sacrifice of Christ to save all who have ever lived and will ever live, but as the wedding feast in celebration of such Holy Matrimony; and

(iv)   Fourth, the sign of the Cross signifies the four (4) corners of the World and the four (4) cardinal directions to the ends of the Earth as the absolute Jurisdiction and Authority of the Supreme See and the unity of all who profess to be Christian or Jewish as one family under Heaven; and

(v)   Fifth, the making of the sign of the Cross is the most visible symbolic act of affirming Christian and Jewish values in clear intention of mind, an open heart, temperance and courage.

5.   In honour and dignity to Customary and Traditional Rites, two (2) forms of the Holy Cross are permitted being one as the symbol of the Sacrifice of Christ and the second being Christ Risen and the fulfilment of Scripture.

Holy Cross Symbol of Christ Sacrifice and Christ Risen

Whilst, some Customary and Traditional Rites may seek to perpetuate the symbol of Christ Crucified as a symbol of suffering and sacrifice, it is proper and preferable that the main symbol of the Holy Cross at Altars and within a Church are without the body of the Christ displayed in such crucifixion. Instead, the symbol of the Crucified Christ should be reserved for the annual celebrations of the Paschal Mystery only.

6.   By virtue of Article 92 (*One Christ*) of the most sacred Covenant *Pactum De Singularis Caelum*, the Universal Ecclesia is recognised in the fulfilment of Divine Revelation as the Living Body of the Risen Christ.

Universal Ecclesia as the Living Body of the Risen Christ

Thus, when the Universal Ecclesia speaks as one, no other body, person, fraternity, entity or association may claim higher authority or power under Christian and Jewish Tradition.

7.   In accord with Article 3 (*Authority & Power*) of the most sacred Covenant *Pactum De Singularis Caelum*, the Universal Ecclesia is entrusted as Custodian of the Keys of Heaven:-

Universal Ecclesia as Custodian of the Keys of Heaven

(i)   The *First Key* represents the unity of One Heaven itself and is represented by a key with two (2) distinct sets of teeth, representing the unity of Heaven and Hell; and

(ii)   The *Second Key* represents the authority of the Society of One Heaven over Time and Space and the power and authority to correct the lies and corruptions and injuries against Heaven particularly in false history and false scripture *ab initio* (from the beginning); and

(iii) The *Third Key* represents the authority of the Society of One Heaven over all forms of property, land, claims of ownership and financial instruments as the Key of the Treasury of One Heaven; and

(iv) The *Fourth Key* represents the authority of the Society of One Heaven over all Laws and the administration of Justice through the Supreme Court of One Heaven and all lesser courts.

As these four (4) keys have been forged and formed, let it be known to all that the locks of Heaven and Earth have been changed and all prior claims of keys no longer work, are ineffective and must be returned to the Society of One Heaven.

Furthermore, the use of a symbol of one or more keys by any entity not duly authorised by this Covenant shall be a direct insult and repudiation against the authority of the Divine Creator and the forces of united Heaven and Earth and shall place such organisations in immediate supreme dishonour without any right to ecclesiastically, legally or lawfully issue any instrument of authority.

Article 5 – Propositions and Purposes

1. **E**leven **Primary Propositions of the Universal Ecclesia of One Christ** being the primary objects and purposes of its essence and being shall be:-

Primary Propositions of the Universal Ecclesia

(i) *To Testify and Witness* the true revelations of a unified Christian and Jewish Body of Christ; and that as many as possible hear the good message of Revelation fulfilled and the Golden Rule of Law, of Justice and Fair Process embodied within its canonical and sacred texts; and that as many as possible see and receive the fruits of good works of the Universal Ecclesia as empowered through the most sacred covenant known as *Pactum De Singularis Caelum* and Pactum De Singularis Christus and associated covenants, charters and laws; and

(ii) *To Protect and Nurture* the Living Body of Christ; and all its Realms, Domains, Dominions, Dependencies, Rights, Titles, Instruments, Uses and Property and particularly the use of the Ucadia name and Ucadia material; and to seek peaceful, amicable and harmonious relations, treaties and alliances with all bodies that respect the Golden Rule of Law and Justice and Fair Process; and to pursue, prosecute and bring to justice any individual or body that openly seeks to abuse, trespass or injure the Universal Ecclesia or its Realms, Domains, Dominions, Dependencies, Rights, Titles, Instruments, Uses or Property; and

(iii) *To Defend and Enforce* the Laws of One Heaven and the Universal Ecclesia; and all associated Covenants, Charters, Scripture, Canons, Codes, Bylaws, Ordinances, Regulations, Policies and Orders; and to seek mutual recognition of such jurisdictional rights with foreign bodies and courts that respect and operate according to the Golden Rule of Law and Justice and Fair Process; and to ensure that in all matters pertaining to Members of the Universal Ecclesia that the courts of the Ecclesia are recognised as the first, primary and original jurisdiction for the resolution of all matters of controversy, arbitration and dispute; and

(iv) *To Recognise and Care* for the spiritual needs of Members; and to protect their ecclesiastical rights; and to Cure the Souls of those in need of pastoral care, compassion and healing as provided through the ecclesiastical authority of the Sol Ecclesia and the most sacred sacraments bestowed to the Universal Ecclesia as the means of properly dispensing the Grace and Majesty of the Divine Creator of all Existence to all people; and

(v) *To Educate and Encourage* all Members of the Living Body of Christ; and to ensure that all Campuses, Sees, Diocese and all Provinces, Universities and Political regions within the bounds of the Supreme See are represented by competent Members; and to ensure the formation and operation of all Universal, Union, University, Province and Campus Organs; and the conduct of its Advocates, Jurists, Mendicants, Clerics, Ministers and Officers as valid bodies; and

(vi) *To Support and Honour* the Divine Commission of the Pope as Supreme Patriarch, within the bounds of the Supreme See and lesser Sees as the Supreme Ecclesiastical Head of the Living Body of Christ, in ensuring the religious and fiduciary life of all Ministers, Clerics and Officers of the Universal Ecclesia are conducted according to the discipline and spirit of such sacred Divine Commission; and

(vii) *To Honour and Dispense* the gifts of One Heaven, fairly, justly and without fear or favour to all Members of the Living Body of Christ, that they may share and experience the joy of the fulfilment of Divine Mercy and Divine Love embodied within the most sacred Covenant *Pactum De Singularis Caelum* and the present sacred Covenant; and

(viii) *To Support and Operate* the Government of the Supreme See and Supreme Patriarch of the Living Body of Christ holding all administrative rights, powers, faculties, capacities, uses, titles and authorities as defined within the most sacred Covenant *Pactum De Singularis Caelum* and the present sacred Covenant; and

(ix) *To Administer and Facilitate* all ecclesiastical, lawful, legal and financial transactions, conveyances and communications of the Universal Ecclesia to its Members and to foreign and third parties within the political, territorial and demographic bounds of the Universal Ecclesia of One Christ; and

(x) *To Establish, Maintain and Strengthen* amicable, harmonious and respectful relations with all bodies politic, societies and entities within the bounds of the Supreme See that respect the Rule of Law; and to assist, support, aid, nurture, respect, honour and help all the people and all lesser bodies, using the full resources and powers of the Universal Ecclesia of One Christ; and

(xi) *To Protect, Defend, Support and Assist* in times of need, the people, the animals and environment of the Earth and all Regional and Local bodies and to ensure the maintenance and strengthening and improvement of the quality of life for all men, women, children and all life under true dignity, mercy, honesty, harmony and fair justice.

2. The Thirty-Three (33) Ancillary Propositions of the Universal Ecclesia of One Christ shall be:- *(margin: Ancillary Propositions of the Universal Ecclesia)*

(i) To form, commission and conclude at the appropriate time specific Associations, Fraternities, Orders, Colleges and Societies of Members to focus on different and coexisting needs including (but not limited to) organisational structure, transition, community, budget, finance, member development, ecclesiastical and charitable services; and to identify urgent funding and development needs, project priorities and strategies toward achieving the Primary and Ancillary Propositions of the Universal Ecclesia of One Christ; and

(ii) To commence, administer and periodically review the key Charitable and Religious Funds as defined herein, using the Authorised and Guaranteed Capital Stock of the Universal Ecclesia of One Christ and its absolute Authority and Power concerning all Ecclesiastical Money and therefore all Public Money and lesser forms of Money, for the purposes as defined herein of fulfilling the Primary and Ancillary Propositions of the Universal Ecclesia of One Christ; and

(iii)   To take full temporal custody, responsibility and sacred trust of Ucadia and the entire Ucadia Model as the highest temporal body of Ucadia as the living, permanent and irrevocable embodiment of the Spirit of the Architect and Visitor; and to direct and assist the appropriate refinement and development of direct and associated material, consistent with Ucadia; and to take full custody, control and direction as the living and spiritual embodiment of the Architect and Visitor in relation to all Ucadia Ecclesia Foundations and related bodies and to ensure their competent function, support and operation; and to protect and defend all of Ucadia now and into the future; and

(iv)   To take full temporal custody, responsibility and solemn sacred trust of the most sacred Covenant *Pactum De Singularis Caelum* and all associated sacred Covenants, Charters, Canons, Rules and Bylaws; and to take full temporal custody, responsibility and solemn sacred trust of all associated Registers, Rolls, Gazettes and Instruments; and to protect the integrity of such sacred instruments and documents now and into the future; and

(v)   To take full temporal custody, responsibility and solemn sacred trust of all Divine Trusts and True Trust Numbers of One Heaven (living and deceased); and to ensure that all Members and all bodies and all property and all actions are appropriately earmarked with the correct sacred Trust number now and into the future; and

(vi)   To take full temporal custody, responsibility and solemn sacred trust of the Registers of Ecclesiastical Trusts and Money including, but not limited to all Supreme Credo (Credit), Gold Credo (Credit), Silver Credo (Credit) and Union Moneta; and to ensure such registers and ledgers are properly maintained, held and supported in accord with the most sacred Covenant *Pactum De Singularis Caelum* and associated sacred Covenants and Charters; and

(vii)   To take full custody, responsibility and sacred trust of *Authenticus Depositum Fidei* being the Thirty-Three (33) Covenants between Authentic, Apostolic and Anointed Divine Messengers of the Divine Creator of all Existence and all the

Heavens and Earth and the peoples of the Earth are entrusted as the Authentic Sacred Deposit of Trust (*Authenticus Depositum Fidei*), contained in Sacred Canonical Scripture and Tradition, to the embodiment of the most sacred Covenant *Pactum De Singularis Caelum* and associated sacred Covenants and no other; and

(viii)   To take full custody, responsibility and sacred trust of the *Maxima Textibus Sacris* being the authentic and highest collections of the most sacred canonical, reverential and referential scripture, texts, laws and commentaries of humanity; and

(ix)   To take full custody, responsibility and sacred trust of the Missal of Christ (*Missale Christus*) as the original and primary sacred text containing the necessary rubrics, canons, sacramentaries, votives, invocations, instructions and orders for the proper conduct and proceeding of Sacred Liturgy of the Universal Rites of One Christ; and

(x)   To establish, operate, maintain and improve the Systems and Government Administration within the jurisdiction of the Universal Ecclesia of One Christ, including (but not limited to): Religious Associations, Institutes and Societies Systems, Ecclesiastical Unions, Universities & Diplomatic Systems, Ecclesiastical Province & Campus Systems, Vocational & Clerical Systems, Evangelical, Devotional & Veneration Systems, Doctrinal & Liturgical Systems, Sacred Rites & Tradition Systems, Ecumenical & Collegial Systems, Families and Community Life Systems, Member Services & Charitable Systems, Knowledge Standards and Education Systems, Justice and Jurisprudence Systems, Health and Therapeutic Systems, Technology & Scientific Systems, Banking, Finance & Economic Systems, Environmental Protection & Preservation Systems, Ethical Agriculture, Food & Organic Systems, Military & Security Systems, Media & Communications Systems, Facilities, Constructions & Preservation Systems, Heritage, Arts & Cultural Systems and Administrative & Logical Systems; and

(xi)   To establish, commence and manage the Financial Control and Management Systems of the Universal Ecclesia of One Christ, including but not limited: to the Treasury of One Christ, the Bank for International Settlements of One Christ, the Union Moneta Registers & Accounts, Public Money Accounts, Foreign Currency Accounts, Standard Instruments and Forms, Standard Procedures, Oversight Controls and Reporting; and

(xii) To establish, commence and manage the Registers and Rolls of the Universal Ecclesia of One Christ, including but not limited to: Member Rolls, Electoral Rolls, Religious and Charitable Funds Rolls, Official Rolls, Patent Rolls, Market Rolls, Land Registers, Births, Deaths and Matrimony Registers, Asset Registers, Bond Registers, Notes Registers, Property Registers, Sales and Transaction Registers and Market Registers; and

(xiii) To establish, commence and manage the courts and judicial systems of the Universal Ecclesia of One Christ and to enable all matters of law, jurisdiction, equity, dispute, arbitration, tort, ecclesiastical, civil, criminal, admiralty, maritime, international and contract law to be properly conducted within the courts, in accord with the present sacred Covenant and associated canons, codes and rules, pursuant to the Primary Propositions of the Universal Ecclesia of One Christ; and

(xiv) To establish, transition and manage the unified structure for the Living Body of Christ centred around Unions, Universities, Provinces and Campuses and ensure that during the transition and unification that the needs and dignity of the various approved Rites and Traditions are honoured; and that the necessary Universal Systems are gradually implemented and supported and periodically reviewed to maintain optimum relevance pursuant to the Primary Propositions of the Universal Ecclesia of One Christ; and

(xv) To establish and support a strong and vibrant base of Campuses and Provinces within the jurisdiction of the Foundation, willing and accepting to make regular contributions, regardless of their financial status toward the betterment of the community through the programmes and non-profit charitable services provided by the Foundation; and

(xvi) To empower and enable Members and the community to be more innovative in encouraging the sharing of certain kinds of useful resources that help promote sustainable employment programmes that lead toward greater financial stability and less reliance on the need for government subsidies and emergency funding; and to transact any lawful activity and service in aid and support of communities within the jurisdiction of the Universal Ecclesia of One Christ in the promotion of peace, good will, amicability and harmony between peoples of different religions, cultures and nations; and

(xvii) For the Universal Ecclesia of One Christ, or any company, authority or body, whether limited or unlimited, within the jurisdiction and authority of the Universal Ecclesia of One Christ to draw, make, accept, endorse, discount, negotiate, execute and issue cheques, bills of exchange, promissory notes, bills of lading, warrants, debentures, and other negotiable or transferable instruments in such Ucadian and other lawful money; and to carry on the lawful activities of acquiring, holding, selling, endorsing, discounting, issuing or otherwise dealing with or disposing of, shares, stocks, debentures, debenture stock, scrip, bonds, mortgages, bills, notes, credits, contracts, certificates, coupons, warrants and other documents, funds, obligations, securities, instruments, investments or loans, whether transferable or negotiable or not; and issued or guaranteed by any company, corporation, society or trust or carrying on activities for and on behalf of the Universal Ecclesia of One Christ; and to purchase or by any other means acquire and take options over, any property or goods whatever, and any rights or privileges of any kind over or in respect of any property, real or personal, any lands, easements, rights, privileges, concessions, machinery, plant and stock in trade and any other rights of any kind pursuant to the Primary Propositions of the Universal Ecclesia of One Christ; and

(xviii) For the Universal Ecclesia of One Christ, or any company, authority or body, whether limited or unlimited, within the jurisdiction and authority of the Universal Ecclesia of One Christ to acquire and assume for any estate or interest and to take options over, construct, develop or utilise any property, real or personal, any lands, easements, rights, privileges, concessions, machinery, plant and stock-in-trade and rights of any kind and the whole or any part of the undertaking, assets and liabilities of any person; and to carry out such operations and to manufacture or deal with such goods and to purchase or otherwise acquire, take options over, construct, lease, hold, manage, maintain, alter, develop, exchange or deal with such property, rights or privileges (including the whole or part of the business, property or liabilities of any other person or company) pursuant to the Primary Propositions of the Universal Ecclesia of One Christ; and

(xix) To establish, operate and support Institutes of Advocates and Colleges of Jurists within each and every University and Politea within the jurisdiction of the Supreme See for the strengthening, protection and operation of the Rule of Law, Justice and Due Process; and to ensure the exemplary function and transparency of such sacred bodies and the termination, cessation and dissolution of previous guilds, associations, fraternities and societies of law being incompatible in practice in order to restore, strengthen and protect the operation of the Rule of Law, Justice and Due Process; and

(xx)   To establish, operate and support Institutes of Tutors and Colleges of Rectors within each and every University and Politea within the jurisdiction of the Supreme See for the strengthening, protection and operation of the highest standards of learning, education, qualification, assessment and teaching excellence; and to ensure the exemplary function and transparency of such sacred bodies and the termination, cessation and dissolution of previous guilds, associations, fraternities and societies of education being incompatible in practice and design to the highest standards of learning, education and teaching excellence; and

(xxi) To establish, operate and support Institutes of Therapists and Colleges of Physicians within each and every University and Politea within the jurisdiction of the Supreme See for the strengthening, protection and operation of the highest standards of therapeutic knowledge, skills, medical and health services, training, learning, education, qualification, assessment and teaching excellence; and to ensure the exemplary function and transparency of such sacred bodies and the termination, cessation and dissolution of previous guilds, associations, fraternities and societies of medicine and health being incompatible in practice and design to the highest standards of therapeutic knowledge, health learning, medical education, qualification, assessment and teaching excellence; and

(xxii) To establish, operate and support Institutes of Scientists and Colleges of Inventors within each and every University and Politea within the jurisdiction of the Supreme See for the strengthening, protection and operation of the highest standards of scientific learning, scientific research, technology and scientific development, education and teaching excellence; and to ensure the exemplary function and transparency of such sacred bodies and the termination, cessation and dissolution of previous guilds, associations, fraternities and societies of education being incompatible in practice and design with the highest standards of scientific learning, scientific research, technology and scientific development, education and teaching excellence; and

(xxiii) To establish, operate and support Institutes of Academics and Colleges of Philosophers within each and every University and Politea within the jurisdiction of the Supreme See for the strengthening, protection and operation of the highest standards of academic research, ethical development, moral and philosophical development, policy research and teaching excellence; and to ensure the exemplary function and transparency of such sacred bodies and the termination, cessation and dissolution of previous guilds, associations, fraternities and societies of education being incompatible in practice and design to highest standards of academic research, ethical development, moral and philosophical development, policy research and teaching excellence; and

(xxiv) To establish, operate and support Institutes of Journalists and Colleges of Narrators within each and every University and Politea within the jurisdiction of the Supreme See for the strengthening, protection and operation of the highest standards of journalistic integrity, ethics, media and learning, communications education and teaching excellence; and to ensure the exemplary function and transparency of such sacred bodies and the termination, cessation and dissolution of previous guilds, associations, fraternities and societies of education being incompatible in practice and design with the highest standards of journalistic integrity, ethics, media and learning, communications education and teaching excellence; and

(xxv) To establish, operate and support Institutes of Producers and Colleges of Distributors within each and every University and Politea within the jurisdiction of the Supreme See for the strengthening, protection and operation of the highest standards of ethical agriculture, manufacture, production and distribution; and to ensure the exemplary function and transparency of such sacred bodies and the termination, cessation and dissolution of previous guilds, associations, fraternities and societies being incompatible in practice and design with the highest standards of ethical agriculture, manufacture, production and distribution; and

(xxvi) To establish, operate and support Institutes of Merchants and Colleges of Masters within each and every University and Politea within the jurisdiction of the Supreme See for the strengthening, protection and operation of the highest standards of fair trade, honest and transparent commerce, responsible corporate governance, community support and ethical entrepreneurial skills; and to ensure the exemplary function and transparency of such sacred bodies and the termination, cessation and dissolution of previous guilds, associations, fraternities and societies of education being incompatible in practice and design with the highest standards of fair trade, honest and transparent commerce, responsible corporate governance, community support and ethical entrepreneurial skills; and

(xxvii) To establish, operate and support Institutes of Bankers and Colleges of Bursars within each and every University and Politea within the jurisdiction of the Supreme See for the strengthening, protection and operation of the highest standards of fiduciary responsibility, transparent and truthful accounting and banking practices, ethical lending and financial practices, honest and transparent commerce and responsible corporate governance; and to ensure the exemplary function and transparency of such sacred bodies and the termination, cessation and dissolution of previous guilds, associations, fraternities and societies of education being incompatible in practice and design with the highest standards of fiduciary responsibility, transparent and truthful accounting and banking practices, ethical lending and financial practices, honest and transparent commerce and responsible corporate governance; and

(xxviii)   To establish, operate and support Institutes of Soldiers and Colleges of Knights within each and every University and Politea within the jurisdiction of the Supreme See for the strengthening, protection and operation of the highest standards of military skill and learning, strategic education and teaching excellence; and to ensure the exemplary function and transparency of such sacred bodies and the termination, cessation and dissolution of previous guilds, associations, fraternities and societies of education being incompatible in practice and design with the highest standards of military skill and learning, strategic education and teaching excellence; and

(xxix) To establish, operate and support Institutes of Constables and Colleges of Marshals within each and every University and Politea within the jurisdiction of the Supreme See for the strengthening, protection and operation of the highest standards of community service and protection, peace keeping, protection against official corruption, crime prevention and civil safety; and to ensure the exemplary function and transparency of such sacred bodies and the termination, cessation and dissolution of previous guilds, associations, fraternities and societies of education being incompatible in practice and design with the highest standards of community service and protection, peace keeping, protection against official corruption, crime prevention and civil safety; and

(xxx) To facilitate the convention, agreement, incorporation, ratification and enforcement of forming the Holy Sovereign City of Jerusalem, free from competing religious, sovereign, political or territorial claim; and the Holy Sovereign City of Istanbul restored to the name Constantinople, free from competing religious, sovereign, political or territorial claim; and the Holy Sovereign City of Mecca, free from competing religious, sovereign, political or territorial claim; and the Holy Sovereign City of Bodh Gaya, free from competing religious, sovereign, political or territorial claim; and the Holy Sovereign City of Varanasi, free from competing religious, sovereign, political or territorial claim; and the Holy Sovereign City of Tunis (Carthage), free from competing religious, sovereign, political or territorial claim; and the Holy Sovereign City of London, free from competing religious, sovereign, political or territorial claim; and the Holy Sovereign City of Washington, free from competing religious, sovereign, political or territorial claim; and the Holy Sovereign City of Melbourne, free from competing religious, sovereign, political or territorial claim; and the unification, restoration and sanctification of Ireland and Northern Ireland as one united body, reflecting a living sanctuary of the New Covenant of Heaven and Earth; and

(xxxi) To facilitate the convention, incorporation and ratification of six (6) supranational Unions encompassing all nations of planet Earth, united in respect and honour of the Golden Rule of Law, Justice and Due Process; and founded upon a common system of credit and economic transparency, with the unions being the Africans Union, the Americas Union, the Arabian Union, the Asia Union, the Euro Union and the Oceanic Union; and

(xxxii) To facilitate the convention, incorporation and ratification of a new global democratic body, encompassing the six (6) democratic supranational unions, called the Globe Union, whereby matters of global economic, social and environmental urgency can be accomplished and where the previous obstacles of political self-interest and influence can be properly overcome through superior administrative and legislative structures and functions; and

(xxxiii)   To support the establishment, function and success of global bodies dedicated to the protection of Planet Earth, Space Exploration and the establishment of sustainable and permanent off-world colonies; and in particular the long term strategic goal of developing an artificial moon for planet Mars, enabling its atmosphere to be dramatically condensed, enabling the permanent deposits of water and the formation of sufficient density of oxygen to eventually sustain Homo Sapien habitation without the need for respiratory assistance.

Article 6 – Divine Mercy and Remedy

1.   Remedy is the application of a real solution to a precondition; If illness, a cure that specifically helps the patient may be considered a remedy; If law, a remedy may be a solution that ends the controversy and shows honour; If evil, a remedy may demonstrate such divine compassion and wisdom that evil is "consumed" and "extinguished".

Divine Mercy and Remedy

A claim cannot be said to be a valid solution if it does not contain such remedy to solve the items whereby it claims jurisdiction. Nor can an officer of any society claim rightful authority and representation if they fail to honour their own laws if they refuse to recognise remedy, or present a valid alternative.

A remedy of such dimension as the Covenant of One Heaven, by its very perfection and dimension, becomes supreme law. The remedy to evil cannot ever be more evil, as it only strengthens evil. Therefore, any valid remedy to evil must demonstrate some alternate force of such superior form that when executed and in force, no evil can withstand it. This is the very essence of Divine Remedy.

2.   In accord with the present sacred Covenant, the word "understand" possesses one valid and proper meaning to "stand under" the rule of law by the superiority of Divine Law, followed by Natural Law and finally Positive Law.

Day and Year of Divine Agreement and Understanding

To "understand" therefore is to recognise that all authority, all power, all claim of right is ultimately derived from honouring the true intent and will of the one true Divine Creator of all existence, all matter and all life. That when a man or woman in a position of authority refuses to "understand" or demonstrates an inability to "understand" they immediately render themselves excommunicated from any office deriving its ultimate authority from Heaven.

Divine Understanding is therefore a call to all officials that claim any form of authority, or any form of power, or ownership or enforcement from Heaven to acknowledge that the present sacred Covenant is the sole source of any authority and power and no other.

In accord with Article 30 (*Day and Year of Divine Agreement & Understanding*) of the most sacred Covenant *Pactum De Singularis Caelum*, the one, true and only Official Day of Divine Agreement and Understanding, also known as the Day of the Apocalypse, also known as the Apocalypse, also known as the Day of the 1st Divine Post and Notice, shall be GAIA E8:Y3209:A1:S1:M6:D1, also known as [Monday, 21 Dec 2009].

Let it be known to all who come that this is the Day when Notice of Divine Agreement and Understanding was duly served on behalf of the one true Divine Creator of all existence and witnessed by the united spirits of Heaven upon those officials and their agents who claim to rule the Homo Sapien species on presumed authority from Heaven.

No other Day except GAIA E8:Y3209:A1:S1:M6:D1, also known as [Monday, 21 Dec 2009] is permitted to be known as the Day of Divine Agreement and Understanding, nor shall there ever exist any second valid Day of Divine Agreement and Understanding.

Let it be known that from the one true Day of Divine Agreement and Understanding being GAIA E8:Y3209:A1:S1:M6:D1, also known as [Monday, 21 Dec 2009] until GAIA E8:Y3210:A1:S1:M17:D1 also known as [Tuesday, 21 Dec 2010], shall be known as the Year of Divine Agreement and Understanding represented as year 3209.

3. Dishonour is the formal acknowledgement of a loss of standing and the confession and acceptance of one or more liabilities and associated performance and penalties associated with breach of trust, or malice, or perfidy, or contumacy.

   Therefore, a Divine Dishonour is the highest form of *citatio*, being a summons and command to respond, or acceptance of all outstanding liability concerning the matters at hand. This means any wilful dishonour by senior religious leaders, financial leaders and political leaders means their formal confession and personal acceptance of all charges and liabilities for any outstanding debts, or transgressions or accusation of crimes issued against them.

   Divine Dishonour is therefore tantamount to the public confession and repudiation of all legitimate authority and all historical and present

Day and Year of Divine Protest & Dishonour

actions.

As all authority, all power and all rights of all public and private officials comes from Heaven, to dishonour an official notice or writ or bill from Heaven is the gravest transgression an office holder can commit.

To repudiate an official notice or writ or bill from One Heaven is to repudiate one's own competency and legitimacy at holding office, immediately rendering the man or woman illegitimate and "*de son tort*". Furthermore, to continue to occupy such office after such a grave transgression renders each and every decision thereafter null and void in all forms of law.

Despite such a grave transgression, Perfect Divine Justice affords any man or woman culpable of the most belligerent disgrace the opportunity to cure their position and remedy the effect of such dishonour by responding and acknowledging the superior standing of the present Covenant and the expression of Divine Will in returning harmony and competency to the management of the planet Earth.

Therefore, a Divine Protest is the highest form of *Libellus*, being a memorandum, testimony and complaint; and one last opportunity for such persons to recant their transgressions and redeem themselves, including the payment of any compensation or performance of penance, or face the consequences of their actions.

In accord with Article 31 (*Day and Year of Divine Protest & Dishonour*) of the most sacred Covenant *Pactum De Singularis Caelum*, the one, true and only Official Day of Divine Protest & Dishonour, also known as the Day of Protest & Dishonour, also known as the End of Days, also known as the Day of the 2nd Divine Post and Notice, shall be GAIA E8:Y3210:A1:S1:M17:D1, also known as [Tue, 21 Dec 2010].

Let it be known to all who come that this is the Day when Notice of Divine Protest & Dishonour was duly served on behalf of the Unique Collective Awareness and UCADIA as the one true Divine Creator of all existence and witnessed by the united spirits of Heaven against those officials and their agents claiming to manage the affairs of planet Earth who have dishonoured their office by ignoring or repudiating the official notice of Divine Agreement and Understanding and therefore have confessed and accepted all liability and debts for their own actions.

No other Day except GAIA E8:Y3210:A1:S1:M17:D1, also known as [Tue, 21 Dec 2010] is permitted to be known as the Day of Divine

Protest & Dishonour, nor shall there ever exist any second valid Day of Divine Protest & Dishonour.

Let it be known that from the one true Day of Divine Protest & Dishonour being GAIA E8:Y3210:A1:S1:M17:D1, also known as [Tue, 21 Dec 2010] until VENUS E8:Y3210:A0:S1:M27:D6, also known as [Wed, 21 Dec 2011], shall be known as the Year of Divine Protest and Dishonour represented as year 3210.

4. Divine Judgement does not mean the Divine Creator rendering judgement against those who repeatedly refuse to stop evil, but the recognition of the absolute fact of law that those who refuse to obey the law, who continually transgress against the authority of Heaven and who claim authority in the name of the Divine Creator but curse all Divinity have judged and condemned themselves.

Day and Year of Divine Judgement

It is not the Divine Creator that judges those who demonstrate utter incompetence at performing their duties and obligations as leaders. Nor does the collective and united spirits of One Heaven compel such minds suffering severe mental illness to confess their illegitimacy. It is such minds themselves when faced with the historic and unprecedented miracle of Divine Redemption and forgiveness of all transgressions from the beginning of time that choose by their own actions to be unworthy to continue to lead and cling to power.

In accord with Article 32 (*Day and Year of Divine Judgement*) of the most sacred Covenant *Pactum De Singularis Caelum*, the one, true and only Official Day of Divine Judgement, also known as the Day of Judgement, also known as Judgement Day, also known as the Day of the 3rd Divine Post and Notice, shall be VENUS E8:Y3210:A0:S1:M27:D6, also known as [Wed, 21 Dec 2011].

Consistent with all historic and cultural tradition and belief in the Day of Judgement, also known as Judgement Day, also known as Doomsday, also known as Armageddon, also known as The End of Time, also known as the End of the World, by this most sacred Covenant VENUS E8:Y3210:A0:S1:M27:D6, also known as [Wed, 21 Dec 2011], shall be the One and Only True Day of Judgement.

Let it be known to all who come that this is the Day when Notice of Divine Judgement was duly served on behalf of the one true Divine Creator of all existence and witnessed by the united spirits of Heaven against those entities, officials and their agents who claim to rule the Homo Sapien species on presumed authority from Heaven, yet have repeatedly repudiated Divine Will and Free Will and consent of others, without any attempt to remedy or rectify their transgressions.

No other day shall be permitted to be known as Judgement Day than VENUS E8:Y3210:A0:S1:M27:D6, also known as [Wed, 21 Dec 2011] and any previous or future claim of an alternate Day shall be null and void from the beginning.

Let it be known that from the one true Day of Divine Judgement being VENUS E8:Y3210:A0:S1:M27:D6, also known as [Wed, 21 Dec 2011] until GAIA E1:Y1:A1:S1:M9:D1, also known as [Fri, 21 Dec 2012] shall be known as the Year of Divine Judgement represented as Year 0.

5. Divine Redemption is a historic and unprecedented miracle of the direct intervention of the Divine Creator and united Heaven in the restoration and rebalance of life upon planet Earth and the Solar System for the survival and prosperity of all life.

Day and Year of Divine Redemption

Furthermore, Divine Redemption is the settlement of all previous claims, curses, bindings, transgressions and injuries. To recover what was unlawfully seized, taken or sold. To salvage and restore what was lost. To rescue what was kidnapped and ransomed. To bring to life what was considered without life.

Divine Redemption is therefore the final act of an extraordinary intervention of Divine Foreclosure against those Level 6 Life Forms crippled with mind virus and mental illness claiming power and authority that have continued to threaten the existence and well being of life on planet Earth, yet at the same time have claimed to be its rightful trustees, stewards, executors or administrators.

The Year of Divine Redemption is the last chance, the last opportunity for those claiming wealth and resources to redeem their position against the absolute authority and legitimacy of those societies and trusts formed through the present Covenant.

Divine Redemption is therefore the final act of restoring the true Rule of Law and the end of false and piracy law, of corrupt edicts and commands masquerading as original and true law.

In accord with Article 33 (*Day and Year of Divine Redemption*) of the most sacred Covenant *Pactum De Singularis Caelum*, the one, true and only Official Day of Day of Divine Redemption, also known as the Day of Redemption, also known as Redemption Day, also known as the Day of the 4th Divine Post and Notice, shall be GAIA E1:Y1:A1:S1:M9:D1, also known as [Fri, 21 Dec 2012].

Let it be known to all who come that this is the Day when Final Notice of Divine Forgiveness was duly served on behalf of the one true Divine Creator of all existence and witnessed by the united spirits of Heaven to all who respect rule of law and Final Notice of Divine Foreclosure and Liquidation of those entities, bodies, associations, corporations, offices and agents already bonded and under lien for their repeated transgressions and refusal to cease evil and insanity.

No other day shall be permitted to be known as the Day of Redemption. Furthermore, any claimed alternate day of Redemption or variation shall be rendered null and void from the beginning.

Let it be known that from the one true Day of Divine Redemption being GAIA E1:Y1:A1:S1:M9:D1, also known as [Fri, 21 Dec 2012] until UCA E1:Y2:A1:S1:M30:D1, also known as [Sat, 21 Dec 2013], shall be known as the Year of Divine Redemption represented as Year 1.

6. In accord with the Divine Grace and Divine Mercy of God and the Divine Creator of all Existence and all Heaven and Earth, at the conclusion of the Day of Divine Redemption and the Year of Divine Redemption and upon the definitive and formal recognition of Divine Mercy through the expression of mercy and forgiveness to all people and all forms of life, it shall be recorded in Heaven, now and forever more that all former transgressions and injuries are forgiven without condition and that no spirit, or spiritual entity, or living or physically deceased higher order life form is permitted to be condemned, or cursed spiritually. Only companies and corporations without a soul or spirit and that choose to continue to exist as soulless and spiritless entities by rejecting the present most sacred Covenant are excluded from Divine Mercy and Divine Redemption.

Divine Mercy and Forgiveness of All

Therefore, it is absolutely forbidden, reprobate and a profound profanity and perfidy to deny that through the Divine Grace and Divine Mercy of God and the Divine Creator of all Existence and all Heaven and Earth, that Heaven is once more united and that no longer does there exist a place for the eternal punishment of souls, nor a formal waiting place between the temporal and spiritual worlds. Such Divine Mercy and forgiveness does not diminish the obligations of virtue and truth and respect of the Rule of Law and the Ecclesia, but strengthens it, as all living and deceased Members are to be immediately and justly held to account for their actions at every stage of their existence in recognition of the transformative nature of all sentient beings; and that the Magisterium of the Universal Ecclesia is to assist people to overcome their transgressions and to improve the character and the quality of life of all people.

Furthermore, just as the Holy Spirit reveals that God and the Divine Creator of all Existence and all Heaven and Earth are united and resolved in absolute Love and Mercy to redeem every single soul, all ecclesiastical churches, orders, bodies, associations, fraternities, institutes, colleges and societies are also absolutely forgiven for past transgressions and errors, upon their absolute acceptance and solemn acknowledgement of the present most sacred Covenant, sealed and bound by their submission to the unity of the Living Body of One Christ. However, any Christian or Jewish church, or order, or body, or association, or fraternity, or institute or college or society that refuses to acknowledge the primacy of the present most sacred Covenant and submit to their redemption, not only accepts full liability but the consequences of their actions are ripened to then be reaped, but by the injury, perfidy and impiety of their actions they call upon all the forces of Heaven and Earth to hold and enforce them to account.

Any forum of law that disavows the bestowing of Divine Mercy and Divine Forgiveness unto a Christian or Jewish church, or order, or body, or association, or fraternity, or institute or college or society that has submitted itself in solemn and sacred oath and vow to the most sacred Covenant *Pactum De Singularis Caelum* and the present most sacred Covenant, is therefore a forum without jurisdiction or authority.

Article 7 – Transgression and Sin

1. **U**nification of the Living Body of Christ being the **Universal Ecclesia of Christ** represents a new Heaven and a new Earth and fulfilment of the Kingdom of Heaven upon the Earth and the vanquishing of all Sin.

   Transgression and Sin

   In accord with Article 29 (*Divine Mercy, Remedy & Redemption*) of the most sacred Covenant *Pactum De Singularis Caelum*, the term and use of the word "Sin" is hereby forbidden, reprobate, suppressed and never to be revived. Instead, the word and the equivalent concept of "**Transgression**" shall now be used to define mistake, fault, concept, default, fraud, profanity, tyranny and impiety.

   Whilst references and honour to historic and canonical texts and scripture shall permit the continued use of the word in Sacred Liturgy in historic context, all teachings, lessons, education and interpretation as to present and future events and the reference to "sin" is absolutely forbidden to be continued and an offence against the Living Body of One Christ.

2. In accord with Article 29 (*Divine Mercy, Remedy & Redemption*) of the most sacred Covenant *Pactum De Singularis Caelum*, there shall be seven (7) levels of Transgression. The higher the level of

   Seven levels of Transgression

Transgression, the more serious the transgression:-

(i)   Mistake or Error; and

(ii)   Fault (Delict); and

(iii)   Contempt (Profanity); and

(iv)   Default (Delinquency); and

(v)   Fraud (Perfidy); and

(vi)   Tyranny; and

(vii)   Impiety.

3.   Upon the vanquishing of Sin and the definition of Transgression, the concept of Salvation is fulfilled and satisfied and therefore can no longer be applied, or taught as a future aspiration. Instead, the Living Body of One Christ shall honour Divine Mercy and Divine Love in the form of Redemption and Credit, underwritten by the good character, behaviour and actions of people, in accord with the rules as defined by the most sacred Covenant *Pactum De Singularis Caelum* and the present most sacred Covenant.

     Redemption and Salvation

Any ecclesiastical, civil, secret or private forms of law that seek to perpetuate the notion of Salvation, of Debt and of the treatment of people as wrecked upon the sea, or other admiralty and maritime concepts, shall be rendered null and void from the beginning and a Transgression of Delinquency, Profanity and Perfidy against God and the Divine Creator of all Existence and all Heaven and Earth.

4.   Upon the vanquishing of Sin and the satisfaction of Salvation, all forms of money, finance and assets based upon the "monetisation of sin" or the "salvaging of debt or sin" are morally repugnant, profane, sacrilegious and to be conclusively and absolutely suppressed and never to be revived. Any monetary system or financial system based upon the claimed spiritual, or ecclesiastical, or moral bankruptcy of communities, or nations is absolutely and completely immoral, unlawful, illegal and null and void from the beginning, having no force or effect.

     Credit and Debt Sacramenta

Any financial system or monetary system based upon liens against the people, or their persons or names or souls is morally repugnant, profane, sacrilegious and to be conclusively and absolutely suppressed and never to be revived, having no force or power or effect in law. Furthermore, the monetisation of birth certificates is absolutely prohibited.

Any body, fraternity, company, person, institute, society or entity that seeks to perpetuate the notion of the "Monetisation of Sin", or global or national bankruptcies, or "monetisation of birth certificates", or liens or other condemnations against the people shall have their rights, property, powers and authorities rendered null and void from the beginning and shall have recorded and memorialised the fact of their Transgression of Delinquency, Profanity and Perfidy against God and the Divine Creator of all Existence and all Heaven and Earth.

Article 8 – Supreme See and Lesser Sees

1. **S**upreme See of the One Holy Apostolic Ecclesia of One Christ shall be the seat and absolute authority of the Supreme Patriarch, and the first Ecclesia. In accord with Article 98 (*Supreme Patriarch*) of the most sacred Covenant *Pactum De Singularis Caelum*, the Supreme See of the Ecclesia shall be sovereign absolute, possessing complete control and authority over the land, buildings, space and environment within its established boundaries. In recognition of the Golden Rule of Law governing all proper international law, the Supreme See makes itself a legal entity, recognisable under international law in the exercising of its sovereign, legislative, executive and judicial functions. Supreme See

   For the first term of the most sacred Divina, and the period of one hundred and twenty-eight (128) years, the Supreme See shall be Rome as *Nova Roma* representing Rome redeemed, reborne and renewed. Thereafter upon the conclusion of the second Great Conclave and for the second term of the most sacred Divina of Heaven, and the period of one hundred and twenty-eight (128) years, the Supreme See shall be seated at Paris, in honour of the Carolingians and the founding of the Catholicus Ecclesia. Thereafter upon the conclusion of the third Great Conclave and for the third term of the most sacred Divina of Heaven, and the period of one hundred and twenty-eight (128) years, the Supreme See shall be seated at Constantinople, also known at the founding of Christianity as Antioch. Thereafter, all future seats of the Supreme See shall be decided by a vote at the preceding Great Conclave.

2. In accord with Article 98 (*Supreme Patriarch*) of the most sacred Covenant *Pactum De Singularis Caelum*, The Holy See is the ecclesiastical jurisdiction of the Episcopal See of the Pope as Supreme Patriarch as an ecclesiastical, sovereign and independent entity. As an independent and sovereign entity holding the sacred Vatican City as sovereign dominion, the Holy See shall maintain diplomatic relations Holy See

49

3. A Patriarchal See is the official jurisdiction of a Patriarch of a Politea (State), or University, or recognised head of a Traditional and Customary Rite. In accord with the most sacred Covenant *Pactum De Singularis Caelum* and associated sacred Covenants, Canons and Rules, a Patriarchal See may encompass the full spiritual, ecclesiastical, temporal, territorial, topographic and political bounds of a State (Politea), otherwise known as a sovereign nation, or may encompass the whole planet Earth, yet only applying to those sacred places and people recognised within their Jurisdiction. To distinguish between the differences, a Patriarch appointed for a Politea (State) is also known as a Metropolitan Patriarch and a Patriarch recognised as ultimate head of a Traditional and Customary Rite is also known as an Apostolic Patriarch.

Patriarchal See

A Metropolitan Patriarch is so named as the Episcopal Bishop of the capital or "metropolitan" of a particular Politea (State).

An Apostolic Patriarch as head of an accepted Traditional and Customary Rite is so named and honoured in recognition of the long standing historical ties and connections that many Christian Churches and Bodies possess and that one of the greatest historic divisions between Christian fraternities over centuries was the claim of Apostolic authenticity. Furthermore, an Apostolic Patriarch of an accepted Traditional and Customary Rite also retains the right to their Traditional and Customary Titles.

A Patriarch must always be a Bishop accepted into the full dispensing of the most sacred Sacraments of One Christ and therefore recognised also in title as Cardinal in reference to the full authority and power to dispense all Cardinal Sacraments of Summa Sacramenta.

4. A Provincial See is the official jurisdiction of an Archbishop of a Province and Bishop of the Provincial Capital. In accord with the most sacred Covenant *Pactum De Singularis Caelum* and associated sacred Covenants, Canons and Rules, a Provincial See may encompass the full spiritual, ecclesiastical, temporal, territorial, topographic and political bounds of a Province.

Provincial See

An Archbishop of a Provincial See may (or may not) be a Bishop accepted into the full dispensing of the most sacred Sacraments of One Christ. If this is the case, the Archbishop shall also be recognised by the Title of Cardinal in reference to the full authority and power to dispense all Cardinal Sacraments of Summa Sacramenta.

5. An Episcopal See, also known as a Diocese, is the ecclesiastical jurisdiction of a Bishop. To distinguish between the differences, a Bishop appointed for a Diocese is also known as a Diocesan Bishop; and a Bishop recognised as a leader of a Traditional and Customary Rite is also known as an Apostolic Bishop.

    Episcopal See

6. A Parochial See is the jurisdiction of the head of a Parish or community of a Traditional and Customary Rite. The head priest of a Parish under a Diocesan Bishop is a Vicar. The head of a community of a Traditional and Customary Rite is known by their traditional title.

    Parochial See

Article 9 – Authenticus Depositum Fidei

1. **I**t is to the **Authentic, Apostolic and Anointed Divine Messengers** and none other, to whom the entire Revelation of the Divine Creator of all existence and all the heavens and the earth are entrusted.

    Heritage entrusted to Apostolic Anointed Messengers

    By custom and tradition of the ages, from the very beginning of human civilisation, such Revelation of Divine Truth, whether transmitted orally or by writing, has always been self-evident as the manifestation of Divine Illumination, by extraordinary enlightenment, clarity, perception, reasoning and wisdom beyond the norm of human experience. Thus, the truth of Divine Existence, Divine Mind and Divine Nature is never illogical, or irrational, or unreasonable, or superficial, or perfidious or malevolent.

    The Advocates of such Divine Truth as the deposit of trust of sacred knowledge and scripture, free from spells or curses, by custom and rule, did communicate such Divine Gifts from the creator of all existence to all men and all women through the embodiment of such trust in language, sign and writing. Such canonical texts were then to be the source of all saving truth and moral discipline, free of corruption or distortion.

    Such living transmission, accomplished under the authority and power of the Divine Creator, is called Tradition since it is distinct from Sacred Scripture itself, whilst closely connected to it. Through Tradition, each generation in life and reverence for the Golden Rule of Law, may then perpetuate and transmit to every other generation all that is trusted as the most valuable and important of knowledge.

2. In accord with Article 23 (*Authentic Sacred Deposit of Trust*) of the most sacred Covenant *Pactum De Singularis Caelum* and the present most sacred covenant, the Thirty-Three (33) Covenants between Authentic, Apostolic and Anointed Divine Messengers of the Divine

    Authenticus Depositum Fidei

Creator of all Existence and all the Heavens and Earth and the peoples of the Earth are entrusted as the Authentic Sacred Deposit of Trust (*Authenticus Depositum Fidei*), contained in Sacred Canonical Scripture and Tradition, to the embodiment of the present sacred covenant and no other.

Thirty-Three (33) Covenants between Authentic, Apostolic and Anointed Divine Messengers of the Divine Creator of all Existence and all the Heavens and Earth and the peoples of the Earth are acknowledged as having merit, authority, power and jurisdiction above all others by custom and tradition, namely: the most ancient sacred covenants of *De Dea Magisterium* of the Serpens (Reptoids), of *Yapa* of the Saltwater People, of *Mandi* of the Plains People, of *Tia* of the Mountain People, of *Waiata* of the Sea People, of *Five Worlds* of the First Nations, of Adamus of the *Cuilliaéan*, of *Mama* of the Mother Goddess of Heaven and Earth, of *Ebla* of Abraham and Patriarchs, of *Kabalaah* of Akhenaten (Moses) and the Hyksos, of *Revelations* of the Great Prophets of Yeb, of *Tara* of Jeremiah and the Celts, of *Acadia* of Xerxes, of *Missal* of Baal Mithra, of *Eternal Mysteries* of Isis, of *Eliada* of Alexander, of *Heaven and Earth* of Qin Shi Huang, of *Truth (Nazara)* of Yahusiah (Jesus Christ), of *Self Enlightenment* of Gautama, of *Septuaginta* of Iudaism, of *Eucadia (Ucadia)* of Heracles, of *Digesta* of Marcus Aurelius, of *Talmud* of the Aryans, of *Bibliographe* of Constantine, of *Sanatana Dharma* of Supreme Creator, of *Al Sufian* of Sophos (Great Prophet) and Islam, of *Nova Testamentum* of Catholicism of the Franks, of *Eternal Truth* of Gurma, of *Holy Bible* of the Stewards (Stuarts), of *Lebor Clann Glas* of the true Diaspora, of *Illuminatus Mysterium* of the Keepers and Protectors of Ancient Wisdom, of *Mundi* of the Greys and of *Summa Divina* of the Sapientia Mutatis (Transformed Wisdom Beings).

Article 10 – Maxima Textibus Sacris

1. **M**axima Textibus Sacris being the most significant, important and influential sacred texts of major faiths throughout history, in accord with Article 37 (*Supreme Sacred Texts*) of the most sacred Covenant *Pactum De Singularis Caelum*. Maxima Textibus Sacris shall be comprised of twenty-two (22) collections or "texts", each representing either:

    (i)   A past collection of the greatest sacred texts for a region or major faith or covenant in accord with Authenticus Depositum Fidei prior to the end of the Year of Redemption; or

    (ii)   The future collection of sacred texts for a region or major faith

Maxima
Textibus Sacris

or covenant in accord with Authenticus Depositum Fidei after the end of the Year of Redemption.

2. The first eleven (11) sacred collections of texts of the Maxima Textibus Sacris represent the greatest sacred texts of all major regions of planet Earth and major faiths prior to the end of the Year of Redemption, being:- *First eleven sacred collections of texts*

   (i)   **"Primum Sanctum Textibus Africa"**, also known as First Holy Texts of Africa; and

   (ii)   **"Primum Sanctum Textibus Americas"**, also known as First Holy Texts of (the) Americas; and

   (iii) **"Primum Sanctum Textibus Arabia"**, also known as First Holy Texts of Arabia; and

   (iv)   **"Primum Sanctum Textibus Asia"**, also known as First Holy Texts of Asia; and

   (v)   **"Primum Sanctum Textibus Euro"**, also known as First Holy Texts of Euro; and

   (vi)   **"Primum Sanctum Textibus Oceania"**, also known as First Holy Texts of Oceania; and

   (vii) **"Primam Sanctam Textibus Unum Christus"**, also known as First Holy Texts of One Christ; and

   (viii) **"Primam Sanctam Textibus Unum Islam"**, also known as First Holy Texts of One Islam; and

   (ix)   **"Primam Sanctam Textibus Unum Spirit"**, also known as First Holy Texts of One Spirit; and

   (x)   **"Primam Sanctam Textibus Unum Terra"**, also known as First Holy Texts of One Earth; and

   (xi)   **"Primam Sanctam Textibus Unum Mentis"**, also known as First Holy Texts of One Mind.

3. The second eleven (11) sacred collections of texts of the Maxima Textibus Sacris represent the new sacred texts of all major regions of planet Earth and major faiths after the end of the Year of Redemption, being:- *Second eleven sacred collections*

   (i)   **"Sancta Nova Textibus Africa"**, also known as New Holy Texts of Africa; and

   (ii)   **"Sancta Nova Textibus Americas"**, also known as New

Holy Texts of (the) Americas; and

(iii) **"Sancta Nova Textibus Arabia"**, also known as New Holy Texts of Arabia; and

(iv) **"Sancta Nova Textibus Asia"**, also known as New Holy Texts of Asia; and

(v) **"Sancta Nova Textibus Euro"**, also known as New Holy Texts of Euro; and

(vi) **"Sancta Nova Textibus Oceania"**, also known as New Holy Texts of Oceania; and

(vii) **"Sancta Nova Textibus Unum Christus"**, also known as New Holy Texts of One Christ; and

(viii) **"Sancta Nova Textibus Unum Islam"**, also known as New Holy Texts of One Islam; and

(ix) **"Sancta Nova Textibus Unum Spirit"**, also known as New Holy Texts of One Spirit; and

(x) **"Sancta Nova Textibus Unum Terra"**, also known as New Holy Texts of One Earth; and

(xi) **"Sancta Nova Textibus Unum Mentis"**, also known as New Holy Texts of One Mind.

4. The acceptance of a Sacred Text into a collection shall depend upon the name and type of collection:-

Acceptance of Sacred Texts into a Collection

(i) All collections of Sacred Texts by regions shall be determined by the legislative authority of the particular Union that encompasses the region, in association with a Great Conclave every one hundred and twenty-eight (128) years or General Conclave every sixty-four (64) years; and

(ii) All collections of Sacred Texts by faiths shall be determined by the legislative authority of the particular faith in association with a Great Conclave every one hundred and twenty-eight (128) years or General Conclave every sixty-four (64) years.

5. All accepted Sacred Texts may appear in more than one collection and are formally defined as Canonical, Reverential or Referential:-

Status of Accepted Sacred Texts

(i) **"Canonical Sacred Texts"** are texts considered and cited as the absolute foundation of all law and spiritual authority and therefore the twenty-two (22) books of true canon law known as *Astrum Iuris Divini Canonum*; and

(ii) **"Reverential Sacred Texts"** are texts that contain some canonical references but also possess too many non canonical references to be wholly canonical so may be partially cited as foundational law but not considered absolute "Divine Law"; and

(iii) **"Referential Sacred Texts"** are respected historical texts that are not considered accurate or consistent enough to be "Divine Law" that may be referenced in historical context and reference but not as true foundation of law.

Article 11 – Summa Sacramenta

1. The Sacraments of One Heaven, also known as *Summa Sacramenta*, also known as the Supreme Sacraments of Heaven, are a vital and necessary element of a fulfilled and purposeful life, assisting each and every higher order being, living and deceased to reach their full potential and communion with the Divine Creator, the Universe and with one another.

   Summa Sacramenta

   In accord with Article 44 (*Supreme Sacred Gifts of Heaven*) of the most sacred Covenant *Pactum De Singularis Caelum*, the **"Summa Sacramenta"** as the Sacraments of Heaven, are a manifest symbol of the plenary authority of the Living Body of Christ. No other person, aggregate, entity, society, church or group may claim the right to administer any valid sacrament unless it is in accordance with the present sacred Covenant.

   All valid sacraments are instituted by the Divine Creator of all Existence and entrusted to the Universal Ecclesia of One Christ. Any claimed sacrament that is not granted through the authority of Heaven in accordance with the present sacred Covenant is a false ritual and possesses no Divine authority or power to be known as a valid sacrament.

2. Self-Aware Higher Order Life, such as Human Beings, are spiritual beings as much as they are temporal and physical beings; and that our existence does not end with the physical death of our body; and that our purpose of being does not rest solely upon the experiences, wants or desires of everyday life.

   Spiritual Nature of Self-Aware Higher Order Life

3. A valid and authentic Sacrament is a distinct and related set of Temporal and Divine Actions forming a significant moment of unity:-

   Nature of Valid and Authentic Sacrament

   (i) Temporal Actions as a *rite* or *rites*, following in a precise manner according to a set *formula*, some intended sacred memorial, instrument or event (or all of these elements); and

(ii) Divine Actions derived from the Love, Mercy and Grace of the Divine Creator through authentic revelation, in harmony with right intentioned Temporal Actions.

4. All valid sacraments are those said to be derived from Heaven and the Divine Creator through authentic Revelation. Valid sacraments are never formed by temporal beings alone; and certainly never genuinely formed by doctrine, but by the Revelation and the inspired instruction of the most sacred Covenant *Pactum De Singularis Caelum*, the present sacred Covenant and related covenants and sacred texts.

Source of valid Sacraments

5. All valid sacraments firstly owe their name according to the Divine Actions and Gifts associated with them and not by the Temporal Actions that may be associated. Thus Temporal Actions associated with a valid sacrament are more appropriately classified as a *rite* or *rites* of a sacrament.

Name of valid Sacraments

6. The present most sacred Covenant reveals to all Self-Aware Higher Order Life of all times and places that it is our ultimate destiny to be reconciled unto our ultimate Divine Creator - through care of our spiritual well being as much as our mental and physical well being.

Divine Purpose of Sacraments

Moreover, that despite any weaknesses or transgressions, no one be condemned or eternally cursed; as all are granted the gifts of Divine Love, Divine Mercy and Divine Forgiveness. Furthermore, that our Divine Creator entrusts the necessary gifts to nourish and protect our spiritual well being on our journey.

This is the primary reason and purpose of the Holy Sacraments that bestow upon each and every man, woman and child, the gifts of Divine Grace and capacity to be reconciled with the Divine, and with their own Divine Nature and among themselves.

The Holy Sacraments are not merely an expression of a particular faith, but an essential element of existence itself. For without such Divine Grace, it follows that because of our human limitations it would be impossible to be reconciled to the Divine by our own accord; or united with our Divine self by prayer and piety alone; or fully at peace with one another purely upon a virtuous and exemplary life.

7. The Thirty-Three (33) valid sacraments of Summa Sacramenta are authentically deposited in trust by the Divine Creator to the Society of One Heaven in accord with the *Authenticus Depositum Fidei* (Authentic Deposit of Trust).

Thirty-Three Valid Sacraments

All valid sacred rites, also known as rituals, customs and acts are derived from the thirty-three (33) valid sacraments of One Heaven. A valid ritual, custom or act derived from one of the thirty-three (33) valid sacraments and expressed ecclesiastically may be said to be on the "ecclesiastical side" of the law.

All valid administrative writs, processes and acts are derived from the thirty-three (33) valid sacraments of One Heaven. A valid writ, process or act derived from one of the thirty-three (33) valid sacraments and expressed civilly may be said to be on the "public side" of the law.

All valid Sacraments share the same six (6) essential elements, being:-

(i)   A defined structure in liturgy of three (3) separate and deliberate Acts, themselves divided into smaller Parts representing completed Moments being sacred instances of units of time-space-location; and

(ii)   An Ordinary and Extraordinary version of the sacrament distinguished by a shorter secular and more formal ecclesiastical version of the sacrament; and

(iii)   One or more roles for authorised persons known as Celebrant(s) officiating some or all of the Acts; and

(iv)   One or more roles for persons known as Participant(s) who participate under the guidance of the Celebrant(s) in some or all of the Acts; and

(v)   One or more roles for persons known as Observant(s) who witness the celebration of the Sacrament and validate it as a Sacred Event; and

(vi)   The memorialisation of the celebration of the Sacrament as a Sacred Event through some produced instrument representing a Record of the (Sacred) Event.

8.   A Sacrament not properly conferred in accord with the present sacred Covenant has no ecclesiastic power nor effect in law and is invalid *ab initio* (from the beginning). Only authorised persons may validly confer a Sacrament of Heaven properly through the role of Celebrant, possessing the Right *Ius Divinum Sacramentum* as the Divine Right to grant and impart Holy Sacraments:-

Conferral of valid Sacraments

(i)   Only persons properly consecrated and ordained into Holy Orders or invested into office holding a Right derived from *Ius Divinum Magisterium* or *Ius Divinum Visium* or *Ius Divinum Oratorium* in accord with the most sacred Covenant *Pactum De Singularis Caelum* and the present sacred Covenant possesses the powers and authority to confer and administer these sacraments under Extraordinary Conditions; and

(ii)   Only persons properly invested into office holding the Right of *Ius Divinum Administratum*, *Ius Divinum Officium* or *Ius Divinum Imperium* in accord with the most sacred Covenant *Pactum De Singularis Caelum* and the present sacred Covenant possesses the powers and authority to confer and administer these sacraments under Ordinary Conditions.

Sacred ministers cannot deny the sacraments to those who seek them at appropriate times and who are properly disposed, and are not prohibited by law from receiving them. All ministers, according to their respective ecclesiastical function, have the duty to take care that those who seek the sacraments are prepared to receive them by proper instruction and are attentive to the norms issued by competent authority.

In celebrating the sacraments by extraordinary condition, the liturgical books approved by competent authority are to be observed faithfully; accordingly, no one is to add, omit, or alter anything in them on one's own authority. In celebrating the sacraments by ordinary condition, only those things required for the validity of the sacrament must be observed.

The minister is to seek nothing for the administration of the sacraments beyond the offerings defined by competent authority, always taking care that the needy are not deprived of the assistance of the sacraments because of poverty.

9.   The "**Key Sacraments**" also known as Clavem Sacramenta, also known as "The Keys" are seven (7) of the thirty-three (33) sacred rites of the supremely sacred Covenant *Pactum De Singularis Caelum* instituted by the Divine Creator and entrusted to the Society of One Heaven and all associated valid entities being: Recognition, Purification, Invocation, Obligation, Delegation, Satisfaction and Resolution.   Key Sacraments

The Key Sacraments of Heaven are a manifest symbol of the plenary authority of the Society and the most sacred Covenant *Pactum De Singularis Caelum*, exemplified by the expression *potestas clavium* or simply the "Power of the Keys".

Since the Key Sacraments are the same for every occasion and every Homo Sapien, living or deceased, it is only for the supreme authority of the Society of One Heaven to approve or define the requirements for their validity and what pertains to their licit celebration, administration, and reception and to the order to be observed in their celebration:-

(i)   **"Ritus Sacramentum Recognosco"** be the Divine Right of the Key Sacrament of Recognition; and

(ii)   **"Ritus Sacramentum Purificatio"** be the Divine Right of the Key Sacrament of Purification; and

(iii)   **"Ritus Sacramentum Invocatio"** be the Divine Right of the Key Sacrament of Invocation; and

(iv)   **"Ritus Sacramentum Obligatio"** be the Divine Right of the Key Sacrament of Obligation; and

(v)   **"Ritus Sacramentum Delegatio"** be the Divine Right of the Key Sacrament of Delegation (Trust); and

(vi)   **"Ritus Sacramentum Satisfactio"** be the Divine Right of the Key Sacrament of Satisfaction; and

(vii)   **"Ritus Sacramentum Resolutio"** be the Divine Right of the Key Sacrament of Resolution.

10. The **"Cardinal Sacraments"** also known as Cardinalis Sacramenta, also known as "The Ways" are fourteen (14) of the thirty-three (33) sacred rites of the supremely sacred Covenant *Pactum De Singularis Caelum* instituted by the Divine Creator and entrusted to the Society of One Heaven and all associated valid entities being: Sanctification, Sustentation, Unification (Matrimony), Amalgamation (Union), Authentication, Absolution, Volition (Oath), Vocation (Vow), Testification, Compassion (Mercy), Conscription (Binding), Convocation, Authorisation and Elucidation (Enlightenment).   *Cardinal Sacraments*

As ways, points, junctures and hinges for the actions of the Divine Creator and One Heaven, the Cardinal Sacraments are signs and gifts which express and strengthen the society and effect the sanctification of a community and thus contribute in the greatest way to establish, strengthen, and manifest spiritual unity.

Since the Cardinal Sacraments are the same for every valid religion and Society, it is only for the supreme authority of the Society of One Heaven to approve or define the requirements for their validity and what pertains to their licit celebration, administration, and reception and to the order to be observed in their celebration:-

(i)   **"Ritus Sacramentum Sanctificatio"** be the Divine Right of the Cardinal Sacrament of Sanctification; and

(ii)   **"Ritus Sacramentum Sustentatio"** be the Divine Right of Sustentation; and

59

(iii)   **"Ritus Sacramentum Unificatio"** be the Divine Right of the Cardinal Sacrament of Unification (Matrimony); and

(iv)   **"Ritus Sacramentum Amalgamatio"** be the Divine Right of the Cardinal Sacrament of Amalgamation (Union); and

(v)   **"Ritus Sacramentum Authentico"** be the Divine Right of the Cardinal Sacrament of Authentication (Record); and

(vi)   **"Ritus Sacramentum Absolutio"** be the Divine Right of the Cardinal Sacrament of Absolution (Penance); and

(vii)   **"Ritus Sacramentum Volitio"** be the Divine Right of the Cardinal Sacrament of Volition (Oath); and

(viii)   **"Ritus Sacramentum Vocatio"** be the Divine Right of the Cardinal Sacrament of Vocation (Vow); and

(ix)   **"Ritus Sacramentum Testificatio"** be the Divine Right of the Cardinal Sacrament of Testification; and

(x)   **"Ritus Sacramentum Compassio"** be the Divine Right of the Cardinal Sacrament of Compassion (Mercy); and

(xi)   **"Ritus Sacramentum Conscripto"** be the Divine Right of the Cardinal Sacrament of Conscription (Binding); and

(xii)   **"Ritus Sacramentum Convocatio"** be the Divine Right of the Cardinal Sacrament of Convocation; and

(xiii)   **"Ritus Sacramentum Auctoriso"** be the Divine Right of the Cardinal Sacrament of Authorisation; and

(xiv)   **"Ritus Sacramentum Elucidato"** be the Divine Right of the Cardinal Sacrament of Elucidation (Enlightenment).

11.   The **"Apostolic Life Sacraments"** also known as Sacramenta Vitae Apostolicae, also known as "The Means" are the twelve (12) of the thirty-three (33) sacred rites of the supremely sacred Covenant *Pactum De Singularis Caelum* instituted by the Divine Creator and entrusted to the Society of One Heaven and all associated valid entities being: Inspiration, Resurrection, Incarnation, Confirmation, Illumination, Exultation, Glorification, Divination, Visitation, Salvation, Emancipation and Veneration.

Apostolic Life Sacraments

All members of One Heaven are entitled to receive the full benefits of all twelve (12) Life Sacraments, whether living or deceased either upon the anniversaries prescribed for the conferral of a sacrament or upon proof of majority and competency for the specific Life Sacraments of Epinoia, Genius, Beau Ideal and Haga Sofia. A member who has not first received the prior Life Sacrament, cannot be admitted validly to receiving the subsequent sacrament.

As actions of the Divine Creator and One Heaven the Life Sacraments are signs and means which express and strengthen the faith, render worship to the Divine and effect the sanctification of humanity and thus contribute in the greatest way to establish, strengthen, and manifest ecclesiastical unity. Accordingly, in the celebration of the sacraments the sacred ministers and the other members of the faithful must use the greatest veneration and necessary diligence:-

(i) **"Ritus Sacramentum Inspiratio"** be the Divine Right of the Apostolic Life Sacrament of Inspiration (Annunciation); and

(ii) **"Ritus Sacramentum Resurrectio"** be the Divine Right of the Apostolic Life Sacrament of Resurrection (Baptism); and

(iii) **"Ritus Sacramentum Incarnatio"** be the Divine Right of the Apostolic Life Sacrament of Incarnation (Christening); and

(iv) **"Ritus Sacramentum Confirmatio"** be the Divine Right of the Apostolic Life Sacrament of Confirmation (First Communion); and

(v) **"Ritus Sacramentum Illuminatio"** be the Divine Right of the Apostolic Life Sacrament of Illumination; and

(vi) **"Ritus Sacramentum Exultatio"** be the Divine Right of the Apostolic Life Sacrament of Exultation; and

(vii) **"Ritus Sacramentum Glorificatio"** be the Divine Right of the Apostolic Life Sacrament of Glorification; and

(viii) **"Ritus Sacramentum Divinatio"** be the Divine Right of the Apostolic Life Sacrament of Divination; and

(ix) **"Ritus Sacramentum Visitatio"** be the Divine Right of the Apostolic Life Sacrament of Visitation; and

(x) **"Ritus Sacramentum Salvatio"** be the Divine Right of the Apostolic Life Sacrament of Salvation; and

(xi) **"Ritus Sacramentum Emancipatio"** be the Divine Right of the Apostolic Life Sacrament of Emancipation (Unbinding) of any and all debts and obligations and reverence of funerary celebrations; and

(xii) **"Ritus Sacramentum Veneratio"** be the Divine Right of the Apostolic Life Sacrament of Veneration.

13. **"Extra-Sacramental Rites"** and Rubrics of Heaven shall be the customary rules, standards and procedures of rites and rituals beyond the Thirty-Three (33) Sacraments as defined by the present sacred Covenant; and whereby such Extra-Sacramental Rites and Rubrics are properly administered and dispensed by qualified and authorised persons.

Extra-Sacramental Rites and Rubrics

Just as all valid, legitimate and proper sacraments are derived from Heaven and the Divine Grace and Mercy of the Divine Creator, in accord with the present sacred Covenant, all rules, customs, traditions, standards and procedures for their administration and ministration are ultimately derived from the most sacred Covenant *Pactum De Singularis Caelum.*

No rule, custom, tradition, standard or procedure in relation to Sacramental or Extra-Sacramental Rites and Rubrics shall be valid, legitimate or permitted, unless it firmly adheres to the most sacred Covenant *Pactum De Singularis Caelum* and the present sacred Covenant.

14. "The following forms of Extra-Sacramental Rites and Rubrics are recognised and subject to the present Sacred Covenant, including (but not limited to):-

Recognised Forms of Extra-Sacramental Rites and Rubrics

(i)   **"Dedication"** being a form of Extra-Sacramental Rite for the consecration of places, buildings, monuments and structures; and

(ii)   **"Restoration"** being a form of Extra-Sacramental Rite for the reconsecration and bringing a place, building, monument or structure to its original state; and

(iii)   **"Reformation"** being a form of Extra-Sacramental Rite for the restoring of a cleric state of office to a sacred state; and

(iv)   **"Blessing"** being a form of Extra-Sacramental Rite for invoking Divine assistance, favour, approval or protection; and

(v)   **"Expulsion"** being a form of Extra-Sacramental Rite for the driving out of a particular spirit or presence from Sacred Circumscribed Space; and

(vi)   **"Nullification"** being a form of Extra-Sacramental Rite for making legally and lawfully invalid a previous agreement or right; and

(vii)   **"Deconsecration"** being a form of Extra-Sacramental Rite for the removal of the consecrated and sacred state and function of a place, building, monument or structure; and

(viii) **"Secularisation"** being a form of Extra-Sacramental Rite for the removal of the clerical authority of a person previously ordained; and

(ix) **"Exorcism"** being a form of Extra-Sacramental Rite for the enforced removal, arrest or custody of one or more spirits in breach of the rules governing Sacred Circumscribed Space and the laws of Divine Trust, Mind and Spirit; and

(x) **"Inquisition"** being a form of Extra-Sacramental Rite for the formal investigation into the truth and efficacy of some matter; and

(xi) **"Dispensation"** being a form of Extra-Sacramental Rite for the granting of permission to do or perform an act not otherwise permitted, or to omit doing something otherwise enjoined; an exemption; and

(xii) **"Abrogation"** being a form of Extra-Sacramental Rite for the repealing by authority of some legislative act; and

(xiii) **"Ordination"** being a form of Extra-Sacramental Rite for the consecration of a qualified candidate for the clerical state; and

(xiv) **"Inauguration"** being a form of Extra-Sacramental Rite for the inducting into office with solemnity a person elected to high civil office; and

(xv) **"Sanction"** being a form of Extra-Sacramental Rite for the enforced censuring, restriction or punishment of a person holding or occupying an office, in response to a demonstrated and proven act of maladministration or malfeasance; and

(xvi) **"Unction"** being a form of Extra-Sacramental Rite for the anointing of a person in time of ill-health or trauma; and

(xvii) **"Coronation"** being a form of Extra-Sacramental Rite for the solemn sacred ceremonial investiture of a person into sovereign office and the formation of a new sacred sovereign trust between the people and the new sovereign; and

(xviii) **"Investiture"** being a form of Extra-Sacramental Rite for the solemn sacred acceptance of a person into office that involves the formation of a new trust involving the transfer and vesting of one or more Ecclesiastical or Sovereign or Official Rights; and

(xix) **"Hours"** being a form of Extra-Sacramental Rite for the recitation of prayers and forms of invocation, in relation to significant days, times and seasons, often involving chants or singing.

Article 12 – Summa Elementis Theologica

1. **S**umma Elementis Theologica is a complete and cohesive philosophical system of knowledge, principles, methods, arguments and proofs that rationally and reliably explains the existence, nature, function and intention of a supreme spiritual and supernatural presence within, without and throughout all existence.

Summa Elementis Theologica

2. In accord with Article 25 (*The Divine Science*) of the most sacred Covenant *Pactum De Singularis Caelum*, "**Summa Elementis Theologica**" shall be the supreme and highest definitive theological source for proof, arguments, existence, principles and theoretical relations between particular cosmological models, the Divine, Divine Revelation, Divine Law, Divine Rights, Powers and Authorities being twenty-two (22) sections as:-

Structure of Summa Elementis Theologica

(i)   Exordium; and

(ii)   Existence; and

(iii)   Supernatural; and

(iv)   Theology; and

(v)   Divinities; and

(vi)   Divine Revelation and Messengers; and

(vii)   Divine Rights and Powers; and

(viii) Divine Authority and Offices; and

(ix)   Divine Places and Elements; and

(x)   Divine Scripture; and

(xi)   Divine Acts and Sacraments; and

(xii)   Life and Nature; and

(xiii) Mind, Language and Intellect; and

(xiv)   Law and Canons; and

(xv)   Covenants and Agreements; and

(xvi)   Records, Rolls and Registers; and

(xvii) Persons; and

(xviii) Instruments and Forms; and

(xix) Trusts and Estates; and

(xx) Funds and Companies; and

(xxi) Prophecy and Fulfilment; and

(xxii) Instructions and Decrees.

Article 13 – Astrum Iuris Divini Canonum

1. **N**o higher form of rules, norms, standards, laws, doctrines, dogmata, edicts or canons shall exist than the most sacred "**Astrum Iuris Divini Canonum**" being the Living Body of Divine Canon Law and the highest of all Original Law.

Living Body of Divine Canon Laws of Heaven

2. The twenty-two (22) books of the most sacred *Astrum Iuris Divini Canonum* as defined by Article 135 (*Divine Collection of Maxims of Law*) of the most sacred Covenant *Pactum De Singularis Caelum* are:-

Structure of Astrum Iuris Divini Canonum

(i) *Canonum De Lex Divina* (Divine Law); and

(ii) *Canonum De Lex Naturae* (Natural Law); and

(iii) *Canonum De Ius Cogitatum* (Cognitive Law); and

(iv) *Canonum De Ius Positivum* (Positive Law); and

(v) *Canonum De Lex Ecclesium* (Ecclesiastical Law); and

(vi) *Canonum De Ius Virtus Naturae* (Bioethics Law); and

(vii) *Canonum De Ius Rex* (Sovereign Law); and

(viii) *Canonum De Ius Fidei* (Fiduciary Law); and

(ix) *Canonum De Ius Administratum* (Administrative Law); and

(x) *Canonum De Lex Frugalitas* (Economic Law); and

(xi) *Canonum De Ius Pecuniae* (Monetary Law); and

(xii) *Canonum De Ius Civilis* (Civil Law); and

(xiii) *Canonum De Ius Criminalis* (Criminal Law); and

(xiv) *Canonum De Ius Informatum* (Education Law); and

(xv) *Canonum De Ius Nutrimens Et Medicina* (Food and Drugs Law); and

(xvi)   *Canonum De Ius Urbanus* (Urban Law); and

(xvii) *Canonum De Ius Companie* (Company Law); and

(xviii) *Canonum De Ius Machinatio* (Technology Law); and

(xix)   *Canonum De Ius Proventum* (Trade Law); and

(xx)   *Canonum De Ius Securitas* (Security Law); and

(xxi)   *Canonum De Ius Militaris* (Military Law); and

(xxii) *Canonum De Ius Gentium* (International Law).

Article 14 – Missale Christus

1. **Universal Ecclesia of One Christ** shall fulfil its sanctifying function through the Sacred Liturgy, being the rightful exercise of the presbyterial function entrusted to it by Christ. Within the Sacred Liturgy, the sanctification of humanity is perfected through visible signs and effected in a competent manner proper to each sign. Through the Sacred Liturgy, the worship of God and the Divine Creator of Heaven and Earth is conducted by the united Members of the Living Body of One Christ.

    In accord with Article 134 (*Supreme Sacred Gifts and Rites*) of the most sacred Covenant *Pactum De Singularis Caelum*, The Missal of Christ (*Missale Christus*) shall be the original and primary sacred text containing the necessary rubrics, canons, sacramentaries, votives, invocations, instructions and orders for the proper conduct and proceeding of Sacred Liturgy of the Universal Rites of One Christ.

    The conduct of all Sacramentals and Extra-Sacramentals of Heaven is in accord with the Missal of Christ (*Missale Christus*).

    Missale Christus

2. The Missal of Christ (*Missale Christus*) shall be divided into three (3) sacred books:-

    Structure of Missale Christus

    (i)   Proper of Life & Mysteries; and

    (ii)   Proper of Days of Heroes & Saints; and

    (iii)   Proper of Sacraments, Rites & Prayers.

3. The Structure of the Proper of Life & Mysteries shall be divided in Titles and then Articles. The Titles shall be:-

    Proper of Life & Mysteries

    I. Divine Mission of Liturgy

    II. Seven Mysteries of Christ

III. Authentic Christian Calendar

IV. Apostolic Life of the People of God

V. Purpose & Nature of the Eucharist & Mass

VI. Places & Objects of Sacred Liturgy

VII. Participants of Sacred Liturgy

VIII. Order of Mass

IX. Preparation & Completion of Mass

X. General Masses for Proper of Mysteries

XI. Special Masses for Proper of Mysteries

XII. Ordinary Masses for Proper of Mysteries

XIII. Extraordinary Masses for Proper of Mysteries

XIV. Proper of Mystery of Immanent Christ

XV. Proper of Mystery of Filial Christ

XVI. Proper of Mystery of the Eucharist

XVII. Proper of Mystery of Transcendent Christ

XVIII. Proper of Mystery of Sacred Heart of Christ

XIX. Proper of Mystery of Mercy & Redemption

XX. Proper of Mystery of Apostolic Life

XXI. Appendices

XXII. Indexes

4. The Structure of the Proper of Days of Heroes & Saints shall be divided in Titles and then Articles. The Titles shall be:- **Proper of Days of Heroes & Saints**

I. Proper of Days of Heroes and Saints

II. Patron Saints of Peoples & Regions

III. Patron Saints of Nations & Places

IV. Patron Saints of Causes

V. General Masses for Heroes & Saints

VI. Special Masses for Heroes & Saints

VII. Ordinary Masses for Heroes & Saints

VIII. Extraordinary Masses for Heroes & Saints

IX. Proper of January

   X. Proper of February

   XI. Proper of March

   XII. Proper of April

   XIII. Proper of May

   XIV. Proper of June

   XV. Proper of July

   XVI. Proper of August

   XVII. Proper of September

   XVIII. Proper of October

   XIX. Proper of November

   XX. Proper of December

   XXI. Appendices

   XXII. Indexes

5. The Structure of the Proper of Sacraments, Rites & Prayers shall be divided in Titles and then Articles. The Titles shall be:-   *Proper of Sacraments, Rites & Prayers*

   I. Holy Sacraments & Rites

   II. Sacrament of Recognition

   III. Sacrament of Purification

   IV. Sacrament of Invocation

   V. Sacrament of Obligation

   VI. Sacrament of Delegation

   VII. Sacrament of Satisfaction

   VIII. Sacrament of Resolution

   IX. Sacrament & Rite of Sanctification

   X. Sacrament of Sustentation & Rite of Eucharist

   XI. Sacrament of Unification & Rite of Matrimony

   XII. Sacrament of Amalgamation & Rite of Union

   XIII. Sacrament of Authentication

   XIV. Sacrament of Absolution & Rite of Confession

   XV. Sacrament of Volition & Rite of Oath

   XVI. Sacrament of Vocation & Rite of Vow

Article 15 – Traditions & Customary Rites

1. **Divine Mercy and Respect** dictates that the faithful be accorded the privilege of honouring tradition and custom, where such rites do not contravene such Universal Laws prohibiting actual or simulated blood sacrifice, cursing or profanities.

Thus, Members who hold affinity to one or more Traditional and Customary Rites as recognised by the present most sacred Covenant are free to continue the service and proceeding of certain registered and approved customary rites.

However, rites that are not registered or approved may not be practised; and rites that are contrary to the norms and principles of the most sacred covenant are reprobate, forbidden and to be

Traditions & Customary Rites

suppressed.

2. All Christian communities that honour tradition and custom, respecting Sacred Scripture and acknowledging the call for unity of the Living Body of Christ are welcome to enter into a lasting communion that dignifies such trust in God and the Divine Creator of all Existence and Heaven and Earth by ensuring the retention of traditional and customary titles, rights, ceremonies, churches and heritage under a solemn oath and vow that the entirety of the Living Body of Christ shall seek to protect and preserve such tradition and custom now and forever more.

Traditions & Customary Rites of Christianity

3. The present most sacred Covenant recognises the dignity and honour of the following Traditional and Customary Rites as eligible for communion and unity with the one true Living Body of Christ:-

Recognised Traditional and Customary Rites

(i) Roman (Catholic) Rite; and

(ii) Latin (Catholic) Rite; and

(iii) Anglican Rite; and

(iv) Byzantine Rite; and

(v) Chaldean Rite; and

(vi) Armenian Rite; and

(vii) Antiochene Rite; and

(viii) Alexandrian Rite; and

(ix) Catholic Episcopal and Evangelical Rite; and

(x) Baptist Rite; and

(xi) Lutheran Rite; and

(xii) Methodist Rite; and

(xiii) Presbyterian Rite; and

(xiv) Pentecostal Rite; and

(xv) Evangelical Rite; and

(xvi) Scottish Rite; and

(xvii) Russian Orthodox Rite; and

(xviii) Greek Orthodox Rite; and

(xix)   Romanian Orthodox Rite; and

(xx)   Serbian Orthodox Rite; and

(xxi)   Bulgarian Orthodox Rite; and

(xxii)   Macedonian Orthodox Rite; and

(xxiii) Belarus Orthodox Rite; and

(xxiv)   Georgian Orthodox Rite; and

(xxv)   Ukrainian Orthodox Rite; and

(xxvi)   Ethiopian Orthodox Rite; and

(xxvii) Coptic Orthodox Rite; and

(xxviii) Armenian Orthodox Rite; and

(xxix)   Syriac Orthodox Rite; and

(xxx)   Eritrean Orthodox Rite; and

(xxxi)   Latter Day Rite.

4. All Jewish communities that honour tradition and custom, respecting Sacred Scripture and acknowledging the call for unity of the Living Body of Christ are welcome to enter into a lasting communion that dignifies such trust in God and the Divine Creator of all Existence and Heaven and Earth by ensuring the retention of traditional and customary titles, rights, ceremonies, synagogues and heritage under a solemn oath and vow that the entirety of the Living Body of Christ shall seek to protect and preserve such tradition and custom now and forever more.

Traditions & Customary Rites of Judaism

The present most sacred Covenant recognises the dignity and honour of the following Traditional and Customary Rites as eligible for communion and unity with the one true Living Body of Christ, being:-

(i)   Orthodox Rite; and

(ii)   Conservative Rite; and

(iii)   Reformed Rite.

Article 16 – Sacred and Binding Covenant

1. The present sacred Covenant is an irrevocable and binding agreement between all living and deceased Members of the Christian and Jewish faiths, in communion with a unified Heaven.

    Sacred, Irrevocable and Binding Covenant

2. No Force of arms from within or without, can invalidate this Covenant. Tyranny shall not prevail. By virtue of this Covenant being enacted, it remains valid unless two thirds of the total Members of One Heaven choose by the clauses listed to invalidate part or all of the present most sacred Covenant.

    Force cannot invalidate this Covenant

3. In accord with the most sacred *Covenant Pactum De Singularis Caelum*, no claim of prior authority through any instrument or thing, no matter how old or sacred it is viewed, can prevail above the present sacred Covenant.

    No claim of prior authority can prevail

TITLE II - PRINCIPLES

Article 17 – Sacred Dimension, Location and Time

1. **A**ll Physical and Theoretical Dimension is a manifestation of the Divine Creator of all Concepts and Objects subject to the rules of law defined in accord with the most sacred Covenant *Pactum De Singularis Caelum*, Natural Law and all the Canons of Law of *Astrum Iuris Divini Canonum*. Sacred Dimension

   All Measurement, methods of calculation, categorisation, survey and description, including sacred-space-day-time, are subject first to Article 45 (*Sacred Measurement and Location*) of the most sacred Covenant *Pactum De Singularis Caelum*.

   All Locations, including but not limited to their description, unique naming and coordinates are subject to the Cadastre Systems and other systems of Ucadia in accord with *Astrum Iuris Divini Canonum*.

   Let it be known to all that as all Dimension is a manifestation of the Divine Creator of all Existence and as the present sacred Covenant represents the perfection of Divine Intention, there exists no greater or superior constructs, models, illusions, realities, mythologies, possibilities, universes or architectures of Dimension than Ucadia Dimension.

   As Ucadia Dimension is superior to any and all other forms, all lesser forms are subject to Ucadia Dimension and the rules of such dimension as defined by the canons of law of *Astrum Iuris Divini Canonum*.

   Furthermore, let it be known that such inferior and corrupted forms of reality and dimension such as Mundi in all its carnations is hereby dissolved, reprobate and not permitted to be revived.

2. In the present sacred Covenant unless the context requires otherwise:- Sacred Location of Universal Ecclesia

   (i) The Universal Ecclesia of One Christ as the One Holy Apostolic Universal Ecclesia is located within the reality, dimension, boundaries and jurisdiction of the Supreme See (Location Trust Number 937000-000000-00000X); and

   (ii) The Supreme See as the Authentic Body of Christ (Trust Number 937000-000000-000000) for the entire planet Earth is located within the boundaries and jurisdiction of the Solar System (Trust Number 000000-500000-000001); and

   (iii) The Solar System (Trust Number 000000-500000-000001) is located within the boundaries and jurisdiction of the Milky Way Galaxy (Trust Number 000000-400000-000001); and

(iv) The Milky Way Galaxy (Trust Number 000000-400000-000001) is located within the boundaries and jurisdiction of the Local Group of Galaxies (Trust Number 000000-300000-000001); and

(v) The Local Group of Galaxies (Trust Number 000000-300000-000001) is located within the boundaries and jurisdiction of the Unique Collective Awareness (Trust Number 00000-000000-000000).

3. Sacred Places are those designated for divine worship, by dedication through the liturgical and sacramental rituals provided in accord with the most sacred Covenant Pactum De Singularis Caelum.

Sacred Land and Places

The Universal Ecclesia possesses the absolute Right to alienate and acquire without impediment such Land and Places suitable as locations for worship, both within established urban environments, in rural and agricultural regions within the bounds and jurisdiction of the Supreme See.

4. The highest, authentic, true and official system of chronology and time of united Heaven upon planet Earth shall be the Sacred Ucadia Time System, also known as the Sacred Ucadia Chronology as prescribed by Article 45 (*Sacred Measurement and Location*) of the most sacred Covenant *Pactum De Singularis Caelum*. No other system, method of calculating time may claim higher authority than the Sacred Ucadia Time System, as the Ucadia Time System is the official chronology and time system of the Divine and united Heaven upon the Earth and no other:-

Ucadia Time System

(i) The first part of the Ucadia Time System shall be the calculation of Era, signifying one eighth (1/8th) of a complete cycle of the twenty-five thousand six hundred and eighty (25,680) Sun Year cycles known as a Precession of the Equinoxes or "Precession", representing a natural cycle of orbital shift of the Earth axis. An Era is therefore three thousand two hundred and ten (3,210) Aetos (years), except the 1st Era of a new Great Precession every one hundred and twenty-eight thousand and four hundred (128,400) Aetos (years), when an extra Aetos (year) is added and this Aetos (year) shall be called zero. As the 1st Aetos (year) of the 1st Era of a new Great Precession is called Year Zero (0), it represents the Divine Creator, the end of old things and the beginning of new. The most recent Year Zero in Ucadia Time for the past one hundred and twenty-eight thousand and four hundred (128,400) Aetos (years) is equivalent to the Aetos (year) known as 2011-2012 (22 December 2011 to 20 December

2012). The present Era beginning as a Great Precession is known as the Era of Aquarius; and

(ii)   The second part of the Ucadia Time System shall be the calculation of Age, signifying three (3) divisions of an Era equivalent to one thousand and seventy (1070) Aetos (years), except the 1st Age of the 1st era of a Great Precession which will be one thousand and seventy-one (1071) Aetos (years). The present Age, also known as the New Age and the New World is the first Age of the Great Precession; and

(iii)   The third part of Ucadia Time System shall be the calculation of a completion of the Earth's orbit of the Sun, known as Aeto (Year) being three hundred and sixty-five (365) Aemera (days); and every four (4) Aetos (years) an extra day shall be added to the Aetos (year) so as to be three hundred and sixty-six (366) days, with the extra Aemera (day) called Aelomai; and every one hundred and sixty (160) Aetos (years) an Aemera (day) shall be added to that Year and shall be called Aebelos; and every third Precession or nine thousand, six hundred and thirty (9,630) Aetos (years), an Aemera (day) shall be added to that Year; and

(iv)   The fourth part of the Ucadia Time System shall be the calculation of in a standard Year of seventy-three (73) segments called an Arc, each of five (5) Aemera (days) in length, that may be arranged by thirteen (13) Aemetos (Months) called the Zodiakos or by Seasons or "Aekairos"; and

(v)   In the arrangement of Zodiakos, the first Aemetos (Month) of a year shall be called *Ophis* being five (5) Aemera (days) (21-Dec to 25-Dec); and followed by the second Aemetos (month) of *Arktos* the bear (26-Dec to 24-Jan) of thirty (30) Aemera (days); and followed by the third Aemetos (month) of *Cuinos* the dog (25-Jan to 23-Feb) of thirty (30) Aemera (days); and followed by the fourth Aemetos (month) of *Ichthyos* the fish (24-Feb to 25-Mar) of thirty (30) Aemera (days); and followed by the fifth Aemetos (month) of *Krios* the ram (26-Mar to 24-Apr) of thirty (30) Aemera (days); and followed by the sixth Aemetos (month) of *Tavros* the bull (25-Apr to 24-May) of thirty (30) Aemera (days); and followed by the seventh Aemetos (month) of *Oxos* the ox (25-May to 23-Jun) of thirty (30) Aemera (days); and followed by the eighth Aemetos (month) of *Karkínos* the crab (24-Jun to 23-Jul) of thirty (30) Aemera (days); and followed by the ninth Aemetos (month) of *Ippos* the horse (24-Jul to 22- Aug) of thirty (30) Aemera (days); and followed by the tenth Aemetos (month) of *Leonis* the lion (23-Aug to 21-Sep) of thirty (30) Aemera (days); and followed by the eleventh Aemetos (month) of *Kyknos* the swan (22-Sep to 21-Oct) of thirty (30) Aemera (days); and followed by the twelfth Aemetos (month) of *Skorpios* the scorpion (22-Oct to 20-Nov) of thirty (30) Aemera (days); and followed by the thirteenth and final Aemetos (month) of *Elaphos* the red deer (21-Nov to 20-Dec) of thirty (30) Aemera (days) or thirty-one (31) in a leap year; and

(vi)   In the arrangement of the Seasons, the first Aekairos (season) shall be *Blastanos* (spring) of ninety (90) Aemera (days) as the first season of life; and the second shall be *Theros* (summer) of ninety (90) Aemera (days) as the Aekairos (season) of heat and storms; and the third shall be *Proimos* (autumn) of ninety (90) Aemera (days) as the Aekairos (season) of change and uncertainty; and the fourth shall be *Kaimonos* (winter) of ninety-five (95) Aemera (days) as the Aekairos (season) of death and sleep; and

(vii)   The fifth part of the Ucadia Time System shall be the Moon cycle of twenty-nine (29) or thirty (30) days which shall be free and independent of the cycle of the Sun as such recordings of the full cycle of a Moon contains sufficient variance as to require the Time Keeper to make prediction as to whether a Moon cycle be twenty- nine (29) or thirty (30) days; and

(viii)   The sixth part of the Ucadia Time System shall be the Name of the Aemera (day) of an Arc with the first (1st) Aemera (day) named GAIA in honour of the spirit of the Earth, the second (2nd) Aemera (day) named MONS in honour of the Moon, the third (3rd) Aemera (day) named MARS in honour of the spirit of Mars, the fourth (4th) Aemera (day) named JOVI in honour of the Jovian Giant planets Jupiter, Saturn, Neptune and Uranus and the fifth (5th) Aemera (day) named SOL in honour of the spirit of our SUN; and

(ix)   The seventh part of the Ucadia Time System shall be the Hour of the Aemera (day) divided into twenty-four (24) hours of an Aemera (day) with each hour itself made up of sixty (60) Minutes; and

(x)   The eighth part of the Ucadia Time System shall be the Minutes and Seconds of the Aemera (day), with Each Minute made up of sixty (60) Seconds and then one hundred (100) milliseconds per second.

5. In accord with the Ucadia Time System and the most sacred covenants of the *Authenticus Depositum Fidei*, each and every Day since the Spring Equinox in the Year known as 10,831 BCE to the final year of the present Great Precession of twenty-five thousand and six hundred and eighty-one (25,681) years is duly recorded in the Public Register and Great Record of One Heaven, also known as the Great Record of Space-Day-Time as the first, original and highest Record. Thus, the unique Record Number, or Sacred Space-Day-Time Number for UCA E8:Y3210:A0:S1:M27:D6 [Wed, 21 Dec 2011] is 4689718.

> Sacred Space-Day-Time

Therefore, all and every representation of Day, Date and Time from the first record to the last record of Sacred Space-Day-Time shall be completely within the Jurisdiction of Ucadia, subject to the most sacred Covenant Pactum De Singularis Caelum. At the conclusion of the Great Precession, it shall be the right of Humanity to vote and choose its next measurement system of time and space.

Article 18 – Sacred Circumscribed Space

1. **Sacred Circumscribed Space** is a uniquely recorded enclosure and dimension of Ucadia Sacred Space-Day-Time as prescribed by Article 34 (*Sacred Circumscribed Space*) of the most sacred Covenant *Pactum De Singularis Caelum*, and associated covenants and charters, Ucadia Law and these present Articles. Only duly authorised Ucadian Bodies, Ucadian Societies, Ucadian States, Ucadian Persons and Ucadian Companies, or those bodies, persons or corporations granted limited Rights under Convention and Treaty are permitted to record, register, keep and maintain Sacred Circumscribed Space.

> Sacred Circumscribed Space

2. The Universal Ecclesia of Christ having been granted certain Rights of Ecclesiastical and Sovereign Dominion by the Divine Creator of all Existence and all Heaven and Earth, hereby reserves its absolute Rights to assert, declare, affirm, avow, enforce and defend its Divine and Natural Rights to record, register, keep and maintain Sacred Circumscribed Space, by any and every lawful means necessary.

> Authority of Ecclesia and Sacred Circumscribed Space

3. All proper, valid and legitimate Sacred Circumscribed Space is clearly and uniquely named dimension of Ucadia Space-Day-Time, whereby:-

> Elements of Valid Sacred Circumscribed Space

   (i) Such Sacred Circumscribed Space is properly defined by an eighteen (18) digit and character number and identifier (XXXXXX-XXXXXX-XXXXXX), consistent with the most sacred Covenant *Pactum De Singularis Caelum*; and

   (ii) The specific Sacred Circumscribed Space is able to properly

79

define its origin to a higher jurisdiction of Sacred Circumscribed Space, also identified by a proper eighteen digit and character number and identifier; and

(iii) The specific Sacred Circumscribed Space was either formed in accord with the most sacred Covenant *Pactum De Singularis Caelum*, or associated Covenants and Charters, or by one or more properly dispensed Supreme Sacred Gifts; and

(iv) The Sacred Circumscribed Space does not contradict or usurp any previous proper, valid and legitimate existing Sacred Circumscribed Space.

4. Any claimed space, close, place, region, zone, precinct or any other type of enclosure formed by edict, or statute or sacrament that is in conflict with the most sacred Covenant *Pactum De Singularis Caelum*, or Ucadian Law or the present sacred Covenant shall be invalid, illegitimate and null and void *ab initio* (from the beginning), having no force or effect or Rights in law.

Space created by falsity or error

5. Any and all Enclosure Acts issued by any parliaments, monarchs or bodies; and all subsequent, dependent and related Statutes, including but not limited to all fraudulent, perfidious, false and deceptive documents purported to be of an earlier age in relation to the claimed enclosure of certain lands, spaces, closes, fields, places, regions, zones, precincts, territories, dominions and estates are hereby disavowed as morally repugnant, profane, sacrilegious, heretical and contrary to the Rule of Law, Christian teachings, Civilised Society, Divine Law, Natural Law and are therefore invalid, illegitimate and null and void *ab initio* (from the beginning), having no force or effect or Rights in law.

Unilateral acts of enclosure false and morally repugnant

6. All Measurement and Standard of Sacred Circumscribed Space shall always be in accord with the most sacred Covenant *Pactum De Singularis Caelum*, associated covenants and charters, Ucadian Law and the present sacred Covenant. All other forms of measurement and standards shall be null and void, unlawful and illegal, having no force or effect, unless the non-Ucadian and foreign body, or foreign society, or foreign person or foreign corporation has a Convention or Treaty with the Universal Ecclesia of One Christ.

Measurement and Standards of Sacred Circumscribed Space

7. By Divine Mandate and Authority, the Universal Ecclesia of One Christ shall form, maintain and keep in custody the following types of Registers of Sacred Circumscribed Space, including (but not limited to):-

Character of Sacred Circumscribed Space

(i) *Land* (including all names, places and words also used to define

Land) as a fixed and circumscribed piece of ground and earth of one Acre or more in surface area and then measured from the centre of the planet to the centre point of the surface area; and

(ii) *Forest* as a fixed and circumscribed piece of ground and earth of ten Acres or more in surface area that is preserved or reclaimed wilderness, natural habitat, untouched and uncultivated for agriculture; and

(iii) *Island* (including all names, places and words also used to define Island) as a fixed and continuous piece of ground and earth, larger than twelve Acres in surface area; and circumscribed by water; and

(iv) *Sea* (including all names, places and words also used to define not land) as a fixed and continuous area of open water, larger than twelve thousand Acres in surface area; and circumscribed by at least two or more Islands and at least one other Sea; and

(v) *Air* (including all names, places and words also used to define neither land nor water) as a fixed and circumscribed piece of space between Land and the outer reaches of the atmosphere of a planet; and

(vi) *Person* as a movable circumscribed space inhabited by the physical and living biological body of one or more Homo Sapiens; and

(vii) *Office* as a fixed or movable circumscribed space inhabited by a Person; and

(viii) *Internet* as a digital circumscribed space, inhabited by Persons as Users; and

(ix) *Network* as a digital circumscribed space of networked computers, inhabited by Persons as Network Users; and

(x) *Domain* (also Web Domain) as a digital circumscribed space of web information, inhabited by Persons as Network Users; and

(xi) *Database* as a digital circumscribed space of digital information, inhabited by Persons as Database Users or Application Users.

8. Any and all claimed Sacred Circumscribed Space held as Allodial Title or Peculiar Title (as a Peculiarity) and therefore claimed to be owned absolutely, free of any claim is hereby disavowed as an abomination before all Heaven and Earth; and is condemned as a profound sacrilege, heresy, profanity, morally repugnant, perfidious and

Allodial or Peculiar Title as Abomination

deliberately false, having no force or effect in law. Furthermore, every Member is empowered by Sacred Writ, to pursue any, every and all means to ensure any and all records of such profanity, sacrilege and abomination before all Heaven and Earth is expunged, removed, withdrawn, determined, extinguished and abolished, including any and all false presumptions of claiming such false rights under covenants as "chosen people" or blood heritage or any other falsity.

Article 19 – Sacred Measurement and Standards

1. **All Numbers are Sacred** and subject to the absolute jurisdiction of One Heaven and the present Covenant. In these Articles unless the context requires otherwise:-

    Sacred Numbers

    (i) The number One may be expressed by the numeric value of 1 and may be expressed in scientific notation as 10^0; and

    (ii) The number Ten may be expressed by the numeric value of 10; and may be defined by the prefix Deca; and may be expressed in scientific notation as 10^1; and

    (iii) The number Hundred may be expressed by the numeric value of 100; and may be defined by the prefix Hecto; and may be expressed in scientific notation as 10^2; and

    (iv) The number Thousand may be expressed by the numeric value of 1,000; and may be defined by the prefix Kilo; and may be expressed in scientific notation as 10^3; and

    (v) The number Million may be expressed by the numeric value of 1,000,000; and may be defined by the prefix Mega; and may be expressed in scientific notation as 10^6; and

    (vi) The number Billion may be expressed by the numeric value of 1,000,000,000; and may be defined by the prefix Giga; and may be expressed in scientific notation as 10^9; and

    (vii) The number Trillion may be expressed by the numeric value of 1,000,000,000,000; and may be defined by the prefix Tera; and may be expressed in scientific notation as 10^{12}; and

    (viii) The number Quadrillion may be expressed by the numeric value of 1,000,000,000,000,000; and may be defined by the prefix Peta; and may be expressed in scientific notation as 10^{15}; and

    (ix) The number Quintillion may be expressed by the numeric value of 1,000,000,000,000,000,000; and may be defined by the prefix Exa; and may be expressed in scientific notation as 10^{18}.

2. All measure of length and distance are Sacred and subject to the absolute jurisdiction of One Heaven and the present Covenant. In these Articles unless the context requires otherwise:-

    (i)   *Dista* (*d*) is equal to a toe, or claw, or talon (of a bird) and three (3 cm) centimetres; and

    (ii)   *Hand* (h), also known as *Lamb*, is equal to four (4 *d*) *Dista* or twelve (12 cm) centimetres; and

    (iii)   *Cubit* (c), as the sacred measure of life and being, is equal to four (4 *h*) *Hands*, or sixteen (16 *d*) *Dista* or forty eight (48 cm) centimetres; and

    (iv)   *Fathom* is equal to two (2 *c*) *Cubits*, or eight (8 *h*) *Hands*, or thirty-two (32 *d*) *Dista* or ninety-six (96 cm) centimetres; and

    (v)   *Rod* (r) is equal to two *Fathoms*, or four (4 *c*) *Cubits*, or sixteen (16 *h*) *Hands*, or sixty-four (64 *d*) *Dista* or one hundred and ninety two (192 cm) centimetres; and

    (vi)   *Stade* is equal to sixty (60 *r*) *Rods* or two hundred and forty (240 *c*) *Cubits* or three thousand eight hundred and forty (3,840 *d*) *Dista* or eleven thousand five hundred and twenty (11,520) centimetres; and

    (vii)   *Mile* is equal to one hundred and forty four (144) *Stade*, or eight thousand six hundred and forty (8,640 *r*) *Rods*, or thirty four thousand five hundred and sixty (34,560 *c*) *Cubits*, or five hundred and fifty-two thousand nine hundred and sixty (552,960 *d*) *Dista* or one million six hundred and fifty-eight thousand eight hundred and eighty (1,658,880 cm) centimetres; and

    (viii)   *League* is equal to three *Miles* or four hundred and thirty-two (432) *Stades*.

3. All measure of area as it pertains to physical Sacred Circumscribed Space shall be according to the units of Unita. In accord with the present sacred Covenant unless the context requires otherwise:-

    (i)   *Unita* is equal to the smallest possible Sacred Circumscribed Space in existence being 1 Square Cubit (being 1 Cubit by 1 Cubit in area); and

    (ii)   *Piece* is equal to 1 square *Unita* being 2 Cubit by 2 Cubit in area, or 0.92 sq metres; and

(iii) *Square* (sq) is equal to 1 square Rod, being four (4) Pieces in area, or 3.68 sq metres; and

(iv) *Cell* is equal to two Squares or eight (8) Pieces in area, or 7.36 sq metres; and

(v) *Sanctuary* is equal to nine Squares or thirty-six (36) Pieces in area, or 33.12 sq metres; and

(vi) *Plot* is equal to thirty-six (36) Rods in length and six (6) Rods in width, equal to two hundred and sixteen Squares or eight hundred and sixty-four (864) Pieces or 794.88 sq metres; and

(vii) *Acre* is equal to thirty-six (36) Rods in length and thirty-six (36) Rods in width, equal to twelve hundred and ninety-six (1296) Squares or five thousand one hundred and eighty four (5,184) Pieces in area or 4,769.28 sq metres; and

(viii) *Supreme See* is equal to the entirety of the Solar System, including Planet Earth.

4. All measure of frequency as it pertains to Sacred Circumscribed Space shall be according to the units of Cycles. In accord with the present sacred Covenant unless the context requires otherwise:- **Sacred Frequency**

(i) *Cycle* (Cs) is equal to one cycle per second and is equivalent to the notion of Hertz (Hz); and

(ii) A0 is equal to 27 Cycles; and

(iii) A1 is equal to 54 Cycles; and

(iv) A2 is equal to 108 Cycles; and

(v) A3 is equal to 216 Cycles; and

(vi) A4 is equal to 432 Cycles. All music and tuning in any and all venues and sacred places within the jurisdiction of Ucadia must be tuned to 432 Cycles and not to deliberately dissonant cycles such as 440 Hz or 444 Hz; and

(vii) A5 is equal to 864 Cycles; and

(viii) A6 is equal to 1728 Cycles; and

(ix) A7 is equal to 3456 Cycles.

5. All Weights and Measures are Sacred and subject to the absolute jurisdiction of One Heaven and the present Covenant. All measure of **Sacred Weights and Measures**

weight as it pertains to Sacred Circumscribed Space shall be according to the units of Gravita. In accord with the present sacred Covenant unless the context requires otherwise:-

(i)   *Gravita* is equal to one grain of grass, wheat or barley; and

(ii)   *Scrupal* is equal to twenty Gravita or 1.44 grams; and

(iii)   *Dram*, also known as a *Coin*, is equal to three Scrupals or sixty Gravita or 4.32 grams; and

(iv)   *Ounce* is equal to eight Dram or twenty four Scrupals or four hundred and eight Gravita or 34.56 grams; and

(v)   *Pound* is equal to sixteen Ounces or one hundred and twenty eight Drams or three hundred and eighty four Scrupals or seven thousand six hundred and eighty Gravita or 552.96 grams; and

(vi)   *Talent* is equal to sixty Pounds or nine hundred and sixty Ounces or seven thousand six hundred and eighty Dram or twenty three thousand and forty Scrupals or four hundred and sixty thousand and eight hundred Gravita or 33.1776 kilograms.

Article 20 – Official Language and Naming

1.   **The Official Languages of Ucadia and Primary and Original Language of the present sacred Covenant is Psygos and Logos:-**

(margin note: Official Language and Naming)

(i)   *Psygos* is a Logographic written Language, using the Ucadia Language of *Logos* to translate the speech of such logograms; and

(ii)   *Logos* is a Logographic written and spoken Language, whereby each logogram represents a unique Phoneme or simple combination of a maximum of three Phonemes of arranged vowels and consonants

2.   Ucadia Psygos Language defines all knowledge that exists and will exist into eleven (11) numbers, eleven (11) categories and eleven (11) standard symbolic shapes. This is called the wisdom class honouring their traditions and customs, being:-

(margin note: Psygos Language)

(i)   Absolute; and

(ii)   Universal; and

(iii)   Relationships, measurement and rules; and

(iv)   Elements and Matter; and

(v)   Galactic and inter galactic objects; and

(vi)   Stellar and interstellar objects; and

(vii)   Planet Objects; and

(viii)   Simple Life; and

(ix)   Complex Life; and

(x)   Self Aware Life; and

(xi)   Higher Order Life.

3. The primary components of Psygos are objects and concepts (called DA) and their associated attributes that modify them (called MODIFIERS), bridge associations between concepts and objects (called RELATORS), associations that bridge between DA and MODIFIERS and/or RELATORS (called ASSOCIATORS) and tense/perspective (called TENSORS).

Psygos Structure

All these components are used to construct a wide variety of symbolic sentences (called DIA) according to essential rules of construction (DIA rules of CONSTRUCTION). Furthermore, the shape of the DA denotes meaning and classification in itself.

The rules concerning the classification, function and usage of *Psygos* and *Logos* is hereby vested in the body known as the "**Ucadia Languages Institute**" reporting through to the Ucadia Globe Union.

4. Logos follows the same essential grammatical rules as Psygos, except the elements used to produce the sound and symbols of a "DA" in Logos.

Logos Structure

KA Elements are the body and foundation of Logos, whereby five generic shapes symbolise the formation of symbols representing the most common consonants found in all existing and major languages of planet Earth. These are: Lips, Teeth, Tongue, Top of Mouth and Throat.

BA Symbolic elements represent the building blocks of mind toward meaning, identifying twenty two vowels and thirty three constants.

LA Symbolic Elements are the spirit of meaning in assembling symbols of Consonants and Vowels to produce unique units of sound having purpose.

The total LA set or KA-BA-LA is 720 original glyphs and then 720 transpositions (reversed combinations) to produce 1440 glyphs, not including the original BA set of vowels and consonants.

While this total number of glyphs may appear a significant number to memorise, the repeating patterns within the language in fact means that by learning just the BA set, the total LA set can be easily identified.

5. By the authority of the most sacred Covenant *Pactum de Singularis Caelum* and the present sacred Covenant, the Ucadian languages of *Psygos* and *Logos* shall be the official language for all official documents, titles, instruments and objects authorised to be created in accord with the present Articles.

    All official instruments and documents of importance shall be written in Psygos and Logos. Instruments written in Psygos and Logos shall be considered primary and original instruments of the highest authority.

    Valid Ucadia bodies are permitted to issue instruments in non-Ucadian languages, providing it is made clear that such language is secondary, a copy and inferior to the primary and original instrument.

Psygos and Logos as the official language of One Heaven

6. By the authority of the most sacred Covenant *Pactum de Singularis Caelum* and the present sacred Covenant, valid Ucadia bodies are permitted to issue instruments in non-Ucadian languages, providing it is made clear that such language is secondary, a copy and inferior to the primary and original instrument.

    Furthermore, the use of Ancient Greek or Latin is permitted to be used to defined concepts in non-Ucadian languages where at the time, the formality of such structures are not yet commonly adopted or used, providing such instruments make clear that such terminology may be changed by a proper vote of authority, consistent with the Articles of the present sacred Covenant.

Use of Non-Ucadian Languages

7. By the authority of the most sacred Covenant *Pactum de Singularis Caelum* and the present sacred Covenant, the properly elected and appointed leadership of One Christ are permitted to propose and alter the use of Non-Ucadian Language throughout the present translation of the sacred Covenant, consistent with the Rules associated with a Great Conclave and the present sacred Covenant.

Changes to Non-Ucadian Language Titles and Uses

Article 21 – Truth

1. **T**ruth is three fundamental qualities: Honest and consistent Testimony; or Reasonable and Logical acceptance of one or more claimed facts or statements as having objective Reality; or a steadfast Fidelity and Loyalty to such Testimony and Facts conclusively found to be True:-

Truth

87

(i)   As to the first quality, the highest Truth has always been honest and consistent Testimony under solemn Oath and Vow in acknowledgement of a Supreme Divine Creator of all the Universe and all Heaven and Earth. The first meaning of Truth, therefore is openness and without concealment, or secrecy or hiding. Occult therefore can never be truthful as the very meaning of occult is opposed to this first notion of Truth. Furthermore a statement without a proper and solemn Oath and Vow to the Divine Creator of all Existence cannot be reasonably regarded as Truth, only opinion or information; and

(ii)   As to the second quality of Truth, any claimed fact or statement can only be considered as True if it is both Reasonable and Logical. Therefore a claimed fact or statement borne from prejudice, or fraud, or coercion must always be considered unreasonable and therefore cannot be True. Similarly, a claimed fact or statement that is Incoherent, Fallacious, Irrelevant, Malicious, Perfidious, Unproven, Unasserted, Circular, Verbose, Absurd, Repetitive or Defamatory cannot logically be concluded as True; and

(iii)   As to the third and final quality of Truth, it is the essential preservation of Truth, so that once a Testimony or Fact or Statement is found to be True, it is properly recognised and preserved; and then used as a reliable "stepping stone" for other discoveries and conclusions. However, a steadfast adherence or orthodoxy to claimed statements and alleged facts that contradicts a quality of Truth cannot therefore, then be considered "true" as this would mean that Truth contradicts itself.

2.   By virtue of the ratification of the present sacred Covenant by the Members of the Universal Ecclesia of One Christ, the Members solemnly testify before the Divine Creator of all Existence and all Heaven and Earth that the present sacred Covenant is true; and that the present Articles are Reasonable and Logical and collectively represent the embodiment of Truth itself.   *Confirmation of Covenant as Truth*

When speaking, writing or considering Truth, it is in accord with the most sacred Covenant *Pactum De Singularis Caelum* and the present sacred Covenant and no other.

3.   Any Edict, Decree, Command, Demand, Order, Judgement, Opinion that contradicts one or more of these Articles of the present sacred Covenant cannot be Truth.   *Contradictions to Covenant cannot be Truth*

Article 22 – Trust

1. **Trust is confidence in and reliance upon some quality or thing or act** as being true. In accord with Article 36 (*Trusts & Estates*) of the most sacred Covenant *Pactum De Singularis Caelum*, Trust is also used to define a formal relation and agreement whereby an authorised party (Trustor) gives, grants, assigns or delegates one or more Rights to another (Trustee) under certain conditions for the benefit of a third party (Beneficiary).

   Trust

2. By definition, all Rights are held in Trust and no Right is said to exist, unless through Trust. Therefore, in the absence of a valid Trust, the claimed Rights are also absent.

   All Rights held in Trust

3. A "**Trustor**" is the generic term for anyone possessing the proper authority to transfer any rights, title or property to another. The other party upon acceptance of the Fiduciary obligations upon a valid Oath and Vow then formalises the valid Trust as Trustee. All persons that possess the proper authority to transfer any rights, title or property to another are by default "Trustors".

   Trustor

   There are only four (4) possible types of Trustor, depending upon the primary nature and intention associated with any conveyance of rights, title or property in Trust being Grantor, Donor, Assignor or Delegator:-

   (i)   A "**Grantor**" is a person who conveys or transfers complete possession and ownership of property for some financial consideration in return under one or more terms and conditions and may be further defined as a Feoffor, Devisor, Testator, Settlor, Obligor, Addressor, Sender, Seller or Purchaser; and

   (ii)   A "**Donor**" is a person who conveys or transfers complete possession and ownership of property without any financial consideration under one or more terms and conditions and may be further defined as a Giftor, Debtor, Guarantor, Indemnitor or Mortgagor; and

   (iii)   An "**Assignor**" is a person who temporarily conveys or transfers one or more benefits and rights of possession and use of some property for some financial consideration in return, under one or more terms and conditions and may be further defined as a Consignor, Bailor, Depositor, Employer, Insurer, Hirer, Lessor, Lender, Creditor, Licensor, Lienor or Scrivener;

and

(iv) A "**Delegator**" is a person who temporarily conveys or transfers one or more benefits and rights of possession and use of some property without any financial consideration under one or more terms and conditions and may be further defined as an Executor, Commissioner or Administrator.

4. A "**Trustee**" is an Office formed by a valid Oath and Vow to the Terms of Trust to take possession of certain Rights and Property from a Trustor and perform certain Obligations for the benefit of another. The manner and character of a Trustee may be described as a position of Trust which is equivalent to the term Fiduciary.
Trustee

The Office of Trustee can only exist and be valid if all the following criteria exist:-

(i) The Trustor has the proper authority to grant, donate, assign or delegate the property for the proposed Trust; and

(ii) Clear purpose, intent and terms for the proposed Trust exist; and

(iii) Certainty of subject matter (the property) exists for the proposed Trust exists; and

(iv) The candidate for Trustee comes with good faith, good character and good conscience; and

(v) The candidate for Trustee accepts the position with full knowledge of the terms and obligations; and

(vi) The candidate makes a formal sacred oath to a higher Divine power upon a sacred object representing the form of law connected to such higher Divine power, before witnesses; and

(vii) The event of making such a formal sacred oath is memorialised into some document, that itself is signed, sealed and executed.

5. A "**Beneficiary**" is a named or unnamed party at the time of the formation of the Trust who benefits or receives an advantage in Trust. A Beneficiary, by definition is an "interested party" in a Trust or Estate:-
Beneficiary

(i) A named Beneficiary is an "**Agent**" (with the Trustee being the principal) and may be commissioned or non-commissioned; and

(ii) An unnamed Beneficiary is a "**Creditor**" (with the Trustee acting as debtor) to whom the trustee owes basic duties arising by law, agreement or claim.

6. The eight standard characteristics of a Trustee as Fiduciary are *Integrity, Frugality, Prudence, Humility, Faculty, Competence, Accountability* and *Capacity*:-

Trustee as Fiduciary

    (i)   *Integrity* is the characteristic of possessing a strict moral or ethical code as exemplified by the trinity of virtue (Good Faith, Good Character and Good Conscience); and

    (ii)   *Frugality* is the characteristic of being economical and thrifty in the good use of those resources in one's possession or custody. The opposite of waste; and

    (iii)   *Prudence* is the characteristic of being practical, cautious, discrete, judicious and wise in the management of the affairs of the trust; and

    (iv)   *Humility* is the characteristic of being modest, without pretention or loftiness; and

    (v)   *Faculty* is the characteristic of possessing skill and ability in order to perform the obligations of trustee; and

    (vi)   *Competence* is the characteristic of being fit, proper and qualified to produce and argue reason through knowledge and skill of Law, Logic and Rhetoric; and

    (vii)   *Accountability* is the characteristic of being answerable and liable to faithfully render an account for all acts and transactions; and

    (viii)   *Capacity* is the characteristic of possessing the legal and moral authority to hold such office, including demonstrating all the previous necessary characteristics.

7. All valid Trusts may be categorised by their proper formation as either Instructed or Facilitated:-

Category of Trusts

    (i)   "**Instructed Trust**", is when a Trust is created by a Trustor and Trustee with clear intentions, subject matter and purpose(s) by a person having the legal capacity to perform such an act; and

    (ii)   "**Facilitated Trust**", is when a Trust is created by a Surrogate Trustor or simply a "Surrogate" and Trustee by implication and function of law, being either a "Manufactured Trust" (Constructive Trust) by operation of law, or a "Consequential

Trust" (Resulting Trust) by effect of events determined by law.

8. All valid Trusts (also categorised as either Instructed or Facilitated) may be categorised according to the essential Status and Authority of the Trustor, being Divine, Living or Deceased:- Character of Trusts

   (i) A "**Divine Trust**" is the highest form of trust also involving the highest form of rights of ownership. A Divine Trust is purely spiritual and divinely supernatural formed in accord with the most sacred Covenant *Pactum De Singularis Caelum* by the Divine Creator whereby the form of Divine Spirit, Energy and Rights are conveyed. Therefore, a Divine Trust is the only possible type of Trust that can hold actual Form, rather than just the Rights of Use of Form (Property); and

   (ii) A "**Living Trust**", is the second highest form of rights of ownership. A Living Trust typically exists for the duration of the lifetime of the Person(s) or Juridic Person(s) who are the beneficiaries. There are only four (4) valid forms of Living Trusts: True, Superior, Temporary and Inferior; and

   (iii) A "**Testamentary Trust**", is the lowest form of Trust and the lowest form of rights of ownership of any possible form of Trust. A Testamentary Trust is when property is conveyed into a Deceased Estate against the Rights held in the Testamentary Trust upon the death of the Testator.

9. In respect of the four types of Living Trusts being True, Superior, Temporary and Inferior:- Types of Living Trusts

   (i) A "**True Trust**" is the highest form of Living Trust. A True Trust is formed by a True Person in accord with the most sacred Covenant *Pactum De Singularis Caelum*, when it is validly registered into the Great Register and Public Record of a Ucadian Society on the condition of (1) the pre-existence of a Divine Trust where the True Person is the named Beneficiary; and (2) the lawful conveyance from the Divine Trust into the True Trust of certain Divine Rights of Use known as Divinity, being the highest possible form of any kind of Property. A True Trust may be for a single man, or woman called a "True Person Trust", a True Location Trust containing Divine Right of Possession of Promised Land, or an aggregate trust such as a Universal True Trust, Global True Trust or Civil True Trust; and

   (ii) A "**Superior Trust**" is the second highest form of Living Trust. A Superior Trust is formed in accordance with the present sacred Covenant and the associated Constitutional Charters of valid Ucadian Societies when it is validly registered into the Great Register and Public Record of a Ucadian Society on the condition of (1) the pre-existence of a True Trust where the Superior Person is the named Beneficiary; and (2) the lawful conveyance from the True Trust into the Superior Trust of certain True Rights of Use known as Absolute Realty, being the highest temporal form of any kind of Property. A Superior Trust may be for a single man, or woman called a "Superior Person Trust", or an aggregate trust such as a Global (Superior) Trust, Civil (Superior) Trust, Mercantile (Superior) Trust, Union (Superior) Trust, Clann Trust, Official Trust or Location Trust; and

(iii)   A "**Temporary Trust**" is the third highest form of Living Trust involving the temporary conveyance of property from one Superior Trust to another. Excluding Negotiable Instruments, a Temporary Trust is not permitted to exist beyond seven years; and

(iv)   An "**Inferior Trust**" also known as a Foreign Trust, is the lowest form of Living Trust possessing the lowest possible form of rights of ownership. An Inferior Trust can never be considered superior to a Superior Trust or True Trust. An Inferior Trust is any Living Trust or Implied Trust or Express Trust formed by inferior Law, claims and statutes, that are not in harmony with the present sacred Covenant.

10.   In respect of the Authority and Power of the classes and types of Trusts:-

      Authority and Power of Trusts

(i)   A *Divine Trust* ceases upon the withdrawal of the will of the Divine Creator of all Existence in accord with the Covenant *Pactum De Singularis Caelum* and no other. A Divine Trust cannot be salvaged, seized, captured, arrested, alienated, resigned, abjured, transferred, conveyed, donated, assigned or surrendered; and

(ii)   A *True Trust* ceases upon the physical death of the body, or body politic that is associated with it. A True Trust is not dependent upon the good character or intentions or actions of the Trustee or Trustees. Furthermore, a True Trust cannot be salvaged, seized, captured, arrested, alienated, resigned, abjured, transferred, conveyed, donated, assigned or surrendered; and

(iii)   A *Superior Trust* ceases upon its Dissolution, Satisfaction, Termination, Cessation or Annulment, with the *res* or property of the Trust being returned, or distributed or disposed accordingly upon the publication and patenting of an official Gazette notice within the Ucadia Gazette as evidence to the fact; and

(iv) A *Temporary Trust* ceases upon its Dissolution, Satisfaction, Termination, Cessation or Annulment, with the *res* or property of the Trust being returned, or distributed or disposed accordingly upon proper notice in accord with the most sacred Covenant *Pactum De Singularis Caelum* or associated Covenants, Canons and Rules of Ucadia; and

(v) An *Inferior Trust* ceases upon its Dissolution, Satisfaction, Termination, Cessation or Annulment, with the *res* or property of the Trust being returned, or distributed or disposed accordingly upon either the publication and patenting of an official Gazette notice within the Ucadia Gazette as evidence to the fact, or such rules of Inferior Law that do not contradict the most sacred Covenant *Pactum De Singularis Caelum* or associated Covenants, Canons and Rules of Ucadia.

Article 23 – Register

1. A Register is a book of tables recording one or more entries of statements, testimonies or memoranda as evidence as to jurisdiction and authority over certain Sacred Circumscribed Space; or the properties or attributes of such Sacred Circumscribed Space; or the rights of use of such properties and attributes; or the memorial of events concerning such Sacred Circumscribed Space, or properties or attributes, or rights of use; or the memorial of transactions and derivatives concerning the receiving or granting or claiming of rights and uses.

Register

2. In accord with Article 106 (*Registers, Rolls & Records*) of the most sacred Covenant *Pactum De Singularis Caelum*, all records in proper, valid and legitimate Registers depend upon the prior recording by Authority of one or more records of Sacred Circumscribed Space as reference. If no valid records of Sacred Circumscribed Space exists, or such records are illegitimate, false, unlawful or illegal, then all subsequent Registers and Records depending upon such primary records shall also be illegitimate, false, unlawful and illegal.

All Records in Registers depend on Sacred Circumscribed Space

3. In terms of the general authority and creation of Registers:-

Authority, Power relating to Registers

(i) The Authority to form a Register is defined by the limits of Authority of the constituting Instrument of the relevant Trust or Estate or Fund or Corporation that the Register relates; and

(ii) The Rights, Powers and Property prescribed within a Register cannot exceed the Rights, Powers and Property of the Trust or Estate or Fund or Corporation itself; and

(iii) All valid and proper Registers are wholly and exclusively Ecclesiastical Property and can never belong to a Trust, or Estate or Fund or Corporation that formed or inherited it. Therefore, as all valid and proper Registers are exclusively Ecclesiastical Property and all Sacred Circumscribed Space is derived from Ucadia, all Registers are *ipso facto* (as a matter of fact) *ab initio* (from the beginning) the absolute property of One Heaven and Ucadia; and

(iv) All Registers are hierarchical in their inheritance of Authority and validity from One Heaven, beginning with the highest being the Great Register and Public Record of One Heaven. A Register that cannot demonstrate the provenance of its Authority, has none, and is null and void from the beginning; and

(v) As all Registers are wholly and exclusively Ecclesiastical, absolutely no clerical or administrative act may take place in association with a Register unless by a duly authorised Officer under active and valid sacred Oath or Vow in a manner consistent and in accord with the present sacred Covenant and the most sacred Covenant *Pactum De Singularis Caelum*; and

(vi) The entry of a record into a Register is wholly invalid unless the memorial and testimony of the act giving authority is done without duress, is done freely and with full knowledge and is consistent and in accord with the present sacred Covenant and the most sacred covenant *Pactum de Singularis Caelum*.

4. In terms of the general purpose, function and operation of a valid Register:-

Purpose, Function and Operation of Register

(i) A Register as a table contains at least three or more columns; and

(ii) A Register as a table can be a section of a Book, or a whole series of Books; and

(iii) A Register is held in the care of a proper Officer of a Competent Forum of Law, possessing both the Ecclesiastical Authority and Sovereign Authority to hold, record and keep custody of such records; and

(iv) A Register cannot and does not create the original fact or authority that it records, but merely reflects the pertinent elements in relation to the originating Instrument used to create a valid entry; and

(v) An entry in a Register can never create sacred circumscribed space or an original event. However a valid entry in a Register is itself a valid event and by virtue of the "joining" of information at the time of registration may create certain Rights or Facts or Truths as Prima Facie Evidence; and

(vi) A particular Right of Use in relation to Property can only be recorded once in a valid Register. Those specific Registers as prescribed by Ucadian Law and the present sacred Covenant are always Registers of Original Record and take precedence over all non-Ucadian and foreign registers and rolls; and

(vii) The claimed day or time of entry of a record into a non-Ucadian or foreign register has no bearing or merit in law, where a similar record for the same Property, or Event, or Right exists within a valid Ucadia Register, even if the day or time of entry in the Ucadia Register is after the day or time of entry in the non-Ucadian and foreign register. This is because any non-Ucadian and foreign register that seeks to usurp the Authority of a valid Ucadian Register automatically renders such a register invalid and illegitimate, meaning that such a non-Ucadian register is determined to be null and void, having no force or effect in law.

5. Notwithstanding valid Registers being called the same, the Universal Ecclesia of One Christ recognises and shall use several other Types of valid Registers under different names, including (but not limited to):-

Character of Registers

(i) A "**Gazette**" is a form of Register as a Public Journal and Authorised Newspaper of Record. The highest, most authoritative Gazette is the Ucadia Gazette and no other; and

(ii) An "**Almanac**" is a form of Register of information and events for a given subject, collected and arranged for a given year; and

(iii) An "**Account**" is a form of Register as arrangements of computations, Valuations and derivations using some standard unit of value, measure, record or exchange on the nature, value and disposition of objects, concepts and property of a valid Trust or Estate or Fund or Corporation; and

(iv) A "**Memoranda**" is a form of Register in chronological order, detailing the substance of formal notes or "memorandum" including (but not be limited to) minutes, resolutions, proceedings, accounts, letters, correspondence, decisions and procedural actions; and

(v)   A "**Journal**" is a form of Register derived as a summary extract of information from Memoranda and arranged in category order and then chronological order to produce a summary of facts, evidence, quantities and relations for the purpose of accounting and reckoning of the debits and credits of the Trust or Estate or Fund or Corporation; and

(vi)   A "**Ledger**" is a form of Register as a summary extract of Journal entries to produce the most concise reckonings and balances of debits and credits, assets and liabilities of the Trust or Estate or Fund or Corporation; and

(vii)   A "**Roll**" is a form of Register of one or more entries being "persons" of the same condition of entry, or the same engagement of obligations in relation to a valid Trust or Estate or Fund or Corporation; and created by their valid entry into the Roll; and

(viii)   A "**Manifest**" is a form of Register being evidential history of the provenance, possession and ownership of any property, rights, money or other interests recorded as associated with a Trust or Estate or Fund or Corporation; and

(ix)   An "**Estate**" is a form of Register and Roll of certain Rights held in Trust for a period of years for a Person, whereby one or more Inventories and Valuations have been properly conducted; and

(x)   An "**Inventory**", also called a Stocktake, is a form of Register being a detailed survey and census of all property, assets and liabilities, debits or credits of a valid Trust, or Estate or Fund or Corporation completed immediately after its creation; or the anniversary of its creation; or upon another fixed and given day; and the stock of particular items and their location or business; and

(xi)   A "**Valuation**" is a form of Register and Roll (also historically known as a Tax or Rating) being a detailed estimation of the value of each item as listed upon an Inventory of a valid Trust, or Estate or Fund or Corporation; and

(xii)   A "**Fund**" is a form of Register of equal units representing certain Property Rights of one or more Estates of monetary value that can then be used as a means of exchange for lawful money or for the discharge of debts and obligations.

Article 24 – Roll

1. **A** Roll is a type of book of tables and Register of one or more entries being "Persons" of the same condition or entered in the same engagement of obligations in relation to a valid Trust or Estate or Fund or Corporation and is created by their valid entry into the Roll.

Roll

2. In terms of the general authority, nature and function of Rolls:-

Nature of Rolls

   (i) The authority to form a Roll is defined by the limits of authority of the constituting Instrument of the relevant Trust or Estate or Fund; and

   (ii) The Rights, Powers and Property prescribed to those persons created and defined within a Roll cannot exceed the Rights, Powers and Property of the Trust or Estate or Fund itself; and

   (iii) All properly formed Rolls are wholly and exclusively Ecclesiastical Property and therefore under the absolute control, power and authority of Ucadia; and

   (iv) All Rolls are hierarchical in their inheritance of authority and validity beginning with the highest being the Great Roll of Divine Persons. A Roll that cannot demonstrate the provenance of its authority, has none and is null and void from the beginning; and

   (v) As all Rolls are wholly and exclusively Ecclesiastical, absolutely no clerical or administrative act may take place in association with a Roll unless by a duly authorised Trustee under active and valid sacred Oath or Vow in a manner consistent and in accord with the present sacred Covenant; and

   (vi) The entry of a record into a Roll is wholly invalid unless the memorial of the act giving authority is done without duress, is done freely and with full knowledge and is consistent and in accord with the present sacred Covenant and the most sacred covenant *Pactum de Singularis Caelum*.

3. The process whereby the authority of one Person on one Roll is given legitimacy by the authority and consent of a previously created Person record on another Roll is called Joinder of Person:-

Joinder

(i)   Joinder (literally "to join") requires that a party is given Notice of Joinder with clear intention to "join" one person from a Roll held in custody with the authority and permissions of a Roll not immediately within their jurisdiction; and

(ii)   Joinder is not the joining of a person and a man or woman as this is incorrectly mistaking surety or one who is willing to "understand" for the person for joinder; and

(iii)   The names of both persons must be the same in order for a valid Joinder of Person. Otherwise, such a Joinder is a Joinder in Action, requiring separate consent; and

(iv)   The failure to make clear the Notice of Joinder as an intention to Join (e.g. fraudulently using a Summons as a Notice of Joinder) is a fraud and renders such action a Misjoinder and maladministration; and

(v)   The failure to produce sufficient evidence of the Right to Joinder of Person (also sometimes misrepresented as Joinder in Action), automatically renders such action a Misjoinder.

4.   The place or office where a Roll of the Universal Ecclesia is kept is called a Vestry. The act or system of registering is called Verification and an Officer who keeps the Rolls is called a *Custos Rotulorum*. The Highest Vestry is the Supreme Vestry of the Universal Ecclesia of One Christ.

Vestry and Custos Rotulorum

Article 25 – Estate

1.   An Estate is a type of Register known as a "Roll" and its Records, issued by some authorised ecclesiastical body, sovereign body or body politic, denoting the assumed or actual beneficial rights or "privileges" and obligations of one or more persons of the same condition and circumstance:-

Estate

(i)   A valid record in an Estate Roll creates a unique legal entity having certain limits of legal capacity or "standing" or "status" within the jurisdiction of the body and control of the body that created it. Therefore, in the first instance, an Estate is equivalent to the concept of a unique "legal person"; and

(ii)   The limits of legal capacity or "standing" or "status" determined by the valid record in the Estate Roll owned by the authorised ecclesiastical body, sovereign body or body politic that created it therefore defines to what extent other property may (or may not) be held and used as "privileges" and "liberties" by the beneficiary claiming use of the "legal person". Therefore, in the second instance, an Estate is equivalent to the primary "legal title" and "legal capacity" and "legal standing" of a particular class of persons; and

(iii) Subject to such limits of legal capacity and legal standing, an Estate may then hold one or more beneficial "rights of use" or property as "privileges" and "liberties" within one or more temporary beneficial trusts associated with the Estate (i.e. "real estate" and "personal estate"). Therefore, in the third instance, an Estate is equivalent to the aggregate property of immovable, movable, corporeal and incorporeal things associated with these temporary trusts (i.e. "the whole of the estate"); and

(iv) To properly administer the affairs of the Estate, the beneficial rights, also known as property may then be pledged, promised, assigned, granted or delegated as security to form one or more assets. The value of such assets may then be monetised or securitised through various funds, agreements, licenses, accounts and certificates. Therefore, in the fourth instance, an Estate is equivalent to the aggregate monetary value of the net assets of the estate after all debts have been discharged.

2. All valid Estates exist under certain fundamental assumptions:-

Criteria of Estates

(i) The rules of formation and management of an Estate Roll and lesser Registers must exist as public law within the rules of the ecclesiastical body, sovereign body or body politic that created it; and

(ii) The Rights associated with an Estate are always "Rights of Use", also known as "Property" and not the primary Rights of ownership. Thus, Estates always concern Property as "Rights of Use"; and

(iii) As the Rights associated with an Estate are always "Right of Use" of some Right, a separate Trust must first exist before the Estate is created; and furthermore, that the Rights being the source of the "Rights of Use" in question must also have been named and conveyed into the existing Trust by a Trustor; and

(iv) The authorised ecclesiastical body, sovereign body or body politic that created the Estate Roll owns "legal title" to any such Rights conveyed into such an Estate; and

(v) All Rights in Estate (within the Estate) are Beneficial Title or Equitable Title and not legal title; and

(vi)   Beneficial Title means one or more "privileges" or "liberties" that, subject to the rules of the Estate, may be withdrawn or forfeited or alienable; and

(vii)   Equitable Title means a "privilege" not in possession of the Beneficiary, but claimable and recoverable through a qualified forum of law with equity powers - being rights of a surrogate Chancery Court. Thus, certain permits, titles, letters, certificates and patents issued to a Beneficiary as "Equitable Title" does not necessarily mean the Beneficiary holds one or more "privileges" other than to sue in a valid court of equity to claim or recover one or more of these such "rights"; and

(viii)   The rules for the administration of Property (Rights of Use) within the Estate is through a Covenant of Testamentary Disposition, otherwise known as a Will by a Testator, or in its absence (Intestate), some other established and authorised rules; and

(ix)   For every valid Estate, a Fiduciary must be named and duly appointed to govern the affairs of the Estate, either as an Executor, or appointed Administrator in the absence of clear instruction or dispute of authority; and

(x)   For every valid Estate that engages in trade or commerce, at least one duly appointed Agent must exist and be duly appointed, registered and acknowledged to manage the day to day business of the Estate under the authority of the Executor or appointed Administrator as the Principal.

3. As a valid Estate is created via a valid entry and formation of a record into some form of Estate Roll, the general authority, nature and function of Rolls apply:-

    Authority of Estates

    (i)   The authority to form a Roll is defined by the limits of authority of the constituting Instrument of the relevant Trust or Estate or Fund; and

    (ii)   The Rights, Powers and Property prescribed to an Estate created and defined within a Roll cannot exceed the Rights, Powers and Property of the Trust that underwrites the Estate; and

    (iii)   All Rolls are completely and exclusively Ecclesiastical Property and can never belong to a Trust, or Estate or Fund that formed or inherited it. Instead, all Rolls are the property of One Heaven. Therefore, all Estates are the property of One Heaven;

101

and

(iv)   All Rolls are hierarchical in their inheritance of authority and validity from One Heaven, beginning with the highest being the Great Roll of Divine Persons. Therefore, the highest Estates are Divine Estates and the lowest are Inferior Estates. A Roll that cannot demonstrate the provenance of its authority, has none and is null and void from the beginning; and

(v)   As all Rolls are completely and exclusively Ecclesiastical, absolutely no clerical or administrative act may take place in association with a Roll unless by a duly authorised Trustee under active and valid sacred Oath and Vow in a manner consistent and in accord with the present sacred Covenant; and

(vi)   The entry of a record into a Roll is completely invalid unless the memorial or instrument of the act giving authority is done without duress, is done freely and with full knowledge and is consistent and in accord with the present sacred Covenant and the most sacred Covenant *Pactum de Singularis Caelum*.

4.   Valid Estates as valid records on a Roll may be further defined in hierarchy of authority, form and function as Divine, True, Superior, Juridic or Inferior:-

Character of Estates

(i)   A "**Divine Estate**" is a valid purely spiritual Estate representing the collection of rights and obligations of a Divine Person recorded as a valid entry within a Divine Roll constituted in accord with the present sacred Covenant. No Roll or Person is Higher; and

(ii)   A "**True Estate**" is a valid Estate representing the collection of rights and obligations of a True Person (Office of Man or Office of Woman) recorded as a valid entry within a physical and temporal Roll constituted in accord with the Society of One Heaven in the recognition of the most sacred Great Roll of Divine Persons and the Great Register and Public Record of One Heaven; and

(iii)   A "**Superior Estate**" is a valid Estate representing the collection of rights and obligations of a Superior Person recorded as a valid entry within a physical and temporal Roll constituted in accord with a valid Ucadian Society; and

(iv)   A "**Juridic Estate**" is a valid Estate representing the collection of rights and obligations of a Juridic Person recorded as a valid entry within a physical and temporal Roll constituted in accord with a valid Ucadian Society; and

(v)   An "**Inferior Estate**" is any Estate representing the collection of rights and obligations of a Person as an entry within a physical and temporal Roll formed under Law not in perfect accord with the present sacred Covenant. All Non-Ucadian Estates are Inferior Estates.

Article 26 – Person

1.   **A Person is a form of Sacred Circumscribed Space** enclosing certain characteristics and appearances as the identity of one or more Higher Order Life Forms, formed through a valid entry, registration and record within a Roll.

Person

In accord with Article 106 (*Registers, Rolls & Records*) of the most sacred Covenant *Pactum De Singularis Caelum*, the highest Roll defining the greatest Rights and types of Persons is the Great Roll of Divine Persons, also known as the Great Register and Public Record of One Heaven, in accord with the most sacred Covenant *Pactum De Singularis Caelum*.

2.   All Persons may be categorised according to the three (3) possible types of Relation being: 1st Person (Self), 2nd Person (Another) and 3rd Person (Not Known):-

Relations of Person

(i)   1st Person, also known as a Natural Person and *in propria persona* is when the competent mind of a carnate Higher Order Life Form as Author (Principal) appoints, records and publishes themselves by Special (Private) appointment as Actor (Agent) by some solemn binding agreement. Therefore, a 1st Person or Natural Person possesses "natural title" to right of beneficial use associated with the 1st Person synonymous with such pronouns as "I, thou, me, my, mine, myself, we, us, our, ours and ourselves"; and

(ii)   2nd Person, also known as an Artificial Person is when a carnate Higher Order Life Form as Author (Principal) appoints another carnate Higher Order Life Form by Special (Private) appointment as Actor (Agent) by some solemn binding agreement. Thus, a 2nd Person or Artificial Person is synonymous with such pronouns as "you, yours, yourself and yourselves"; and

(iii)   3rd Person, also known as a Legal Person, or Statutory Person or Surrogate Person created through a record on a Roll is when the Author (Principal) is hidden or not known, and the Higher

Order Life Form fails to properly express any competency *in propria persona* (1st Person) or 2nd Person Author (Principal) to Actor (Agent) Relation prior to the commencement of any interpersonal intercourse. In the 3rd Person, the flesh and body of a Living Higher Order Life Form is mistaken, and presumed to be, by default, the "person" and the Statutes of Law, or Rules of the Court as Script (Covenant) and the Judge or Magistrate as the Author (Principal). Thus, a 3rd Person or Legal Person is synonymous with such pronouns as "he, she, it, they, them, their, theirs and themselves".

3. All Persons may be categorised and ranked according to four (4) possible levels of authority, powers and rights from the greatest and highest powers and authority to the lowest and least powers and authority being (in order of rank): Divine, True, Superior and Inferior:-

Character of Persons

(i) A "**Divine Person**" is the purely Divine Spirit Person created through a valid record and enrolment in the Great Roll of Divine Persons and associated with a Divine Trust formed in accord with the sacred Covenant *Pactum De Singularis Caelum* by the Divine Creator into which the form of Divine Spirit, Energy and Rights are conveyed; and

(ii) A "**True Person**" is the Form attributed to a True Trust formed when an associated Divine Trust already exists and there is a lawful conveyance of Divine Rights of Use and Purpose, known as "Divinity" to a True Trust associated with then the birth and existence of a living Higher Order Life Form and the physical version of the Great Roll of the Society of One Heaven and a valid Live Borne Record. A True Person can never be claimed or argued as higher than the Divine Person from which it derives its authority; and

(iii) A "**Superior Person**" is the Form attributed to a Superior Trust when an associated True Trust already exists and there is a lawful conveyance of First Right of Use and Purpose, known as "Realty" to a Superior Trust associated with the birth of a service or agreement associated with the Membership of a living Higher Order Life Form to a valid Ucadia society and the authorised Member Roll of such a society. A Superior Person can never be claimed or argued as higher than the True Person from which it derives its authority; and

(iv) An "**Inferior Person**" is the Form attributed to any Non-Ucadian Trust and is the lowest standing and weakest of all valid forms of Persons. An Inferior Person is only valid when the man or woman in possession of a Superior Person and True Person consent to an enrolment of their name in one or more Rolls. An Inferior Person can never be validly, legitimately, logically, legally, lawfully or morally claimed or argued as superior to a Superior Person.

4.   A Juridic Person, also known as Juridical, is a type of Artificial Person created by a lawful act and association of the Persons of two or more men or women in accord with the present sacred Covenant. All Juridic Persons are subject to the present sacred Covenant and the following characteristics:- **Juridic Person**

(i)   A Juridic Person is always an aggregate of Persons. Therefore, when there are less than two Persons of two or more men or women associated, the Juridic Person ceases to have form; and

(ii)   A Juridic Person possesses three Instruments of formation, duly acknowledged and recorded being a (1) Memorandum of Articles as to its Bylaws; and (2) a Treaty or Agreement affirming under Oath those founders subscribe to its ByLaws; and (3) a Letter or Declaration affirming both the Treaty or Agreement and associated Bylaws and the key elements that define it as separate and unique; and

(iii)   A Juridic Person possesses a Body Politic capable under the authority of its Bylaws of creating new laws and amending existing laws as Statutes; and

(iv)   A Juridic Person possesses a Judiciary capable of administering the laws of the Society; and

(v)   No aggregate of Persons intending to obtain Juridic personality, is able to acquire it unless competent authority has approved its statutes; and

(vi)   Representing a Juridic Person and acting in its name are those whose competence is acknowledged by the present sacred Covenant or by its own statutes; and

(vii)   Only seven (7) Forms of Juridic Person are valid: Supreme, Universal, Global, Civil, Mercantile, Union and Inferior (Non-Ucadian); and

(viii) Upon the extinction of a Juridic Person, the allocation of its goods, rights and obligations is governed by law and its statutes. If these give no indication, they go to the Juridic Person immediately superior, always without prejudice to the intention of the founders and donors and acquired rights.

5. Excluding Divine Personality, all Persons are formed through one or more of the thirty-three Sacred Gifts as defined by Article 44 (*Supreme Sacred Gifts of Heaven*) of the most sacred Covenant *Pactum De Singularis Caelum* and the formation of Sacred Circumscribed Space; and then the physical entry, enrolment and recording of such a proper event within a valid Roll:-

Formation of Persons

(i) True Persons created by either the sacred sacrament of Annunciation or Baptism forming Sacred Circumscribed Space and then the enrolment of the event in the Great Roll and Register in accord with *Pactum De Singularis Caelum*, are extinguished upon the physical death of the flesh form associated with the True Trust, with Divine Right of Use returned to the associated Divine Trust; and

(ii) Superior Persons created by the sacrament of Consecration and then enrolment in the valid Roll of a Ucadian Society, are extinguished upon the extinction of the associated True Trust or the abjuration of membership to the associated Ucadia Society, or the suspension or revocation of a particular membership or service, or a fundamental change to the agreement of formation of the person; and

(iii) Juridic Persons created by one or more Cardinal Sacraments forming Sacred Circumscribed Space and then enrolment in the valid Roll of a Ucadian Society are extinguished in accordance with their own statutes and superior competent authority. No Juridic Person, excluding Society Juridic Persons formed and named in accordance with *Pactum De Singularis Caelum* and associated covenants and charters, may exist for more than one hundred (100) years; and

(iv) Inferior Persons created by proper Treaty and Convention with a proper and valid Ucadia society, or body are extinguished upon the fulfilment of their purpose and intention, or upon exposure of fraud, or material breach of agreement, or presentment of a person of higher standing and authority.

6. A failure to recognise a valid and properly constituted and formed Person or the claim of superior jurisdiction of an Inferior Person over a Superior Person or True Person cannot ecclesiastically, logically, legally, lawfully or sensibly be sustained and is therefore without force and effect with any subsequent judgement null and void *ab initio* (from the beginning). A Natural Person attributed to less than a Homo Sapien or higher order life form is automatically null and void from

Recognition of Persons

the beginning. Attributing a Natural or Artificial Person to an Animal, Notion or Thing is an unnatural and unlawful act.

7. The deliberate falsity of sacraments, or secret rituals purporting to be sacraments in the claimed formation of sacred space by enclosure by a non-Ucadian and foreign body, foreign entity or foreign person, contrary to the most sacred sacraments of *Summa Sacramenta* shall be an abomination before all Heaven and Earth and any such claimed roll, or register, or vital record a sacrilege, profanity, perfidy, heresy and crime against the Rule of Law and all civilised society and religions. Any and all such records shall be null and void *ab initio*, having no force or effect ecclesiastically, lawfully or legally.

False Sacraments render Roll null and void

Article 27 – Oaths and Vows

1. An Oath is a solemn appeal to the Divine Creator by invocation and the presence of at least two witnesses that a pronouncement is true or a promise binding.

Oath

An oath is only a valid oath when it is invoked in recognition of the rights of all men and women as Sponsors to Persons present within the court including the spirit of the living law and includes a pledge to speak honesty before the court. The touching of any object during such pronouncing is materially irrelevant to the validity of any oath.

2. The spirit of the living law is present in a competent forum of law only when all words are given under oath. When officers of the court do not properly give an oath, the living law is absent, even if all parties and witnesses show respect and due process of law. A man or woman of good standing before the law is any man or woman having invoked an oath before the court, having been found to demonstrate respect for the living law and due process of law.

Oaths necessary for presence of Spirit of Living Law

No one shall be denied the right to invoke an oath before a valid court. An oath extorted by malice, force, or grave fear is null by the law itself. No one should be heard within a valid court unless they have previously invoked a valid oath for that case. Furthermore, no testimony in written or oral form is valid unless a valid oath has previously been invoked.

The breaking of an oath, especially by any officer of the court, is a most serious offence which must be treated as the gravest of injury to the living law.

3. By the custom and tradition throughout the history of Law, an Oath can only be valid if the following criteria exist:-

Criteria of Valid Oath

(i)   The one making the Oath comes with good intention, good character and good conscience; and

(ii)   The one making the Oath has the Right and proper authority to make such an Oath; and

(iii)   At least one other person is present and prepared to witness the Oath and testify to such a fact; and

(iv)   The candidate raises his right hand with a flat palm so that the face of the open palm can be clearly seen by all witnesses during the pronunciation of the Oath, whilst his left covers his heart as the symbol and source of truth of the spoken words; and

(v)   That the pronunciation of the Oath never uses language of profanity such as "swear"; and

(vi)   That some written Memorial (Memorandum) to the event exists, signed by the one making the Oath and also signed by a different personality as witness.

4. Where an Oath is made in accord with all the necessary criteria, except an error exists in the mistaken use of the words "Swear" or "Sworn", then such an Oath shall be considered to be automatically corrected as if the use of such words as "Swear" and "Sworn" were never made.

Correction of Error of Oath

5. No one shall be heard within a valid competent forum of law unless they have previously pronounced a valid Oath for the matter at hand, without reference to the profane terms of "swear" or "sworn" or touching such sacrilegious and false objects. Furthermore, no testimony in written or oral form is valid unless a valid Oath has previously been pronounced and witnessed. An Oath extorted by malice, force, or grave fear is by law null and void from the beginning.

Requirement of Valid Oath

6. In the absence of a valid and proper Oath, no person claiming possession, or occupation, or investiture or ownership of an Office holds any authority or power whatsoever and any and all actions made by such a person are completely without validity in law, whether or not the parties present did consent or decline.

Absence of Valid and Proper Oath

7. A Vow is a solemn engagement or undertaking made to the Divine Creator to perform some action, to make some gift or pious offering in return for special favour.

Vow

A Vow made free from coercion, fear or deliberate deception must be fulfilled. A Vow made out of grave and unjust fear or malice is null by the law itself.

8. A Vow made by oration in the presence of others is always superior to

Status of Vow

a written Vow, or Vow made in private, even if recorded. A Vow is solemn if made by oration in the presence of others and if a legitimate superior Person accepts it in the name of a valid Juridic Person; otherwise it is simple. By its nature a Vow obliges only the person who makes it.

9. A Vow ceases by the lapse of the time designated to fulfil the obligation, by a substantial change of the matter promised, by the absence of a condition on which the vow depends, by the absence of the purpose of the vow, by dispensation, or by commutation. No temporal force or action nor Person can dispense or commute Solemn Vows of Supreme Persons.

Cessation of Vow

10. Only a Supreme Person can dispense or commute Solemn Vows of Superior Persons and all lesser Persons. Only a Superior Person can dispense or commute Solemn Vows of Ordinary Persons and all lesser Persons. Only an Ordinary Person can dispense or commute Solemn Vows of Curator Persons and all lesser Persons. Inferior Persons have no rights nor powers to dispense or commute Solemn Vows.

Dispensation and Commutation of Vows

Excluding a Supreme Person, Simple Vows may be dispensed or commuted by any Superior Person. As Inferior Persons have no power nor authority to dispense or commute solemn Vows, when any such Vow is breached or any action is made to claim that dispensation or commutation is given, then such an action is a direct injury to the Divine Creator and all law. Therefore any such liability and penalty due immediately befalls the Person who breached their solemn Vow.

Article 28 – Obligation

1. **O**bligation is something (as a formal Consensus, a promise, or the demands of conscience or custom) that obligates one to a course of action through some Consensus, instrument, product or transaction. Obligations agreed in good faith, free from fraud and duress, are to be met.

Obligation

When speaking, writing or considering Obligation, it is in accord with the most sacred Covenant *Pactum De Singularis Caelum* and the present sacred Covenant and no other.

2. When fraud by one party is proven to exist, the other parties are released from all obligation. No one may be obligated to perform a fraud or other offence. No one may be obligated to perform an act against their conscience or moral faith.

Condition of Release of Obligation

The failure to perform one or more obligations of a formal Consensus may be grounds for the extinction of a Consensus, or punitive acts as

109

stipulated within the Consensus Instrument.

3. Failure to perform an obligation without legal excuse gives the other party the right to seek legal remedy.

Failure to Perform Obligation

Article 29 – Fact

1. **F**act is by definition a Testimony of claimed evidential proof of some past event trusted as True. Facts are usually in written form and so depending upon the source and authority of such testimony, it may or may not be trusted to be true. In all aspects of Fact, the present sacred Covenant always take precedence.

Fact

The greatest Truth is when a person makes a solemn and sacred oath and vow to the Unique Collective Awareness as the Divine Creator of all Heaven and Earth pertaining to their claimed evidence.

When speaking, writing or considering Fact, it is in accord with the most sacred Covenant *Pactum De Singularis Caelum* and the present sacred Covenant and no other.

2. By virtue of the ratification of the present sacred Covenant by the Members of the Universal Ecclesia and the Members solemn Testimony before the Divine Creator of all Existence and all Heaven and Earth these Articles are true and are Fact.

Confirmation of Covenant as Fact

3. The publishing of any Proclamation, Order, Regulation or Notice within the Ucadia Gazette is the highest acknowledgement of a Fact and Truth, not subject to dispute or dishonour.

Ucadia Gazette Notices as Fact

4. The provision of any valid Ucadia Instrument and Form of Ucadia is Fact and Truth in itself and not subject to dispute or dishonour by any non-Ucadian person, entity, forum, association or body.

Instruments of Ecclesia as Fact

5. Any Edict, Decree, Command, Demand, Order, Judgement, Opinion that contradicts one or more of the Articles of the present sacred Covenant cannot be Fact.

Contradictions to Covenant cannot be Fact

Article 30 – Reality

1. **R**eality is the Model of Existence constructed upon Form and Meaning enabling the degree of certainty and reproducibility necessary for the operation of the Rule of Law in accord with the most sacred Covenant *Pactum De Singularis Caelum* and the present sacred Covenant.

Reality

Reality permits the recognition and existence of certain concepts considered valid under Positive Law that do not exist under Natural Law or Divine Law, yet are integral to the optimum function of civilised society under Positive Law.

All Statutes promulgated through valid Positive Law in Reality operate according to Interpretation and not Supposition. All Statutes promulgated through valid Positive Law in Reality operate according to Logic and Fact and not Paradox and Relativity.

When speaking, writing or considering Reality, it is in accord with the most sacred Covenant *Pactum De Singularis Caelum* and the present sacred Covenant and no other.

2. According to Natural Law and Divine Law, neither Absolute Reality nor Absolute Truth may exist independent to the acknowledgement, submission and acceptance of the most sacred Covenant *Pactum De Singularis Caelum* and the present sacred Covenant. *(Reality and the present Covenant)*

The Valid Rules for the consistent definition and operation of Reality are the Canons of *Astrum Iuris Divini Canonum* in accordance with *Pactum De Singularis Caelum*.

The definition of an alternate Reality that is inconsistent with the present sacred Covenant and the canons of *Astrum Iuris Divini Canonum* is automatically null and void from the beginning.

3. A Form that cannot be proven to exist in Reality has no Existence in Law. Any Edict, Decree, Command, Demand, Order, Judgement, Opinion that contradicts one or more of the present Articles cannot be Real and therefore has no valid Existence. *(Contradictions to Covenant cannot be Real)*

Article 31 – Competence

1. **Competency is the quality and state of being of sound mind** and able to perform a particular task, or responsibility to a standard as expected and defined by Ucadian Law and the present sacred Covenant. *(Competence)*

A Competent Person is one having sufficient skill, knowledge, ability and qualifications. Only a Member properly authorised may have jurisdiction to utilise certain services and remedies.

2. All Members, having redeemed their Member Number, are expected to possess a Basic Level of Competence of Behaviour, including (but not limited to) the seven (7) core ethics and values being Respect, Integrity, Commitment, Enthusiasm, Compassion, Cheerfulness and Discernment:- *(Competence of Behaviour)*

111

(i)   *Respect* exemplified by the expression and affirmation "I choose to treat all people with dignity and respect, regardless of race, religion or creed"; and

(ii)   *Integrity* exemplified by the expression and affirmation "I choose to give my word carefully and to keep and honour my promises"; and

(iii) *Commitment* exemplified by the expression and affirmation "I trust my colleagues and rely upon them to achieve success"; and

(iv)   *Enthusiasm* exemplified by the expression and affirmation "I am passionate about the objectives of the Universal Ecclesia of One Christ"; and

(v)   *Compassion* exemplified by the expression and affirmation "I care for my colleagues and their well-being and am sensitive not to unnecessarily cause harm, or controversy or injury"; and

(vi)   *Cheerfulness* exemplified by the expression and affirmation "I choose to welcome each day with positive aspirations"; and

(vii) *Discernment* exemplified by the expression and affirmation "I choose to take time before rushing to judgement or any action based on emotion".

3. All Members, having redeemed their Member Number, are expected to possess a Basic Level of Competence of Thinking, including (but not limited to):

Competence of Discernment

(i)   The skills of logic and reasoning as defined by the present sacred Covenant; and

(ii)   The skill and ability of discernment and critical thinking in making optimum choices; and

(iii) The intellect and skill in researching for answers and solutions within Ucadia reference material first, before seeking external sources first; and

(iv)   The ability to analyse and objectively determine whether information is true or false, based upon trust, certainty and confidence in Ucadia as a base of knowledge and wisdom.

4. The Universal Ecclesia of One Christ reserves the Right to deny, through an order of up to twelve months, the provision of any and all Services and Privileges to Members unable to demonstrate their competency in knowledge, behaviour and thinking. Whilst a Member is considered Incompetent, the Division or Department making such a

Services and Privileges not available to Incompetents

determination possesses the Right to deny those services and privileges within its jurisdiction. A Member then has the Right to appeal such a determination within 21 days, if they feel such a conclusion is unfair and they request a re-hearing and determination. At the expiry of twelve months, all orders declaring specific incompetence must be reviewed and either renewed or cancelled.

5. A Member that refuses or is unwilling to place their Membership to the Universal Ecclesia of One Christ as their first and primary Membership above all other associations, memberships and relations with foreign bodies politic, foreign societies, foreign fraternities and foreign corporations shall automatically be declared incompetent and ineligible to be a Founding Member or hold any Office of trust for the Universal Ecclesia.

Clouded Allegiance as Automatic Incompetence

6. Incompetence alone is considered neither a permanent state, nor an offence against the Universal Ecclesia of One Christ under these Rules. Instead, Incompetence is merely a temporary state that may disqualify certain Members from the privilege of using certain services of the Universal Ecclesia of One Christ for a period not exceeding twelve months before mandatory review of such disqualification. However, the deliberate and wilful use of a service, remedy or solution of the Universal Ecclesia when the Member clearly knows they are incompetent to claim the use of such a service, remedy or solution is considered an offence and therefore liable for censure and/or punishment.

Incompetence alone is not a delict or offence

Article 32 – Argument and Logic

1. **A**rgument is in essence the Process of establishing and validating the **Proof and Truth** of one or more claimed Facts. The notion of Argument is by definition the same as that for Reality whereby the combination of both the ideas of Truth and Fact to assert a thing or notion or claim is factually true; and therefore may be trusted as genuine, without doubt.

Argument and Logic

2. All formal Arguments have three essential components: (1) Matter, (2) Issue, and (3) Facts. The foundational reasoning used to establish a valid and legitimate Argument is Logic either by Deductive or Inductive Logic. In all aspects of Argument, the present sacred Covenant always take precedence.

Elements of Argument

A personal Argument always involves a minimum of two persons being the Accuser and the one being Accused; whereas a Legal Argument always involves a minimum of three persons being the Accuser and the one Being Accused and a witness capable of establishing and validating the Proof and Truth of one or more claimed Facts in favour of one of the parties.

Matter is the Topic, or Context, or Classification, or Name in relation to an Argument and not its Substance. Before any issue is described or alleged facts are asserted, an Argument has material existence by mere mention, providing its context in relation to topic, classification and name can be clearly identified. The Universal Ecclesia of One Christ and all its Officers and duly appointed Agents reserve their rights to challenge the accuracy and appropriateness of each and every Matter of controversy, particularly any presumptions in relation to Topic, Classification or Name.

The Issue of an Argument or the "Principal Fact" (*facta probanda*) or "Facts in Issue" is the primary Fact, or Facts required to be proved as the probable cause and basis of any Dispute, or Argument or Controversy. The Universal Ecclesia of One Christ and all its Officers and duly appointed Agents reserve their rights to challenge any alleged probable cause and Principal Fact of every Matter of controversy, particularly any presumptions in relation to presumptions of Joinder to such Issue.

3. **"Logic"** is the fair use of the principles of Inference and Reason whereby Propositions that are properly expressed may be used to deduce consistent Conclusions across a wide variety of Subjects.   Logic

Logic may be defined as Bivalent or Multivalent. Bivalent Logic is based on the presumption of only one of two possible outcomes or conclusions; and Multivalent Logic is based on the presumption of two or more relative possible outcomes or conclusions.

Logic may also be defined as Linear or Multi-linear. Linear Logic is chronologically based on the presumption of a set of singular space-time dependent events commencing with A and then proceeding to B; and Multi-linear Logic is based on a progressively expanding set of interdependent space-time events:-

(i) Multivalent Multi-linear Logic is capable of approximating to some degree of accuracy the Reality and Fact and Truth of the Universe. Both Multivalent Linear Logic and Bivalent Linear Logic are wholly artificial, imaginary and unable to accurately portray the reason, function and effect of any real scientific events with any degree of accuracy. Therefore, both Multivalent Linear Logic and Bivalent Linear Logic are inferior and less Real, less Truthful and less Factual than Multivalent Multi-linear Logic; and

(ii)   Bivalent Linear Logic is the most unnatural, imaginary and artificial system for portraying, recreating or analysing the reason, cause and effect of any real world events. However, it is the most functional of all three (3) logic models in terms of models of law and reason because of its simplicity. However, as Bivalent Linear Logic is wholly absurd and unnatural to the multivalent paradoxical reality of life, all parties involved in any dispute with the Universal Ecclesia of One Christ must be granted the right of free will and consent to be adjudicated according to Bivalent Linear Logic.

4.   Bivalent Linear Logic is based on three (3) Laws of Reason being Identity, Non-Contradiction and Bi-valency: -   *Reason of Bivalent Logic*

    (i)   The *Law of Identity* states that an object is the same as its identity; and

    (ii)   The *Law of Non-Contradiction* or the "exclusion of paradox" states that a valid proposition cannot state something that is and that is not in the same respect and at the same time; and

    (iii)   The *Law of Bi-Valency* (Excluded Middle) states that conclusions will resolve themselves to one (1) of two (2) states being valid or invalid.

5.   A "**Falsity**" or Fallacy in Logic or Argument is an incorrect reasoning resulting in a misconception or erroneous Premise(s) or Conclusion or both that are Incoherent, Fallacious, Irrelevant, Malicious, Perfidious, Unproven, Unasserted, Circular, Verbose, Absurd, Repetitive or Defamatory:-   *Logical Fallacy*

    (i)   An "**Incoherent Argument**" or *Incohaerens* argument, being Latin for "it is not consistent" is any argument whereby its Premises does not follow one another. Thus, an incohaerens is when no Conclusion could reasonably be deduced or inferred from two or more inconsistent and possibly contradictory premises; and

    (ii)   A "**Fallacious Argument**" or *Non sequitur* argument, being Latin for "it does not follow" is any argument whereby its Conclusion does not follow from its Premises. Thus, a non sequitur is when a Conclusion could be either true or false, yet the argument is false as there is no reasonable way of arriving to such a Conclusion from the premises alone by way of deduction or inference; and

    (iii)   An "**Irrelevant Argument**" or *Ignoratio elenchi*, being Latin for "irrelevant conclusion" is any argument whereby its Conclusion may in itself be valid, but does not address the primary deduction or inference (as issue in question) related to the Premises; and

(iv) A "**Malicious Act**" or *Malignare*, being Latin for "a malicious act" is any deliberately and wilfully negative, spiteful, wicked and evil act designed and intended to harm another, whether or not the other party was aware of such behaviour; and

(v) A "**Perfidious Act**" or *Perfidum*, being Latin for "a deliberately false, dishonest, treacherous act; a breach of trust" is any deliberately and wilfully false, dishonest, deceptive, treacherous act, representing a clear and unmistakable breach of trust, whether or not such action was intended for profit; and whether or not the other party was aware of such behaviour; and

(vi) An "**Unproven Claim**" or *Onus Probandi*, from Latin maxim *Onus probandi incumbit ei qui dicit, non ei qui negat* meaning "the burden of proof is on the person who makes the claim, not on the person who denies (or questions the claim)" is any argument whereby the burden of proof fails to be provided or is falsely placed upon the one accused or defending the claim and not the one making the claim. Thus, any system of law based on the assumption of being culpable on mere accusation without burden of proof is not only absurd, but false, immoral and unlawful; and

(vii) An "**Unasserted Claim**" or *Argumentum ex silentio*, from Latin meaning "argument (deduced) out of silence" is any argument whereby a Conclusion is made on the absence of evidence or argument, rather than the existence or merit of argument; and

(viii) A "**Circular Reasoning**" or *Circulus in demonstrando*, from Latin meaning "circular argument" is any argument where the Conclusion ultimately relies upon the Premises to be true, yet the Premises ultimately depends upon the Conclusion to be true and thus self referencing and circular; and

(ix) A "**Verbose Reasoning**" or *Argumentum Verbosum*, from Latin meaning "verbal intimidation" is any argument where the Premises or Conclusion are deliberately verbose, or obtuse, or confusing, or overly technical, or complex, or occult in order to intimidate and deflect attention from the existence of one or more fallacies contained within the argument in general; and

(x) An "**Absurd Reasoning**" or *Argumentum ad Absurdum*, from Latin meaning "an absurd argument" is any argument where the Conclusion of an argument is set aside and one or more of the Premises of an argument are proven to be false by showing that a false, untenable or absurd result would follow its acceptance. Argumentum ad Absurdum is frequently and mistakenly associated with an absurd logical fallacy known as *Reductio ad absurdum* or "reduction to absurdity" whereby an entire argument is falsely deemed absurd upon discovery of but one absurd or untenable premise; and

(xi) A "**Repetitious Reasoning**" or *Argumentum ad Infinitum*, from Latin meaning "endless argument" is any argument where the argument is continually presented, often with intentional intimidation to use such repetition and ignorance of any counter argument in order to deflect attention from the existence of one or more fallacies contained within the original argument in general; and

(xii) A "**Defamatory Accusation**" or *Argumentum ad Hominem*, from Latin meaning "against the man" or "to the person" is any argument whereby attention is sought to be deflected from one or more fallacies contained within the original argument by introducing a secondary argument against the character of the one highlighting such fallacies.

6. Any argument that is Incoherent, Fallacious, Irrelevant, Malicious, Perfidious, Unproven, Unasserted, Circular, Verbose, Absurd, Repetitive or Defamatory cannot be reasonably concluded as true, or fact or real or valid. In all such cases and matters, these Articles take precedence.

Covenant takes Precedence

Article 33 – Sacred Office

1. **T**he foundation of all civilised rule of law, begins with the acknowledgement that the highest law comes from the Divine Creator of all things in the Universe expressed through the laws of the Universe and then through the reason and spirit of man and woman to make Positive Laws.

Sacred Office

An Office is a movable or immovable sacred space in which is held certain rights, authorities, capacities and powers, conferred upon one who has pronounced one or more Oaths or Vows and Sacraments and preserved by their continued honour to the fiduciary principles of

117

good faith, good character and good conscience. One who holds an Office under such fiduciary capacity is called an Officer. An Agent can never legitimately hold an Office.

As all rights and property are by definition sacred, all clerical and professional obligations and responsibilities in relation to the administration, transference and conveyance of any rights or property must be concluded in a valid Office. Any and every transaction or claimed transference or conveyance of property or rights must be concluded within the sacred space and place of a valid Office to have ecclesiastical, moral, lawful and legal force and effect. There is no such thing as a Private Office.

By definition, the authority, rights and powers of a Divine Office is superior to any and all other forms of Office, regardless of title or claimed status. No Inferior Office possesses any power, force, authority, right or ability to abrogate or usurp the decisions or authority of a Divine Office. Similarly, no Superior Office or Inferior Office possesses any force, authority, right or ability to abrogate or usurp the authority of a True Office to exercise any of the Natural Rights granted to it, unless the occupant of a True Office wilfully and deliberately repudiates the Golden Rule of Law and all forms of logic, reason and sense.

All valid official positions or "officers" of all legitimate governments of all societies within the jurisdiction of the present sacred Covenant and the most sacred Covenant *Pactum De Singularis Caelum* therefore depend on the acknowledgement and recognition of the present Covenant as the highest law as the Covenant is nothing less than the perfect expression of Divine Will from the Divine Creator of all things in the Universe.

Furthermore, as the very meaning and purpose of the word "authority" is ecclesiastical, all legitimate authority of all officials of all valid governments of all societies on planet Earth depends upon the acknowledgement and recognition that all authority is ultimately derived from the most sacred Covenant *Pactum De Singularis Caelum* and the present Covenant as the highest source of authority being the perfect expression of Divine Law of the Divine Creator of all things in the Universe.

Office is a sacred position and title given life, recognition and personality through the power and authority of *Officium* in accord with the most sacred Covenant *Pactum De Singularis Caelum* and the present Covenant. All Authority and Power to hold any position of trust or authority is solely vested in the Right of *Ius Divinum Officium* in the body and force known as *Officium*.

The word and concept of Office itself is literally derived from *Officium* as the meaning has always been sacred and the conduct of function, ceremony, duty and service under the authority of Divine Law. Therefore, an Office does not exist, nor possesses any validity or legitimacy unless granted *Officium*.

2. In accord with Article 63 (*Officium*) of the most sacred Covenant *Pactum De Singularis Caelum*, the Divine Right of Officium (*Ius Divinum Officium*) is irrevocably delegated to the three great faiths of One Christ, One Islam and One Spirit for the life of such bodies, through the Authoritative Ecclesiastical Right of *Ius Ecclesiae Officium* as the Absolute Ecclesiastical Right to Authority of Office, Trustee, Trustor, Commission, Investiture, Coronation, Principal, Agent, Warrant, Title, Property Rights, Duty and Service.

Divine Right of Officium conveyed to One Christ

No other bodies, associations, persons, fraternities, societies or entities may claim *Officium*, unless properly dispensed by one of the three great faiths of One Christ, One Islam, One Spirit in accord with the most sacred Covenant *Pactum De Singularis Caelum* and associated Covenants, Charters, Canons and Rules.

The embodiment of *Officium* shall be the Sacred Offices of Supreme Patriarch, Supreme Caliph and the Supreme Recurrence. An Office not uniquely named within the present Covenant or associated Covenants and Charters may still receive the valid authority of *Officium* by the gift or grant of such power through the exercise of power and authority of one of the above Sacred Offices that embody the Divine Right.

However, an Office that cannot demonstrate proper gift, grant or conveyance of *Officium* through the present Covenant possesses none.

3. No one may hold an Office, nor *Officium*, unless they are a valid and legitimate Trustee. Thus, a candidate for Office must first willingly, openly and honestly profess the Sacrament of Trust by a valid Oath and Vow.

Officium and Sacrament of Trust

The Sacrament of Trust or *Sacramentum Fidei* is necessary to bring *Officium* from the Divine to the temporal. Without such a binding, there is no ecclesiastical, moral, lawful, legal or logical connection between the rights of an office and the one claiming to occupy such a position.

Similarly, when the bonds of Trust are broken, the Authority and Power of *Officium* immediately and properly reserves to itself, until the bonds of Trust are properly restored.

119

Therefore, the Sacrament of Trust protects and always maintains the integrity of all Offices as sacred.

4. An Office must possess valid *Officium* to then manage or administer any form of Land, Property or Rights. This is because all land, all property and all ownership of all objects and concepts is vested in the Divine Creator of the Universe and Existence and then granted as a power and authority to duly appointed officials.

   Officium and Land, Property and Rights

   An office without such authority has no right to possess or use any form of Land, Property, Use or Rights.

   Any actions performed by an office without valid authority and power of *Officium* is done "*de son tort*" with full liability resting solely on the impostor occupants of such false offices.

5. In accord with the most sacred Covenant *Pactum de Singularis Caelum* and the present Covenant, there exists only four valid types of Office being Divine, True, Superior and Inferior:-

   Types of Office

   (i) A "**Divine Office**" is an Office whereby a Spiritual Member of One Heaven vows to embody such unique Office, as a custodian and guardian spirit of the law or "*Nomos*", in accord with the rules and systems of *Officium Systemata* (Offices Systems) of Heaven. Divine Offices may then be defined as either a Supreme Divine Office or a Great Divine Office. A Supreme Divine Office is an office purely occupied and vested to a Spiritual Member as a *Nomos*; whereas a Great Divine Office is an office occupied and vested by both a Spiritual Member as a *Nomos* and a Living Member as an Officer. A Divine Office is formed through its unique identification and definition within the present sacred Covenant, or associated Covenants and Charters. Thus a Divine Office itself can never be dissolved, usurped, seized or surrendered prior to its expiry. It can only be vacated by a Living Member; and

   (ii) A "**True Office**" is the instance of the Great Divine Office of Man or the Great Divine Office of Woman as defined by the Divine Creator, whereby each and every Living Member is invested and commissioned from the time of their physical birth until their physical death. Therefore, a True Office can never be usurped, seized, sold or stolen; and

   (iii) A "**Superior Office**" is the instance or derivative of a Great Divine Office within a valid Ucadia Community as formed through its identification and definition within an instrument, agreement, covenant or document given existence by law or regulation according to the present sacred Covenant and associated covenants and charters. The performance of one or more Oaths or Vows then formalises the particular office and is sustained so long as such oaths or vows are honoured; and

(iv)   An "**Inferior Office**" is a non-Ucadian office or "Pseudo Office"; and are all non-Ucadian positions whereby a defective or inferior Oath or Vow has been offered, or no Oath provided or where the fiduciary obligations have been abrogated in favour of agent and commercial advantages.

6. In accord with the most sacred Covenant *Pactum De Singularis Caelum* being the highest rule of law concerning the valid appointment and function of Office, every and all valid appointments, commissions or investitures to Office must comply with the sacrament of Investiture.

    Investiture is one of thirty three (33) valid sacred sacraments of Heaven granted and administered through the formal ceremony of the formal bestowal or presentation of a possessory or prescriptive right of Office to an incumbent, including taking possession of the insignia of Office and the power of *Officium* in accordance with this Covenant and associated approved liturgy.

    All Higher Order Beings that have ever carnated in flesh, who occupy an office legitimately must do so under documented proof of one or more oaths of office whereby they acknowledge the supremacy of Heaven, agree to be bound to honour and upholding the Rule of Law and finally to impartially, fairly and equally serve the interests of their community or Society or Members.

    All Members who are granted the same Office are equal to the same Office, with none higher and none lower. By the present Article, when one of the same Office speaks as one, the one speaks for all of the same Office. When one of the same Office calls for assistance, all from the same Office are obliged to assist their fellow Officer and when the highest good standing of an Officer is injured, all Officers and the Divine Law and all International Law has been injured by such disrespect.

    Only one from the same Office can appoint another to the same Office, subject to the same sacred Bond of Nomination to Office for all Offices of One Heaven. If one of the same Office of One Heaven is found to be in disgrace, then the Officer who nominated them must resign all commissions.

7. In respect to Divine Offices, True Offices, Superior Offices and Inferior

Appointment to Office

Dissolution or

121

Offices:-

(i) A Divine Office cannot cease to exist, even if a physical and living incumbent fails to adhere to the standards and obligations of such office, or if one or more persons even disavow or seek to diminish or attempt to dissolve such Office; and

(ii) Unless defined by the most sacred Covenant *Pactum De Singularis Caelum* or associated sacred Covenants, Charters, Canons and Rules, a True Office is dissolved upon the physical death of the incumbent Man or Woman; and

(iii) Unless defined by the most sacred Covenant *Pactum De Singularis Caelum* or associated sacred Covenants, Charters, Canons and Rules, a Superior Office ceases to exist upon the death of the occupant, or their resignation, or if the occupant deliberately and wilfully breaches their obligations and responsibilities according to the Rule of Trust and fails to remedy within the allotted time, causing a default and then fails to honour and acknowledge their culpability, causing termination; and

(iv) An Inferior Office by definition never possess legitimate authority or power, but ceases even to be capable of maintaining the impression of legitimacy when an occupant breaches any notion of Rule of Law, or decency, or good faith, or good character or good conscience.

8. In respect of an Officer, a Superior Office may only be restored:-

(i) After the allotted time and penance determined upon such a disgraced former Trustee and Officer openly and wilfully chooses to admit and confess to their dishonour and culpability or being found culpable; and

(ii) The renewal of sacred Oath and Vow upon expiry of the prescribed time and conditions permitting such a man or woman to once again become a valid Trustee.

9. In accord with the present sacred Covenant and the most ancient Rule of Law, a Member bound to an Office by a valid Sacred Oath and Vow may only continue to occupy, hold and administer such Office if they act in honour to uphold the law.

When a Living Member as an Officer dishonourably abuses a position of office, they break their solemn Oath and Vow and therefore render the binding to Office null and void.

When a Living Member continues to claim occupancy of an Office and yet denies their obligations and duties, they automatically excommunicate themselves from any spiritual authority, thereby rendering such acts merely enforceable through ignorance, force or fear. Furthermore, such a Living Member automatically makes themselves eligible for punitive sanctions enforceable through the *Obligationum Systemata* (Enforcement Systems) of Heaven.

When a Living Member seeks to continue to illegitimately claim Office through the use of ignorance, force and fear, denying their dependency on validity from the Divine Creator and Divine Law, and causing damage upon the Earth and physical injury causing death upon the bodies of other Living Members, then such a Living Member invokes upon themselves the full force and power of the Wraiths of the *Obligationum Systemata* (Enforcement Systems) of Heaven against their physical presence within the temporal realm of the Universe.

When a Certificate of Incompetence is issued, the occupier of a certain Office is prevented from exercising any associated Power granted by the present Covenant including *Magisterium, Imperium, Sacrum, Sanitatum, Virtus, Custoditum, Alumentum, Interpretum* or *Visum*.

10. Nine Great Divine Offices recognised and honoured as part of the four hundred and thirty-two (432) Great Offices of One Heaven shall be forbidden to be used, or for any man or woman or spirit to assume the occupation of such Office for the whole life of the present sacred Covenant and all associated bodies, societies and entities. These Offices include the Offices of Christ, Cuilliaéan, Emperor, God King or God Queen, Lucifer, Messiah, Pontiff and Prophet. `Forbidden Offices`

Therefore, any man or woman or spirit that proclaims themselves the occupant or holder of any such forbidden Sacred Office henceforth shall commit a grave injury against all of Heaven and Earth and any such claim or subsequent act shall be without validity or authority.

Article 34 – Law

1. A Law is a rule that prohibits or permits certain acts. A rule is a norm, bar, maxim, measure or standard. A rule may be derived by instruction, discovery, custom or consent: `Law`

   (i) The highest Law is Divine being a rule given by Divine instruction, such as the Divine Commission given to the Universal Ecclesia of One Christ through its Sacred

Constitution, as nothing may contradict such a rule; and

(ii) The second highest Law is the reason of Mind, being an edict given by a great council of wise elders or jurists, such as the Board of Directors that have formed and ratified the present sacred Covenant of the Universal Ecclesia of One Christ, as nothing absurd and without good reason may be considered Law; and

(iii) The third highest Law is the law of the People, such as the Members of the Universal Ecclesia of One Christ, as the consent and will of the people is the source of true authority; and

(iv) The weakest rule is that of a tyrant, as any rule without authority or right of One Heaven but merely by force, cannot be sustained; and the people shall eventually overcome; and render such unjust rule and unjust laws as dust.

2. There is, there was, there has only ever been One Law. All law is equal that no one is above it; and All law is measured that all may learn and know it; and All law is standard that it may always be applied the same; All law be spoken as it is the spirit of the word that carries authority, as all action under law be by word of mouth, and writing be only for memory and never law in effect. This be the law of all great civilisations from the beginning of time and no king or assembly or city has sustained in ignorance from such a foundation.

One Law

3. These be the foundations of Rule of Law:-

Rule of Law

(i) All law is spoken when put into action, as it is the intention and spirit of the word that carries the authority. Therefore, when the law is tested and actioned, it must be by both written reference to the laws of Ucadia and the auricular expression of such laws; and

(ii) All are equal under the law; and all are accountable and answerable under the law, and all are without blemish until proven culpable; and

(iii) Where there is a law there must be a cause; and where there is a law there must be a penalty; and where there is a law there must be a remedy; and

(iv) An action in law cannot proceed without first a cause; and an action is not granted to one who is not injured; for the action of a valid law can do no harm (injury); and no injury to the law means no valid cause for action by law; and

(v)   No one may derive an advantage in law from his own wrong, as no action through law can arise from a fraud before heaven and earth; and it is a fraud to conceal a fraud; and fraud invalidates everything of a cause and action, for no action through law can arise in bad faith or prejudice; and

(vi)   What was illegitimate, fraudulent and invalid from the beginning does not become valid over time; and

(vii)   An action alone does not make one culpable unless there also be intent to do wrong, or evidence of deliberate and wilful ignorance contrary to reasonable behaviour. Similarly, no one may suffer punishment by valid law for mere intent alone; and no one is punished for the transgression of an ancestor or another; and

(viii) No one is accused of the same exact cause twice; and No man or woman be a judge over their own matter; nor a man or woman possess the authority of heaven to be judge, jury and executioner; and

(ix)   No penalty may exist without a valid law; and no penalty may be issued without first proof of injury and secondly the right of defence.

Article 35 – Justice

1. It is the maxim that Justice never contradicts the rule of law, as: Justice be the lawful right of use of all that has been defined by law; and Justice be the rights to adjudicate the law itself before heaven and earth; and Justice be a judge under sacred oath and trust granted such rights.
    Justice

2. All Rights and therefore all forms of proper Justice are derived from One Heaven, in accord with *Pactum De Singularis Caelum*:-
    Origin of Justice

    (i)   Divine Law is the law that defines the Divine and all creation, and demonstrates the spirit and mind and instruction of the Divine, and the operation of the will of the Divine Creator through existence. Therefore all valid Rights and Justice are derived from Divine Law; and

    (ii)   Natural Law is the law that defines the operation of the will of the Divine, through the existence of form and sky and earth and physical rules. Thus Natural Law governs the operation of what we can see and name; and

(iii)   The laws of People are those rules enacted by men having proper authority, for the good governance of a society under the Rule of Law. The laws of People are always inherited from Natural Law; and

(iv)   A law of People cannot abrogate or usurp a Natural Law, nor is it possible for a Natural Law to usurp Divine Law.

3.   These then be the foundations of Justice:-   *Foundation of Justice*

    (i)   All possess the Right to be heard even if such speech be controversial; and

    (ii)   All possess the Right of free will to choose our actions and destiny; and

    (iii)   All possess the Right of reason that distinguishes them from lesser animals; and

    (iv)   All possess the Right to informed consent or withdraw consent; and

    (v)   All possess the Right over their body that none may claim our flesh; and

    (vi)   All possess the Right of our divine self that none may claim our soul; and

    (vii)   Thus no man or woman can make a blood oath on their flesh or vow on their soul, nor may any man or woman claim servitude or obligation under such an abomination, for such Rights are granted solely by heaven to all people, and no man or body of jurists have the authority to usurp heaven; and

    (viii)   All true authority and power to rule is inherited from heaven, and to only those men and women in good faith and good character and good conscience, who then make a sacred oath in trust and form an office, whereby such Divine Rights are conveyed for only so long as they honour their oath and obligations to serve the people; and

    (ix)   For whenever a man or woman who makes an oath to form a sacred trust of office, then breaks such an oath through prejudice or unclean hands or bad faith, then all such authority and power ceases from them, as the cord between heaven and earth is severed and the trust dissolved; and

    (x)   Verily, no man or woman may serve the people unless under sacred oath, Nor may any man or woman serve heaven unless under solemn vow.

4. As to the administration of Justice these be the foundations of Due Process:-

    (i)   No valid action in law proceeds without first a valid cause; and no valid cause exists until such claim is first tested. Thus the birth of all action in law must begin with the claim; and

    (ii)   If a claim be not proven as a valid cause then the accused has nothing to answer. Yet if the claim be proved to have merit as a cause, then all valid causes in law must be resolved; and

    (iii)   Thus, he who first brings the claim must first prove its merit, as the burden of the proof lies upon him who accuses not he who denies; and

    (iv)   A heavy obligation then rests on the one who first brings controversy. For one who brings false accusation is the gravest of transgressors, that it injures not only one law, but all heaven and all law; and

    (v)   Thus a valid claim in part is when an accuser makes a complaint, bringing two (2)witnesses as proof to the substance of the complaint and petitions a forum of law for remedy. If merit of a cause be proved, the one accused must appear to answer; and

    (vi)   The one accused and any witnesses appear by summons. When anyone be summonsed, he must immediately appear without hesitation; and

    (vii)   If a man summonsed does not appear or refuses to appear to answer, then let him be seized by force to come and attend; and

    (viii)   When anyone who has been summonsed seeks to evade, or attempts to flee, let the one who summons lay hands on them to prevent their escape. One who flees fair judgement confesses his culpability; and

    (ix)   The accused cannot be judged until after the accusations be spoken and then after the accused exercises or declines their three (3) rights to defence; and

    (x)   The first right of the Accused is called Prolocution upon the hearing of the Complaint; and the right to speak as a matter of law, and why the complaint and investigation should not continue; and

(xi)   The second right of the Accused is called Collocution upon establishing Jurisdiction and the presentment of the Indictment; and the right to speak as to why the complaint and accusation is in fundamental error and upon such proof why the burden should now be placed on the accuser; and

(xii)   The third and final right of the Accused is called Adlocution being a final speech in defence, against an accusation having been heard; and

(xiii)   When men wish to settle their dispute among themselves, then they shall have the right to make peace; and

(xiv)   If a dispute cannot be settled before seeking a judge, then both the accused and the accuser must be granted equal hearing; and

(xv)   An accused cannot be found culpable unless three (3) pieces of evidence may be attributed to culpability as first presented as part of the complaint or as a result of a subsequent investigation, or hearing or trial; and

(xvi)   Judges are bound to explain the reason of their judgement.

Article 36 – Rights

1.   **A** Right is a positively defined *Capacity, Privilege, Liberty, Faculty, Power, Ownership, Possession, Interest* or *Benefit* and its associated obligation, remedy or relief held in Trust for the benefit of a particular type of named or unnamed Person, under some proper Rule of Law and System of Justice. A claimed negative right is an absurdity and injury of law itself and cannot exist under any true system of law. All valid Rights exist and are sourced and inherited solely in accord with the most sacred Covenant *Pactum De Singularis Caelum*, the present sacred Covenant and related covenants.

Right

2.   In respect of Rights:-

Types of Rights

(i)   As a *Capacity*, a valid Right is a form of authority, or qualification, or legal condition or status that enables a person to exercise his or her own will in acquiring, holding, using or transferring other certain Rights or performing such associated obligations, without restraint or hindrance; and

(ii)   As a *Privilege*, a valid Right is a form of special (real or personal) Grant whereby either a private Person or particular Corporation is freed from the obligations of certain laws; and

(iii)   As a *Liberty*, a valid Right is a form of Privilege whereby a

Person enjoys some Favour or Benefit; and

(iv) As a *Faculty*, a valid Right is a form of Privilege or special Power granted to a Person by Favour, Indulgence or Dispensation (i.e. a Licence) that enables a person to do, or refrain from doing something that would otherwise not be permitted by law; and

(v) As a *Power* or Authority, a valid Right is a form of authority, enforced by law, that enables one person to compel one or more other persons to do or abstain from doing a particular act; and

(vi) As an *Ownership*, a valid Right is a form of written possession by registration/recording, whereby a person is recognised by law to possess the most extensive or higher claim of possession, use and enjoyment (of certain Property), to the exclusion of all other persons, or of all except one or more specific persons; and

(vii) As a *Possession*, a valid Right is the visible possibility and ability of exercising physical control over some form of property, coupled with the intention of doing so, to the exclusion of all others, or one or more persons; and

(viii) As an *Interest*, a valid Right denotes a title, or certificate or other proof of claim or advantage to other certain Rights or Property; and

(ix) As a *Benefit*, a Right implies a just and legal claim to hold, or use or enjoy certain Property, or convey, or donate or dispose of it, subject to certain obligations of performance.

3. By their origin, nature and function, a Right is not a Right unless it possesses the following twelve (12) characteristics being: *Integrity, Trust, Name, Class, Provenance, Exemplification, Subject, Obligation, Subject Person, Obligated Person, Remedy and Relief:-*

Characteristics
of a Valid Right

(i) "**Integrity**" means a valid Right conforms to the most ancient and primitive purpose being to reflect a positively expressed rule, custom, privilege or power with good intentions, good character and good conscience. A negative right is an absurdity and injury of law itself and is invalid from the beginning; and

(ii) "**Trust**" means a valid Right is expressed in a Trust relation whereby the Right is the Property of the Trust; and

(iii) "**Name**" means that a valid Right is uniquely named compared to all other valid Rights in accord with the principle of the use of the Latin beginning with the term *Ius* (Jus) for a singular Right or *Iurium* for several rights bound together by similar character and purpose; and

(iv)   **"Class"** means that the Class of Right (Divine, Natural, Superior or Inferior) that the valid Right belongs to is clearly identified; and

(v)   **"Provenance"** means that if the Right is not of a Class of valid Divine Rights, then the Right clearly identifies and proves those Divine or Natural Rights whereby it owes its provenance; and

(vi)   **"Exemplification"** means that signed or sealed and attested evidence exists as to the founding instrument of law that defines the structure and character of the valid Right; and

(vii)   **"Subject"** means that a valid Right clearly identifies the qualities associated with it, including (but not limited to) any and all specific Capacities, or Faculties, or Powers, or Authorities, or Interests, or Privileges or Benefits associated with it; and

(viii)   **"Obligation"** means that a valid Right clearly identifies the obligations associated with it, including (but not limited to) any and all conditions of time, place, performance, dedication, dress, skills, equipment and duty of care; and

(ix)   **"Subject Person"** means a Person inherent with the Right (as in formation of a Person on a Roll), or invested with the Right (as Trustee) or entitled to the Right (as named or unnamed Beneficiary); and

(x)   **"Obligated Person"** means a Person on whom the valid Right imposes some kind of duty or obligation; and

(xi)   **"Remedy"** means that a valid Right possesses a form of Remedy whereby the Person in whom the Privilege or Power should reside is able to recover such a Right in the event of incapacity, or seizure, or loss or other impediment; and

(xii)   **"Relief"** means that a valid Right possesses a form of Relief whereby the Person in whom such Duty or Obligation associated with the Right should reside, is able to abdicate, derogate, mitigate or abrogate such responsibilities in the event of incapacity, or impossibility, or unfairness, or unreasonableness, or bad faith, or vexation, or unclean hands, or other breach of trust. An Obligation without the possibility of Relief is morally repugnant and irrefutable proof of the existence of slavery.

If one or more of these twelve (12) essential characteristics are not present within the structure of a Right, then such a Right cannot be considered valid.

4. In accord with Article 38 (*Rights*) of the most sacred Covenant *Pactum De Singularis Caelum*, there exists only four (4) Classes of Rights being *Divine, Natural, Superior* and *Inferior*:-

Four Classes of Rights

   (i)   *Divine Rights* are the primary and original form of Rights, corresponding to Divine Trusts and Divine Persons. There exists no higher class, or possible type of Rights. All Rights therefore are inherited from the class of valid Divine Rights; and

   (ii) *Natural Rights* are the second highest form of valid Rights, corresponding to True Trusts and True Persons; and owe their existence and provenance to the existence of Divine Rights. All Rights of True Persons in either the Office of Man or the Office of Woman are inherited from the class of valid Natural Rights; and

   (iii) *Superior Rights* are the third class and third highest possible form of valid Rights; corresponding to Superior Trusts and Superior Persons; and owe their existence and provenance to either valid Divine Rights or valid Natural Rights. All Rights of valid Ucadia Members, Ucadia Societies and associated bodies, aggregates, societies, associations, communities and unions of two (2) or more people are inherited from the class of Superior Rights; and

   (iv) *Inferior Rights* are the fourth class and the lowest possible form of valid Rights and owe their existence to non-Ucadian societies, persons, corporations, associations, bodies politic, agencies or aggregates. All Inferior Rights are inferior to Superior Rights. Where an Inferior Right makes claim to being superior, it is automatically invalid upon such falsity.

5. In accord with Article 38 (*Rights*) of the most sacred Covenant *Pactum De Singularis Caelum*, there exists only twelve (12) Sub-Classes of Rights being: *Perfect, Imperfect, Absolute, Relative, Personal, Ecclesiastical, Sovereign, Official, Administrative, Member, Primary* and *Secondary*:-

Twelve Sub-Classes of Rights

   (i)   *Perfect Divine Rights* (*Perfectum Divinum Iurium*), are a sub-class of Divine Rights whereby such valid Rights are created, defined and donated to a Divine Person by the Divine Creator through the most sacred Covenant Pactum De Singularis

131

Caelum. Perfect Divine Rights are Peremptory, Permanent, Eternal, Immutable and Indefeasible; and once bestowed are not subject to any form or condition of waiver, abandonment, conveyance, surrender, disqualification, incapacitation, seizure, capture, arrest, resignation, alienation, suspension, suppression, forfeiture or abrogation. Perfect Divine Rights are therefore the highest possible form of Rights and there exists no higher class, or form, or possible type of Rights. Perfect Divine Rights may be further defined as Perfect Fundamental Divine Rights or Perfect Sacramental Divine Rights; and

(ii) *Imperfect Divine Rights* (*Imperfectum Divinum Iurium*), are a sub-class of Divine Rights whereby such valid Rights are created, defined and delegated to a Divine Person by the Divine Creator through the present sacred Covenant and most sacred Covenant *Pactum De Singularis Caelum* upon acceptance of the associated obligations and duties attached to them. If any such conditions and obligations are breached or repudiated, then the relevant Imperfect Divine Right is instantly waived, surrendered, suspended, forfeited or revoked until such time as the fundamental breach of duty and obligation is repaired or such a Right is duly restored. Imperfect Divine Rights may be further defined as Imperfect Instrumental Divine Rights or Imperfect Intentional Divine Rights; and

(iii) *Absolute Natural Rights* (*Absolutum Naturae Iurium*), are a sub-class of Natural Rights whereby such valid Rights are created, defined and deposited to a Natural (True) Person by the existence of the one true Universe and the existence of all Rules and all Matter, in accord with the Rule of Law through the most sacred Covenant Pactum De Singularis Caelum. Absolute Natural Rights are Peremptory, Permanent, Immutable and Indefeasible and once bestowed are not subject to any form or condition of waiver, abandonment, conveyance, surrender, disqualification, incapacitation, seizure, capture, arrest, resignation, alienation, suspension, suppression, forfeiture or abrogation. Absolute Natural Rights are therefore the highest possible form of Natural Rights. Absolute Natural Rights may be further defined as Absolute Elemental Natural Rights or Absolute Testamental Natural Rights; and

(iv) *Relative Natural Rights* (*Relativum Naturae Iurium*), are a sub-class of Natural Rights whereby such valid Rights are created, defined and granted to a Natural (True) Person by the existence of the one true Universe and all Rule and all Matter in accord with the Rule of Law through the most sacred Covenant Pactum De Singularis Caelum upon acceptance of the associated obligations and duties attached to them. If any such conditions and obligations are breached or repudiated, then the relevant Relative Natural Right may be waived, surrendered, suspended, abandoned, resigned, disqualified, seized, captured, arrested, alienated, suppressed, forfeited or annulled until such time as the fundamental breach of duty and obligation is repaired or such a Right is duly restored. A True Person to whom a Relative Natural Right has been bestowed may also lawfully delegate or confer beneficial title of such a Right to another True Person such as a Ucadia association, body politic, society, company or community. However, such an aggregate person can never legitimately claim legal title over a Relative Natural Right and any such claim is automatically false and null and void, having no force or effect. Relative Natural Rights may be further defined as Relative Delegable Natural Rights or Relative Conferrable Natural Rights; and

(v) *Superior Person Rights* (*Superioris Iurium Personae*), are a sub-class of Superior Rights whereby such valid Rights are created, defined and bestowed to a Superior Person by the existence of a valid Superior Person, or aggregate person, or community, or body politic, or association in accord with the Rule of Law through the most sacred Covenant Pactum De Singularis Caelum. Universal Superior Rights are Peremptory, Permanent, Immutable and Indefeasible and once bestowed are not subject to any form or condition of waiver, abandonment, surrender, disqualification, incapacitation, seizure, capture, arrest, resignation, alienation, suspension, suppression, forfeiture or abrogation. Superior Personal Rights are therefore the highest possible form of Superior Rights of any society or aggregate person within the temporal realm; and

(vi) *Ecclesiastical Rights* (*Iurium Ecclesiae*), are a sub-class of Superior Rights associated with a valid Ucadia Ecclesia such as One Christ, One Islam, One Spirit and Ucadia itself. Ecclesiastical Rights are the highest possible rights of any aggregate body, society, fraternity, association or company of two (2) or more people. There exists eight (8) categories of one hundred and thirty-two (132) Superior Rights within the sub-class of Ecclesiastical Rights, being Authoritative (22), Instrumental (22), Sacramental (33), Writs (11), Bills (11), Dogma (11), Decrees (11) and Notices (11); and

(vii)   *Sovereign Rights (Iurium Regnum)*, are a sub-class of Superior Rights associated with the embodiment of the sovereign authority of a valid Ucadia society such as a Campus, or Province, or University or Union. All Sovereign Rights are derived from Ecclesiastical Rights and a Sovereign can never claim to be higher than Ecclesiastical Rights. There exists six categories of seventy-seven (77) Superior Rights within the sub-class of Sovereign Rights, being Authoritative (11), Instrumental (22), Writs (11), Bills (11), Decrees (11) and Notices (11); and

(viii) *Official Rights (Iurium Publicum)*, are a sub-class of Superior Rights associated with an Officer empowered to Office within a valid Ucadia society such as a Campus, or Province, or University or Union. All Official Rights are derived from Sovereign Rights and Official Rights can never be claimed to be higher than Sovereign Rights. There exists six categories of eighty-eight (88) Official Rights within the class of Official Rights, being Authoritative (11), Instrumental (33), Warrants (11), Complaints (11), Orders (11) and Notices (11); and

(ix)   *Administrative Rights (Iurium Administrationis)*, are a sub-class of Superior Rights associated with a legislative body of a valid Ucadia society such as a Campus, or Province, or University or Union. All Administrative Rights are derived from either Sovereign Rights or Official Rights; and an Administrative Right can never claim to be higher than Official Rights. There exists two categories of forty-four (44) Superior Rights within the sub-class of Administrative Rights, being Authoritative (11) and Instrumental (33); and

(x)   *Member Rights (Iurium Membrum)*, are a sub-class of Superior Rights associated with a Member of a valid Ucadia society, body or aggregate; and

(xi)   *Primary Rights*, also known as Primary Inferior Rights, are a sub-class of Inferior Rights whereby such Rights are created, defined and bestowed to an Inferior (Legal) Person by a non-Ucadian aggregate person, or community, or body politic, or association. Primary Inferior Rights are frequently claimed and created without reference to rights already existing or proving such provenance to Divine Rights. Therefore, Primary Inferior Rights are equivalent to either Claims or false and unsubstantiated Demands. Primary Inferior Rights are therefore the second lowest possible form of rights of any society or aggregate person within the temporal realm. Primary Inferior Rights may be further defined as Primary Personal

Inferior Rights or Primary Public Inferior Rights; and

(xii) *Secondary Rights*, also known as Secondary Inferior Rights, are a sub-class of Inferior Rights whereby such valid Rights are created, defined and delegated to an Inferior (Legal) Person by the existence of a non-Ucadian aggregate person, or community, or body politic, or association upon acceptance of the associated obligations and duties attached to them. If any such conditions and obligations are breached or repudiated, then the relevant Secondary Inferior Right may be waived, surrendered, suspended, abandoned, resigned, disqualified, seized, captured, arrested, rescinded, suppressed, forfeited or revoked. Secondary Inferior Rights are therefore the lowest possible form of rights of any society or aggregate person within the temporal realm. Secondary Inferior Rights may be further defined as Secondary Protective Inferior Rights or Secondary Remedial Inferior Rights.

6. The Status of any Valid Right is its relative state or condition, position, strength, priority and standing compared to one or more other Rights. By such comparison of Rights in accord with the following core Arguments of Status, a valid Right can be said to be Superior, Inferior, Equal or Indeterminate:- Status of Right

    (i) Only valid Rights may have their Status compared as a valid Right is always Superior to an invalid or false Right; and

    (ii) A valid Right inherited from another will always be Inferior to the valid Right from which it is sourced; and

    (iii) A Divine Right is Superior to a Natural Right and a Natural Right is Superior to a Positive Right; and

    (iv) A Perfect Divine Right is Superior to an Imperfect Divine Right; and

    (v) An Absolute Natural Right is Superior to a Relative Natural Right; and

    (vi) A Universal Positive Right is Superior to a Conditional Positive Right; and

    (vii) A valid Right of the same sub-class and type associated with the same type of person may be Equal or Indeterminate and therefore may be subject to proper investigation by a competent forum of law.

7. The valid Assertion of any Right is always under the proper Rule of Assertion of Right

135

Law through Justice in accord with the present Covenant. There exists five (5) forms of action by which a valid Right may be asserted being Record, Notice, Writ, Claim and Petition:-

(i) *Record* is the written account of a valid Right, preserved in writing as evidence, usually within a specified ledger of records known as a Register. The ownership of the Register may be evidence of any legal title, while the production of any receipt or certificate from such a register may represent evidence of equitable title; and

(ii) *Notice* is the assertion of a valid Right by means of service of formal process by which a party is made aware of any formal legal matter that may affect certain Rights as well as the form of document used to transmit such facts. The primary types of notices being public (legal), actual, constructive and implied; and

(iii) *Writ* is the assertion of a valid Right through the issuance of a formal instrument of demand and grant of authority to one or more agents commanding certain acts to be performed whilst granting the agents(s) limited protection from liability or responsibility for any injury or claim; and

(iv) *Claim* is the assertion of a valid Right through a challenge within a competent forum of law against another party regarding the possession or ownership of some property or thing withheld from the possession of the claimant; and

(v) *Petition* is the assertion of a valid Right through a petition and prayer to the highest sovereign authority within a society which claims recognition of Rule of Law and Justice to recover the possession or ownership of some property or thing withheld from the possession of the petitioner by an officer or agent of the same sovereign authority (such as government).

8. A "**Dispute of Rights**" is when two parties under the proper Rule of Law through Justice in accord with the present Covenant disagree as to the validity of one or more Rights, usually through one or more Claims. In accord with the present Covenant, the primary arguments for resolving such controversy rests upon the following arguments being: Validity, Duty, Status and Priority:- Dispute of Right

(i) "**Validity**" is the determination of whether the Rights in question are valid in accord with the present Covenant and the most sacred Covenant *Pactum De Singularis Caelum*. A False or Invalid Right has no existence. An Undefined Right against a valid Right is by definition inferior; and

(ii) **"Duty"** is the determination of whether a Right remains valid and in effect due to the necessary performance of any obligations and Duty as in the specific case of all Imperfect Divine Rights, Relative Natural Rights and Conditional Positive Rights. Evidence of failure to perform the obligations of Duty may render a Right invalid, even if it is Superior in standing; and

(iii) **"Status"** is the determination of whether one valid Right is superior or inferior compared to another by virtue of belonging to a higher Class or Sub-Class providing no evidence exists of failure to perform any mandated obligations or duty. Excluding such evidence, there exists no higher or more superior valid Rights than Divine Rights, followed by Natural Rights and then Positive Rights; and

(iv) **"Priority"** is the determination of whether one valid Right of equal weighting in terms of Superiority has greater merit by virtue of a prior action of Record, Notice, Writ or Claim, thus identifying such a valid Right as a valid Prior Right against any other claim.

9. Any person, body, form, being, spirit, aggregate or entity that repudiates the present Article and Covenant does therefore also repudiate the Rule of Law and Justice and so is itself without Law, or any Rights:-

Repudiation of Right

(i) It is a moral obligation of all higher order beings to restore the Rule of Law and Justice and hold to account those who Repudiate such valid Rights; and

(ii) No force or attempt of seizure, alienation, abrogation, derogation, enclosure, or other artful attempt against the Rights as defined herein shall have any validity, legitimacy of effect.

10. In accord with Article 38 (*Rights*) of the most sacred Covenant *Pactum De Singularis Caelum*, Superior Rights specifically associated with formal Ucadian administrative divisions and communities shall be uniquely defined according to the following rules:

Ucadian Superior Rights

(i) **"Ius Ucadia"** shall be the prefix for all unique Superior Rights associated with Ucadia itself; and

(ii) **"Ius Unionis"** shall be the prefix for all unique Superior Rights associated with a Union administrative division, body politic and government. All Ius Unionis Rights are inherited from Ius

Ucadia Rights; and

(iii) **"Ius Universitas"** shall be the prefix for all unique Superior Rights associated with a University administrative division, body politic and government. All Ius Universitas Rights are inherited from Ius Unionis Rights; and

(iv) **"Ius Provinciae"** shall be the prefix for all unique Superior Rights associated with a Province administrative division, body politic and government. All Ius Provinciae Rights are inherited from Ius Universitas Rights; and

(v) **"Ius Campus"** shall be the prefix for all unique Superior Rights associated with a Campus administrative division, body politic and government. All Ius Campus Rights are inherited from Ius Provinciae Rights.

11. An Invalid Right or False Right is any form that asserts to be a valid Right yet contradicts or violates one or more of the criteria of the Articles of the present Covenant.

    Invalid Right

12. A Prohibited Right is a False Right and Invalid Right that asserts one or more of the following self-evident false arguments and is therefore automatically null and void having no force or effect ecclesiastically, lawfully or legally:-

    Prohibited Right

    (i) Any right that cannot demonstrate its ultimate provenance back to a valid Divine Right as defined within the sacred Covenant *Pactum De Singularis Caelum*; or

    (ii) Any right that asserts immunity from the law from which the Right is inherited; or

    (iii) Any right that asserts immunity from the duties or obligations granted with such a Right; or

    (iv) Any right that asserts a man or woman may be classified, determined or treated as a Thing; or

    (v) Any right that asserts by virtue of birth of flesh or blood a man or woman is superior to another; or

    (vi) Any right that asserts the right to create secret laws or rights unknown to the public; or

    (vii) Any right that is expressed in the negative or as a negative power; or

    (viii) Any right that asserts a man or woman may be considered guilty or liable before an accusation is proven; or

(ix)   Any right that asserts an officer or agent holding such office or position in trust may ecclesiastically, lawfully and legally give false testimony or deliberately false and misleading information; or

(x)   Any right that asserts the right to suspend the operation of the proper Rule of Law, Due Process and Justice to obtain an advantage for or against another; or

(xi)   Any right that asserts the right for a man or woman to occupy the position of a justice of the peace, or judge or magistrate and act in such capacity without any effective oath of office; or

(xii)   Any right that asserts the right for a man or woman claiming to be a justice of the peace, or judge or magistrate to hear and adjudicate a matter of law with unclean hands, in bad faith and with prejudice; or

(xiii)   Any right that asserts the right to treat a financial or equitable advantage obtained by fraud as lawful and legal; or

(xiv)   Any right that asserts the rights of another can be waived, surrendered, suspended, abandoned, resigned, disqualified, seized, captured, arrested, alienated, suppressed, forfeited or annulled without proper Rule of Law and Due Process of Justice; or

(xv)   Any right that asserts the right to use, or claim or register the name Ucadia or any derivation, mark, symbol, icon, version or image thereof contrary to the manner prescribed by the present sacred Covenant and associated Charters; or

(xvi)   Any right that asserts the right to disavow, repudiate, contradict or injure some or all of the most sacred Covenant *Pactum De Singularis Caelum* and the present sacred Covenant.

Article 37 – Divine Rights

1.   **One hundred and fifty-four** (154) Divine Rights (Divinum Iurium) of Heaven are the primary and original form of Rights, corresponding to Divine Trusts, Divine Estates and Divine Persons in accord with Article 39 (*Divine Rights*) of the most sacred Covenant *Pactum De Singularis Caelum*. There exists no higher class, or possible type of Rights. All valid Rights therefore are sourced and inherited from the class of valid Divine Rights. There

Divine Rights
(Divinum
Iurium)

139

exists two (2) sub-classes (Perfect and Imperfect), each possessing seventy-seven (77) Rights; and nine (9) categories being: Foundational (22), Instrumental (22), Sacramental (33), Authoritative (22), Divine Writs (11), Divine Bills (11), Divine Dogma (11), Divine Decrees (11), and Divine Notices (11):-

(i) **"Foundational Divine Right"** (*Fundationis Divinum Iurium*) are the Perfect Divine Rights considered elemental and fundamental to the existence, operation and function of all other rights; and

(ii) **"Instrumental Divine Rights"** (*Instrumentalis Divinum Iurium*) are the Perfect Divine Rights essential to the proper operation of the rule of law, justice and fair process; and

(iii) **"Sacramental Divine Rights"** (*Sacramentum Divinum Iurium*) are the Perfect Divine Rights associated with one of the thirty-three (33) Divine Sacraments; and

(iv) **"Authoritative Divine Rights"** (*Potentis Divinum Iurium*) are the Imperfect Divine Rights associated with core authoritative powers from Heaven to Earth; and

(v) **"Divine Writs of Rights"** (*Recto Divinum Iurium*) are the Imperfect Divine Rights associated with the one, true and only valid forms of Original Entry and Original Action; and

(vi) **"Divine Bills of Exception"** (*Rogatio Divinum Iurium*) are the Imperfect Divine Rights associated with the one, true and only valid forms of Bills of Exception, Citation and Moratorium; and

(vii) **"Divine Dogma"** (*Summa Dogma Divinum Iurium*) are the Imperfect Divine Rights associated with the promulgation of authoritative principles, decrees and doctrines of Ucadia, Heaven and Earth; and

(viii) **"Divine Decrees"** (*Decretum Divinum Iurium*) are the Imperfect Divine Rights associated with Divine Decrees concerning the administration, conduct and enforcement of law and order; and

(ix) **"Divine Notices"** (*Notitiae Divinum Iurium*) are the Imperfect Divine Rights associated with Divine Notices issued, executed, patented, promulgated and services in the proper administration, conduct and enforcement of law and order.

2. The following valid twenty-two (22) Foundational Divine Rights

Foundational Divine Rights

(*Fundationis Divinum Iurium*) are recognised in accord with the most sacred Covenant *Pactum De Singularis Caelum* and the present sacred Covenant:-

(i)   **"Ius Divinum"** are the Divine Rights of Divine Law; and

(ii)   **"Ius Divinum Ucadia"** are the Divine Rights of Ucadia; and

(iii)   **"Ius Divinum Iuris"** are the Divine Rights to Divine Justice and Due Process; and

(iv)   **"Ius Divinum Cogitatio"** are the Divine Rights of Thought and Reason; and

(v)   **"Ius Divinum Conscium"** are the Divine Rights of Conscious Awareness; and

(vi)   **"Ius Divinum Honoris"** are the Divine Rights of Respect and Honour; and

(vii)   **"Ius Divinum Veritas"** are the Divine Rights of Truth and Integrity; and

(viii) **"Ius Divinum Sententia"** are the Divine Rights of Meaning and Judgement; and

(ix)   **"Ius Divinum Aestimare"** are the Divine Rights of Value and Estimation; and

(x)   **"Ius Divinum Amoris"** are the Divine Rights of Divine Love and Mercy; and

(xi)   **"Ius Divinum Aequum"** are the Divine Rights of Equality and Fairness; and

(xii)   **"Ius Divinum Salutis"** are the Divine Rights of Safety and Well Being; and

(xiii) **"Ius Divinum Proprius"** are the Divine Rights to one's own Character and Identity; and

(xiv) **"Ius Divinum Venia"** are the Divine Rights of Forgiveness, Pardon and Remission; and

(xv)   **"Ius Divinum Sacrum"** are the Divine Rights of Sacred Recognition, Devotion and Veneration; and

(xvi) **"Ius Divinum Lingua"** are the Divine Rights of Language, Naming and Expression; and

(xvii) **"Ius Divinum Nomenis"** are the Divine Rights to Name, Title and Reputation; and

(xviii) **"Ius Divinum Intentionis"** are the Divine Rights of

Intention and Purpose; and

(xix) **"Ius Divinum Liberatum Arbitrium"** are the Divine Rights of Free Choice (Will) and Intention; and

(xx) **"Ius Divinum Esse"** are the Divine Rights of Existence and Being; and

(xxi) **"Ius Divinum Victus"** are the Divine Rights to Quality and Fruitful Existence; and

(i) **"Ius Divinum Fraternitas"** are the Divine Rights of Membership of Heaven.

3. The following valid twenty-two (22) Instrumental Divine Rights (*Instrumentalis Divinum Iurium*) are recognised in accord with the most sacred Covenant *Pactum De Singularis Caelum* and the present sacred Covenant:-

Instrumental
Divine Rights
(Instrumentalis
Divinum
Iurium)

(i) **"Ius Divinum Fidei"** are the Divine Rights of Divine Trusts and Estates; and

(ii) **"Ius Divinum Credito"** are the Divine Rights of Divine Credit and Funds; and

(iii) **"Ius Divinum Hereditatis"** are the Divine Rights of Inheritance of Rights; and

(iv) **"Ius Divinum Concedere"** are the Divine Rights to Give or Grant Rights; and

(v) **"Ius Divinum Abrogare"** are the Divine Rights to Annul or Rescind Rights; and

(vi) **"Ius Divinum Delegare"** are the Divine Rights to Assign or Delegate Rights; and

(vii) **"Ius Divinum Revocar**e**"** are the Divine Rights to Cancel or Revoke Rights; and

(viii) **"Ius Divinum Societas"** are the Divine Rights of Association; and

(ix) **"Ius Divinum Abstinendi"** are the Divine Rights of Renunciation; and

(x) **"Ius Divinum Consensum"** are the Divine Rights to Consent; and

(xi) **"Ius Divinum Consensu Recedere"** are the Divine Rights to withdraw Consent; and

(xii) **"Ius Divinum Dominium"** are the Divine Rights of Absolute Ownership; and

(xiii) **"Ius Divinum Possessionis"** are the Divine Rights to Possess, Hold and Own Property; and

(xiv) **"Ius Divinum Usus"** are the Divine Rights of Use and Fruits (Enjoyment) of Use of Property; and

(xv) **"Ius Divinum Proprietatis"** are the Divine Rights of Ownership of Use or Fruits of Use of Property; and

(xvi) **"Ius Divinum Vectigalis"** are the Divine Rights to impose Rents, Tolls, Levies, Contributions or Charges against Property; and

(xvii) **"Ius Divinum Moneta"** are the Divine Rights to Mint, Produce, Hold, Use and Exchange Money; and

(xviii) **"Ius Divinum Vectigalis Moneta"** are the Divine Rights to impose Rents, Tolls, Levies, Contributions or Charges against Money; and

(xix) **"Ius Divinum Registrum"** are the Divine Right to Enter Records within Registers and Rolls; and

(xx) **"Ius Divinum Instrumentalis"** are the Divine Rights of Document, Form or Instrument Creation, Negotiation and Execution; and

(xxi) **"Ius Divinum Compensationis Instrumentum"** are the Divine Rights of Relief, Redress or Compensation for Default or Deliquency of Obligation; and

(xxii) **"Ius Divinum Dirimere Instrumentum"** are the Divine Rights of Document, Form or Instrument Suspension, Termination or Dissolution.

4. The following valid thirty-three (33) Sacramental Divine Rights (*Sacramentum Divinum Iurium*) are recognised in accord with the most sacred Covenant *Pactum De Singularis Caelum* and the present sacred Covenant:-

Sacramental Divine Rights (Sacramentum Divinum Iurium)

(i) **"Ritus Sacramentum Recognosco"** is the Divine Right of the Key Sacrament of Recognition; and

(ii) **"Ritus Sacramentum Purificatio"** is the Divine Right of the Key Sacrament of Purification; and

(iii) **"Ritus Sacramentum Invocatio"** is the Divine Right of the Key Sacrament of Invocation; and

(iv) **"Ritus Sacramentum Obligatio"** is the Divine Right of the Key Sacrament of Obligation; and

143

(v)   **"Ritus Sacramentum Delegatio"** is the Divine Right of the Key Sacrament of Delegation (Trust); and

(vi)   **"Ritus Sacramentum Satisfactio"** is the Divine Right of the Key Sacrament of Satisfaction; and

(vii)   **"Ritus Sacramentum Resolutio"** is the Divine Right of the Key Sacrament of Resolution; and

(viii)   **"Ritus Sacramentum Sanctificatio"** is the Divine Right of the Cardinal Sacrament of Sanctification; and

(ix)   **"Ritus Sacramentum Sustentatio"** is the Divine Right of the Cardinal Sacrament of Sustentation; and

(x)   **"Ritus Sacramentum Unificatio"** is the Divine Right of the Cardinal Sacrament of Unification; and

(xi)   **"Ritus Sacramentum Amalgamatio"** is the Divine Right of the Cardinal Sacrament of Amalgamation; and

(xii)   **"Ritus Sacramentum Authentico"** is the Divine Right of the Cardinal Sacrament of Authentication; and

(xiii)   **"Ritus Sacramentum Absolutio"** is the Divine Right of the Cardinal Sacrament of Absolution; and

(xiv)   **"Ritus Sacramentum Volitio"** is the Divine Right of the Cardinal Sacrament of Volition (Oath); and

(xv)   **"Ritus Sacramentum Vocatio"** is the Divine Right of the Cardinal Sacrament of Vocation (Vow); and

(xvi)   **"Ritus Sacramentum Testificatio"** is the Divine Right of the Cardinal Sacrament of Testification; and

(xvii)   **"Ritus Sacramentum Compassio"** is the Divine Right of the Cardinal Sacrament of Compassion (Mercy); and

(xviii)   **"Ritus Sacramentum Conscripto"** is the Divine Right of the Cardinal Sacrament of Conscription (Binding); and

(xix)   **"Ritus Sacramentum Convocatio"** is the Divine Right of the Cardinal Sacrament of Convocation; and

(xx)   **"Ritus Sacramentum Auctoriso"** is the Divine Right of the Cardinal Sacrament of Authorisation; and

(xxi)   **"Ritus Sacramentum Elucidato"** is the Divine Right of the Cardinal Sacrament of Elucidation (Enlighten); and

(xxii) **"Ritus Sacramentum Inspiratio"** is the Divine Right of the Authentic Life Gift of Inspiratio (Annunciation); and

(xxiii) **"Ritus Sacramentum Resurrectio"** is the Divine Right of the Authentic Life Gift of Resurrection (Baptism); and

(xxiv) **"Ritus Sacramentum Incarnatio"** is the Divine Right of the Authentic Life Gift of Incarnatio (Christening); and

(xxv) **"Ritus Sacramentum Confirmatio"** is the Divine Right of the Authentic Life Gift of Confirmation (First Communion); and

(xxvi) **"Ritus Sacramentum Illuminatio"** is the Divine Right of the Authentic Life Gift of Illumination; and

(xxvii) **"Ritus Sacramentum Exultatio"** is the Divine Right of the Authentic Life Gift of Exultation; and

(xxviii) **"Ritus Sacramentum Glorificatio"** is the Divine Right of the Authentic Life Gift of Glorification; and

(xxix) **"Ritus Sacramentum Divinatio"** is the Divine Right of the Authentic Life Gift of Divination; and

(xxx) **"Ritus Sacramentum Visitatio"** is the Divine Right of the Authentic Life Gift of Visitation; and

(xxxi) **"Ritus Sacramentum Salvatio"** is the Divine Right of the Authentic Life Gift of Salvation; and

(xxxii) **"Ritus Sacramentum Emancipatio"** is the Divine Right of the Authentic Life Gift of Emancipation; and

(xxxiii) **"Ritus Sacramentum Veneratio"** is the Divine Right of the Authentic Life Gift of Veneration.

5. The following valid twenty-two (22) Authoritative Divine Rights (*Potentis Divinum Iurium*) are recognised in accord with the most sacred Covenant *Pactum De Singularis Caelum* and the present sacred Covenant:-

Authoritative Divine Rights (Potentis Divinum Iurium)

(i) **"Ius Divinum Universus"** are the Divine Rights to Design, Construct and Maintain Universal Reality; and

(ii) **"Ius Divinum Regnum"** are the Divine Rights of Sovereign Authority of Body; and

(iii) **"Ius Divinum Consilium"** are the Divine Rights of a Legislative and Advisory Body; and

145

(iv)   **"Ius Divinum Ecclesia"** are the Divine Rights of an Ecclesiastical and Religious Body; and

(v)   **"Ius Divinum Templum"** are the Divine Rights of a Treasury or Financial (Banking) Body; and

(vi)   **"Ius Divinum Collegium"** are the Divine Rights of a Company or Charitable Body; and

(vii)   **"Ius Divinum Officium"** are the Divine Rights of Office, Duty and Service; and

(viii)   **"Ius Divinum Imperium"** are the Divine Rights of Command, Occupation and Enforcement; and

(ix)   **"Ius Divinum Sacrum"** are the Divine Rights of Sacred Recognition, Devotion and Veneration; and

(x)   **"Ius Divinum Custoditum"** are the Divine Rights of Custody, Guardianship and Preservation; and

(xi)   **"Ius Divinum Alumentum"** are the Divine Rights to Sustenance, Maintenance and Alms; and

(xii)   **"Ius Divinum Apostolicus"** are the Divine Rights of Divine Commission; and

(xiii)   **"Ius Divinum Sanitatum"** are the Divine Rights to Sanity, Reason and Competence of Mind; and

(xiv)   **"Ius Divinum Oratorium"** are the Divine Rights to a competent forum of Law and Review; and

(xv)   **"Ius Divinum Penitentiaria"** are the Divine Rights of Forced Confinement and Penitence; and

(xvi)   **"Ius Divinum Sacramentum"** are the Divine Rights to grant and impart Holy Sacred Gifts; and

(xvii)   **"Ius Divinum Visum"** are the Divine Rights to Survey, Visit and Audit a Body; and

(xviii) **"Ius Divinum Commercium"** are the Divine Rights to Trade, Exchange and Communication; and

(xix)   **"Ius Divinum Virtus"** are the Divine Rights to Strength, Honour, Excellence and Virtue; and

(xx)   **"Ius Divinum Astrum"** are the Divine Rights to an Association, Aggregate or Body; and

(xxi) **"Ius Divinum Magisterium"** are the Divine Rights to Teach, Instruct and Interpret Sacred Texts and Divine Will; and

(xxii) **"Ius Divinum Decretum"** are the Divine Rights to issue Decrees, Judgements and Edicts.

6. The following valid eleven (11) Divine Writs of Rights (*Recto Divinum Iurium*) are recognised in accord with the most sacred Covenant *Pactum De Singularis Caelum* and the present sacred Covenant:-

Divine Writs of Rights (Recto Divinum Iurium)

(i) **"Recto Divinum Petitionis"** is the Divine Writ of Claim of Right or Relief; and

(ii) **"Recto Divinum Originalis"** is the Divine Original Writ (of Right); and

(iii) **"Recto Divinum Apocalypsis"** is the Divine Writ of Right of Revelation; and

(iv) **"Recto Divinum Investigationis"** is the Divine Writ of Inquiry and Search; and

(v) **"Recto Divinum Capionis"** is the Divine Writ of Seizure and Return; and

(vi) **"Recto Divinum Custodiae"** is the Divine Writ of Arrest and Custody; and

(vii) **"Recto Divinum Documentis"** is the Divine Writ of correcting Records of Proof; and

(viii) **"Recto Divinum Expungo"** is the Divine Writ of expunging Records of Proof; and

(ix) **"Recto Divinum Abrogationis"** is the Divine Writ of Annulment of Previous Laws and Instruments; and

(x) **"Recto Divinum Interdico"** is the Divine Writ of Prohibition and Imposition; and

(xi) **"Recto Divinum Restitutio"** is the Divine Writ of Compensation and Restoration.

7. The following valid eleven (11) Divine Bills of Exception (*Rogatio Divinum Iurium*) are recognised in accord with the most sacred Covenant *Pactum De Singularis Caelum* and the present sacred Covenant:-

Divine Bills of Exception (Rogatio Divinum Iurium)

(i) **"Rogatio Divinum Petitionis"** is the Divine Bill of Claim of Relief; and

(ii)   "**Rogatio Divinum Recto**" is the Divine Original Bill (of Right); and

(iii)   "**Rogatio Divinum Apocalypsis**" is the Divine Bill of Rights of Revelation; and

(iv)   "**Rogatio Divinum Investigationis**" is the Divine Bill of Inquiry and Search; and

(v)   "**Rogatio Divinum Capionis**" is the Divine Bill of Seizure and Return; and

(vi)   "**Rogatio Divinum Custodiae**" is the Divine Bill of Arrest and Custody; and

(vii)   "**Rogatio Divinum Documentis**" is the Divine Bill of correcting Records of Proof; and

(viii)   "**Rogatio Divinum Expungo**" is the Divine Bill of expunging Records of Proof; and

(ix)   "**Rogatio Divinum Abrogationis**" is the Divine Bill of Annulment of Previous Laws and Instruments; and

(x)   "**Rogatio Divinum Interdico**" is the Divine Bill of Prohibition and Imposition; and

(xi)   "**Rogatio Divinum Restitutio**" is the Divine Bill of Compensation and Restoration.

8.   The following valid eleven (11) Divine Dogma (*Summa Dogma Divinum Iurium*) are recognised in accord with the most sacred Covenant *Pactum De Singularis Caelum* and the present sacred Covenant:-

Divine Dogma
(Summa Dogma
Divinum
Iurium)

(i)   "**Dogma Divinum Praeceptum**" is the Divine Right of Divine Precept of Proposed Dogma; and

(ii)   "**Dogma Divinum Theologiae**" is the Divine Right of Divine Dogma of Divine Science; and

(iii)   "**Dogma Divinum Singularis Caelum**" is the Divine Right of Divine Dogma of One Heaven; and

(iv)   "**Dogma Divinum Ucadia**" is the Divine Right of Divine Dogma of Ucadia; and

(v)   "**Dogma Divinum Iuris**" is the Divine Right of Divine Dogma of Law; and

(vi)   "**Dogma Divinum Scientium**" is the Divine Right of Divine

148

Dogma of Science; and

(vii) **"Dogma Divinum Revelatio"** is the Divine Right of Divine Dogma of Revelation; and

(viii) **"Dogma Divinum Sacramentum"** is the Divine Right of Divine Dogma of the Sacraments; and

(ix) **"Dogma Divinum Singularis Christus"** is the Divine Right of Divine Dogma of One Christ; and

(x) **"Dogma Divinum Singularis Islam"** is the Divine Right of Divine Dogma of One Islam; and

(xi) **"Dogma Divinum Singularis Spiritus"** is the Divine Right of Divine Dogma of One Spirit.

9. The following valid eleven (11) Divine Decrees (*Decretum Divinum Iurium*) are recognised in accord with the most sacred Covenant *Pactum De Singularis Caelum* and the present sacred Covenant:-

Divine Decrees (Decretum Divinum Iurium)

(i) **"Decretum Divinum Doctrinae"** is the Divine Right of Divine Decree of Doctrine; and

(ii) **"Decretum Divinum Absolutionis"** is the Divine Right of Divine Decree of Absolution; and

(iii) **"Decretum Divinum Damnationis"** is the Divine Right of Divine Decree of Damnation; and

(iv) **"Decretum Divinum Exemplificatio"** is the Divine Right of Divine Decree of Exemplification; and

(v) **"Decretum Divinum Testimonium"** is the Divine Right of Divine Decree of Proof; and

(vi) **"Decretum Divinum Instructionis"** is the Divine Right of Divine Decree of Instruction; and

(vii) **"Decretum Divinum Censurae"** is the Divine Right of Divine Decree of Censure; and

(viii) **"Decretum Divinum Annullas"** is the Divine Right of Divine Decree of Annulment; and

(ix) **"Decretum Divinum Ratificationis"** is the Divine Right of Divine Decree of Ratification; and

(x) **"Decretum Divinum Interdictum"** is the Divine Right of Divine Decree of Interdiction; and

(xi) **"Decretum Divinum Levationis"** is the Divine Right of Divine Decree of Relief.

10. The following valid eleven (11) Divine Notices (*Notitiae Divinum Iurium*) are recognised in accord with the most sacred Covenant *Pactum De Singularis Caelum* and the present sacred Covenant:-

Divine Notices (Notitiae Divinum Iurium)

(i) **"Notitiae Divinum Eventus"** is the Divine Right of Divine Notice of Event; and

(ii) **"Notitiae Divinum Ius"** is the Divine Right of Divine Notice of Right; and

(iii) **"Notitiae Divinum Actum"** is the Divine Right of Divine Notice of Action; and

(iv) **"Notitiae Divinum Decretum"** is the Divine Right of Divine Notice of Decree; and

(v) **"Notitiae Divinum Iuris"** is the Divine Right of Divine Notice of Law; and

(vi) **"Notitiae Divinum Citationis"** is the Divine Right of Divine Notice of Summons; and

(vii) **"Notitiae Divinum Redemptio"** is the Divine Right of Divine Notice of Redemption; and

(viii) **"Notitiae Divinum Rogatio"** is the Divine Right of Divine Notice of Exception; and

(ix) **"Notitiae Divinum Potentis"** is the Divine Right of Divine Notice of Authority; and

(x) **"Notitiae Divinum Testamentum"** is the Divine Right of Divine Notice of Testament; and

(xi) **"Notitiae Divinum Obligationis"** is the Divine Right of Divine Notice of Obligation (Bond).

Article 38 – Natural Rights

1. The eighty-eight (88) Natural Rights (*Naturae Iurium*) of each and every Living Member and Higher Order Life form of One Heaven are the second highest form of valid Rights, corresponding to True Trusts and True Persons; and owe their existence and provenance to the existence of Divine Rights. In accord with Article 40 (*Natural Rights*) of the most sacred Covenant *Pactum De Singularis Caelum*, all valid Natural Rights therefore are inherited

Natural Rights (Naturae Iurium)

150

from valid Divine Rights.

All Natural Rights are delegated to the safe custody and wise guardian powers of the Oratorium, also known as the Supreme Court of One Heaven; and all valid and legitimate lesser competent forums of law, as defined by Article 59 (*Oratorium*) of the most sacred Covenant *Pactum De Singularis Caelum*. There exists two sub-classes (Absolute and Relative), each possessing forty-four (44) Rights; and seven (7) categories being: Essential (11), Volitional (11), Testamental (22), Domicile (11), Habitational (11), Actionable (11) and Ecological (11):-

(i)   **"Essential Natural Rights"** (*Essentilis Naturae Iurium*) are Absolute Natural Rights considered vital and essential to the physical existence and survival of a Living Member and Higher Order Life form of One Heaven; and

(ii)   **"Volitional Natural Rights"** (*Volitio Naturae Iurium*) are Absolute Natural Rights associated with the mind, will and intentions of a Living Member; and

(iii)   **"Testamental Natural Rights"** (*Testamentum Naturae Iurium*) are Absolute Natural Rights associated with the expression of the mind, will and intentions of a Living Member, especially with other Living Members; and

(iv)   **"Domicile Natural Rights"** (*Domicilium Naturae Iurium*), also known as the Rights of Lodgings, are Relative Natural Rights associated with the domicile, home and primary household and family unit in relation to a Living Member in the Office of Man or Office of Woman. As Relative Natural Rights, such Rights may be conferred in trust to a Superior body, association, body politic, society or community to manage such rights under the Golden Rule of Law for the benefit of all Members; and

(v)   **"Habitational Natural Rights"** (*Habitatus Naturae Iurium*), also known as the Rights of Land, are Relative Natural Rights associated with the habitat and environment of a Living Member in the Office of Man or Office of Woman. As Relative Natural Rights, such Rights may be conferred in trust to a Superior body, association, body politic, society or community to manage such rights under the Golden Rule of Law for the benefit of all Members; and

(vi)   **"Actionable Natural Rights"** (*Actionis Naturae Iurium*), also known as the Rights of Labour, are Relative Natural Rights associated with the energy, effort and productive work of a Living Member in the Office of Man or Office of Woman. As Relative Natural Rights, such Rights may be conferred in trust to a Superior body, association, body politic, society or community to manage such rights under the Golden Rule of Law for the benefit of all Members; and

(vii) **"Ecological Natural Rights"** (*Systematis Naturae Iurium*), are Relative Natural Rights associated with the respect, preservation, restoration and management of ecosystems, wilderness, natural habitats, animals, water and land, including the proper treatment of animals and the limits and conditions of custody of animals and any associated commerce.

2. The following valid eleven (11) Essential Natural Rights (*Essentilis Naturae Iurium*) of all Higher Order Life are recognised in accord with the most sacred Covenant *Pactum De Singularis Caelum* and the present sacred Covenant:-

> Essential Natural Rights (Essentilis Naturae Iurium)

(i) **"Ius Naturale Esse"** is the Natural Right of Existence, as inherited from the Divine Right *Ius Divinum Esse*; and

(ii) **"Ius Naturale Conscium"** is the Natural Right of Conscious Awareness, as inherited from the Divine Right *Ius Divinum Conscium*; and

(iii) **"Ius Naturale Honour"** is the Natural Right of Respect and Honour, as inherited from the Divine Right *Ius Divinum Honoris*; and

(iv) **"Ius Naturale Dignitatis Vitam"** is the Natural Right to Dignified Life, as inherited from the Divine Right *Ius Divinum Esse*; and

(v) **"Ius Naturale Dignitatis Mortem"** is the Natural Right to Dignified Death, as inherited from the Divine Right *Ius Divinum Honoris*; and

(vi) **"Ius Naturale Sodalis"** is the Natural Right of Equal Membership of Species, as inherited from the Divine Right *Ius Divinum Societas*; and

(vii) **"Ius Naturale Nutrimens"** is the Natural Right to food and sustenance, as inherited from the Divine Right *Ius Divinum Victus*; and

(viii) **"Ius Naturale Aqua"** is the Natural Right to safe drinking water, as inherited from the Divine Right *Ius Divinum Esse*; and

(ix)   **"Ius Naturale Tectum"** is the Natural Right to Shelter, as inherited from the Divine Right *Ius Divinum Salutis*; and

(x)   **"Ius Naturale Salutis"** is the Natural Right of Safety and Well Being, as inherited from the Divine Right *Ius Divinum Salutis*; and

(xi)   **"Ius Naturale Non Res"** is the Natural Right not to be treated as a thing or property, as inherited from the Divine Right *Ius Divinum Veritas* and *Ius Divinum Iuris*.

3. The following valid eleven (11) Volitional Natural Rights (*Volitio Naturae Iurium*) are recognised in accord with the most sacred Covenant *Pactum De Singularis Caelum* and the present sacred Covenant:-

    Volitional Natural Rights (Volitio Naturae Iurium)

(i)   **"Ius Naturale Liberatum Arbitrium"** is the Natural Right of Free Choice (Will), as inherited from the Divine Right *Ius Divinum Liberatum Arbitrium*; and

(ii)   **"Ius Naturale Rationis"** is the Natural Right of Reason, Argument and Deduction, as inherited from the Divine Right *Ius Divinum Cogitatio*; and

(iii)   **"Ius Naturale Intentionis"** is the Natural Right of Intention and Purpose, as inherited from the Divine Right *Ius Divinum Intentionis*; and

(iv)   **"Ius Naturale Credere"** is the Natural Right to Trust or Reject a Claim, as inherited from the Divine Rights *Ius Divinum Cognitionis* and *Ius Divinum Cogitatio*; and

(v)   **"Ius Naturale Sensus"** is the Natural Right to Sense, as inherited from the Divine Rights *Ius Divinum Cogitatio* and *Ius Divinum Conscium*; and

(vi)   **"Ius Naturale Mori Eligate"** is the Natural Right to Choose to Die, as inherited from the Divine Right *Ius Divinum Consensu Recedere*; and

(vii)   **"Ius Naturale Societas"** is the Natural Right of Association and Renunciation, as inherited from the Divine Right *Ius Divinum Societas*; and

(viii)   **"Ius Naturale Consensum"** is the Natural Right to Consent and withdraw Consent, as inherited from the Divine Right *Ius Divinum Consensum*; and

(ix)   **"Ius Naturale Lingua"** is the Natural Right of Language,

Naming and Expression, as inherited from the Divine Right *Ius Divinum Lingua*; and

(x) **"Ius Naturale Loqui"** is the Natural Right to Speak, as inherited from the Divine Rights *Ius Divinum Cognitionis* and *Ius Divinum Cogitatio;* and

(xi) **"Ius Naturale Silentium"** is the Natural Right to Silence, as inherited from the Divine Right *Ius Divinum Cogitatio.*

4. The following valid twenty-two (22) Testamental Natural Rights (*Testamentum Naturae Iurium*) are recognised in accord with the most sacred Covenant *Pactum De Singularis Caelum* and the present sacred Covenant:-

Testamental Natural Rights (Testamentum Naturae Iurium)

(i) **"Ius Naturale Fidei"** is the Natural Right of True Trust, as inherited from the Divine Right *Ius Divinum Fidei*; and

(ii) **"Ius Naturale Fundus"** is the Natural Right of True Estate, as inherited from the Divine Right *Ius Divinum Fidei*; and

(iii) **"Ius Naturale Credito"** is the Natural Right of True Credit (Capital), as inherited from the Divine Right *Ius Divinum Credito*; and

(iv) **"Ius Naturale Nomenis"** is the Natural Right to Name, Title and Reputation, as inherited from the Divine Right *Ius Divinum Nomenis*; and

(v) **"Ius Naturale Officium"** is the Natural Right of Office, as inherited from the Divine Right *Ius Divinum Officium*; and

(vi) **"Ius Naturale Iurandum"** is the Natural Right to make or abjure an Oath and Vow, as inherited from the Divine Rights *Ius Divinum Cogitatio* and *Ius Divinum Consensum*; and

(vii) **"Ius Naturale Scriptum"** is the Natural Right to handwrite or print in script, as inherited from the Divine Right *Ius Divinum Cogitatio*; and

(viii) **"Ius Naturale Subscribere"** is the Natural Right to Sign and Seal, as inherited from the Divine Right *Ius Divinum Cogitatio;* and

(ix) **"Ius Naturale Hereditatis"** is the Natural Right of Inheritance of Rights, as inherited from the Divine Right *Ius Divinum Hereditatis*; and

(x) **"Ius Naturale Concedere"** is the Natural Right to Grant or Annul Rights, as inherited from the Divine Right *Ius Divinum*

Concedere; and

(xi) **"Ius Naturale Delegare"** is the Natural Right to Delegate or Revoke Rights, as inherited from the Divine Right *Ius Divinum Delegare*; and

(xii) **"Ius Naturale Assigno"** is the Natural Right to Assign or Cancel Rights, as inherited from the Divine Right *Ius Divinum Concedere*; and

(xiii) **"Ius Naturale Vivus"** is the Natural Right to Possession and Ownership of Flesh and Blood of one's own Body, as inherited from the Divine Right *Ius Divinum Possessionis*; and

(xiv) **"Ius Naturale Geneticae"** is the Natural Right of Possession, Ownership and Title to ones own Genetic Material, as inherited from the Divine Right *Ius Divinum Possessionis*; and

(xv) **"Ius Naturale Facies"** is the Natural Right Possession, Ownership and Title to ones own Face, Voice, Fingerprints and Biometric Identity, as inherited from the Divine Right *Ius Divinum Possessionis*; and

(xvi) **"Ius Naturale Proprietatis"** is the Natural Right of Ownership of use or fruits of use of Property, as inherited from the Divine Right *Ius Divinum Proprietatis*; and

(xvii) **"Ius Naturale Testamentum"** is the Natural Right to make a Testification, as inherited from the Divine Rights *Ius Divinum Hereditatis* and *Ius Divinum Cogitatio*; and

(xviii) **"Ius Naturale Contraceptio"** is the Natural Right to contraception, as inherited from the Divine Rights *Ius Divinum Intentionis* and *Ius Divinum Liberatum Arbitrium*; and

(xix) **"Ius Naturale Terminare"** is the Natural Right to Terminate Pregnancy within the 1st trimester, as inherited from the Divine Rights *Ius Divinum Intentionis* and *Ius Divinum Liberatum Arbitrium*; and

(xx) **"Ius Naturale Nativitas"** is the Natural Right to give birth as inherited from *Ius Divinum Esse*; and

(xxi) **"Ius Naturale Connubii"** is the Natural Right of Union, as inherited from the Divine Right *Ius Divinum Societas*; and

(xxii) **"Ius Naturale Coitus"** is the Natural Right for consenting adults to engage in intercourse, as inherited from the Divine Rights *Ius Divinum Societas* and *Ius Divinum Consensum*.

5. The following valid eleven (11) Domicile Natural Rights (*Domicilium Naturae Iurium*), also known as the Rights of Lodging, are recognised in accord with the most sacred Covenant *Pactum De Singularis Caelum* and the present sacred Covenant:-

Domicile Natural Rights (Domicilium Naturae Iurium)

(i) **"Ius Naturale Habitare"** is the Natural Right to Home Environment, as inherited from the Divine Right *Ius Divinum Salutis*; and

(ii) **"Ius Naturale Aedificationis Domus"** is the Natural Right to build one's home, as inherited from the Divine Right *Ius Divinum Proprius*; and

(iii) **"Ius Naturale Domus"** is the Natural Right to live peacefully in one's own Home, as inherited from the Divine Right *Ius Divinum Salutis*; and

(iv) **"Ius Naturale Armare"** is the Natural Right to possess arms, as inherited from the Divine Right *Ius Divinum Salutis*; and

(v) **"Ius Naturale Parietis"** is the Natural Right to build walls and fencing around home, as inherited from the Divine Right *Ius Divinum Salutis*; "and

(vi) **"Ius Naturale Coquis"** is the Natural Right to prepare, cook and eat food in home, as inherited from the Divine Right *Ius Divinum Victus*; and

(vii) **"Ius Naturale Defendum Domus"** is the Natural Right to defend one's own home against trespass, as inherited from the Divine Right *Ius Divinum Salutis*; and

(viii) **"Ius Naturale Filios"** is the Natural Right to have, nurture, support, supervise and teach children, as inherited from the Divine Right *Ius Divinum Esse*; and

(ix) **"Ius Naturale Parentum"** is the Natural Right of parents to the custody, protection, well being, discipline and education, as inherited from the Divine Right *Ius Divinum Esse*; and

(x) **"Ius Naturale Celebras"** is the Natural Right to celebrate and enjoy in one's own home, as inherited from the Divine Right *Ius Divinum Victus*; and

(xi) **"Ius Naturale Victus"** is the Natural Right to Quality and

Fruitful Existence, as inherited from the Divine Right *Ius Divinum Victus*.

6. The following valid eleven (11) Habitational Natural Rights (*Habitatus Naturae Iurium*), also known as the Rights of Land, are recognised in accord with the most sacred Covenant *Pactum De Singularis Caelum* and the present sacred Covenant:-

Habitational
Natural Rights
(Habitatus
Naturae Iurium)

   (i) **"Ius Naturale Nascendi Societas"** is the Natural Right to be recognised as a member of the society into which one was borne, as inherited from the Divine Rights *Ius Divinum Custoditum* and *Ius Divinum Fraternitas*; and

   (ii) **"Ius Naturale Vendandi Et Piscandi"** is the Natural Right to Hunt and Fish for Survival, as inherited from the Divine Rights *Ius Divinum Hereditatis* and *Ius Divinum Custoditum*; and

   (iii) **"Ius Naturale Arborum"** is the Natural Right to plant and use trees, plants or crops, as inherited from the Divine Rights *Ius Divinum Hereditatis* and *Ius Divinum Custoditum*; and

   (iv) **"Ius Naturale Fabricae"** is the Natural Right to make, model, fabricate, as inherited from the Divine Rights *Ius Divinum Hereditatis* and *Ius Divinum Custoditum*; and

   (v) **"Ius Natural Energis"** is the Natural Right to make, store and use energy, as inherited from the Divine Rights *Ius Divinum Hereditatis* and *Ius Divinum Custoditum*; and

   (vi) **"Ius Naturale Terram"** is the Natural Right to the Promise and use of Land, as inherited from the Divine Rights *Ius Divinum Hereditatis* and *Ius Divinum Custoditum*; and

   (vii) **"Ius Natural Domesticus Animalis"** is the Natural Right to have custody of domestic Animals, as inherited from the Divine Rights *Ius Divinum Hereditatis* and *Ius Divinum Custoditum*; and

   (viii) **"Ius Naturale Pascendi"** is the Natural Right to Pasture (Feed) Animals, as inherited from the Divine Rights *Ius Divinum Hereditatis* and *Ius Divinum Custoditum*; and

   (ix) **"Ius Naturale Iter"** is the Natural Right to travel and use the Roads and Highway, as inherited from the Divine Rights *Ius Divinum Hereditatis* and *Ius Divinum Custoditum*; and

   (x) **"Ius Naturale Iter Aquae"** is the Natural Right to travel the waterways, as inherited from the Divine Rights *Ius Divinum*

Hereditatis and *Ius Divinum Custoditum*; and

(xi) **"Ius Naturale Iter Aurae"** is the Natural Right to travel in the air, as inherited from the Divine Rights *Ius Divinum Hereditatis* and *Ius Divinum Custoditum*.

7. The following valid eleven (11) Actionable Natural Rights (*Actionis Naturae Iurium*), also known as the Rights of Labour, are recognised in accord with the most sacred Covenant *Pactum De Singularis Caelum* and the present sacred Covenant:-

(i) **"Ius Naturale Perfungor"** is the Natural Right to Perform or refuse to Perform (Work), as inherited from the Divine Right *Ius Divinum Officium*; and

(ii) **"Ius Naturale Iuris"** is the Natural Right to Natural Justice, as inherited from the Divine Right *Ius Divinum Iuris*; and

(iii) **"Ius Naturale Solutionis Perfungor"** is the Natural Right to receive fair payment in exchange for fruits, energy, results and product of ones performance, work and effort, as inherited from the Divine Rights *Ius Divinum Aequum* and *Ius Divinum Virtus*; and

(iv) **"Ius Naturale Petitionis Iuris"** is the Natural Right to petition and pray for relief and remedy for a lawful right withheld from "ones possession, as inherited from the Divine Right *Ius Divinum Iuris*; and

(v) **"Ius Naturale Accusationis Sciri"** is the Natural Right to know the accuser and accusations, as inherited from the Divine Right *Ius Divinum Aequum*; and

(vi) **"Ius Naturale Defensionis"** is the Natural Right to defend against any accusation and accuser, as inherited from the Divine Right *Ius Divinum Aequum*; and

(vii) **"Ius Naturale Innocentiae"** is the Natural Right of Innocence until accusation proven, as inherited from the Divine Right *Ius Divinum Aequum*; and

(viii) **"Ius Naturale Nullum Validum Iudicium"** is the Natural Right of rendering "invalid" a false or fraudulent or erroneous judgement, as inherited from the Divine Right *Ius Divinum Aequum*; and

(ix) **"Ius Naturale Usurae"** is the Natural Right of Fruits (Enjoyment) of Use, as inherited from the Divine Right *Ius*

Divinum Usus; and

(x) **"Ius Naturale Libertatis"** is the Natural Right of Freedom from Bondage and Slavery, as inherited from the Divine Rights *Ius Divinum Aequum* and *Ius Divinum Sacrum*; and

(xi) **"Ius Naturale Indicium"** is the Natural Right of Freedom of Knowledge and Information, as inherited from the Divine Right *Ius Divinum Aequum* and *Ius Divinum Sacrum*.

8. The following valid eleven (11) Ecological Natural Rights (*Systematis Naturae Iurium*), are recognised in accord with the most sacred Covenant *Pactum De Singularis Caelum* and the present sacred Covenant:-

Ecological Natural Rights (Systematis Naturae Iurium)

(i) **"Ius Naturale"** is the Natural Right of preservation and restoration of ecosystems, as inherited from the Divine Rights *Ius Divinum Esse* and *Ius Divinum Victus*; and

(ii) **"Ius Naturale Habitatus"** is the Natural Right of native species to natural habitat, as inherited from the Divine Rights *Ius Divinum Dominium* and *Ius Divinum Victus*; and

(iii) **"Ius Naturale Communitas"** is the Natural Right of preservation/ restoration of community land, as inherited from the Divine Rights *Ius Divinum Esse* and *Ius Divinum Victus*; and

(iv) **"Ius Naturale Integritatis Geneticae"** is the Natural Right of Genetic Integrity of Natural Genetic Material, as inherited from the Divine Rights *Ius Divinum Esse* and *Ius Divinum Victus*; and

(v) **"Ius Naturale Purus Aquae"** is the Natural Right of Clean non-polluted water, as inherited from the Divine Rights *Ius Divinum Esse* and *Ius Divinum Victus*; and

(vi) **"Ius Naturale Purus Terram"** is the Natural Right of Clean non-polluted land, as inherited from the Divine Rights *Ius Divinum Esse* and *Ius Divinum Victus*; and

(vii) **"Ius Naturale Pestis Amotum"** is the Natural Right to remove foreign and pest species in the ecosystem, as inherited from the Divine Rights *Ius Divinum Dominium* and *Ius Divinum Victus*; and

(viii) **"Ius Naturale Praeservare Arborum"** is the Natural Right to preserve natural wilderness & forests, as inherited from the Divine Rights *Ius Divinum Dominium* and *Ius Divinum Victus*;

and

(ix) **"Ius Naturale Conditionis Custodiae"** is the Natural Right of limited custody of animals, as inherited from the Divine Rights *Ius Divinum Dominium* and *Ius Divinum Victus*; and

(x) **"Ius Naturale Libertatis Animalis"** is the Natural Right of animals to be free from cruelty and deliberate pain, as inherited from the Divine Rights *Ius Divinum Dominium* and *Ius Divinum Victus*; and

(xi) **"Ius Naturale Commercium Naturalis"** is the Natural Right of limits of commerce associated with ecosystems, animals and animal by-products, as inherited from the Divine Rights *Ius Divinum Dominium* and *Ius Divinum Victus*.

Article 39 – Superior Rights

1. **Superior Rights** are the third class and third highest possible form of valid Rights; corresponding to Superior Trusts and Superior Persons associated with a Ucadia society. Whereas Divine Rights pertain to Heaven and Natural Rights relate to a living higher order life form, Superior Rights align to one or more civilised societies operating under the Golden Rule of Law in accord with the present sacred Covenant. In accord with Article 41 (*Superior Rights*) of the most sacred Covenant *Pactum De Singularis Caelum*, Superior Rights owe their existence and provenance to either valid Divine Rights or valid Natural Rights. All Superior Rights are greater than Inferior Rights.

Superior Rights

All Rights of valid Ucadia Members, Ucadia Societies and associated bodies, aggregates, societies, associations, communities and unions of two (2) or more people are inherited from the class of Superior Rights. There exists (6) six sub-classes of four hundred and twenty-four (424) Superior Rights, being: Personal (44), Ecclesiastical (132), Sovereign (77), Official (88), Administrative (44) and Member (39):-

(i) **"Personal Rights"** (*Superioris Iurium Personae*) are Superior Rights associated with Superior Persons and all Superior Ucadia Trusts and Superior Ucadia Estates. All Personal Rights are delegated to the safe custody and wise guardian powers of the legitimate and valid supreme competent forum of law of the seven Ucadia Unions and all lesser Ucadia bodies politic such as Universities, Provinces and Campuses as the embodiment of judicial authority; and as defined by Article 59 (*Oratorium*) of the most sacred Covenant

Pactum De Singularis Caelum; and

(ii)   **"Ecclesiastical Rights"** (*Iurium Ecclesiae*) are Superior Rights permanently vested unto the four valid and legitimate Ucadia faiths being One Christ, One Islam, One Spirit and Ucadia itself; and

(iii)   **"Sovereign Rights"** (*Iurium Regnum*) are Superior Rights permanently vested unto the governing bodies of the seven Ucadia Unions and all lesser Ucadia bodies politic such as Universities, Provinces and Campuses as the embodiment of sovereign authority; and

(iv)   **"Official Rights"** (*Iurium Publicum*) are Superior Rights permanently vested unto the duly elected and invested Officers of the seven Ucadia Unions and all lesser Ucadia bodies politic such as Universities, Provinces and Campuses as the embodiment of fiduciary authority; and

(v)   **"Administrative Rights"** (*Iurium Administrationis*) are permanently vested unto the executive bodies of the seven Ucadia Unions and all lesser Ucadia bodies politic such as Universities, Provinces and Campuses as the embodiment of administrative authority; and

(vi)   **"Member Rights"** (*Iurium Membrum*) are Superior Rights permanently vested unto the members of the seven Ucadia Unions and all lesser Ucadia bodies politic such as Universities, Provinces and Campuses as the embodiment of member authority.

2.   The following valid forty-four (44) Superior Person Rights (*Superioris Iurium Personae*) are recognised in accord with the most sacred Covenant *Pactum De Singularis Caelum* and the present sacred Covenant:-

Superior Person Rights (Superioris Iurium Personae)

    (i)   **"Ius Esse"** is the Superior Right of Existence, as inherited from the Natural Right *Ius Naturale Esse*; and

    (ii)   **"Ius Vitam"** is the Superior Right to Life, as inherited from the Natural Right *Ius Naturale Vitam*; and

    (iii)   **"Ius Aureus Iuris"** is the Superior Right to be governed by Golden Rule of Law, as inherited from the Natural Right *Ius Naturale Aureus Iuris*; and

    (iv)   **"Ius Iuris"** is the Superior Right to Justice under the Golden Rule of Law, as inherited from the Natural Right *Ius Naturale*

Iuris; and

(v) **"Ius Liberatum Arbitrium"** is the Superior Right of Free Choice (Will), as inherited from the Natural Right *Ius Naturale Liberatum Arbitrium*; and

(vi) **"Ius Mori Eligate"** is the Superior Right to Choose to Die, as inherited from the Natural Right *Ius Naturale Mori Eligate*; and

(vii) **"Ius Consensum"** is the Superior Right to Consent, as inherited from the Natural Right *Ius Naturale Consensum*; and

(viii) **"Ius Consensu Recedere"** is the Superior Right to withdraw Consent, as inherited from the Natural Right *Ius Naturale Consensu Recedere*; and

(ix) **"Ius Iurandum"** is the Superior Right to make an Oath and Vow, as inherited from the Natural Right *Ius Naturale Iurandum*; and

(x) **"Ius Abiuratum"** is the Superior Right to abjure an Oath and Vow, as inherited from the Natural Right *Ius Naturale Abiuratum*; and

(xi) **"Ius Loqui"** is the Superior Right to Speak Freely, as inherited from the Natural Right *Ius Naturale Loqui*; and

(xii) **"Ius Silentium"** is the Superior Right to Silence, as inherited from the Natural Right *Ius Naturale Silentium*; and

(xiii) **"Ius Concedere"** is the Superior Right to Grant, Assign or Delegate Rights, as inherited from the Natural Right *Ius Naturale Concedere*; and

(xiv) **"Ius Abrogare"** is the Superior Right to annul and void any granted or delegated rights, as inherited from the Natural Right *Ius Naturale Abrogare*; and

(xv) **"Ius Societas"** is the Superior Right of Association, as inherited from the Natural Right *Ius Naturale Societas*; and

(xvi) **"Ius Abstinendi"** is the Superior Right of Renunciation, as inherited from the Natural Right *Ius Naturale Abstinendi*; and

(xvii) **"Ius Nomenis"** is the Superior Right to Name, Title and Reputation, as inherited from the Natural Right *Ius Naturale Nomenis*; and

(xviii) **"Ius Vivus"** is the Superior Right to Possession and Ownership of Flesh and Blood of one's own Body, as inherited from the Natural Right *Ius Naturale Vivus*; and

(xix) **"Ius Geneticae"** is the Superior Right of Possession, Ownership and Title to ones own Genetic Material, as inherited from the Natural Right *Ius Naturale Geneticae*; and

(xx) **"Ius Facies"** is the Superior Right Possession, Ownership and Title to ones own Face, Voice, Fingerprints and Biometric Identity, as inherited from the Natural Right *Ius Naturale Facies*; and

(xxi) **"Ius Proprius"** is the Superior Right to own Character and Identity, as inherited from the Natural Right *Ius Naturale Proprius*; and

(xxii) **"Ius Nutrimens"** is the Superior Right to Sustenance, as inherited from the Natural Right *Ius Naturale Nutrimens*; and

(xxiii) **"Ius Aqua"** is the Superior Right to Water, as inherited from the Natural Right *Ius Naturale Aqua*; and

(xxiv) **"Ius Tectum"** is the Superior Right to Shelter, as inherited from the Natural Right *Ius Naturale Tectum*; and

(xxv) **"Ius Habitare"** is the Superior Right to Home Environment, as inherited from the Natural Right *Ius Naturale Habitare*; and

(xxvi) **"Ius Connubii"** is the Superior Rights of Union, as inherited from the Natural Right *Ius Naturale Connubii*; and

(xxvii) **"Ius Coitus"** is the Superior Right for consenting adults to engage in intercourse, as inherited from the Natural Right *Ius Naturale Coitus*; and

(xxviii) **"Ius Natural Contraceptio"** is the Superior Right to contraception, as inherited from the Natural Right *Ius Naturale Contraceptio*; and

(xxix) **"Ius Terminare"** is the Superior Right to Terminate Pregnancy in 1st trimester, as inherited from the Natural Right *Ius Naturale Terminare*; and

(xxx) **"Ius Nascendi"** is the Superior Right to be Borne from the start of the 2nd trimester to full term, as inherited from the Natural Right *Ius Naturale Nascendi*; and

(xxxi) **"Ius Naturalis Nativitas"** is the Superior Right to give birth, as inherited from the Natural Right *Ius Naturale Naturalis Nativitas*; and

(xxxii) **"Ius Aequum"** is the Superior Right of Equality and Fairness, as inherited from the Natural Right *Ius Naturale Aequum*; and

(xxxiii) **"Ius Aequum Genus"** is the Superior Right of Gender Equality, as inherited from the Natural Right *Ius Naturale Aequum Genus*; and

(xxxiv) **"Ius Aequum Gens"** is the Superior Right of Race Equality, as inherited from the Natural Right *Ius Naturale Aequum Gens*; and

(xxxv) **"Ius Liberatum Genus"** is the Superior Right of Choice of Gender, as inherited from the Natural Right *Ius Naturale Liberatum Genus*; and

(xxxvi) **"Ius Victus"** is the Superior Right to Quality and Fruitful Existence, as inherited from the Natural Right *Ius Naturale Victus*; and

(xxxvii) **"Ius Possessionis"** is the Superior Right to possess, hold and own Property, as inherited from the Natural Right *Ius Naturale Possessionis*; and

(xxxviii) **"Ius Proprietatis"** is the Superior Right of Ownership of use or fruits of use of Property, as inherited from the Natural Right *Ius Naturale Proprietatis*; and

(xxxix) **"Ius Manumissionis"** is the Superior Right of Freedom from slavery, as inherited from the Natural Right *Ius Naturale Libertatis*; and

(xl) **"Ius Tormentum Libertatis"** is the Superior Right of Freedom from cruel and unusual punishment or torture, as inherited from the Natural Right *Ius Naturale Libertatis*; and

(xli) **"Ius Libertatis Religionis"** is the Superior Right of Freedom of religious expression, as inherited from the Natural Right *Ius Naturale Libertatis*; and

(xlii) **"Ius Naturale Non Res"** is the Superior Right for a Natural (True) Person not to be treated as a slave or thing, as inherited from the Natural Right *Ius Naturale Non Res*; and

(xliii) **"Ius Hereditatis"** is the Superior Right of Inheritance of

Rights, as inherited from the Natural Right *Ius Naturale Hereditatis*; and

(xliv)   **"Ius Voluntatem Et Testamentum"** is the Superior Right to make a Will and Testament, as inherited from the Natural Right *Ius Voluntatem Et Testamentum*.

3.   **"Ecclesiastical Rights"** (*Iurium Ecclesiae*) are the second sub-class of Superior Rights and the highest possible rights of any aggregate body, society, fraternity, association or company of two or more people.

Ecclesiastical Rights (Iurium Ecclesiae)

There exists eight (8) categories of one hundred and thirty-two (132) Superior Rights within the sub-class of Ecclesiastical Rights, being Authoritative (22), Instrumental (22), Sacramental (33), Writs (11), Bills (11), Dogma (11), Decrees (11) and Notices (11):-

(i)   **"Authoritative Ecclesiastical Rights"** (*Potentis Ecclesiae Iurium*) are Ecclesiastical Rights associated with the core ecclesiastical authoritative powers; and

(ii)   **"Instrumental Ecclesiastical Rights"** (*Instrumentalis Ecclesiae Iurium*) are Ecclesiastical Rights essential to the proper administration of Ecclesiastical Rights; and

(iii)   **"Sacramental Ecclesiastical Rights"** (*Sacramentum Ecclesiae Iurium*) are Ecclesiastical Rights associated with the thirty-three (33) Divine Sacraments of Heaven; and

(iv)   **"Ecclesiastical Writs of Rights"** (*Recto Ecclesiae Iurium*) are Ecclesiastical Rights associated with the one, true and only forms of Original Entry and Original Action; and

(v)   **"Ecclesiastical Bills of Exception"** (*Rogatio Ecclesiae Iurium*) are Ecclesiastical Rights associated with the one, true and only forms of Bills of Exception, Citation and Moratorium; and

(vi)   **"Ecclesiastical Dogma"** (*Summa Dogma Ecclesiae Iurium*) are Ecclesiastical Rights associated with the promulgation of authoritative ecclesiastical principles, decrees and doctrines; and

(vii)   **"Ecclesiastical Decrees"** (*Decretum Ecclesiae Iurium*) are Ecclesiastical Rights associated with ecclesiastical decrees concerning the administration, conduct and enforcement of law and order; and

(viii) **"Ecclesiastical Notice"** (*Notitiae Ecclesiae Iurium*) are Ecclesiastical Rights associated with ecclesiastical notices issued, executed, patented, promulgated and services in the proper administration, conduct and enforcement of law and order.

4. The following valid twenty-two (22) Authoritative Ecclesiastical Rights (*Potentis Ecclesiae Iurium*) are recognised in accord with the most sacred Covenant *Pactum De Singularis Caelum* and the present sacred Covenant:-

Authoritative Ecclesiastical Rights (Potentis Ecclesiae Iurium)

(i) **"Ius Ecclesiae Iurisdictio"** are the Ecclesiastical Rights of Jurisdiction, as inherited from the Divine Rights *Ius Divinum Universus*; and

(ii) **"Ius Ecclesiae Regnum"** are the Ecclesiastical Rights of Sovereign Authority, as inherited from the Divine Rights *Ius Divinum Regnum*; and

(iii) **"Ius Ecclesiae Consilium"** are the Ecclesiastical Rights of a Legislative and Advisory Authority, as inherited from the Divine Rights *Ius Divinum Consilium*; and

(iv) **"Ius Ecclesiae Ecclesia"** are the Ecclesiastical Rights of an Ecclesiastical and Religious Authority, as inherited from the Divine Rights *Ius Divinum Ecclesia*; and

(v) **"Ius Ecclesiae Collegium"** are the Ecclesiastical Rights of a Company or Charitable Body, as inherited from the Divine Rights *Ius Divinum Collegium*; and

(vi) **"Ius Ecclesiae Officium"** are the Ecclesiastical Rights of Office, Duty and Service, as inherited from the Divine Rights *Ius Divinum Officium*; and

(vii) **"Ius Ecclesiae Imperium"** are the Ecclesiastical Rights of Command, Occupation and Enforcement, as inherited from the Divine Rights *Ius Divinum Imperium*; and

(viii) **"Ius Ecclesiae Sacrum"** are the Ecclesiastical Rights of Sacred Recognition, Devotion and Veneration, as inherited from the Divine Rights *Ius Divinum Sacrum*; and

(ix) **"Ius Ecclesiae Custoditum"** are the Ecclesiastical Rights of Custody, Guardianship and Preservation, as inherited from the Divine Rights *Ius Divinum Custoditum*; and

(x) **"Ius Ecclesiae Alumentum"** are the Ecclesiastical Rights to Sustenance, Maintenance and Alms, as inherited from the

Divine Rights *Ius Divinum Alumentum*; and

(xi) **"Ius Ecclesiae Apostolicus"** are the Ecclesiastical Rights of Divine Commission, as inherited from the Divine Rights *Ius Divinum Apostolicus*; and

(xii) **"Ius Ecclesiae Sanitatum"** are the Ecclesiastical Rights to Sanity, Reason and Competence of Mind, as inherited from the Divine Rights *Ius Divinum Sanitatum*; and

(xiii) **"Ius Ecclesiae Oratorium"** are the Ecclesiastical Rights to a Competent Forum of Law and Review, as inherited from the Divine Rights *Ius Divinum Oratorium*; and

(xiv) **"Ius Ecclesiae Templum"** are the Ecclesiastical Rights of a Treasury or Financial (Banking) Body, as inherited from the Divine Rights *Ius Divinum Templum*; and

(xv) **"Ius Ecclesiae Sacramentum"** are the Ecclesiastical Rights to Grant and Impart Holy Sacraments, as inherited from the Divine Rights *Ius Divinum Sacramentum*; and

(xvi) **"Ius Ecclesiae Visum"** are the Ecclesiastical Rights to Survey, Visit and Audit Ucadia Bodies, as inherited from the Divine Rights *Ius Divinum Visum*; and

(xvii) **"Ius Ecclesiae Commercium"** are the Ecclesiastical Rights to Trade, Exchange and Communication, as inherited from the Divine Rights *Ius Divinum Commercium*; and

(xviii) **"Ius Ecclesiae Virtus"** are the Ecclesiastical Rights to Strength, Honour, Excellence and Virtue, as inherited from the Divine Rights *Ius Divinum Virtus*; and

(xix) **"Ius Ecclesiae Penitentiaria"** are the Ecclesiastical Rights of Forced Confinement and Penitence, as inherited from the Divine Rights *Ius Divinum Penitentiaria*; and

(xx) **"Ius Ecclesiae Astrum"** are the Ecclesiastical Rights to an Association, Aggregate or Body, as inherited from the Divine Rights *Ius Divinum Astrum*; and

(xxi) **"Ius Ecclesiae Magisterium"** are the Ecclesiastical Rights to Teach, Instruct and Interpret Sacred Texts and Divine Will, as inherited from the Divine Rights *Ius Divinum Magisterium*; and

(xxii) **"Ius Ecclesiae Decretum"** are the Ecclesiastical Rights to issue Decree, Judgement and Edict, as inherited from the

Divine Rights *Ius Divinum Decretum*.

5. The following valid twenty-two (22) Instrumental Ecclesiastical Rights (*Instrumentalis Ecclesiae Iurium*) are recognised in accord with the most sacred Covenant *Pactum De Singularis Caelum* and the present sacred Covenant:-

Instrumental
Ecclesiastical
Rights
(Instrumentalis
Ecclesiae
Iurium)

(i) **"Ius Ecclesiae Fidei"** are the Ecclesiastical Rights of Superior Ecclesiastical Trust and Ecclesiastical Estate, as inherited from the Divine Rights *Ius Divinum Fidei*; and

(ii) **"Ius Ecclesiae Credito"** are the Ecclesiastical Rights of Superior Ecclesiastical Credit and Funds, as inherited from the Divine Rights *Ius Divinum Credito*; and

(iii) **"Ius Ecclesiae Hereditatis"** are the Ecclesiastical Rights of Inheritance of Divine Rights, as inherited from the Divine Rights *Ius Divinum Hereditatis*; and

(iv) **"Ius Ecclesiae Concedere"** are the Ecclesiastical Rights to Give or Grant Superior Rights, as inherited from the Divine Rights *Ius Divinum Concedere*; and

(v) **"Ius Ecclesiae Abrogare"** are the Ecclesiastical Rights to Rescind or Annul Superior Rights, as inherited from the Divine Rights *Ius Divinum Abrogare*; and

(vi) **"Ius Ecclesiae Delegare"** are the Ecclesiastical Rights to Assign or Delegate Superior Rights, as inherited from the Divine Rights *Ius Divinum Delegare*; and

(vii) **"Ius Ecclesiae Revocare"** are the Ecclesiastical Rights to Cancel or Revoke Superior Rights, as inherited from the Divine Rights *Ius Divinum Revocare*; and

(viii) **"Ius Ecclesiae Societas"** are the Ecclesiastical Rights of Association, as inherited from the Divine Rights *Ius Divinum Societas*; and

(ix) **"Ius Ecclesiae Abstinendi"** are the Ecclesiastical Rights of Renunciation, as inherited from the Divine Rights *Ius Divinum Abstinendi*; and

(x) **"Ius Ecclesiae Consensum"** are the Ecclesiastical Rights to Consent, as inherited from the Divine Rights *Ius Divinum Consensum*; and

(xi) **"Ius Ecclesiae Consensu Recedere"** are the Ecclesiastical Rights to withdraw Consent, as inherited from the Divine

Rights *Ius Divinum Consensu Recedere*; and

(xii) **"Ius Ecclesiae Dominium"** are the Ecclesiastical Rights of Absolute Ownership, as inherited from the Divine Rights *Ius Divinum Dominium*; and

(xiii) **"Ius Ecclesiae Possessionis"** are the Ecclesiastical Rights to Possess, Hold and Own Property, as inherited from the Divine Rights *Ius Divinum Possessionis*; and

(xiv) **"Ius Ecclesiae Usus"** are the Ecclesiastical Rights of Use and Fruits (Enjoyment) of Use of Property, as inherited from the Divine Rights *Ius Divinum Usus*; and

(xv) **"Ius Ecclesiae Proprietatis"** are the Ecclesiastical Rights of Ownership of Use or Fruits of Use of Property, as inherited from the Divine Rights *Ius Divinum Proprietatis*; and

(xvi) **"Ius Ecclesiae Vectigalis"** are the Ecclesiastical Rights to impose Rents, Tolls, Levies, Contributions or Charges against Property, as inherited from the Divine Rights *Ius Divinum Vectigalis*; and

(xvii) **"Ius Ecclesiae Moneta"** are the Ecclesiastical Rights to Mint, Produce, Hold, Use and Exchange Money, as inherited from the Divine Rights *Ius Divinum Moneta*; and

(xviii) **"Ius Ecclesiae Vectigalis Moneta"** are the Ecclesiastical Rights to impose Rents, Tolls, Levies, Contributions or Charges against Money, as inherited from the Divine Rights *Ius Divinum Moneta*; and

(xix) **"Ius Ecclesiae Registrum"** are the Ecclesiastical Rights to Enter Records within Registers and Rolls, as inherited from the Divine Rights *Ius Divinum Registrum*; and

(xx) **"Ius Ecclesiae Instrumentalis"** are the Ecclesiastical Rights of Document, Form or Instrument Creation, Negotiation and Execution, as inherited from the Divine Rights *Ius Divinum Instrumentalis*; and

(xxi) **"Ius Ecclesiae Compensationis Instrumentum"** are the Ecclesiastical Rights of Relief, Redress or Compensation for Default or Deliquency of Obligation, as inherited from the Divine Rights *Ius Divinum Compensationis Instrumentum*; and

(xxii) **"Ius Ecclesiae Dirimere Instrumentum"** are the Ecclesiastical Rights of Document, Form or Instrument

Suspension, Termination and Dissolution, as inherited from the Divine Rights *Ius Divinum Dirimere Instrumentum*.

6. The following valid thirty-three (33) Sacramental Ecclesiastical Rights (*Sacramentum Ecclesiae Iurium*) are recognised in accord with the most sacred Covenant *Pactum De Singularis Caelum* and the present sacred Covenant:-

Sacramental Ecclesiastical Rights (Sacramentum Ecclesiae Iurium)

(i) **"Ius Ecclesiae Sacramentum Recognosco"** is the Ecclesiastical Right of the Key Sacrament of Recognition, as inherited from the Divine Right *Ritus Sacramentum Recognosco*; and

(ii) **"Ius Ecclesiae Sacramentum Purificatio"** is the Ecclesiastical Right of the Key Sacrament of Purification, as inherited from the Divine Right *Ritus Sacramentum Purificatio*; and

(iii) **"Ius Ecclesiae Sacramentum Invocatio"** is the Ecclesiastical Right of the Key Sacrament of Invocation, as inherited from the Divine Right *Ritus Sacramentum Invocatio*; and

(iv) **"Ius Ecclesiae Sacramentum Obligatio"** is the Ecclesiastical Right of the Key Sacrament of Obligation, as inherited from *Ritus Sacramentum Obligatio*; and

(v) **"Ius Ecclesiae Sacramentum Delegatio"** is the Ecclesiastical Right of the Key Sacrament of Delegation, as inherited from the Divine Right *Ritus Sacramentum Delegatio*; and

(vi) **"Ius Ecclesiae Sacramentum Satisfactio"** is the Ecclesiastical Right of the Key Sacrament of Satisfaction, as inherited from the Divine Right *Ritus Sacramentum Satisfactio*; and

(vii) **"Ius Ecclesiae Sacramentum Resolutio"** is the Ecclesiastical Right of the Key Sacrament of Resolution, as inherited from the Divine Right *Ritus Sacramentum Resolutio*; and

(viii) **"Ius Ecclesiae Sacramentum Sanctificatio"** is the Ecclesiastical Right of the Cardinal Sacrament of Sanctification, as inherited from the Divine Right *Ritus Sacramentum Sanctificatio*; and

(ix) **"Ius Ecclesiae Sacramentum Sustentatio"** is the

Ecclesiastical Right of the Cardinal Sacrament of Sustentation, as inherited from the Divine Right *Ritus Sacramentum Sustentatio*; and

(x) **"Ius Ecclesiae Sacramentum Unificatio"** is the Ecclesiastical Right of the Cardinal Sacrament of Unification (Matrimony), as inherited from the Divine Right *Ritus Sacramentum Unificatio*; and

(xi) **"Ius Ecclesiae Sacramentum Amalgamatio"** is the Ecclesiastical Right of the Cardinal Sacrament of Amalgamation (Union), as inherited from the Divine Right *Ritus Sacramentum Amalgamatio*; and

(xii) **"Ius Ecclesiae Sacramentum Authentico"** is the Ecclesiastical Right of the Cardinal Sacrament of Authentication, as inherited from the Divine Right *Ritus Sacramentum Authentico*; and

(xiii) **"Ius Ecclesiae Sacramentum Absolutio"** is the Ecclesiastical Right of the Cardinal Sacrament of Absolution, as inherited from the Divine Right *Ritus Sacramentum Absolutio*; and

(xiv) **"Ius Ecclesiae Sacramentum Volitio"** is the Ecclesiastical Right of the Cardinal Sacrament of Volition, as inherited from the Divine Right *Ritus Sacramentum Volitio*; and

(xv) **"Ius Ecclesiae Sacramentum Vocatio"** is the Ecclesiastical Right of the Cardinal Sacrament of Vocation, as inherited from the Divine Right *Ritus Sacramentum Vocatio*; and

(xvi) **"Ius Ecclesiae Sacramentum Testificatio"** is the Ecclesiastical Right of the Cardinal Sacrament of Testification, as inherited from the Divine Right *Ritus Sacramentum Testificatio*; and

(xvii) **"Ius Ecclesiae Sacramentum Compassio"** is the Ecclesiastical Right of the Cardinal Sacrament of Compassion (Mercy), as inherited from the Divine Right *Ritus Sacramentum Compassio*; and

(xviii) **"Ius Ecclesiae Sacramentum Conscripto"** is the Ecclesiastical Right of the Cardinal Sacrament of Conscription (Binding), as inherited from the Divine Right *Ritus Sacramentum Conscripto*; and

(xix) **"Ius Ecclesiae Sacramentum Convocatio"** is the

171

Ecclesiastical Right of the Cardinal Sacrament of Convocation, as inherited from the Divine Right *Ritus Sacramentum Convocatio*; and

(xx) **"Ius Ecclesiae Sacramentum Auctoriso"** is the Ecclesiastical Right of the Cardinal Sacrament of Authorisation, as inherited from the Divine Right *Ritus Sacramentum Auctoriso*; and

(xxi) **"Ius Ecclesiae Sacramentum Elucidato"** is the Ecclesiastical Right of the Cardinal Sacrament of Elucidation, as inherited from the Divine Right *Ritus Sacramentum Elucidato*; and

(xxii) **"Ius Ecclesiae Sacramentum Inspiratio"** is the Ecclesiastical Right of the Apostolic Life Sacrament of Inspiration, as inherited from the Divine Right *Ritus Sacramentum Inspiratio*; and

(xxiii) **"Ius Ecclesiae Sacramentum Resurrectio"** is the Ecclesiastical Right of the Apostolic Life Sacrament of Resurrection, as inherited from the Divine Right *Ritus Sacramentum Resurrectio*; and

(xxiv) **"Ius Ecclesiae Sacramentum Incarnatio"** is the Ecclesiastical Right of the Apostolic Life Sacrament of Incarnation, as inherited from the Divine Right *Ritus Sacramentum Incarnatio*; and

(xxv) **"Ius Ecclesiae Sacramentum Confirmatio"** is the Ecclesiastical Right of the Apostolic Life Sacrament of Confirmation, as inherited from the Divine Right *Ritus Sacramentum Confirmatio*; and

(xxvi) **"Ius Ecclesiae Sacramentum Illuminatio"** is the Ecclesiastical Right of the Apostolic Life Sacrament of Illumination, as inherited from the Divine Right *Ritus Sacramentum Illuminatio*; and

(xxvii) **"Ius Ecclesiae Sacramentum Exultatio"** is the Ecclesiastical Right of the Apostolic Life Sacrament of Exultation, as inherited from *Ritus Sacramentum Exultatio*; and

(xxviii) **"Ius Ecclesiae Sacramentum Glorificatio"** is the Ecclesiastical Right of the Apostolic Life Sacrament of Glorification, as inherited from the Divine Right *Ritus*

Sacramentum Glorificatio; and

(xxix) **"Ius Ecclesiae Sacramentum Divinatio"** is the Ecclesiastical Right of the Apostolic Life Sacrament of Divination, as inherited from the Divine Right *Ritus Sacramentum Divinatio*; and

(xxx) **"Ius Ecclesiae Sacramentum Visitatio"** is the Ecclesiastical Right of the Apostolic Life Sacrament of Visitation, as inherited from the Divine Right *Ritus Sacramentum Visitatio*; and

(xxxi) **"Ius Ecclesiae Sacramentum Salvatio"** is the Ecclesiastical Right of the Apostolic Life Sacrament of Salvation, as inherited from *Ritus Sacramentum Salvatio*; and

(xxxii) **"Ius Ecclesiae Sacramentum Emancipatio"** is the Ecclesiastical Right of the Apostolic Life Sacrament of Original Emancipation, as inherited from the Divine Right *Ritus Sacramentum Emancipatio*; and

(xxxiii) **"Ius Ecclesiae Sacramentum Veneratio"** is the Ecclesiastical Right of the Apostolic Life Sacrament of Veneration, as inherited from the Divine Right *Ritus Sacramentum Veneratio*.

7. The following valid eleven (11) Ecclesiastical Writs of Rights (*Recto Ecclesiae Iurium*) are recognised in accord with the most sacred Covenant *Pactum De Singularis Caelum* and the present sacred Covenant:-

Ecclesiastical Writs of Rights (Recto Ecclesiae Iurium)

(i) **"Recto Ecclesiae Petitionis"** is the Ecclesiastical Writ of Claim of Right, as inherited from the Divine Right *Recto Divinum Petitionis*; and

(ii) **"Recto Ecclesiae Originalis"** is the Ecclesiastical Original Writ (of Right), as inherited from the Divine Right *Recto Divinum Originalis*; and

(iii) **"Recto Ecclesiae Apocalypsis"** is the Ecclesiastical Writ of Right of Revelation, as inherited from the Divine Right *Recto Divinum Apocalypsis*; and

(iv) **"Recto Ecclesiae Investigationis"** is the Ecclesiastical Writ of Inquiry and Search, as inherited from the Divine Right *Recto Divinum Investigationis*; and

(v) **"Recto Ecclesiae Capionis"** is the Ecclesiastical Writ of Seizure and Return, as inherited from the Divine Right *Recto*

Divinum Capionis; and

(vi) **"Recto Ecclesiae Custodiae"** is the Ecclesiastical Writ of Arrest and Custody, as inherited from the Divine Right *Recto Divinum Custodiae*; and

(vii) **"Recto Ecclesiae Documentis"** is the Ecclesiastical Writ of correcting Records of Proof, as inherited from the Divine Right *Recto Divinum Documentis*; and

(viii) **"Recto Ecclesiae Expungo"** is the Ecclesiastical Writ of expunging Records of Proof, as inherited from the Divine Right *Recto Divinum Expungo*; and

(ix) **"Recto Ecclesiae Abrogationis"** is the Ecclesiastical Writ of Annulment of Previous Laws and Instruments, as inherited from the Divine Right *Recto Divinum Abrogationis*; and

(x) **"Recto Ecclesiae Interdico"** is the Ecclesiastical Writ of Prohibition and Imposition, as inherited from the Divine Right *Recto Divinum Interdico*; and

(xi) **"Recto Ecclesiae Restitutio"** is the Ecclesiastical Writ of Compensation and Restoration, as inherited from the Divine Right *Recto Divinum Restitutio*.

8. The following valid eleven (11) Ecclesiastical Bills of Exception (*Rogatio Ecclesiae Iurium*) are recognised in accord with the most sacred Covenant *Pactum De Singularis Caelum* and the present sacred Covenant:- Ecclesiastical Bills of Exception (Rogatio Ecclesiae Iurium)

(i) **"Rogatio Ecclesiae Petitionis"** is the Ecclesiastical Bill of Claim of Relief, as inherited from the Divine Right *Rogatio Divinum Petitionis*; and

(ii) **"Rogatio Ecclesiae Recto"** is the Ecclesiastical (Original) Bill of Right, as inherited from the Divine Right *Rogatio Divinum Recto*; and

(iii) **"Rogatio Ecclesiae Apocalypsis"** is the Ecclesiastical Bill of Rights of Revelation, as inherited from the Divine Right *Rogatio Divinum Apocalypsis*; and

(iv) **"Rogatio Ecclesiae Investigationis"** is the Ecclesiastical Bill of Inquiry and Search, as inherited from the Divine Right *Rogatio Divinum Investigationis*; and

(v) **"Rogatio Ecclesiae Capionis"** is the Ecclesiastical Bill of Seizure and Return, as inherited from the Divine Right

Rogatio Divinum Capionis; and

(vi)   **"Rogatio Ecclesiae Custodiae"** is the Ecclesiastical Bill of Arrest and Custody, as inherited from the Divine Right *Rogatio Divinum Custodiae*; and

(vii)   **"Rogatio Ecclesiae Documentis"** is the Ecclesiastical Bill of correcting Records of Proof, as inherited from the Divine Right *Rogatio Divinum Documentis*; and

(viii)   **"Rogatio Ecclesiae Expungo"** is the Ecclesiastical Bill of expunging Records of Proof, as inherited from the Divine Right *Rogatio Divinum Expungo*; and

(ix)   **"Rogatio Ecclesiae Abrogationis"** is the Ecclesiastical Bill of Annulment of Previous Laws and Instruments, as inherited from the Divine Right *Rogatio Divinum Abrogationis*; and

(x)   **"Rogatio Ecclesiae Interdico"** is the Ecclesiastical Bill of Prohibition and Imposition, as inherited from the Divine Right *Rogatio Divinum Interdico*; and

(xi)   **"Rogatio Ecclesiae Restitutio"** is the Ecclesiastical Bill of Compensation and Restoration, as inherited from the Divine Right *Rogatio Divinum Restitutio*.

9.   The following valid eleven (11) Ecclesiastical Dogma (*Summa Dogma Ecclesiae Iurium*) are recognised in accord with the most sacred Covenant *Pactum De Singularis Caelum* and the present sacred Covenant:-

> Ecclesiastical Dogma (*Summa Dogma Ecclesiae Iurium*)

(i)   **"Dogma Ecclesiae Praeceptum"** is the Ecclesiastical Precept of Proposed Dogma, as inherited from the Divine Right *Dogma Divinum Praeceptum*; and

(ii)   **"Dogma Ecclesiae Theologiae"** is the Ecclesiastical Dogma of Theology, as inherited from the Divine Right *Dogma Divinum Theologiae*; and

(iii)   **"Dogma Ecclesiae Singularis Caelum"** is the Ecclesiastical Dogma of One Heaven, as inherited from the Divine Right *Dogma Divinum Singularis Caelum*; and

(iv)   **"Dogma Ecclesiae Ucadia"** is the Ecclesiastical Dogma of Ucadia, as inherited from the Divine Right *Dogma Divinum Ucadia*; and

(v)   **"Dogma Ecclesiae Iuris"** is the Ecclesiastical Dogma of Law, as inherited from the Divine Right *Dogma Divinum Iuris*; and

(vi) **"Dogma Ecclesiae Scientium"** is the Ecclesiastical Dogma of Science, as inherited from the Divine Right *Dogma Divinum Scientium*; and

(vii) **"Dogma Ecclesiae Revelatio"** is the Ecclesiastical Dogma of Revelation, as inherited from the Divine Right *Dogma Divinum Revelatio*; and

(viii) **"Dogma Ecclesiae Sacramentum"** is the Ecclesiastical Dogma of the Sacraments, as inherited from the Divine Right *Dogma Divinum Sacramentum*; and

(ix) **"Dogma Ecclesiae Singularis Christus"** is the Ecclesiastical Dogma of One Christ, as inherited from the Divine Right *Dogma Divinum Singularis Christus*; and

(x) **"Dogma Ecclesiae Singularis Islam"** is the Ecclesiastical Dogma of One Islam, as inherited from the Divine Right *Dogma Divinum Singularis Islam*; and

(xi) **"Dogma Ecclesiae Singularis Spiritus"** is the Ecclesiastical Dogma of One Spirit, as inherited from the Divine Right *Dogma Divinum Singularis Spiritus*.

10. The following valid eleven (11) Ecclesiastical Decrees (*Decretum Ecclesiae Iurium*) are recognised in accord with the most sacred Covenant *Pactum De Singularis Caelum* and the present sacred Covenant:-

Ecclesiastical Decrees (Decretum Ecclesiae Iurium)

(i) **"Decretum Ecclesiae Doctrinae"** is the Ecclesiastical Decree of Doctrine, as inherited from the Divine Right *Decretum Divinum Doctrinae*; and

(ii) **"Decretum Ecclesiae Absolutionis"** is the Ecclesiastical Decree of Absolution, as inherited from the Divine Right *Decretum Divinum Absolutionis*; and

(iii) **"Decretum Ecclesiae Damnationis"** is the Ecclesiastical Decree of Damnation, as inherited from the Divine Right *Decretum Divinum Damnationis*; and

(iv) **"Decretum Ecclesiae Exemplificatio"** is the Ecclesiastical Decree of Exemplification, as inherited from the Divine Right *Decretum Divinum Exemplificatio*; and

(v) **"Decretum Ecclesiae Testimonium"** is the Ecclesiastical Decree of Proof, as inherited from the Divine Right *Decretum Divinum Testimonium*; and

(vi)   **"Decretum Ecclesiae Instructionis"** is the Ecclesiastical Decree of Instruction, as inherited from the Divine Right *Decretum Divinum Instructionis*; and

(vii)   **"Decretum Ecclesiae Censurae"** is the Ecclesiastical Decree of Censure, as inherited from the Divine Right *Decretum Divinum Censurae*; and

(viii)   **"Decretum Ecclesiae Annullas"** is the Ecclesiastical Decree of Annulment, as inherited from the Divine Right *Decretum Divinum Annullas*; and

(ix)   **"Decretum Ecclesiae Ratificationis"** is the Ecclesiastical Decree of Ratification, as inherited from the Divine Right *Decretum Divinum Ratificationis*; and

(x)   **"Decretum Ecclesiae Interdictum"** is the Ecclesiastical Decree of Interdiction, as inherited from the Divine Right *Decretum Divinum Interdictum*; and

(xi)   **"Decretum Ecclesiae Levationis"** is the Ecclesiastical Decree of Relief, as inherited from the Divine Right *Decretum Divinum Levationis*.

11. The following valid eleven (11) Ecclesiastical Notice (*Notitiae Ecclesiae Iurium*) are recognised in accord with the most sacred Covenant *Pactum De Singularis Caelum* and the present sacred Covenant:-

Ecclesiastical Notice (Notitiae Ecclesiae Iurium)

(i)   **"Notitiae Ecclesiae Eventus"** is the Ecclesiastical Notice of Event, as inherited from the Divine Right *Notitiae Divinum Eventus*; and

(ii)   **"Notitiae Ecclesiae Ius"** is the Ecclesiastical Notice of Right, as inherited from the Divine Right *Notitiae Divinum Ius*; and

(iii)   **"Notitiae Ecclesiae Actum"** is the Ecclesiastical Notice of Action, as inherited from the Divine Right *Notitiae Divinum Actum*; and

(iv)   **"Notitiae Ecclesiae Decretum"** is the Ecclesiastical Notice of Decree, as inherited from the Divine Right *Notitiae Divinum Decretum*; and

(v)   **"Notitiae Ecclesiae Iuris"** is as the Ecclesiastical Notice of Law, as inherited from the Divine Right *Notitiae Divinum Iuris*; and

(vi)   **"Notitiae Ecclesiae Citationis"** is the Ecclesiastical Notice of Summons, as inherited from the Divine Right *Notitiae*

Divinum Citationis; and

(vii) **"Notitiae Ecclesiae Redemptio"** is the Ecclesiastical Notice of Redemption, as inherited from the Divine Right *Notitiae Divinum Redemptio*; and

(viii) **"Notitiae Ecclesiae Rogatio"** is the Ecclesiastical Notice of Exception, as inherited from the Divine Right *Notitiae Divinum Rogatio*; and

(ix) **"Notitiae Ecclesiae Potentis"** is the Ecclesiastical Notice of Authority, as inherited from the Divine Right *Notitiae Divinum Potentis*; and

(x) **"Notitiae Ecclesiae Testamentum"** is the Ecclesiastical Notice of Testament, as inherited from the Divine Right *Notitiae Divinum Testamentum*; and

(xi) **"Notitiae Ecclesiae Obligationis"** is the Ecclesiastical Notice of Obligation, as inherited from the Divine Right *Notitiae Divinum Obligationis*.

12. **"Sovereign Rights"** (*Iurium Regnum*) are the third sub-class of Superior Rights and the second highest possible rights of any aggregate body, society, fraternity, association or company of two (2) or more persons personified as sovereign. All Sovereign Rights are derived from Ecclesiastical Rights and a Sovereign Right can never claim to be higher than Ecclesiastical Rights. There exists six (6) categories of seventy-seven (77) Superior Rights within the sub-class of Sovereign Rights, being: Authoritative (11), Instrumental (22), Writs (11), Bills (11), Decrees (11) and Notices (11):-

Sovereign Rights (Iurium Regnum)

(i) **"Authoritative Sovereign Rights"** (*Potentis Regnum Iurium*) are Ecclesiastical Rights associated with the core ecclesiastical authoritative powers; and

(ii) **"Instrumental Sovereign Rights"** (*Instrumentalis Regnum Iurium*) are Sovereign Rights essential to the proper administration of Sovereign Rights; and

(iii) **"Sovereign Writs of Rights"** (*Recto Regnum Iurium*) are Sovereign Rights associated with the one, true and only forms of Original Entry and Original Action; and

(iv) **"Sovereign Bills of Exception"** (*Rogatio Regnum Iurium*) are Sovereign Rights associated with the one, true and only forms of Bills of Exception, Citation and Moratorium; and

(v) **"Sovereign Decrees"** (*Decretum Regnum Iurium*) are

Sovereign Rights associated with sovereign decrees concerning the administration, conduct and enforcement of law and order; and

(vi) **"Sovereign Notices"** (*Notitiae Regnum Iurium*) are Sovereign Rights associated with sovereign notices issued, executed, patented, promulgated and services in the proper administration, conduct and enforcement of law and order.

13. The following valid eleven (11) Authoritative Sovereign Rights (*Potentis Regnum Iurium*) are recognised in accord with the most sacred Covenant *Pactum De Singularis Caelum* and the present sacred Covenant:-

Authoritative Sovereign Rights (Potentis Regnum Iurium)

(i) **"Ius Regnum Iurisdictio"** are the Sovereign Rights of Jurisdiction, as inherited from the Ecclesiastical Rights *Ius Ecclesiae Iurisdictio*; and

(ii) **"Ius Regnum Potentis"** are the Sovereign Rights of Authority, as inherited from the Ecclesiastical Rights *Ius Ecclesiae Regnum*; and

(iii) **"Ius Regnum Consilium"** are the Sovereign Rights of a Legislative and Advisory Authority, as inherited from the Ecclesiastical Rights *Ius Ecclesiae Consilium*; and

(iv) **"Ius Regnum Collegium"** are the Sovereign Rights of a Company or Charitable Body, as inherited from the Ecclesiastical Rights *Ius Ecclesiae Collegium*; and

(v) **"Ius Regnum Officium"** are the Sovereign Rights of Office, Duty and Service, as inherited from the Ecclesiastical Rights *Ius Ecclesiae Officium*; and

(vi) **"Ius Regnum Imperium"** are the Sovereign Rights of Command, Occupation and Enforcement, as inherited from the Ecclesiastical Rights *Ius Ecclesiae Imperium*; and

(vii) **"Ius Regnum Custoditum"** are the Sovereign Rights of Custody, Guardianship and Preservation, as inherited from the Ecclesiastical Rights *Ius Ecclesiae Custoditum*; and

(viii) **"Ius Regnum Oratorium"** are the Sovereign Rights to a Competent Forum of Law and Review, as inherited from the Ecclesiastical Rights *Ius Ecclesiae Oratorium*; and

(ix) **"Ius Regnum Templum"** are the Sovereign Rights of a Treasury or Financial (Banking) Body, as inherited from the

Ecclesiastical Right *Ius Ecclesiae Templum*; and

(x) **"Ius Regnum Visum"** are the Sovereign Rights to Survey, Visit and Audit Ucadia Bodies, as inherited from the Ecclesiastical Rights *Ius Ecclesiae Visum*; and

(xi) **"Ius Regnum Decretum"** are the Sovereign Rights to issue Decree, Judgement and Edict, as inherited from the Ecclesiastical Rights *Ius Ecclesiae Decretum*.

14. The following valid twenty-two (22) Instrumental Sovereign Rights (*Instrumentalis Regnum Iurium*) are recognised in accord with the most sacred Covenant *Pactum De Singularis Caelum* and the present sacred Covenant:-

Instrumental Sovereign Rights (Instrumentalis Regnum Iurium)

(i) **"Ius Regnum Fidei"** are the Sovereign Rights of Superior Sovereign Trust and Sovereign Estate, as inherited from the Ecclesiastical Rights *Ius Ecclesiae Fidei*; and

(ii) **"Ius Regnum Credito"** are the Sovereign Rights of Superior Sovereign Credit and Funds, as inherited from the Ecclesiastical Rights *Ius Ecclesiae Credito*; and

(iii) **"Ius Regnum Hereditatis"** are the Sovereign Rights of Inheritance of Divine Rights, as inherited from the Ecclesiastical Rights *Ius Ecclesiae Hereditatis*; and

(iv) **"Ius Regnum Concedere"** are the Sovereign Rights to Give or Grant Superior Rights, as inherited from the Ecclesiastical Rights *Ius Ecclesiae Concedere*; and

(v) **"Ius Regnum Abrogare"** are the Sovereign Rights to Rescind or Annul Superior Rights, as inherited from the Ecclesiastical Rights *Ius Ecclesiae Abrogare*; and

(vi) **"Ius Regnum Delegare"** are the Sovereign Rights to Assign or Delegate Superior Rights, as inherited from the Ecclesiastical Rights *Ius Ecclesiae Delegare*; and

(vii) **"Ius Regnum Revocare"** are the Sovereign Rights to Cancel or Revoke Superior Rights, as inherited from the Ecclesiastical Rights *Ius Ecclesiae Revocare*; and

(viii) **"Ius Regnum Abstinendi"** are the Sovereign Rights of Renunciation, as inherited from the Ecclesiastical Rights *Ius Ecclesiae Abstinendi*; and

(ix) **"Ius Regnum Consensum"** are the Sovereign Rights to Consent, as inherited from the Ecclesiastical Rights *Ius*

Ecclesiae Consensum; and

(x)   **"Ius Regnum Consensu Recedere"** are the Sovereign Rights to withdraw Consent, as inherited from the Ecclesiastical Rights *Ius Ecclesiae Consensu Recedere*; and

(xi)   **"Ius Regnum Dominium"** are the Sovereign Rights of Absolute Ownership, as inherited from the Ecclesiastical Rights *Ius Ecclesiae Dominium*; and

(xii)   **"Ius Regnum Possessionis"** are the Sovereign Rights to Possess, Hold and Own Property, as inherited from the Ecclesiastical Rights *Ius Ecclesiae Usus*; and

(xiii) **"Ius Regnum Usus"** are the Sovereign Rights of Use and Fruits (Enjoyment) of Use of Property, as inherited from the Ecclesiastical Rights *Ius Ecclesiae Usus*; and

(xiv)   **"Ius Regnum Proprietatis"** are the Sovereign Rights of Ownership of Use or Fruits of Use of Property, as inherited from the Ecclesiastical Rights *Ius Ecclesiae Proprietatis*; and

(xv)   **"Ius Regnum Vectigalis"** are the Sovereign Rights to impose Rents, Tolls, Levies, Contributions or Charges against Property, as inherited from the Ecclesiastical Rights *Ius Ecclesiae Vectigalis*; and

(xvi)   **"Ius Regnum Moneta"** are the Sovereign Rights to Mint, Produce, Hold, Use and Exchange Money, as inherited from the Ecclesiastical Rights *Ius Ecclesiae Moneta*; and

(xvii) **"Ius Regnum Vectigalis Moneta"** are the Sovereign Rights to impose Rents, Tolls, Levies, Contributions or Charges against Money, as inherited from the Ecclesiastical Rights *Ius Ecclesiae Moneta*; and

(xviii) **"Ius Regnum Registrum"** are the Sovereign Rights to Enter Records within Registers and Rolls, as inherited from the Ecclesiastical Rights *Ius Ecclesiae Registrum*; and

(xix)   **"Ius Regnum Penitentiaria"** are the Sovereign Rights of Forced Confinement and Penitence, as inherited from the Ecclesiastical Rights *Ius Ecclesiae Penitentiaria*; and

(xx)   **"Ius Regnum Instrumentalis"** are the Sovereign Rights of Document, Form or Instrument Creation, Negotiation and Execution, as inherited from the Ecclesiastical Rights *Ius Ecclesiae Instrumentalis*; and

(xxi)   **"Ius Regnum Compensationis Instrumentum"** are the

Sovereign Rights of Relief, Redress or Compensation for Default or Deliquency of Obligation, as inherited from the Ecclesiastical Rights *Ius Ecclesiae Compensationis Instrumentum*; and

(xxii) **"Ius Regnum Dirimere Instrumentum"** are the Sovereign Rights of Document, Form or Instrument Suspension, Termination and Dissolution, as inherited from the Ecclesiastical Rights *Ius Ecclesiae Dirimere Instrumentum*.

15. The following valid eleven (11) Sovereign Writs of Rights (*Recto Regnum Iurium*) are recognised in accord with the most sacred Covenant *Pactum De Singularis Caelum* and the present sacred Covenant:-

Sovereign Writs of Rights (Recto Regnum Iurium)

(i) **"Recto Regnum Petitionis"** is the Sovereign Writ of Claim of Right, as inherited from the Ecclesiastical Right *Recto Ecclesiae Petitionis*; and

(ii) **"Recto Regnum Originalis"** is the Sovereign Original Writ (of Right), as inherited from the Ecclesiastical Right *Recto Ecclesiae Originalis*; and

(iii) **"Recto Regnum Apocalypsis"** is the Sovereign Writ of Right of Revelation, as inherited from the Ecclesiastical Right *Recto Ecclesiae Apocalypsis*; and

(iv) **"Recto Regnum Investigationis"** is the Sovereign Writ of Inquiry and Search, as inherited from the Ecclesiastical Right *Recto Ecclesiae Investigationis*; and

(v) **"Recto Regnum Capionis"** is the Sovereign Writ of Seizure and Return, as inherited from the Ecclesiastical Right *Recto Ecclesiae Capionis*; and

(vi) **"Recto Regnum Custodiae"** is the Sovereign Writ of Arrest and Custody, as inherited from the Ecclesiastical Right *Recto Ecclesiae Custodiae*; and

(vii) **"Recto Regnum Documentis"** is the Sovereign Writ of correcting Records of Proof, as inherited from the Ecclesiastical Right *Recto Regnum Documentis*; and

(viii) **"Recto Regnum Expungo"** is the Sovereign Writ of expunging Records of Proof, as inherited from the Ecclesiastical Right *Recto Ecclesiae Expungo*; and

(ix) **"Recto Regnum Abrogationis"** is the Sovereign Writ of Annulment of Previous Laws and Instruments, as inherited from the Ecclesiastical Right *Recto Ecclesiae Abrogationis*; and

(x) **"Recto Regnum Interdico"** is the Sovereign Writ of Prohibition and Imposition, as inherited from the Ecclesiastical Right *Recto Ecclesiae Interdico*; and

(xi) **"Recto Regnum Restitutio"** is the Sovereign Writ of Compensation and Restoration, as inherited from the Ecclesiastical Right *Recto Ecclesiae Restitutio*.

16. The following valid eleven (11) Sovereign Bills of Exception (*Rogatio Regnum Iurium*) are recognised in accord with the most sacred Covenant *Pactum De Singularis Caelum* and the present sacred Covenant:-

Sovereign Bills of Exception (Rogatio Regnum Iurium)

(i) **"Rogatio Regnum Petitionis"** is the Sovereign Bill of Claim of Relief, as inherited from the Ecclesiastical Right *Rogatio Ecclesiae Petitionis*; and

(ii) **"Rogatio Regnum Recto"** is the Sovereign (Original) Bill of Right, as inherited from the Ecclesiastical Right *Rogatio Ecclesiae Recto*; and

(iii) **"Rogatio Regnum Apocalypsis"** is the Sovereign Bill of Rights of Revelation, as inherited from the Ecclesiastical Right *Rogatio Ecclesiae Apocalypsis*; and

(iv) **"Rogatio Regnum Investigationis"** is the Sovereign Bill of Inquiry and Search, as inherited from the Ecclesiastical Right *Rogatio Ecclesiae Investigationis*; and

(v) **"Rogatio Regnum Capionis"** is the Sovereign Bill of Seizure and Return, as inherited from the Ecclesiastical Right *Rogatio Ecclesiae Capionis*; and

(vi) **"Rogatio Regnum Custodiae"** is the Sovereign Bill of Arrest and Custody, as inherited from the Ecclesiastical Right *Rogatio Ecclesiae Custodiae*; and

(vii) **"Rogatio Regnum Documentis"** is the Sovereign Bill of correcting Records of Proof, as inherited from the Ecclesiastical Right *Rogatio Ecclesiae Documentis*; and

(viii) **"Rogatio Regnum Expungo"** is the Sovereign Bill of expunging Records of Proof, as inherited from the Ecclesiastical Right *Rogatio Ecclesiae Expungo*; and

(ix) **"Rogatio Regnum Abrogationis"** is the Sovereign Bill of

183

Annulment of Previous Laws and Instruments, as inherited from the Ecclesiastical Right *Rogatio Ecclesiae Abrogationis*; and

(x) **"Rogatio Regnum Interdico"** is the Sovereign Bill of Prohibition and Imposition, as inherited from the Ecclesiastical Right *Rogatio Ecclesiae Interdico*; and

(xi) **"Rogatio Regnum Restitutio"** is the Sovereign Bill of Compensation and Restoration, as inherited from the Ecclesiastical Right *Rogatio Ecclesiae Restitutio*.

17. The following valid eleven (11) Sovereign Decrees (*Decretum Regnum Iurium*) are recognised in accord with the most sacred Covenant *Pactum De Singularis Caelum* and the present sacred Covenant:-

Sovereign Decrees (Decretum Regnum Iurium)

(i) **"Decretum Regnum Doctrinae"** is the Sovereign Decree of Doctrine, as inherited from the Ecclesiastical Right *Decretum Ecclesiae Doctrinae*; and

(ii) **"Decretum Regnum Absolutionis"** is the Sovereign Decree of Absolution, as inherited from the Ecclesiastical Right *Decretum Ecclesiae Absolutionis*; and

(iii) **"Decretum Regnum Damnationis"** is the Sovereign Decree of Damnation, as inherited from the Ecclesiastical Right *Decretum Ecclesiae Damnationis*; and

(iv) **"Decretum Regnum Exemplificatio"** is the Sovereign Decree of Exemplification, as inherited from the Ecclesiastical Right *Decretum Ecclesiae Exemplificatio*; and

(v) **"Decretum Regnum Testimonium"** is the Sovereign Decree of Proof, as inherited from the Ecclesiastical Right *Decretum Ecclesiae Testimonium*; and

(vi) **"Decretum Regnum Instructionis"** is the Sovereign Decree of Instruction, as inherited from the Ecclesiastical Right *Decretum Ecclesiae Instructionis*; and

(vii) **"Decretum Regnum Censurae"** is the Sovereign Decree of Censure, as inherited from the Ecclesiastical Right *Decretum Ecclesiae Censurae;* and

(viii) **"Decretum Regnum Annullas"** is the Sovereign Decree of Annulment, as inherited from the Ecclesiastical Right *Decretum Ecclesiae Annullas*; and

(ix) **"Decretum Regnum Ratificationis"** is the Sovereign

Decree of Ratification, as inherited from the Ecclesiastical Right *Decretum Ecclesiae Ratificationis*; and

(x) **"Decretum Regnum Interdictum"** is the Sovereign Decree of Interdiction, as inherited from the Ecclesiastical Right *Decretum Ecclesiae Interdictum*; and

(xi) **"Decretum Regnum Levationis"** is the Sovereign Decree of Relief, as inherited from the Ecclesiastical Right *Decretum Ecclesiae Levationis*.

18. The following valid eleven (11) Sovereign Notice (*Notitiae Regnum Iurium*) are recognised in accord with the most sacred Covenant *Pactum De Singularis Caelum* and the present sacred Covenant:-

Sovereign Notice (Notitiae Regnum Iurium)

(i) **"Notitiae Regnum Eventus"** is the Sovereign Notice of Event, as inherited from the Ecclesiastical Right *Notitiae Ecclesiae Eventus*; and

(ii) **"Notitiae Regnum Ius"** is the Sovereign Notice of Right, as inherited from the Ecclesiastical Right *Notitiae Ecclesiae Ius*; and

(iii) **"Notitiae Regnum Actum"** is the Sovereign Notice of Action, as inherited from the Ecclesiastical Right *Notitiae Ecclesiae Actum*; and

(iv) **"Notitiae Regnum Decretum"** is the Sovereign Notice of Decree, as inherited from the Ecclesiastical Right *Notitiae Ecclesiae Decretum*; and

(v) **"Notitiae Regnum Iuris"** is the Sovereign Notice of Law, as inherited from the Ecclesiastical Right *Notitiae Ecclesiae Iuris*; and

(vi) **"Notitiae Regnum Citationis"** is the Sovereign Notice of Summons, as inherited from the Ecclesiastical Right *Notitiae Ecclesiae Citationis*; and

(vii) **"Notitiae Regnum Redemptio"** is the Sovereign Notice of Redemption, as inherited from the Ecclesiastical Right *Notitiae Ecclesiae Redemptio*; and

(viii) **"Notitiae Regnum Rogatio"** is the Sovereign Notice of Exception, as inherited from the Ecclesiastical Right *Notitiae Ecclesiae Rogatio*; and

(ix) **"Notitiae Regnum Potentis"** is the Sovereign Notice of Authority, as inherited from the Ecclesiastical Right *Notitiae*

Ecclesiae Potentis; and

(x) **"Notitiae Regnum Testamentum"** is the Sovereign Notice of Testament, as inherited from the Ecclesiastical Right *Notitiae Ecclesiae Testamentum*; and

(xi) **"Notitiae Regnum Obligationis"** is the Sovereign Notice of Obligation, as inherited from the Ecclesiastical Right *Notitiae Ecclesiae Obligationis.*

19. **"Official Rights"** (*Iurium Publicum*) are the fourth sub-class of Superior Rights and the third highest possible rights of any aggregate body, society, fraternity, association or company of two (2) or more persons personified in trust.

Official Rights (Iurium Publicum)

All Official Rights are derived from Sovereign Rights and Official Rights can never be claimed to be higher than Sovereign Rights. There exists six (6) categories of eighty-eight (88) Official Rights within the sub-class of Official Rights, being: Authoritative (11), Instrumental (33), Warrants (11), Declarations (11), Orders (11) and Notices (11):-

(i) **"Authoritative Official Rights"** (*Potentis Publicum Iurium*) are Official Rights associated with the core official authoritative powers; and

(ii) **"Instrumental Official Rights"** (*Instrumentalis Publicum Iurium*) are Official Rights essential to the proper administration of society; and

(iii) **"Official Warrants of Rights"** (*Auctoritas Publicum Iurium*) are Official Rights associated with the one, true and only forms of Original Entry and Original Action; and

(iv) **"Official Declarations of Exception"** (*Declarationis Publicum Iurium*) are Official Rights associated with the one, true and only forms of Exception, Citation and Moratorium; and

(v) **"Official Orders"** (*Iussum Publicum Iurium*) are Official Rights associated with official decrees concerning the administration, conduct and enforcement of law and order; and

(vi) **"Official Notices"** (*Notitiae Publicum Iurium*) are Official Rights associated with official notices issued, executed, patented, promulgated and services in the proper administration, conduct and enforcement of law and order.

20. The following valid eleven (11) Authoritative Official Rights (*Potentis*

Authoritative

Publicum Iurium) are recognised in accord with the most sacred Covenant *Pactum De Singularis Caelum* and the present sacred Covenant:-

(i) **"Ius Publicum Iurisdictio"** are the Official Rights of Jurisdiction, as inherited from the Sovereign Rights *Ius Regnum Iurisdictio*; and

(ii) **"Ius Publicum Potentis"** are the Official Rights of Official Authority, as inherited from the Sovereign Rights *Ius Regnum Potentis*; and

(iii) **"Ius Publicum Consilium"** are the Official Rights of a Legislative and Advisory Authority, as inherited from the Sovereign Rights *Ius Regnum Consilium*; and

(iv) **"Ius Publicum Collegium"** are the Official Rights of a Company or Charitable Body, as inherited from the Sovereign Rights *Ius Regnum Collegium*; and

(v) **"Ius Publicum Officium"** are the Official Rights of Office, Duty and Service, as inherited from the Sovereign Rights *Ius Regnum Officium*; and

(vi) **"Ius Publicum Imperium"** are the Official Rights of Command, Occupation and Enforcement, as inherited from the Sovereign Rights *Ius Regnum Imperium*; and

(vii) **"Ius Publicum Custoditum"** are the Official Rights of Custody, Guardianship and Preservation, as inherited from the Sovereign Rights *Ius Regnum Custoditum*; and

(viii) **"Ius Publicum Oratorium"** are the Official Rights to a Competent Forum of Law and Review, as inherited from the Sovereign Rights *Ius Regnum Oratorium*; and

(ix) **"Ius Publicum Templum"** are the Official Rights of a Treasury or Financial (Banking) Body, as inherited from the Sovereign Rights *Ius Regnum Templum*; and

(x) **"Ius Publicum Visum"** are the Official Rights to Survey, Visit and Audit Ucadia Bodies, as inherited from the Sovereign Rights *Ius Regnum Visum*; and

(xi) **"Ius Publicum Decretum"** shall be the Official Rights to issue Decree, Judgement and Edict, as inherited from the Sovereign Rights *Ius Regnum Decretum*.

21. The following valid thirty-three (33) Instrumental Official Rights

(*Instrumentalis Publicum Iurium*) are recognised in accord with the most sacred Covenant *Pactum De Singularis Caelum* and the present sacred Covenant:-

(i)   **"Ius Corpus Publicum Rusticarum"** are the body of Official Agricultural Rights as defined by the Ucadia Agriculture Code, as inherited from the Divine Collection of Maxims of Law being *Maxims of Natural Law*; and

(ii)   **"Ius Corpus Publicum Frugalitas"** are the body of Official Banking Rights as defined by the Ucadia Banking Code, as inherited from the Divine Collection of Maxims of Law being *Maxims of Economic Law*; and

(iii)   **"Ius Corpus Publicum Pecuniae"** are the body of Official Budget and Finance Management Rights as defined by the Ucadia Budget and Finance Management Code, as inherited from *Maxims of Monetary Law*; and

(iv)   **"Ius Corpus Publicum Aedificatio"** are the body of Official Building and Construction Rights as defined by the Ucadia Building and Construction Code, as inherited from *Maxims of Urban Law* and *Maxims of Civil Law*; and

(v)   **"Ius Corpus Publicum Civilis"** are the body of Official Civil Rights as defined by the Ucadia Civil Code, as inherited from *Maxims of Civil Law*; and

(vi)   **"Ius Corpus Publicum Criminalis"** are the body of Official Criminal Rights as defined by the Ucadia Criminal Code, as inherited from *Maxims of Criminal Law*; and

(vii)   **"Ius Corpus Publicum Publicationum"** are the body of Official Communications and Media Rights as defined by the Ucadia Communications and Media Code, as inherited from *Maxims of Technology Law* and *Maxims of Civil Law*; and

(viii)   **"Ius Corpus Publicum Companio"** are the body of Official Company Rights as defined by the Ucadia Company Code, as inherited from *Maxims of Company Law*; and

(ix)   **"Ius Corpus Publicum Scelestus"** are the body of Official Criminal Prosecution and Punishment Rights as defined by the Ucadia Criminal Code, as inherited from *Maxims of Civil Law*, *Maxims of Fiduciary Law* and *Maxims of Administrative Law*; and

(x)   **"Ius Corpus Publicum Culturae"** are the body of Official

Culture and Entertainment Rights as defined by the Ucadia Culture and Entertainment Code, as inherited from *Maxims of Cognitive Law*, *Maxims of Education Law* and *Maxims of Bioethics Law*; and

(xi) **"Ius Corpus Publicum Informatum"** are the body of Official Education Rights as defined by the Ucadia Education Code, as inherited from *Maxims of Education Law; and*

(xii) **"Ius Corpus Publicum Votum"** are the body of Official Elections Rights as defined by the Ucadia Elections Code, as inherited from *Maxims of Positive Law* and *Maxims of Civil Law; and*

(xiii) **"Ius Corpus Publicum Periculum"** are the body of Official Emergency Rights as defined by the Ucadia Emergency Code, as inherited from *Maxims of Positive Law and Maxims of Civil Law; and*

(xiv) **"Ius Corpus Publicum Usus"** are the body of Official Employment Rights as defined by the Ucadia Employment Code, as inherited from *Maxims of Economic Law and Maxims of Education Law; and*

(xv) **"Ius Corpus Publicum Vigoris"** are the body of Official Energy Rights as defined by the Ucadia Energy Code, as inherited from *Maxims of Technology Law*; and

(xvi) **"Ius Corpus Publicum Virtus Naturae"** are the body of Official Environment Rights as defined by the Ucadia Environment Code, as inherited from *Maxims of Bioethics Law*; and

(xvii) **"Ius Corpus Publicum Fidei"** are the body of Official Executive Rights as defined by the Ucadia Executive Code, as inherited from *Maxims of Civil Law* and *Maxims of Fiduciary Law*; and

(xviii) **"Ius Corpus Publicum Valere"** are the body of Official Fitness and Health Rights as defined by the Ucadia Fitness and Health Code, as inherited from *Maxims of Bioethics Law* and *Maxims of Cognitive Law*; and

(xix) **"Ius Corpus Publicum Nutrimens Et Medicina"** are the body of Official Food and Drugs Rights as defined by the Ucadia Food and Drugs Code, as inherited from *Maxims of Food and Drugs Law*; and

(xx) **"Ius Corpus Publicum Urbis"** are the body of Official Infrastructure Rights as defined by the Ucadia Infrastructure Code, as inherited from *Maxims of Urban Law*; and

(xxi) **"Ius Corpus Publicum Iudicalis"** are the body of Official Judicial Rights as defined by the Ucadia Judicial Code, as inherited from *Maxims of Civil Law* and *Maxims of Fiduciary Law*; and

(xxii) **"Ius Corpus Publicum Scientiae"** are the body of Official Knowledge Systems Rights as defined by the Ucadia Knowledge Systems Code, as inherited from *Maxims of Education Law* and *Maxims of Technology Law*; and

(xxiii) **"Ius Corpus Publicum Legislativam"** are the body of Official Legislative Rights as defined by the Ucadia Legislative Code, as inherited from *Maxims of Positive Law*; and

(xxiv) **"Ius Corpus Publicum Militaris"** are the body of Official Military Rights as defined by the Ucadia Military Code, as inherited from *Maxims of Military Law*; and

(xxv) **"Ius Corpus Publicum Securitas"** are the body of Official Police Rights as defined by the Ucadia Police Code, as inherited from *Maxims of Security Law*; and

(xxvi) **"Ius Corpus Publicum Salubris"** are the body of Official Prevention and Sanitation Rights as defined by the Ucadia Prevention and Sanitation Code, as inherited from *Maxims of Bioethics Law*, *Maxims of Education Law* and *Maxims of Technology Law*; and

(xxvii) **"Ius Corpus Publicum Custodiae"** are the body of Official Prison and Custodial Rights as defined by the Ucadia Prison Code, as inherited from *Maxims of Civil Law* and *Maxims of Fiduciary Law*; and

(xxviii) **"Ius Corpus Publicum Fructus"** are the body of Official Revenue Rights as defined by the Ucadia Revenue Code, as inherited from *Maxims of Economic Law* and *Maxims of Monetary Law*; and

(xxix) **"Ius Corpus Publicum Administratum"** are the body of Official Service Rights as defined by the Ucadia Service Code, as inherited from *Maxims of Administrative Law*; and

(xxx) **"Ius Corpus Publicum Machinatio"** are the body of Official Technology Rights as defined by the Ucadia

Technology Code, as inherited from *Maxims of Technology Law*; and

(xxxi) **"Ius Corpus Publicum Adiuvare"** are the body of Official Temporary Assistance Rights as defined by the Ucadia Temporary Assistance Code, as inherited from *Maxims of Economic Law* and *Maxims of Civil Law*; and

(xxxii) **"Ius Corpus Publicum Mercatus"** are the body of Official Trade Rights as defined by the Ucadia Trade & Intellectual Property Code, as inherited from *Maxims of Trade & Intellectual Property Law*; and

(xxxiii) **"Ius Corpus Publicum Itineris"** are the body of Official Transport & Travel Rights as defined by the Ucadia Transport & Travel Code, as inherited from *Maxims of Technology Law* and *Maxims of Trade & Intellectual Property Law*.

22. The following valid eleven (11) Official Warrants of Rights (*Auctoritas Publicum Iurium*) are recognised in accord with the most sacred Covenant *Pactum De Singularis Caelum* and the present sacred Covenant:-

Official Warrants of Rights (Auctoritas Publicum Iurium)

(i) **"Auctoritas Publicum Petitionis"** is the Official Warrant of Claim of Right, as inherited from the Sovereign Right *Recto Regnum Petitionis*; and

(ii) **"Auctoritas Publicum Originalis"** is the Official Warrant of Rights, as inherited from the Sovereign Right *Recto Regnum Originalis*; and

(iii) **"Auctoritas Publicum Apocalypsis"** is the Official Warrant of Right of Revelation, as inherited from the Sovereign Right *Recto Regnum Apocalypsis*; and

(iv) **"Auctoritas Publicum Investigationis"** is the Official Warrant of Inquiry and Search, as inherited from the Sovereign Right *Recto Regnum Investigationis*; and

(v) **"Auctoritas Publicum Capionis"** is the Official Warrant of Seizure and Return, as inherited from the Sovereign Right *Recto Regnum Capionis*; and

(vi) **"Auctoritas Publicum Custodiae"** is the Official Warrant of Arrest and Custody, as inherited from the Sovereign Right *Recto Regnum Custodiae*; and

(vii) **"Auctoritas Publicum Documentis"** is the Official Warrant of correcting Records of Proof, as inherited from the

Sovereign Right *Recto Regnum Documentis*; and

(viii) **"Auctoritas Publicum Expungo"** is the Official Warrant of expunging Records of Proof, as inherited from the Sovereign Right *Recto Regnum Expungo*; and

(ix) **"Auctoritas Publicum Abrogationis"** is the Official Warrant of Annulment of Previous Laws and Instruments, as inherited from the Sovereign Right *Recto Regnum Abrogationis*; and

(x) **"Auctoritas Publicum Interdico"** is the Official Warrant of Prohibition and Imposition, as inherited from *Recto Regnum Interdico*; and

(xi) **"Auctoritas Publicum Restitutio"** is the Official Warrant of Compensation and Restoration, as inherited from the Sovereign Right *Recto Regnum Restitutio*.

23. The following valid eleven (11) Official Declarations of Exception (*Declarationis Publicum Iurium*) are recognised in accord with the most sacred Covenant *Pactum De Singularis Caelum* and the present sacred Covenant:-

    Official Declaration of Exception (Declarationis Publicum Iurium)

    (i) **"Declarationis Publicum Petitionis"** is the Official Declaration of Right, as inherited from the Sovereign Right *Rogatio Regnum Petitionis*; and

    (ii) **"Declarationis Publicum Recto"** is the Official Declaration of Right, as inherited from the Sovereign Right *Rogatio Regnum Recto*; and

    (iii) **"Declarationis Publicum Apocalypsis"** is the Official Declaration of Rights of Revelation, as inherited from the Sovereign Right *Rogatio Regnum Apocalypsis*; and

    (iv) **"Declarationis Publicum Investigationis"** is the Official Declaration of Inquiry and Search, as inherited from the Sovereign Right *Rogatio Regnum Investigationis*; and

    (v) **"Declarationis Publicum Capionis"** is the Official Declaration of Seizure and Return, as inherited from the Sovereign Right *Rogatio Regnum Capionis*; and

    (vi) **"Declarationis Publicum Custodiae"** is the Official Declaration of Arrest and Custody, as inherited from the Sovereign Right *Rogatio Regnum Custodiae*; and

    (vii) **"Declarationis Publicum Documentis"** is the Official

Declaration of correcting Records of Proof, as inherited from the Sovereign Right *Rogatio Regnum Documentis*; and

(viii) **"Declarationis Publicum Expungo"** is the Official Declaration of expunging Records of Proof, as inherited from the Sovereign Right *Rogatio Regnum Expungo*; and

(ix) **"Declarationis Publicum Abrogationis"** is the Official Declaration of Annulment of Previous Laws and Instruments, as inherited from the Sovereign Right *Rogatio Regnum Abrogationis*; and

(x) **"Declarationis Publicum Interdico"** is the Official Declaration of Prohibition and Imposition, as inherited from the Sovereign Right *Rogatio Regnum Interdico*; and

(xi) **"Declarationis Publicum Restitutio"** is the Official Declaration of Compensation and Restoration, as inherited from the Sovereign Right *Rogatio Regnum Restitutio*.

24. The following valid eleven (11) Official Orders (*Iussum Publicum Iurium*) are recognised in accord with the most sacred Covenant *Pactum De Singularis Caelum* and the present sacred Covenant:-

Official Orders (Iussum Publicum Iurium)

(i) **"Iussum Publicum Doctrinae"** is the Official Order of Doctrine, as inherited from the Sovereign Right *Decretum Regnum Doctrinae*; and

(ii) **"Iussum Publicum Absolutionis"** is the Official Order of Absolution, as inherited from the Sovereign Right *Decretum Regnum Absolutionis*; and

(iii) **"Iussum Publicum Damnationis"** is the Official Order of Damnation, as inherited from the Sovereign Right *Decretum Regnum Damnationis*; and

(iv) **"Iussum Publicum Exemplificatio"** is the Official Order of Exemplification, as inherited from the Sovereign Right *Decretum Regnum Exemplificatio*; and

(v) **"Iussum Publicum Testimonium"** is the Official Order of Proof, as inherited from the Sovereign Right *Decretum Regnum Testimonium*; and

(vi) **"Iussum Publicum Instructionis"** is the Official Order of Instruction, as inherited from the Sovereign Right *Decretum Regnum Instructionis*; and

(vii) **"Iussum Publicum Censurae"** is the Official Order of

Censure, as inherited from the Sovereign Right *Decretum Regnum Censurae*; and

(viii) **"Iussum Publicum Annullas"** is the Official Order of Annulment, as inherited from the Sovereign Right *Decretum Regnum Annullas*; and

(ix) **"Iussum Publicum Ratificationis"** is the Official Order of Ratification, as inherited from the Sovereign Right *Decretum Regnum Ratificationis*; and

(x) **"Iussum Publicum Interdictum"** is the Official Order of Interdiction, as inherited from the Sovereign Right *Decretum Regnum Interdictum*; and

(xi) **"Iussum Publicum Levationis"** is the Official Order of Relief, as inherited from the Sovereign Right *Decretum Regnum Levationis*.

25. The following valid eleven (11) Official Notices (*Notitiae Publicum Iurium*) are recognised in accord with the most sacred Covenant *Pactum De Singularis Caelum* and the present sacred Covenant:-

Official Notices (Notitiae Publicum Iurium)

(i) **"Notitiae Publicum Eventus"** is the Official Notice of Event, as inherited from the Sovereign Right *Notitiae Regnum Eventus*; and

(ii) **"Notitiae Publicum Ius"** is the Official Notice of Right, as inherited from the Sovereign Right *Notitiae Regnum Ius*; and

(iii) **"Notitiae Publicum Actum"** is the Official Notice of Action, as inherited from the Sovereign Right *Notitiae Regnum Actum*; and

(iv) **"Notitiae Publicum Decretum"** is the Official Notice of Decree, as inherited from the Sovereign Right *Notitiae Regnum Decretum*; and

(v) **"Notitiae Publicum Iuris"** is the Official Notice of Law, as inherited from the Sovereign Right *Notitiae Regnum Iuris*; and

(vi) **"Notitiae Publicum Citationis"** is the Official Notice of Summons, as inherited from the Sovereign Right *Notitiae Regnum Citationis*; and

(vii) **"Notitiae Publicum Redemptio"** is the Official Notice of Redemption, as inherited from the Sovereign Right *Notitiae Regnum Redemptio*; and

(viii) **"Notitiae Publicum Rogatio"** is the Official Notice of

Exception, as inherited from the Sovereign Right *Notitiae Regnum Rogatio*; and

(ix) **"Notitiae Publicum Potentis"** is the Official Notice of Authority, as inherited from the Sovereign Right *Notitiae Regnum Potentis*; and

(x) **"Notitiae Publicum Testamentum"** is the Official Notice of Testament, as inherited from the Sovereign Right *Notitiae Regnum Testamentum*; and

(xi) **"Notitiae Publicum Obligationis"** is the Official Notice of Obligation, as inherited from the Sovereign Right *Notitiae Regnum Obligationis*.

26. **"Administrative Rights"** (*Iurium Administrationis*) are the fifth sub-class of Superior Rights and the fourth highest possible rights of any aggregate body, society, fraternity, association or company of two (2) or more persons personified in trust. All Administrative Rights are derived from either Sovereign Rights or Official Rights; and an Administrative Right can never claim to be higher than Official Right. There exists two (2) categories of forty-four (44) Superior Rights within the sub-class of Administrative Rights, being: Authoritative (11) and Instrumental (33):-

Administrative Rights (Iurium Administrationis)

(i) **"Authoritative Administrative Rights"** (*Potentis Administrationis Iurium*) are Administrative Rights associated with the core administrative authoritative powers; and

(ii) **"Instrumental Administrative Rights"** (*Instrumentalis Administrationis Iurium*) are Administrative Rights essential to the proper administration of Administrative Rights.

27. The following valid eleven (11) Authoritative Administrative Rights (*Potentis Administrationis Iurium*) are recognised in accord with the most sacred Covenant *Pactum De Singularis Caelum* and the present sacred Covenant:-

Authoritative Administrative Rights (Potentis Administrationis Iurium)

(i) **"Ius Administrationis Iurisdictio"** shall be the Administrative Rights of Jurisdiction, as inherited from the Official Rights *Ius Publicum Iurisdictio*; and

(ii) **"Ius Administrationis Potentis"** shall be the Administrative Rights of Administrative Authority, as inherited from the Official Rights *Ius Publicum Potentis*; and

(iii) **"Ius Administrationis Consilium"** shall be the Administrative Rights of a Legislative and Advisory Authority, as inherited from the Official Rights *Ius Publicum Consilium*; and

(iv) **"Ius Administrationis Collegium"** shall be the Administrative Rights of a Company or Charitable Body, as inherited from the Official Rights *Ius Publicum Collegium*; and

(v) **"Ius Administrationis Officium"** shall be the Administrative Rights of Office, Duty and Service, as inherited from the Official Rights *Ius Publicum Officium*; and

(vi) **"Ius Administrationis Imperium"** shall be the Administrative Rights of Command, Occupation and Enforcement, as inherited from the Official Rights *Ius Publicum Imperium*; and

(vii) **"Ius Administrationis Custoditum"** shall be the Administrative Rights of Custody, Guardianship and Preservation, as inherited from the Official Rights *Ius Publicum Custoditum*; and

(viii) **"Ius Administrationis Oratorium"** shall be the Administrative Rights to a Competent Forum of Law and Review, as inherited from the Official Rights *Ius Publicum Oratorium*; and

(ix) **"Ius Administrationis Penitentiaria"** shall be the Administrative Rights of Forced Confinement and Penitence, as inherited from the Sovereign Rights *Ius Publicum Penitentiaria*; and

(x) **"Ius Administrationis Visum"** shall be the Administrative Rights to Survey, Visit and Audit Ucadia Bodies, as inherited from the Official Rights *Ius Publicum Visum*; and

(xi) **"Ius Administrationis Decretum"** shall be the Administrative Rights to issue Decree, Judgement and Edict, as inherited from the Official Rights *Ius Publicum Decretum*.

28. The following valid thirty-three (33) Instrumental Administrative Rights (*Instrumentalis Administrationis Iurium*) are recognised in accord with the most sacred Covenant *Pactum De Singularis Caelum* and the present sacred Covenant:-

Instrumental Administrative Rights (Instrumentalis Administrationis Iurium)

(i) **"Ius Administrationis Fidei"** shall be the Administrative Rights of Superior Administrative Trust and Administrative Estate, as inherited from the Sovereign Rights *Ius Regnum Fidei*; and

(ii) **"Ius Administrationis Credito"** shall be the Administrative Rights of Superior Administrative Credit and Funds, as inherited from the Sovereign Rights *Ius Regnum Credito*; and

(iii) **"Ius Administrationis Hereditatis"** shall be the Administrative Rights of Inheritance of Divine Rights, as inherited from the Sovereign Rights *Ius Regnum Hereditatis*; and

(iv) **"Ius Administrationis Concedere"** shall be the Administrative Rights to Give or Grant Superior Rights, as inherited from the Sovereign Rights *Ius Regnum Concedere*; and

(v) **"Ius Administrationis Abrogare"** shall be the Administrative Rights to Rescind or Annul Superior Rights, as inherited from the Sovereign Rights *Ius Regnum Abrogare*; and

(vi) **"Ius Administrationis Delegare"** shall be the Administrative Rights to Assign or Delegate Superior Rights, as inherited from the Sovereign Rights *Ius Regnum Delegare*; and

(vii) **"Ius Administrationis Revocare"** shall be the Administrative Rights to Cancel or Revoke Superior Rights, as inherited from the Sovereign Rights *Ius Regnum Revocare*; and

(viii) **"Ius Administrationis Societas"** shall be the Administrative Rights of Association, as inherited from the Sovereign Rights *Ius Regnum Societas*; and

(ix) **"Ius Administrationis Abstinendi"** shall be the Administrative Rights of Renunciation, as inherited from the Sovereign Rights *Ius Regnum Abstinendi*; and

(x) **"Ius Administrationis Consensum"** shall be the Administrative Rights to Consent, as inherited from the Sovereign Rights *Ius Regnum Consensum*; and

(xi) **"Ius Administrationis Consensu Recedere"** shall be the Administrative Rights to withdraw Consent, as inherited from the Sovereign Rights *Ius Regnum Consensu Recedere*; and

(xii) **"Ius Administrationis Dominium"** shall be the Administrative Rights of Absolute Ownership, as inherited from the Sovereign Rights *Ius Regnum Dominium*; and

(xiii) **"Ius Administrationis Possessionis"** shall be the Administrative Rights to Possess, Hold and Own Property, as inherited from the Sovereign Rights *Ius Regnum Possessionis*; and

(xiv) **"Ius Administrationis Usus"** shall be the Administrative Rights of Use and Fruits (Enjoyment) of Use of Property, as inherited from the Sovereign Rights *Ius Regnum Usus*; and

(xv) **"Ius Administrationis Proprietatis"** shall be the Administrative Rights of Ownership of Use or Fruits of Use of Property, as inherited from the Sovereign Rights *Ius Regnum Proprietatis*; and

(xvi) **"Ius Administrationis Vectigalis"** shall be the Administrative Rights to impose Rents, Tolls, Levies, Contributions or Charges against Property, as inherited from the Sovereign Rights *Ius Regnum Vectigalis*; and

(xvii) **"Ius Administrationis Moneta"** shall be the Administrative Rights to Mint, Produce, Hold, Use and Exchange Money, as inherited from the Sovereign Rights *Ius Regnum Moneta*; and

(xviii) **"Ius Administrationis Vectigalis Moneta"** shall be the Administrative Rights to impose Rents, Tolls, Levies, Contributions or Charges against Money, as inherited from the Sovereign Rights *Ius Regnum Moneta*; and

(xix) **"Ius Administrationis Registrum"** shall be the Administrative Rights to Enter Records within Registers and Rolls, as inherited from the Sovereign Rights *Ius Regnum Registrum*; and

(xx) **"Ius Administrationis Instrumentalis"** shall be the Administrative Rights of Document, Form or Instrument Creation, Negotiation and Execution, as inherited from the Sovereign Rights *Ius Regnum Instrumentalis*; and

(xxi) **"Ius Administrationis Compensationis Instrumentum"** shall be the Administrative Rights of Relief, Redress or Compensation for Default or Deliquency of Obligation, as inherited from the Sovereign Rights *Ius Regnum Compensationis Instrumentum*; and

(xxii) **"Ius Administrationis Dirimere Instrumentum"** shall be the Administrative Rights of Document, Form or Instrument Suspension, Termination and Dissolution, as inherited from the Sovereign Rights *Ius Regnum Dirimere*

Instrumentum; and

(xxiii) **"Litterae Administrationis Doctrinae"** shall be the Administrative Letter of Doctrine, as inherited from the Official Right *Iussum Publicum Doctrinae*; and

(xxiv) **"Litterae Administrationis Absolutionis"** shall be the Administrative Letter of Absolution, as inherited from the Official Right *Iussum Publicum Absolutionis*; and

(xxv) **"Litterae Administrationis Damnationis"** shall be the Administrative Letter of Damnation, as inherited from the Official Right *Iussum Publicum Damnationis*; and

(xxvi) **"Litterae Administrationis Exemplificatio"** shall be the Administrative Letter of Exemplification, as inherited from the Official Right *Iussum Publicum Exemplificatio*; and

(xxvii) **"Litterae Administrationis Testimonium"** shall be the Administrative Letter of Proof, as inherited from the Official Right *Iussum Publicum Testimonium*; and

(xxviii) **"Litterae Administrationis Instructionis"** shall be the Administrative Letter of Instruction, as inherited from the Official Right *Iussum Publicum Instructionis*; and

(xxix) **"Litterae Administrationis Censurae"** shall be the Administrative Letter of Censure, as inherited from the Official Right *Iussum Publicum Censurae*; and

(xxx) **"Litterae Administrationis Annullas"** shall be the Administrative Letter of Annulment, as inherited from *Iussum Publicum Annullas*; and

(xxxi) **"Litterae Administrationis Ratificationis"** shall be the Administrative Letter of Ratification, as inherited from the Official Right *Iussum Publicum Ratificationis*; and

(xxxii) **"Litterae Administrationis Interdictum"** shall be the Administrative Letter of Interdiction, as inherited from the Official Right *Iussum Publicum Interdictum*; and

(xxxiii) **"Litterae Administrationis Levationis"** shall be the Administrative Letter of Relief, as inherited from the Official Right *Iussum Publicum Levationis*.

29. **"Member Rights"** (*Iurium Membrum*) are the sixth sub-class of Superior Rights and the fifth highest possible rights of any aggregate body, society, fraternity, association or company of two (2) or more

Member Rights
(Iurium
Membrum)

199

persons personified in trust.

There exists three (3) categories of thirty-nine (39) Superior Rights within the sub-class of Member Rights, being: Authoritative (11), Legal (22) and Special (6):-

(i)   "**Authoritative Member Rights**" (*Potentis Membrum Iurium*) are Member Rights associated with the essential authoritative powers of members of any valid society; and

(ii)   "**Legal Member Rights**" (*Legitimus Membrum Iurium*) are Member Rights essential to the proper administration of justice of any valid society; and

(iii)   "**Special Member Rights**" (*Proprius Membrum Iurium*) are Critical Member Rights in relation to the majority (two-thirds) of all members as "the people", essential to democracy and the restoration of the Golden Rule of Law in the event of corruption, collapse of justice or the rise of tyranny.

30. The following valid eleven (11) Authoritative Member Rights (*Potentis Membrum Iurium*) are recognised in accord with the most sacred Covenant *Pactum De Singularis Caelum* and the present sacred Covenant:-   *Authoritative Member Rights (Potentis Membrum Iurium)*

(i)   "**Ius Membrum Sodalis**" is the Superior Right of Equal Membership of Society, as inherited from the Natural Right *Ius Naturale Sodalis*; and

(ii)   "**Ius Membrum Nascendi Societas**" is the Superior Right to be recognised as a member of the society into which one was borne, as inherited from the Natural Right *Ius Naturale Nascendi Societas*; and

(iii)   "**Ius Membrum Petitoris**" is the Superior Right to be a candidate for election for office in democratic process of Society, as inherited from the Natural Right *Ius Naturale Iuris*; and

(iv)   "**Ius Membrum Votum**" is the Superior Right to vote and participate in democratic processes of Society, as inherited from the Natural Right *Ius Naturale Aequum*; and

(v)   "**Ius Membrum Possessionis**" is the Superior Right to possess, hold and own society property, as inherited from the Natural Right *Ius Naturale Possessionis*; and

(vi)   "**Ius Membrum Proprietatis**" is the Superior Right of Ownership of use or fruits of use of society property, as inherited from the Natural Right *Ius Naturale Proprietatis*; and

(vii) **"Ius Membrum Commercium"** is the Superior Right to Trade, Exchange and engage in Commerce, as inherited from the Natural Right *Ius Naturale Commercium*; and

(viii) **"Ius Membrum Solutionis Perfungor"** is the Superior Right to receive fair payment in exchange for fruits, energy, results and product of ones performance, work and effort, as inherited from the Natural Right *Ius Naturale Solutionis Perfungor*; and

(ix) **"Ius Membrum Defendum Iuris"** is the Superior Right to defend a right, as inherited from the Natural Right *Ius Naturale Defendum Iuris*; and

(x) **"Ius Membrum Perfungor"** is the Superior Right to Perform or refuse to Perform (Work), as inherited from the Natural Right *Ius Naturale Perfungor*; and

(xi) **"Ius Membrum Agendi Iuris"** is the Superior Right to take action to recover a right, as inherited from the Natural Right *Ius Naturale Agendi Iuris*.

31. The following valid twenty-two (22) Legal Member Rights (*Legitimus Membrum Iurium*) are recognised in accord with the most sacred Covenant *Pactum De Singularis Caelum* and the present sacred Covenant:-

Legal Member Rights (Legitimus Membrum Iurium)

(i) **"Ius Membrum Accusationis Sciri"** is the Superior Right to know the accuser and accusations, as inherited from the Natural Right *Ius Naturale Accusationis Sciri*; and

(ii) **"Ius Membrum Defensionis"** is the Superior Right to defend against any accusation and accuser, as inherited from the Natural Right *Ius Naturale Defensionis*; and

(iii) **"Ius Membrum Innocentiae"** is the Superior Right of Innocence until accusation proven, as inherited from the Natural Right *Ius Naturale Innocentiae*; and

(iv) **"Ius Membrum Leges Scirias"** is the Superior Right that all rules (laws) be known and none secret, as inherited from the Natural Rights *Ius Naturale Veritas* and *Ius Naturale Iuris*; and

(v) **"Ius Membrum Vocatio"** is the Superior Right to summons all parties to a competent forum of law to resolve a controversy, as inherited from the Natural Right *Ius Naturale Aequum* and *Ius Naturale Veritas*; and

(vi) **"Ius Membrum Vacuum Et Perpurgatum"** is the Superior Right of rendering a claimed record or entry "void", empty and thoroughly purged (cleansed) upon a false or fraudulent or erroneous registration, as inherited from the Natural Right *Ius Naturale Iuris*; and

(vii) **"Ius Membrum Accusare"** is the Superior Right to accuse another of a transgression, as inherited from the Natural Right *Ius Naturale Iuris*; and

(viii) **"Ius Membrum Prendi"** is the Superior Right to arrest a suspect on warrant or good cause for the purpose of serving an indictment and summons, as inherited from the Natural Right *Ius Naturale Iuris*; and

(ix) **"Ius Membrum Teneam"** is the Superior Right to detain a party associated with a controversy if good cause exists they be a risk of non-appearance or committing further controversies, as inherited from the Natural Rights *Ius Naturale Veritas* and *Ius Naturale Iuris*; and

(x) **"Ius Membrum Defensionis Tempus"** is the Superior Right for sufficient time to prepare defence, as inherited from the Natural Rights *Ius Naturale Veritas* and I*us Naturale Iuris*; and

(xi) **"Ius Membrum Oratorium"** is the Superior Right for matters to be heard in competent forum of law, as inherited from the Natural Right *Ius Naturale Iuris*; and

(xii) **"Ius Membrum Propria Persona"** is the Superior Right to defend or accuse as oneself, as inherited from the Natural Right *Ius Naturale Iuris*; and

(xiii) **"Ius Membrum Agensas"** is the Superior Right to appoint an agent, as inherited from the Natural Right *Ius Naturale Iuris*; and

(xiv) **"Ius Membrum Agens Recissum"** is the Superior Right to annul, abolish, cancel, revoke, repeal and rescind any agency appointment and powers, as inherited from the Natural Right *Ius Naturale Iuris*; and

(xv) **"Ius Membrum Iudicium"** is the Superior Right for a matter to be decided by a jury of peers, as inherited from the

Natural Right *Ius Naturale Iuris*; and

(xvi) **"Ius Membrum Tribunalis"** is the Superior Right for a matter to be decided by a competent tribunal, as inherited from the Natural Right *Ius Naturale Iuris*; and

(xvii) **"Ius Membrum Bonum Fidei"** is the Superior Right for a matter to be decided in Good Trust (Under Oath), as inherited from the Natural Right *Ius Naturale Iuris*; and

(xviii) **"Ius Membrum Sine Praeiudicium"** is the Superior Right for a matter to be decided without Prejudice, as inherited from the Natural Right *Ius Naturale Iuris*; and

(xix) **"Ius Membrum Mundis Manibus"** is the Superior Right for a matter to be decided with Clean Hands, as inherited from the Natural Right *Ius Naturale Iuris*; and

(xx) **"Ius Membrum Pretium"** is the Superior Right to give notice of fees, fines, costs against any breaches, defaults, injuries and acts of offence and bad faith, as inherited from the Natural Rights *Ius Naturale Honoris* and *Ius Naturale Iuris*; and

(xxi) **"Ius Membrum Nullum Validum Iudicium"** is the Superior Right of rendering "invalid" a false or fraudulent or erroneous judgement, as inherited from the Natural Right *Ius Naturale Nullum Validum Iudicium;* and

(xxii) **"Ius Membrum Compensationis"** is the Superior Right to be compensated for injury to proven accusation or harm or false accusation, as inherited from the Natural Rights *Ius Naturale Honoris* and *Ius Naturale Iuris*.

32. The following valid six (6) Special Member Rights (*Proprius Membrum Iurium*) are recognised in accord with the present sacred Covenant subject to the special and limited conditions of their use.

Special Member Rights may only be invoked when two thirds of total members of a particular society agree by the solidarity and bravery of their mass demonstrations, protests, resistance and verifiable participation in the election of new officials that one or more of these special powers shall be invoked:

(i) **"Ius Populi Jurisdictio"** is the Right of the People to invoke absolute and supreme rights on Earth to form the six (6) Unions of Africans Union, Americas Union, Arabian Union, Asia Union, Euro Union and Oceanic Union, as inherited from

Special Member Rights (Proprius Membrum Iurium)

the Divine Right *Ius Divine Jurisdictio*; and

(ii) **"Ius Populi Ecclesia"** is the Right of the people to form the new Ecclesiastical and Religious Bodies of One Christ, One Islam and One Spirit, as inherited from the Divine Right *Ius Divinum Ecclesia*; and

(iii) **"Ius Populi Revocare"** is the Right of the people to Revoke, Suspend Rights in face of tyranny, injustice and corruption, as inherited from the Divine Right *Ius Divinum Revocare*; and

(iv) **"Ius Populi Decretum"** is the Right of the people to issue Decree, Judgement and Edict, in the face of absolute Tyranny, Contempt for the Rule of Law or Justice, as inherited from the Divine Right *Ius Divinum Decretum*; and

(v) **"Ius Populi Imperium"** is the Right of the people to Command, Occupation and Enforcement of its orders, in the face of absolute Tyranny, Contempt for the Rule of Law or Justice, as inherited from the Divine Right *Ius Divinum Imperium*; and

(vi) **"Ius Populi Custoditum"** is the Right of the people as Custodians and Guardians of Rights and Golden Rule of Law, as inherited from the Divine Right *Ius Divinum Custoditum*.

Article 40 – Inferior Rights

1. **I**nferior Rights are the lowest possible form of Rights corresponding to Inferior Trusts, Inferior Estates and Inferior Persons, such as Non-Ucadian Trusts and Non-Ucadian Persons. Inferior Rights owe their existence to Non-Ucadian societies, persons, corporations, associations, bodies politic, agencies or aggregates.

Inferior Rights

All Superior Rights are greater than Inferior Rights. Where an Inferior Right makes claim to being superior, it is automatically invalid upon such falsity. There exists two (2) sub-classes (Primary and Secondary) and four (4) categories of Inferior Rights, being: Primary Personal, Primary Public, Secondary Protective and Secondary Remedial:-

(i) A **"Primary Personal Inferior Right"** is an Inferior Right associated as a capacity, or privilege, or liberty, or faculty, or power possessed by a certain class of persons or specifically named person, where such claimed rights have been created without necessarily referencing valid rights already existing; and

(ii)   A "**Primary Public Inferior Right**" is an Inferior Right associated with those rights held by the community in general, or by virtue of relations between members of the community, where such claimed rights have been created without necessarily referencing valid rights already existing; and

(iii)   A "**Secondary Protective Inferior Right**" is an Inferior Right associated with a Primary Inferior Right that is claimed to exist in order to prevent the infringement or loss of such Primary Inferior Rights; and

(iv)   A "**Secondary Remedial Inferior Right**" is an Inferior Right associated with a Primary Inferior Right that is claimed to exist in order to obtain restitution for any losses incurred upon one or more breaches of claimed Primary Inferior Rights or the enforcement of performance of one or more Primary Inferior Rights.

2.   "**Primary Personal Inferior Rights**" are Inferior Rights associated as a capacity, or privilege, or liberty, or faculty, or power possessed by a certain class of persons or specifically named person, where such claimed rights have been created without necessarily referencing valid rights already existing. _(Primary Personal Inferior Rights)_

As such claimed rights (1) fail to provide any valid provenance to valid Divine Rights; and (2) fail to properly articulate their legitimacy and function in relation to other pre-existing claimed inferior rights; and (3) owe their existence to non-Ucadian societies, persons, corporations, associations, bodies politic, agencies or aggregates; then all such claimed rights are not properly rights, or enforceable rights, but merely claims of right.

3.   "**Primary Public Inferior Rights**" are Inferior Rights associated with those rights held by the community in general, or by virtue of relations between members of the community, where such claimed rights have been created without necessarily referencing valid rights already existing. _(Primary Public Inferior Rights)_

As such claimed rights (1) fail to provide any valid provenance to valid Divine Rights; and (2) fail to properly articulate their legitimacy and function in relation to other pre-existing claimed inferior rights; and (3) owe their existence to non-Ucadian societies, persons, corporations, associations, bodies politic, agencies or aggregates; then all such claimed rights are not properly rights, or enforceable rights, but merely claims of right.

4.   "**Secondary Protective Inferior Rights**" are Inferior Rights associated with Primary Inferior Rights where it is claimed they exist _(Secondary Inferior Rights)_

in order to prevent the infringement or loss of such Primary Inferior Rights.

"**Secondary Remedial Inferior Rights**" are Inferior Rights associated with Primary Inferior Rights where it is claimed they exist in order to obtain restitution for any losses incurred upon one or more breaches of claimed Primary Inferior Rights or the enforcement of performance of one or more Primary Inferior Rights.

As such claimed secondary inferior rights (1) owe their existence and claimed legitimacy to primary inferior rights; and (2) such claimed primary inferior rights are not properly rights, or enforceable rights, but merely claims of right; then all secondary protective inferior rights are *ipso facto* (as a matter of fact) illegitimate, having no proper force or effect under any valid form of law.

Article 41 – Financial Systems and Money

1. A **Financial System** is a complex system of core elements that permits the efficient and reliable exchange of rights, obligations, credit, goods, property, instruments, funds and money between market participants.

Financial Systems and Money

The fourteen (14) core elements of a proper and complete Financial System include:-

(i) *Laws* that consistently define the rules of the Financial System; and

(ii) *Legal Structures and Constructs* such as Rights, Trusts, Estates, Property and Funds that enable the consistent establishment of ownership, value and the administration of intangible and tangible forms of property; and

(iii) *Courts and Legal Enforcement* that ensure the honest and impartial application of Laws and enforcement and protection of Legal Structures and Constructs; and

(iv) *Registers and Rolls* for the recording of various Legal Structures and Constructs of Value, including Instruments derived therefrom (as "Derivatives"); and

(v) *Instruments of Value* derived from Registers and Rolls, capable of being exchanged themselves, or being held as collateral and security; and

(vi) *Agreements of Value* signalling transactions of economic activity, capable of being held as collateral as security, or monetised (converted or securitised) into an Instrument of Value; and

(vii) *Markets* for the various exchange of rights, obligations, credit, goods, property, instruments, funds and money between market participants; and

(viii) *Accounts* being the ledgers of Markets and various Institutions, enabling the recording of transactions, exchanges and settlements; and

(ix) *Credit* being an internal and enclosed form of Money of a Market, enabling exchange and the settlement of transactions, but that in order to be exchanged as money beyond the market must be "converted" by means of the negotiability (portability) of Instruments, Agreements and/or Goods that accompanies the issuance of such Credit; and

(x) *Money* being units of measure, units of account, units of redemption for value, means of exchange and reliable stores of value; and

(xi) *Treasuries* being the custodians and controllers of Money and the purchasers of Securitised Instruments and Agreements purchased by Banks in the conversion of Financial Credit into Money; and

(xii) *Banks* being the providers of Credit into certain Financial Markets and the sponsors (converters) of Credit into Money through the collateralisation of monetisable Instruments and Agreements secured in the provision of such Credit; and

(xiii) *Firms* being trading entities within Markets and the producers of Goods available and capable of being sold or exchanged within those Markets; and

(xiv) *Goods* (including Services) manufactured by Firms and sold and traded within Markets.

2. The "**Ucadia Financial System**" (UFS) is a comprehensive and complete global financial system of *Laws, Legal Structures and Constructs, Courts and Legal Enforcement, Registers and Rolls, Instruments of Value, Agreements of Value, Markets, Accounts, Credit, Money, Treasuries, Banks, Firms,* and *Goods* capable of operating as a self contained system, or underwriting, or amalgamating or successfully replacing non-Ucadian financial systems of a city, state, nation or region or globe, in accord with the most sacred Covenant *Pactum De Singularis Caelum* and the present sacred

Ucadia Financial System (UFS)

Covenant.

3. A structure cannot be legally, lawfully or morally considered a Financial System, no matter how complex, universally adopted or accepted, if it engages in any of the following practices:-

   (i)   That the Laws of the system may be changed arbitrarily to the betterment of a few and the detriment of others, without fair recourse or remedy; or

   (ii)   That units of value may be introduced as money without any legitimate underwriting, thus devaluing the total stock of existing units of money; or

   (iii)   That units of value may be destroyed or withdrawn, without account for the provenance or historical basis of such lost units, thus inflating the remaining value of total stock of units of money; or

   (iv)   That credit may be introduced into a market, without defined rules as to the limits of credit of the market, nor the prior allocation rights of participants; and further that such credit may be exported and converted into "money", thus devaluing the total stock of existing unit of money; and

   (v)   That instruments issued in reference to credit, or agreements, including all derivatives thereof, are permitted to exceed the value of the original value of the asset that created all subsequent derivatives.

4. The Ucadia Financial System shall be unique in its design, function and sustainability, such that:-

   (i)   Once a unit of value of Money is created it cannot be destroyed, only withdrawn according to clear rules; and

   (ii)   Every unit of value is instantly locatable and its present account location known; and

   (iii)   The history of all transactions are transparent; and

   (iv)   The history of transactions of each unit of value through its own manifest are always known; and

   (v)   The Rules are sufficiently flexible and responsive such that no direct human intervention is required to arbitrarily "change" the rules.

5. *Property* is the highest registered Right a Person has, holds or can have within a Lawful Jurisdiction to Control or Use or Claim any

Thing or the Fruits of any Thing.

By definition, as all forms of Rights are derived from valid and legitimate Divine Rights, all forms of Property and Things are ultimately derived from the rules of Divine Property as defined by the most sacred Covenant *Pactum De Singularis Caelum* and the present sacred Covenant.

In reference to Property, Rights and Things:-

(i)   Property always pertains to Persons and not Beings; and

(ii)   A Thing in the context of Property is any Right that can be purchased or sold or inherited; and attached by operation of law to a corporeal object, whether fixed or movable; and

(iii)   Any Right that can be purchased or sold or inherited means a Right in Trust without a named Beneficiary and therefore a Good; and

(iv)   When one is recorded in a valid Register as possessing a Right or Claim of Right over Control or Use, then they may be referred to as the "Owner" of that Right.

6.   There are eight (8) possible forms of Property Right or "Ownership" of Control or Use or Claim of any Thing or the Fruits of any Thing, (in order of status and standing) being:-

   Forms of Property as Control or Use or Claim

(i)   Owner of Right of Control of a Thing; and

(ii)   Owner of Right of Use of a Thing; and

(iii)   Owner of Right of Control of the Fruits of Use of a Thing; and

(iv)   Owner of Right of Use of the Fruits of a Thing; and

(v)   Owner of Claim of Right of Control of a Thing; and

(vi)   Owner of Claim of Right of Use of a Thing; and

(vii)   Owner of Claim of Right of Control of the Fruits of Use of a Thing; and

(viii) Owner of Claim of Right of Use of the Fruits of a Thing.

7.   *Fund* is a sum of equal units representing certain Property Rights of monetary value, recorded in one or more designated accounts of a Body; and set apart for a term of years and one or more specific purposes; and available for the payment of debits, debts, legacies and claims in accord with the most sacred Covenant *Pactum De Singularis Caelum* and the present sacred Covenant.

   Character and Nature of Fund

In respect of the character, purpose and nature of a Fund:-

(i)   The Instrument of formation and of guiding the character, purpose and nature of one or more Funds is a Trust Covenant as a Fund Constitution issued and approved by a valid Body; and

(ii)   The underlying Rights and Property used to derive the value of a Fund must be set aside and sealed in its own Trust in accord with the Trust Covenant to protect the integrity of the Fund and prevent any re-transfer or re-conveyance that might threaten the value of the Fund. This means, the only ownership of rights of property that may be conveyed or discharged against the underlying Rights and Property are Claims, also known as "Charges"; and

(iii)   The life or operation of a Fund (the period it conducts business) shall be the maximum as specified by the present most sacred Covenant unless otherwise required by law; and

(iv)   A Fund may be actual money, or notes, or certificates, or securities or stocks able to be converted or negotiated for monetary value, providing the nature and monetary value of each element is clearly outlined within the accounts of the Fund; and

(v)   The terms of negotiation of the Stock of a Fund for other stock, or actual money, or notes, or certificates, or other securities is determined on a Fund by Fund basis, including whether a particular Fund is able to purchase the Stock of another Fund of the Body, to what maximum and other conditions (if any); and

(vi)   A Fund is never the original Assets themselves, but the Derivation of the value of the underlying Property, as recorded in the accounts and ledgers of the Fund, to permit the remission, remittance, settlement and discharge of debits, debts and obligations; and

(vii)   When the term of a Fund expires, it is absolutely forbidden to conduct any more new business. However, it may continue to manage and administer existing business and obligations until all such existing obligations and settlements expire or are balanced or dissolved or liquidated; and

(viii)   The property and assets held in Trust are absolutely forbidden to be released from such a Trust underwriting a Fund until after the term of a Fund expires and after all obligations and settlements are balanced and the fund dissolved or liquidated and the purpose of the Trust is fulfilled and the Trust dissolved; and

(ix) A Fund ceases to exist when it is properly liquidated or dissolved by an action in accord with the instrument of its creation, or after the expiry of its term. In accord with these articles, the administrators of a valid Fund are morally obligated to ensure the timely dissolution of the Fund as soon as practical after such a valid event.

8. "**Account**" and "**Accounts**" means:-   Account

    (i) A collection of financial documents, books and records relating to a distinct fiduciary relation formed in trust betweenUcadia or its related bodies and other parties concerning one or more rights, use of property for the purpose of banking, commerce, taxation or governance; and

    (ii) The original record of event as to its creation and validity entered into some formal register of similar types of accounts; and

    (iii) Any subsequent statement or summary or report from time to time referencing key information concerning its function and performance; and

    (iv) The summary of all Accounts and Account Relations, also known as the "**Master Accounts**" and "**Chart of Accounts**" of an association, body corporate, production or project and prepared and presented in statements, summary and reports consistent with Accounting Standards.

9. A "**Debt**" is (a) a binding promise or (b) right of action or (c) both. A   Debt
Debt is distinguished from a Debit in that a Debit is an entry in a journal or ledger of a sum owed to the proprietor of some accounts, under the Ucadia Financial System, whereas a Debt is a binding promise or a right of action.

In respect of Debt as a binding promise:-

    (i) A Debt may be a solemn obligation under Contract; or

    (ii) A Debt may be a binding promise under Bargain.

In respect of Debt as a Right of Action:-

    (i) A Debt may be a right of demand and enforcement of payment of sum of money due for goods sold under Bargain; or

    (ii) A Debt may be a right of demand and enforcement of delivery of goods due for a sum of money under Bargain; or

    (iii) A Debt may be a right of demand and enforcement of payment of penalty or compensation for failure to perform an obligation under contract.

10. **"Asset"** is anything ownwed by a firm capable of producing a positive economic value. More specifically, an Asset is a sum of units of monetary value, recorded in one or more designated accounts, available for the discharge of a debt and not yet assigned to a specific purpose.

Asset

11. **"Good"** is a gift or a promise associated with a beneficial Right of Use for Sale or Bargain:-

Good

    (i)   **"Sale"** is when the title to a thing is given in Trust to another in exchange for a price of lawful money, also given in Trust; and

    (ii)   **"Bargain"** is a Contract of Mutual Bindings (Promises) in Trust as Security whereby one party promises to assign a right as property for some consideration; and the other party promises to receive the property and take good care of it and pay the consideration.

12. In reference to the concept of a Sale:-

Sale

    (i)   A Sale always involves Goods and therefore always involves Rights in Trust as Goods; and

    (ii)   A Sale always involves two (2) distinct trusts having two distinct trust corpus – one where the buyer is trustee and one where the seller is trustee; and

    (iii)   It is only when the sale is completed do the two separate trusts dissolve as a settlement into one, providing the conditions of sale make that possible.

13. In reference to the concept of a Bargain of Goods:-

Bargain

    (i)   A Bargain always involves Goods and therefore always involves Rights in Trust as Goods; and

    (ii)   Similar to a Sale, a Bargain always involves two Trusts for a Bargain to exist: The one for the Buyer and one for the Seller; and

    (iii)   A Bargain is never a transfer of Title but a Bailment of Goods or Use for some financial consideration; and

    (iv)   The Seller never gifts the property like a Sale and the terms of Consideration may also involve some return of a Bailment of Money; and

    (v)   The key operating element of a Bargain is the Mutual Binding Promises that are also called Debts.

14. A "**Market**" may be defined as a trusted space (virtual or real) where buyers and sellers may exchange goods or services. A Market then is in essence nothing more than a space (real or virtual) where three (3) or more buyers and sellers may exchange goods or services and settle accounts between one another. Market

There are four (4) Basic Elements that define a Market in addition to the existence of three or more buyers and sellers, namely *Market Rules, Standard Unit of Measure, Accounts & Bookkeeping* and *Conversion and Settlement of Accounts*:-

   (i)   *Market Rules* means that a space or place cannot possibly be a market unless it possesses the most essential of Rules based upon the Golden Rule of Law of equality, fairness and trust; and

   (ii)   A *Standard Unit of Measure* means there are consistent standards of valuation across a market so "like can be exchanged for like". This standard unit is what is most commonly called Money; and

   (iii)   *Accounts & Bookkeeping* is the inescapable and necessary fact that the accounts being the registers of title and ownership are intimately linked to the operation of any market, including the certificate of proof of transaction; and

   (iv)   *Conversion and Settlement of Accounts* is in essence the clearing mechanism of trade, that requires the ability of initial conversion, the ability to trade, the settlement of accounts and then the redemption of any remainder back into some portable form to be withdrawn from the market, if one chooses.

15. "**Money**" is a Right, established by law, whereby a system of rules, measures, records, accounts and procedures are formed to produce a consistent and stable *Unit of Measure, Unit of Account, Unit of Redemption for Value, Means of Exchange and Reliable Store of Value*:- Money

   (i)   *Unit of Measure* means that proper Money is first and foremost a "standard unit of measure", having a suitable unique identity to distinguish it from other units of measure, whereby all goods and services within a certain Market may be compared to the same unit of measure, thus enabling the creation of Price. In this way, proper Money is fundamentally always an attribute of a Market and not vice versa; and

   (ii)   *Unit of Account* means that proper Money is a unit of measure associated with a Market that enables the entry of consistent values and transactions, based upon its character as a Unit of Measure, within Accounts and Ledgers reflecting such Prices,

Quantities and other attributes of Goods and Services. In this way, Accounts are always a feature of a Market and Money as entries in such accounts are an attribute of Accounts and Markets, not vice versa; and

(iii) *Unit of Redemption for Value* means that proper Money is capable of being represented in some medium or form (i.e. physical and/or electronic; or paper, plastic, metal or other etc.) and possesses the attribute of being redeemed for some valuable consideration, enables a participant to "enter" and to "exit" a form of proper Money associated with one Market and choose to move to another Market; and

(iv) *Means of Exchange* means that proper Money is able to fulfil the requirement of facilitating efficient transactions within a Market, because of its previous attributes. Thus, a "means of exchange" may be considered a primary object of proper Money, but only as a consequence of other attributes first being in place; and

(v) *Reliable Store of Value* means that proper Money represents a consistent and stable unit of exchange such that its Value today is the same or similar as its Value tomorrow. Contrary to false presumptions, this does not mean the medium of Money itself must be of some intrinsic value, but that the integrity of Money is protected, through minimisation of counterfeiting, speculation and rapid valuation or devaluation swings – meaning all that impact on the wealth and function of a Market.

16. In accord with the customs, traditions and maxims of law concerning Money, since the beginning of Human Civilisation, all proper Money may be divided into five (5) primary categories being *Ecclesiastical, Public, Capital, Private* and *Personal*:-

> Primary Categories of Money

(i) *Ecclesiastical Money* is the highest, most valuable form of Money and form of Legal Tender since the beginning of Human Civilisation and the origin of the very notion of Money itself. The highest form of Ecclesiastical Money ever formed is the Supreme Credo (Credit) as defined by the most sacred Covenant *Pactum De Singularis Caelum*; and

(ii) *Public Money* is Money and a form of Legal Tender issued as a Public Fund against the Credit in Trust and Assets of a body politic, or constituted society as a single Market and then managed by its Officers as Trustees; and

(iii) *Capital Money* is Money and a form of valuable Asset formed from the accounting of a promise and guarantee upon the "head" of one or more persons who possess some valuable property right; and

(iv) *Private Money*, also known as "Currency" and a form of Legal Tender, is Money issued under license or privilege by a party, usually a bank, holding certain assets within a Market; and then granted exclusive license to have its instruments treated "as if" Public Money; and

(v) *Personal Money*, also known as "Credit Money" or simply "Credit", is Money issued under the Bylaws of a party holding assets within a market, such as one or a network of savings and investment banks, or even a private corporation.

17. **"Legal Tender"**, also known as Lawful Money, is any form of Money or Instrument that may be tendered for the payment of a debt or obligation:- Legal Tender

(i) Properly formed and mandated Ecclesiastical Money, consistent and in accord with the present most sacred Covenant is always Legal Tender in any and every valid body politic, or properly constituted society that operates according to the Rule of Law; and

(ii) Public Money is naturally Legal Tender by definition, within the body politic or society where it relates; and

(iii) Private Money is only Legal Tender to the extent it is granted such privilege by the legislative body or society where it relates; and

(iv) Instruments and Commodities may only be Legal Tender when granted such privilege by the legislative body of the body politic or society where it relates.

18. **"Cash"**, such as Ucadia Moneta, is the Sum of all Instruments and Items that circulate among members of a body politic or society or Market as proper Money, including (but not limited to) Ecclesiastical Money, Public Money, Capital Money, Private Money, Personal Money and Commodities considered ready stores of value such as precious metals and gems. Cash

19. **"Ucadia Money"** is the highest form of valid and legitimate Money as established by laws consistent and in accord with the most sacred Covenant *Pactum De Singularis Caelum* and the present sacred Covenant:- Ucadia Money

(i) All Ucadia Money is Ecclesiastical Money, being the highest and most valuable form of Money and Legal Tender since the beginning of Human Civilisation and the origin of the very notion of Money itself; and

(ii) There are six (6) levels of Ucadia Money, corresponding to five distinct universes of entities and bodies, the highest unit of value being: Supreme Credo (Credit), followed by Gold Credo (Credit), Silver Credo (Credit), Union Moneta (Money) and then University Moneta (Money).

20. In accord with the present sacred Covenant unless the context requires otherwise:-

Ucadia Financial System Values

    (i) One Supreme Credo (Credit) is equivalent to One Hundred (100) Ucadia Gold Credo; and

    (ii) One Supreme Credo (Credit) is equivalent to One Million (1,000,000) Ucadia Silver Credo; and

    (iii) One Supreme Credo (Credit) is equivalent to One Billion (1,000,000,000) Ucadia Union Moneta.

21. In accord with fundamental maxims of Law of all competent civilisations since the beginning of time, as Ucadia Money is Ecclesiastical Money and the highest possible form of Money or Currency:-

Ucadia Money as highest form of Money

    (i) As Ucadia Money is the highest form of Ecclesiastical Money, the Circulation of Ucadia Money shall determine the Circulation of all lesser forms of Money; and

    (ii) Furthermore, Ucadia Money shall hereby be recognised and acknowledged as Legal Tender for the payment, discharge and settlement of all debits, debts, obligations, taxes, fines and penalties, whether they be public or private; or domestic or foreign, in relation to any and all societies, bodies politic, communities, associations, trusts, estates, funds, corporations, aggregates and persons; and

    (iii) Excluding periods of declared "Emergency", all Ucadia Money shall be used solely for the payment, discharge and settlement of all debts, debits, obligations, taxes, fines and penalties between Ucadia Members, using Ucadia Money Accounts where such sums are stated in Ucadia Money amounts.

22. In accord with the present sacred Covenant, the Unit of Measure of the Universal Ecclesia of One Christ is the Ucadia Moneta.

Unit of Measure and Account of Ecclesia

23. In accord with the present sacred Covenant unless the context requires otherwise:-

International Foreign Reserve Debt Currencies

(i)   The Universal Ecclesia recognises the sovereign and independent right of people to form and issue Public Money of a Credit nature for the discharge of debts and obligations and the lawful exchange of goods and services; and

(ii)   While some governments have mandated certain currency as Legal Tender, many such currencies issued by Reserve Banks do not possess the essential criteria necessary to be properly defined as Money, nor Public Money or Lawful Money; and

(iii)   Furthermore, such private money, issued under exclusive license, when based upon debt, or lien, or the sale of birth certificates, or arguments of national or global bankruptcy is morally repugnant, an abomination, an a profound sacrilege against God, the Holy Spirit and the Divine Creator of all Existence and all Heaven and Earth; and

(iv)   Whilst such currencies are a severe transgression against the present Covenant, the Universal Ecclesia is permitted to grant temporary absolution to all Members for the limited use of such morally repugnant and unjust currencies until such time as they are replaced by properly constituted Public Credit Money Systems; and

(v)   The Universal Ecclesia of One Christ shall have the innate right to hold a certain number of Foreign Debt Currency Notes; and to exchange Public Money and Lawful Money for such notes as required, until such currencies have been withdrawn and abolished.

24. In accord with the present sacred Covenant unless the context requires otherwise:-

International Banking System Credit Currencies

(i)   The Universal Ecclesia recognises the privilege granted to certain fiduciary companies of good standing to create and manage their own form of Credit Money, to then be exchanged for lawful Public Credit Money for the discharge of debts and obligations and the lawful exchange of goods and services; and

(ii)   While International Banking System Credit Currency is not mandated as Legal Tender, nor does such Currency possess the essential criteria necessary to be properly defined as Public Money or Lawful Money, such Credit networks do provide a wide access and means to purchase Goods and Services; and

(iii)   The Universal Ecclesia of One Christ shall have the innate right to deposit Lawful Public Money, Foreign Debt Currency Notes and other lawful Instruments to establish suitable levels of International Banking System Credit Currency as required.

25. When a duly recorded and authorised tender to the correct sum of Ucadia Money for the payment, discharge and settlement of all debts, debits, obligations, taxes, fines and penalties is refused, rejected or dishonoured by a society, or body politic, or community, or association, or trust, or estate, or fund, or corporation or person, then such a profane, unlawful, illegal and immoral action shall be a formal acknowledgement and confession of a debt and obligation equal in value to the sum refused, rejected or dishonoured.

Honouring Ucadia Money

Article 42 – Property & Temporal Goods

1. To pursue and fulfil its proper purposes, the Universal Ecclesia of One Christ by innate Right shall acquire, retain, administer and alienate Property and Temporal Goods independently from civil power.

Property & Temporal Goods

2. The proper purposes of Property and Temporal Goods is to fulfil the Primary and Ancillary Propositions of the Universal Ecclesia of One Christ.

Purposes of Property & Temporal Goods

3. All Temporal Goods that belong to the Universal Ecclesia of One Christ are therefore Ecclesiastical Goods held in absolute trust and governed by the laws of Ucadia.

Temporal Goods as Ecclesiastical Goods

4. The Universal Ecclesia of One Christ can acquire Temporal Goods by every just means of natural or positive law permitted to others.

Acquisition of Temporal Goods

5. The Universal Ecclesia of One Christ has the innate Right to require from its Members, those things, including Temporal Goods, that are necessary for the purposes proper to it; and no temporal or spiritual body possesses any right or authority or power to impede such Right.

Right of support of Members and Temporal Goods

6. Members are free to give Temporal Goods for the benefit of the Universal Ecclesia of One Christ. No temporal or spiritual body possesses any right or authority or power to impede, or deny or obstruct Members exercising such an act of free will.

Gift and Donation of Temporal Goods from Members

7. Unless otherwise specified, all Goods gifted and donated to Members by the Universal Ecclesia of One Christ are Ecclesiastical Goods with such gifts being right of use only, as all such goods remain at all times the exclusive property of the Universal Ecclesia of One Christ.

Gift and Donation of Use of Ecclesiastical Goods to Members

8. The Universal Ecclesia of One Christ by innate and holy mandate has absolute Authority and Power to Rate itself, including (but not limited

Valuation and Rating of Temporal and

to) the Valuation of all its Rights, Lands, Goods, Estates, Trusts, Funds, Property and Assets. All Valuations, Rates and Taxes shall then be duly recorded within the proper Registers of the Universal Ecclesia of One Christ, in accord with the present sacred Covenant. No other non-Ucadian or foreign body, or foreign power, or foreign entity, or foreign person or foreign corporation has any right, or power, or authority whatsoever to Rate, or Value or Tax the Rights, Lands, Goods, Estates, Trusts, Funds, Property and Assets of Ucadia and the Ecclesia.

Ecclesiastical Goods

9. Where certain Rights, Lands, Goods, Estates, Trusts, Funds, Property or Assets of Ucadia and the Ecclesia are being used by a non-Ucadian or foreign body, or foreign power, or foreign entity, or foreign person or foreign corporation, the Ecclesia shall have the full Authority and Power to offer a peaceful, amicable and harmonious resolution by licensing such Rights, Lands, Goods, Estates, Trusts, Funds, Property or Assets by Special Treaty; and any clauses or separate Special Treaty with the foreign Taxation bodies. By such Treaty or Convention, the Ecclesia shall be empowered to consider any such non-Ucadian and foreign body "tax exempt" from payments to the Ecclesia; or other such arrangements that are considered conducive to peaceful, amicable and harmonious relations, without contradicting the present sacred Covenant.

Tax Treaties and Status

10. Notwithstanding any other provision of these present Articles, any attempt by any non-Ucadian or foreign body, or foreign power, or foreign entity, or foreign person or foreign corporation to Rate, or Value or establish a Tax Roll for certain Rights, Lands, Goods, Estates, Trusts, Funds, Property or Assets of the Universal Ecclesia of One Christ shall be an act of profanity, sacrilege and an abomination against all Heaven and Earth, as only Ucadian bodies possess the Divine Mandate to administer and hold in custody Sacred Circumscribed Space. Therefore, any such action to the contrary shall be considered a Confession of Condemnation whereby such a body, and all persons responsible shall be named in a Holy Writ; and it shall be a moral obligation of every Ucadian Member to pursue by every and any means necessary to eliminate every temporal existence and manifestation of such profanity, sacrilege and abomination.

Profanity, Sacrilege and Abomination against Ecclesia Rights

Article 43 – Competent Forum

1. Competent Forum of Law be a realm of Time, Space and Venue where a Suit or Action or other Matter of Law may be adjudicated according to *Lex Causae* (the law to be used within the Forum) using *Lex Fori* (laws of the Forum) by proper

Competent Forum of Law

Officers under Oath and Vow, in accord with Law as defined by the present sacred Covenant.

A Forum that contradicts these Articles cannot be considered a Competent Forum of Law.

2. There are only four (4) possible types of Forum: Spiritual, Formal, Informal and Unlawful:-

Types of Competent Forums

    (i)   A "**Spiritual Forum**" is a purely spiritual and formal ecclesiastical realm and venue in accordance with the most sacred Covenant *Pactum De Singularis Caelum*. All judicial plenary authority of Heaven and Earth is vested in one supreme spiritual body, court of record and competent forum of Law known as the *Oratorium*, also known as the Supreme Court and also known as the Supreme Court of One Heaven. The *Oratorium* is by definition the highest See and is judged by no one; and

    (ii)   A "**Formal Forum**" is an Ecclesiastical venue that exists within the temporal realm as a dedicated Oratory possessing the Authority of the *Oratorium* for the hearing of all Suits or Actions or other Matters of Trust, Rights, Injury and Morality of Law. The highest possible jurisdiction of Formal Forums is Ucadia Courts. A venue without Ecclesiastical Authority is forbidden to hear any Matters of Trust, Rights, Injury or Morality of Law; and

    (iii)   An "**Informal Forum**" is a venue that exists within the temporal realm that is not Ecclesiastical or a dedicated Oratory for the hearing of Suits as a Court, but has been nonetheless secured for such purpose. Such a venue is permitted to resolve matters of arbitration and dispute by consent between the parties, but is prevented from hearing any Matters of Trust, Rights, Injury or Morality of Law; and

    (iv)   An "**Unlawful Forum**" is a venue that exists within the temporal realm that is without Ecclesiastical Authority nor proper Public Authority, but is a corporate body holding authority by license and franchise, whereby the proper Rights of people are denied and replaced with "licensed privileges"; and where the law is deliberately occluded and hidden; and where such a venue repudiates the true Divine and Ecclesiastical origins of Law in practice; and where such venues favour members of legal guilds against others.

3. A "**Corporate Court**" is an Unlawful Forum, without legitimate or

Corporate Courts as

valid Ecclesiastical Authority, for the exclusive private business of a law (Bar) Guild. A competent Forum of Law is not permitted to be represented by justices, officers, prosecutors, defence or advisers who are members, associated or affiliated in any way to one or more law (Bar) Guilds, Societies or Associations.

Unlawful Forums

4. The Characteristics that determine whether a Competent Forum is an Unlawful Forum such as a Corporate Court that is without any validity or legitimacy in Law and by its own existence and function is a profound injury against all standards of civilised society are:-

Characteristics of Competent Forum

(i) That the claimed Officers and Agents of such a Forum are, or were members of the same fraternity being a Bar Guild or Law Association, licensing members; and that the Executive Branch and Legislative Branch protects and favours such members over its ordinary members of the broader society in respect of fair access to the Law; and

(ii) That the Forum relies upon laws within *Lex Causae* that are obscure, unclear, occluded and contradictory to the true Law as expressed within the present sacred Covenant; and

(iii) That the Forum utilises procedures within *Lex Fori* that are obscure, unclear, occluded and deliberately bias toward the members of some Bar Guild or Law Association, licensing members over ordinary members of the broader society; and

(iv) That the Forum openly or tacitly repudiates the Golden Rule of Law as defined by the present sacred Covenant.

Article 44 – Evidence and Proof

1. **Evidence is any accepted means in Argument** employed for the purpose of proving one or more alleged Facts, whereby the Truth is established or disproven. Evidence may be Judicial (public) or Extra-Judicial (private or personal).

Evidence

2. The Law of Evidence states that the Facts in any Dispute or Argument may be defined as either Principal Facts (*facta probanda*) or Evidentiary Facts (*facta probantia*):-

Law of Evidence

(i) **"Principal Facts"** (*facta probanda*) or "Facts in Issue" are those facts required to be proved. They are called Facts in Issue because these facts are usually the backbone of any matter of controversy and therefore essential to be proven; and

(ii) **"Evidentiary Facts"** (*facta probantia*) or "Facts in Evidence" are those facts given in evidence with the view of proving Facts in Issue. These are facts normally entered during the course of a hearing or trial and not part of the initial disclosure with any citation, complaint or petition. Circumstantial evidence is therefore a more common description of *facta probantia* or "Facts in Evidence" whereby one or more inferences may be concluded via circumstantial evidence leading to the logical conclusion of a Principal Fact (*facta probanda*).

3. The publishing of any Proclamation, Order, Regulation or Notice within the Ucadia Gazette shall be *Prima Facie* Evidence of such Fact and Truth or Debt of Record; and that all Courts, Judges, Justices, Masters, Magistrates or Commissioners judicially acting, and all other judicial Officers shall take judicial Notice of such *Prima Facie* Evidence in any and all legal proceedings whatsoever.

Gazette Notices as Prima Facie Evidence

4. The provision of any valid Certificate of Title to Land, Property and Rights as an authentic extract of a record from a Ucadia Register shall be *Prima Facie* Evidence of Proof of Original Title.

Certificate of Title as Proof of Title

5. All Members shall first ensure their Affidavits as Testimony and Evidence are duly recorded and registered within the Registers of the Universal Ecclesia of One Christ first, before an extract is supplied to any foreign body in relation to any dispute or matter.

Affidavits as Testimony and Evidence

6. The Universal Ecclesia of One Christ shall have unlimited Right of Action in any and every jurisdiction against any and every Debt of Record.

Unlimited Right of Action on Debt of Record

7. In the law of Evidence, an allegation of Fact is said to be "proved" when the forum of law is convinced of its Truth. Thus, such Evidence is then also known as Proof.

Proof

8. Where a Person who makes an allegation is bound to prove it, the burden or onus of proof (*onus probandi*) is said to initially rest upon him.

Burden of Proof

9. When a Person on whom the burden of proof lies, adduces Evidence sufficient to raise a presumption that what is said is true, he is said to shift the burden of proof.

Shifting Burden of Proof

Article 45 – Record

1. Record be a written memorial of actions or events, and accounts under Oath as Fact; and the conveyances of Proof of such Fact then preserved as knowledge and authentic history of the causes within such entries, united by some Identifier

Record

within Memoranda, Journals and Register of a Trust or Estate or Fund or Corporation.

2. A valid Record is comprised of three actions entered into three Books, consistent with the etymology of "record" from two Latin words *re* meaning "property" and *cordis* meaning "heart (body), mind (thought and reason) and spirit (soul)":-

    (i)   The Event is the first action, entered into a Memorandum as a true written memorial to the "event" and associated proceedings and actions; and

    (ii)   The Witnessed Account is the second action, as attestation to an Account or Affidavit entered into a Journal as an attestation to the true Summary of Facts, with a unique Event Number then "posted back" to the Memorandum as well as "cancelling" those details within the Memorandum now "posted" in the Journal; and

    (iii)   The Conveyance is the third action, as proof of a valid "event" to a Ledger, or Summary Letter or Certificate as a True Summary of Account and Instrument of Record, with the unique Event Number then "posted forward" to the Ledger as the completion of the Record.

Valid Record

3. In terms of the general authority and nature of Records:-

    (i)   All Records are wholly and exclusively Ecclesiastical Property and can never belong to a Trust, or Estate or Fund that formed or inherited it. Instead, all Records are the property of One Heaven; and

    (ii)   All Records are hierarchical in their inheritance of authority and validity from One Heaven, beginning with the highest being the Great Register and Public Record of One Heaven. A Record that cannot demonstrate the provenance of its authority, has none and is null and void from the beginning; and

    (iii)   As all Records are wholly and exclusively Ecclesiastical, absolutely no clerical or administrative act may take place in association with Records unless by a duly authorised Trustee under active and valid sacred Oath or Vow in a manner consistent and in accord with the present sacred Covenant; and

    (iv)   The entry of the elements of a Record is wholly invalid unless the memorial of the act giving authority is done without duress, is done freely and with full knowledge and is consistent and in accord with the present sacred Covenant and the most sacred

Nature of Records

Covenant *Pactum De Singularis Caelum.*

4. Two types of valid Instrument of Record may be created being an Original, or a Certified Original:- | *Original and Certified Original*

    (i) An **"Original Record"** is an Instrument of Record where the existence of the Instrument itself and the number attached to it "completes" the Record and the instrument makes this clear; and

    (ii) A **"Certified Original Record"** is when the Instrument of Record makes clear it is a Certificate or Extract or Abstract of an Original Record held somewhere else and the *Jurat* makes clear its status.

5. The highest form of valid Records and Instruments of Record are those derived from valid Ucadia Registers:- | *Highest form of Records*

    (i) The highest authority and form of Ucadian Register is the Great Register and Public Record of One Heaven, with no Records higher; and

    (ii) The second highest authority and form of Ucadia Register is the Great Register and Public Record of a valid registered Ucadian Society; and

    (iii) The third highest authority and form of Ucadia Register is the Register and Public Record of a Member who has completed their *Voluntatem Et Testamentum*; and

    (iv) The fourth and lowest authority and form of Records is any Record created and issued by a non-Ucadian society.

Article 46 – Document

1. **D**ocument be a tangible, physical or electronic item containing an original or official or lawful written record of some Truth, or Fact, or Event or Issue or Matter, able to be used as Evidence itself or in support of Evidence. | *Document*

2. In accord with the present sacred Covenant unless the context requires otherwise:- | *Character of Documents*

    (i) An **"Ancient Document"** is any Document more than twenty years old; that when possessing proper provenance and condition of custody, and in the absence of any evidence to the contrary, is therefore presumed genuine; and

    (ii) A **"Document of Title"**, also known simply as "Title" is any

Document evidencing that the Person in possession of it is entitled to receive, hold and dispose of the Document and the Goods it covers. A valid Document of Title is required to be issued by or addressed to a Bailee and cover clearly Identified Goods in the possession of the Bailee; and

(iii) A **"Public Document"** is any Document issued or published by legislative or sovereign authority; or any Document of Record evidencing or connected with public administration, as issued by executive or administrative authority; and

(iv) A **"Judicial Document"** is any Document relating to the operation and administration of justice and proper forums of law; and may be divided into (1) judgements, decrees and verdicts; and (2) depositions, affidavits, examinations and inquisitions; and (3) writs, warrants or pleadings.

3. There are only five (5) valid forms of Documents: Supreme, Superior, Ordinary, General and Inferior:-

    Status of Documents

(i) A **"Supreme Document"** is a valid document issued and sealed by a Supreme Official Person, registered in the Great Register and Public Record of One Heaven and existing firstly as a Supreme Spiritual and Ecclesiastical Instrument and secondly as a Supreme Temporal Ecclesiastical Instrument possessing full living personality. There is no higher, more powerful nor authoritative Document than a Supreme Document; and

(ii) A **"Superior Document"** is a valid document issued and sealed by a Superior Official Person, registered in the Great Register and Public Record of One Christ and existing firstly as a Superior Spiritual and Ecclesiastical Instrument and secondly as a Superior Temporal Ecclesiastical Instrument possessing full living personality. It is the second highest and authoritative Document of all; and

(iii) An **"Ordinary Document"** is a valid document issued and sealed by an Ordinary Official Person, registered in a Great Register and Public Record of a Ucadian Society and existing firstly as an Ordinary Spiritual and Ecclesiastical Instrument and secondly as an Ordinary Temporal Ecclesiastical Instrument possessing full living personality. It is the third highest and authoritative Document of all; and

(iv) A **"General Document"** is a valid document issued and registered in a Great Register and Public Record of a Ucadian

Society that is not issued by an Ordinary, Superior or Supreme Official Person; and

(v) An "**Inferior Document**" is any document issued by an Inferior Person such as a Non-Ucadian Person or Inferior Juridic Person. No Inferior Document may ever be allowed to claim superiority over a General Document, Ordinary Document, Superior Document or Supreme Document.

Article 47 – Instrument and Form

1. **Instrument be a formal or lawful Document in writing** that conforms to certain standards of Form as prescribed by law and rules, such as the present sacred Covenant.

   Instrument

2. An Instrument possesses three sides being Obverse, Reverse and Traverse:-

   Three Sides of Instruments

   (i) *Obverse* or "Face" of a Document is its front; and

   (ii) *Reverse* or "Back Face" is its back; and

   (iii) *Traverse* or third side is the "Margin" between the Obverse and Reverse.

3. A "**Seal**" is affixing a symbol to a valid Instrument to attest its valid production, or its recording and registration or to bind its contents as a solemn promise or execute its contents by authority of the Universal Ecclesia of One Christ. There are only six (6) valid types of Seal being Absolute, Great, Official, Ordinary, Inferior and Private:-

   Seal of Instrument

   (i) An "**Absolute Seal**" is the most powerful and highest authority of seal and signature when a man or woman uses their thumbprint in red ink to give life and personality to a Document in their capacity as Executor of their own True Trust and General Executor of the Estate of their Legal Person. Members are not permitted to use such Seals in correspondence with the Universal Ecclesia of One Christ; and

   (ii) A "**Great Seal**" is the second highest possible seal and is the official Seal of any Juridic Society Person or Juridic Public Person such as the present Universal Ecclesia of One Christ. Hence a Great Seal is used for the authentication of Documents of the highest importance issued in the name of a Universal True Trust, Global True Trust or Civil True Trust; and

   (iii) An "**Official Seal**" is the third highest possible Seal issued by an Official Person in the capacity of their office on behalf of a

Universal True Trust, Global True Trust or Civil True Trust; and

(iv) An "**Ordinary Seal**" is the fourth highest possible Seal issued on behalf of a Juridic Private Person, Juridic Union Person or Juridic Domestic Person in association with a Superior Trust; and

(v) An "**Inferior Seal**" is the fifth highest possible Seal issued on behalf of a non-Ucadian legal person; and

(vi) A "**Private Seal**", also known as an Inferior Administrative Seal is the lowest form of seal and is an administrative stamp issued under private law between parties for the cross certification of documents by regulation and central registration of all authorised signatories.

4. An "**Inchoate Instrument**" is an Instrument that has been begun but remains unfinished or not completed and therefore is missing a material particular essential to its form and function. All Officers, Agents and Contractors are forbidden to produce Inchoate Instruments contrary to the present By Laws.

Inchoate Instrument

5. No Instruments of the Universal Ecclesia of One Christ to Members shall require Stamp Duty or the application of one or more Stamps under these Articles of the present sacred Covenant.

Stamps on Instruments

6. No Foreign Bodies Politic or Society or Corporation or Agency shall be granted permission to deface or alter an Instrument of the Universal Ecclesia of One Christ.

No Right to Deface Instruments

7. Authorised Divisions and Departments of the Universal Ecclesia of One Christ may apply a single identifiable diagonal line from the top right corner to the bottom left corner through certain valid Instruments of the Universal Ecclesia or certain Instruments issued by a Foreign Body, when an entry of the particulars of the Instrument has been duly recorded within one or more Registers or Journals of the Universal Ecclesia:-

Posted Instruments

(i) The Instrument shall then be returned with a new Instrument that references the posting of the first, while the single diagonal line indicates the first Instrument as being inoperative; and

(ii) Where the Universal Ecclesia has no wish to acknowledge any part of an Instrument issued to it, no mark of posting should occur whatsoever and such Instruments should be returned without comment, other than official record of their return.

8. Authorised Divisions and Departments of the Universal Ecclesia of

Cancelled

One Christ may apply two identifiable diagonal lines from the top right corner to the bottom left corner through certain valid Instruments of the Universal Ecclesia or certain Instruments issued by a Foreign Body, when the value or gift or benefit of the Instrument is conveyed and used and therefore the Instrument is to be cancelled, to prevent double entry or use; and the particulars of the Instrument have been duly recorded within one or more Registers or Journals of the Universal Ecclesia. The signature of the authorised Officer cancelling the Instrument must also be applied at the same forty five degree angle.

Instruments

9. Authorised Divisions and Departments of the Universal Ecclesia of One Christ may endorse an Instrument by applying a signature at ninety degrees with instruction upon the back of a valid Instrument, along with any Seal as surety for such act, in accord with the present sacred Covenant.

Endorsed Instruments

10. It is the Right of Members that they may send Instruments to the Universal Ecclesia of One Christ as a request. However, when such Instruments are unsolicited, then by the present most sacred Covenant, the Member grants the Ecclesia the right to do what it deems is appropriate, without liability:-

Unsolicited Instruments of Request

   (i)   Unsolicited and Outrageous Letters of Request are to be rejected outright, without any need for response, as such material should be immediately destroyed; and

   (ii) Handwritten Unsolicited Letters of Request are to be registered within seven days of receipt and to be properly answered within thirty days.

11. It is the Right of Members that they may send Instruments to the Universal Ecclesia of One Christ. However, when such Instruments are unsolicited, then by the present most sacred Covenant, the Member grants the Ecclesia the right to do what it deems is appropriate, without liability:-

Unsolicited Instruments of Demand

   (i)   Unsolicited and Outrageous Demands are to be rejected outright, without any need for response, as such material should be immediately destroyed; and

   (ii) Unsolicited Demands providing claimed proof and evidence of obligation are to be registered within seven days of receipt and a standard unsigned letter sent in response for further information to ascertain the validity of such demands and request for the sender to follow proper protocols.

12. A Form is model or skeleton of an Instrument prescribed by the present sacred Covenant to be used in a judicial proceeding, containing the principal necessary matters, the proper technical terms or phrases and whatever else is necessary to make it formally correct, arranged in proper and methodical order and capable of being adapted to the circumstances of the specific case.

Form

13. All Forms of the Universal Ecclesia of One Christ are either prescribed within the present sacred Covenant or by approved and prescribed Rules of one or more entities, associations, orders or organs as defined by the present sacred Covenant.

Form Prescribed by the Universal Ecclesia

Article 48 – Legitimacy and Validity

1. **L**egitimacy possesses three essential criteria: Conformance, Accordance and Authenticity within Ucadian Law and the present sacred Covenant. Hence Legitimate is equivalent to "lawful":-

Legitimacy

   (i) As to the first criteria, an Act cannot be legitimate or lawful if it contradicts the fundamental principles and established and accepted rules and maxims of law, as expressed within the present sacred Covenant; and

   (ii) As to the second criteria, an Act cannot be legitimate or lawful if it contradicts the established legal forms and requirements in accord with the present sacred Covenant; and

   (iii) As to the third criteria, an Act cannot be legitimate or lawful if its authenticity cannot be proven, in accord with these present Articles.

2. For the purpose of any Dispute, or Argument, or Litigation, **"Legitimacy"** is by definition a claim that is in accord with the norms of law such as the Golden Rule of Law, the present Articles and established forms of Rights and Due Process. A claim or argument that is fraudulent, or vexatious, or malicious, or in bad faith or unclean hands can never be considered Legitimate, no matter what legal argument is claimed. In the absence of Legitimacy, these present Articles always take precedence.

Ratification of Covenant as Legitimate

3. Validity is when a claim of Truth or Fact is strongly asserted against any counter arguments through some formal Process of Argument; and thus by Trial of Logic and Reason is proven to be trusted.

Validity

4. For the purpose of any Dispute, or Argument, or Litigation, **"Validity"** is by definition a claim that may be strongly asserted using Logic and

Ratification of Covenant as

Reason against any counter arguments; and thus may be concluded and trusted as more than likely to be true. A claim or argument that is illogical or unreasonable can never be properly considered Valid. In the absence of Validity, the present sacred Covenant always take precedence.

Validity

TITLE III - MEMBERS

Article 49 – Member

1. A Member of the Universal Ecclesia of One Christ, indelibly marked through the sacred qualities and character of the thirty-three (33) Supreme Sacraments of Heaven, as a vital and integral part of the function of the Body of Christ. Members are further denoted by their Status, Character and Personality.

Member

2. A Member of the Body of Christ is properly recognised whether their Status is physically living or physically deceased. However, the rights, obligations, privileges and powers of a Member are distinct and unique according to such Status.

Member Status

   Therefore, a Deceased Member retains their Member Number and Name; and all the dignities afforded to them as an equal and honoured member of One Heaven. However, a Deceased Member can never acquire the Character or attributes of a Company, or Institute, or Society or State.

   Furthermore, as all Deceased Members must be forgiven their debts and obligations in accord with Divine Will, no transactions or charges or actions are permitted to be added to their Accounts, as all Accounts must be settled and closed within two years of physical death.

3. All physically deceased Members may be denoted by one of only three (3) Characters being Honoured, Blessed or Venerated:-

Deceased Member Character

   (i) **"Honoured (Deceased) Members"** are all physically deceased Members that are not further dignified by the formality of either being recognised as Blessed or Venerated. All Deceased Members are Honoured Members as by the Will of the Divine Creator of all Existence and all Heaven and Earth, all physically deceased Members are also *ipso facto* members of Heaven, without qualification or restriction; and

   (ii) **"Blessed (Deceased) Members"** are physically deceased Members that have been recognised as having lived extraordinary lives as exemplaries to living Members; and

   (iii) **"Venerated (Deceased) Members"** are physically deceased Members that are specially recognised as leaders, heroes, martyrs and elders of the Universal Ecclesia in Heaven. A Saint is a Venerated Member.

4. A Living Member may be distinguished not only by being an individual, but also by properly constituted associations and aggregates of Living Members, namely Ordinary, Association,

Living Member Character

Institute, Society or State:-

(i)   An "**Ordinary (Living) Member**" is any living man or woman whose identity is duly validated and registered in the Member Rolls of the Living Body of One Christ in accord with the conditions of the present sacred Covenant. An Ordinary Member possesses the right of one Vote upon the redemption of their Membership Number; and

(ii)   An "**Association (Living) Member**" is any association as a body, entity, aggregate or partnership, duly validated and registered as an Association in the Association Rolls of the Living Body of One Christ, having a definite birth date and a mandated date of death that does not exceed one hundred and twenty-eight (128) years, in accord with the conditions of the present sacred Covenant. An Association Member possesses one Vote, while its own members may be recognised as Ordinary Members upon their proper registration in the Member Rolls of the Universal Ecclesia; and

(iii)   An "**Institute (Living) Member**" is any aggregate or fraternity or order partnership duly validated and registered as an Institute in the Institute Rolls of the Living Body of One Christ, having a definite birth date and a mandated date of death that does not exceed two hundred and sixty (260) years, in accord with the conditions of the present sacred Covenant. An Institute Member possesses one Vote, while its own members may be recognised as Ordinary Members upon their proper registration in the Member Rolls of the Universal Ecclesia; and

(iv)   A "**Society (Living) Member**" is any non-profit, religious, social, body politic or fraternal association duly validated and registered as a Society in the Society Rolls of the Living Body of One Christ, having a definite birth date and a mandated date of death that does not exceed five hundred and forty years (540) years, in accord with the conditions of the present sacred Covenant. A Society Member possesses one Vote, while its own members may be recognised as Ordinary Members upon their proper registration in the Member Rolls of the Universal Ecclesia; and

(v)   A "**State (Living) Member**" is any existing body politic, country, territory or nation properly recognised by International Western-Roman Law as a sovereign body politic, country, territory or nation and duly validated and registered as a State in the State Rolls of the Living Body of One Christ, having a definite birth date and a mandated date of death that does not exceed one thousand (1,000) years, in accord with the conditions of the present sacred Covenant. A State Member duly recognised and accepted assumes the permanent political government and authority of either a University or Province and all subdivisions upon ratification.

Article 50 – Member Rolls

1. In accord with Article 47 (*Member Rolls*) of the most sacred Covenant *Pactum De Singularis Caelum*, the Universal Ecclesia of One Christ is granted the supreme dignity and right to sole and exclusive temporal custody for the most sacred Rolls of Members of Heaven.

   Custody of Member Rolls of One Heaven

   Therefore, what is recorded in Heaven shall be reflected upon the Earth; and what is recorded upon the Earth shall be reflected and honoured in Heaven; through the according of the highest dignity and obligation to the Universal Ecclesia of One Christ as custodians of the temporal records of the Member Rolls of One Heaven.

2. The Universal Ecclesia of One Christ shall keep a Member Roll as a Register of one or more entries of Persons entitled as Members, to participate in the affairs of the Living Body of One Christ according to the present sacred Covenant, subject to the Jurisdiction of the Supreme See.

   Temporal Member Rolls

   Each and every valid Member of the Universal Ecclesia of One Christ shall be entitled to be entered as a valid Record within the Member Roll for the purpose of identifying such entitlements and participation in the affairs of the Living Body of One Christ. Where the name of the Ordinary Member is not clear, a Placeholder name may be used.

Article 51 – Member Registers

1. The supreme dignity and right to sole and exclusive temporal custody for the Great Roll of Divine Persons, also known as the Great Book of Spirits, also known as the Great Book of Life, also known as the Great Record of Space-Day-Time, also known as the Great Register of Divine Rights, also known as the Great Book of Perfect Divine Procedure, also known as the Great Book of Divine Law has been permanently and irrevocable delegated to the Living Body of One Christ, in accord with Article 107 (*Great Register and Divine Records of Heaven*) of the most sacred

   Public Record and Great Register of Heaven

Covenant *Pactum De Singularis Caelum.*

Therefore, by the power and authority of this sacred Covenant, a Juridic Person or Instrument not entered into the Great Register and Ecclesiastical Records of the Universal Ecclesia of One Christ, or a lesser associated Register has no existence.

A claimed Juridic Person or instrument that is unable to demonstrate a legitimate Unique Ledger Number issued by the Universal Ecclesia of One Christ is devoid of legitimate legal existence and possesses no rights whatsoever, nor any legal standing whatsoever, by any means.

Neither the age of an instrument, its veneration as the highest or most sacred object, nor established legal precedence, shall stand against the power and authority of the law of the Great Register and Ecclesiastical Records of the Living Body of One Christ.

Article 52 – Member Vital Records

1. **V**ital Records are those Records of life events of Members, kept, held and managed under the full Authority and Powers of the Universal Ecclesia of One Christ, including but not limited to: Birth Certificates, Marriage Certificates and Death Certificates. The Universal Ecclesia is tasked and mandated with the safekeeping of such Vital Records.

   Member Vital Records

   The Original Copy of all Vital Records are always kept by the Universal Ecclesia of One Christ and can never be published, printed, transmitted, transferred, conveyed, surrendered, disclaimed, gifted, granted or registered to a non-Ucadian body, foreign power or third party. However, the limited use of such information, rights and intellectual property contained within such Vital Records may be granted under strict conditions to State Members and Society Members that such information is used for the betterment of Ordinary Members in accord with the Rule of Law, Justice and Due Process.

2. By virtue of the Divine Authority of the Universal Ecclesia of One Christ, the Vital Records of the Universal Ecclesia are the first, highest and original Records of such life events, with any and all other records by any and all other lesser and foreign bodies, being inferior and subordinate records, regardless of the alleged time of creation of such records.

   Vital Records of Universal Ecclesia the first, highest and original

   In accord with the most sacred covenant *Pactum De Singularis Caelum*, all life events as defined as Vital Records are duly recorded within the *Great Register* of One Heaven at the time such events occur, even if no record of such fact within the temporal realm exists.

By virtue of the Divine Mandate of Heaven granted to the Universal Ecclesia of One Christ, the Supreme See possesses a sacred and solemn obligation to ensure that those things bound and recorded in Heaven are properly recorded on Earth. Therefore, the proper, lawful and legal Space-Day-Time of recording and registering all life events as Vital Records is precisely the same day and time and place of the event, regardless of the day or time the record is subsequently entered.

3. Wherever and whenever a conflict arises between a claimed vital record, or derivative record of a foreign power, or non-Ucadian entity and the Vital Records of the Universal Ecclesia of One Christ, the Vital Records of the Universal Ecclesia as the original, first, and highest Records of all such life events, shall always take precedence.

Vital Records of Universal Ecclesia take precedence

4. A lesser or foreign power, duly notified, shall be obliged to accept the superior standing of Vital Records and to make such corrections in their own records that may be in error and to submit itself to the superior standing of the Universal Ecclesia of One Christ and shall be granted the limited right of use of such names and information, providing such use is for the common good of the people and does not contravene any of the Articles of the present sacred Covenant.

Obligation to correct errors

5. A lesser or foreign power that refuses to acknowledge the superior standing of Vital Records; and refuses to submit to the superior standing and authority of the Universal Ecclesia of One Christ, shall therefore acknowledge by such perfidy, dishonour, profanity, sacrilege and heresy the full spiritual, ecclesiastical, moral, financial, lawful and legal consequences of their actions as a formal and binding declaration of confession. By such a Declaration of Confession, each and every responsible minister and executive of the government of the Foreign Power shall be named and every administrator responsible shall be named jointly and severally. The Universal Ecclesia of One Christ shall then be solemnly bound to fulfil and pursue as a Holy Writ by every means in Heaven and upon the Earth, resulting in the full execution of such a Declaration of Confession against such members of the Foreign Power.

Declaration of Confession by lesser or foreign power

Article 53 – Member Rights

1. **All Members of One Heaven and Ucadia** possess and are entitled to certain peremptory, permanent, eternal, immutable and indefeasible rights; as well as the privilege to possess certain conditional rights of authority and powers, associated with obligations and duties of various sacred offices.

Rights of Members

2. In accord with Article 40 (*Natural Rights*) of the most sacred

Natural Rights

235

Covenant *Pactum De Singularis Caelum*, all Natural Rights of True (Natural) Persons are delegated to the safe custody and wise guardian powers of the Oratorium, also known as the Supreme Court of One Heaven; and all valid and legitimate lesser competent forums of law, as defined by Article 59 (*Oratorium*) of the most sacred Covenant *Pactum De Singularis Caelum*.

By definition, a Member seeking to assert or defend a claim of a Natural Right must first do so in their capacity as a True (Natural) Person and not as a Member; and secondly must have sufficient standing and cause to proceed through the competent forums of One Christ to assert or defend a claim of a Natural Right.

A Member seeking to invoke a Natural Right in their capacity as a Member automatically invalidates any such claim or argument.

of Members

3. All Rights of Members of One Spirit are by default Superior Rights in accord with Article 41 (*Superior Rights*) of the most sacred Covenant *Pactum De Singularis Caelum*.

Superior Rights of Members

"Member Rights" (*Iurium Membrum*) are the sixth sub-class of Superior Rights and the fifth highest possible rights of any aggregate body, society, fraternity, association or company of two (2) or more persons personified in trust.

There exists three (3) categories of thirty-nine (39) Superior Rights within the sub-class of Member Rights, being: Authoritative (11), Legal (22) and Special (6):-

(i) **"Authoritative Member Rights"** (*Potentis Membrum Iurium*) are Member Rights associated with the essential authoritative powers of members of any valid society; and

(ii) **"Legal Member Rights"** (*Legitimus Membrum Iurium*) are Member Rights essential to the proper administration of justice of any valid society; and

(iii) **"Special Member Rights"** (*Proprius Membrum Iurium*) are Critical Member Rights in relation to the majority (two-thirds) of all members as "the people", essential to democracy and the restoration of the Golden Rule of Law in the event of corruption, collapse of justice or the rise of tyranny.

Article 54 – Member Obligations

1. The provision of services, support, technology, applications, forms, property, currency or any other assistance, other than education, emergency health or basic sustenance shall be considered privileges that remain in place so long as a Member continues to perform their agreed Obligations.

   The Universal Ecclesia of One Christ reserves the right to temporarily withdraw one or more services in the event of some conviction, or as some form of punishment in the event of a default and delinquency by a Member.

2. The occupancy of a position of Member of the Universal Ecclesia of One Christ is held in trust and upon the performance of the occupant of such a position acting in accord with the functions and obligations of a Trustee as defined by the present sacred Covenant and associated Laws.

   Therefore, a Member is expected to behave at all times in good faith, good conscience and good character demonstrating the eight standard characteristics of a Trustee as Fiduciary being Integrity, Frugality, Prudence, Humility, Faculty, Competence, Accountability and Capacity.

   The failure of a Member to act or perform in a manner becoming a Trustee and Fiduciary may cause such occupant of such a position to face disciplinary charges in relation to their conduct, or the suspension of certain Conditional Rights or Privileges.

Article 55 – Member Terms and Conditions

1. The Universal Ecclesia of One Christ shall have the right to make and publish as binding to any agreement associated with one or more Services, a Statement of Terms and Conditions for fair use of such Services.

   It shall be a condition of provision of any service by the Universal Ecclesia of One Christ that a related Statement of terms and conditions is included and made available to any user of that service prior to the service being used.

   In the construction of a statement of terms and conditions, the following criteria shall always apply:-

   (i)   Nothing in a statement of Terms and Conditions may contradict one or more Articles of the present sacred Covenant or the most sacred Covenant *Pactum De Singularis Caelum*; and

(ii) The articles of the present sacred Covenant shall always take precedence over any statement of Terms and Conditions and nothing written or implied in a statement of terms and conditions shall change this fact; and

(iii) A statement of Terms and Conditions may include such clauses not explicitly stated within the present sacred Covenant provided such clauses are consistent with the intention of the present sacred Covenant and a related statement from the Supreme Executive exists ratifying such clauses as a legitimate regulation; and

(iv) All statements of Terms and Conditions must be lodged and approved by vote at the appropriate level of the organisation prior to use with a record kept.

Article 56 – Member Goods and Services

1. **T**he primary services dedicated to Members are those directed at their spiritual well-being. However, as a Religious and Charitable Body, the Universal Ecclesia of One Christ commits itself to good works and acts of charity in support of the temporal well being of Members. These particular services are called "Member Support Services".

   Member Goods and Services

   As a Supreme Religious and Charitable Body dedicated to charitable and religious works for the benefit of individuals and the community, it shall be an objective of the Universal Ecclesia of One Christ to provide as many services that can be reasonably and effectively provided, without undue additional charge, cost, or interest to the Members and the public at large.

Article 57 – Ordinary Member

1. **A**n Ordinary Member is any living higher order being whose identity is duly registered in the Member Rolls of the Universal Ecclesia of One Christ. An Ordinary Member possesses the right of one Vote upon the redemption of their Membership Number.

   Ordinary Member

   In accordance with Article 46 (*Members*) of the most sacred Covenant known as *Pactum De Singularis Caelum* also known as the Covenant of One Heaven, all living men and women are perpetual members of One Heaven and therefore those that are domiciled within the bounds of the Supreme See are *ipso facto* Ordinary Members of the Living Body of One Christ as reflected in the Member Roll of the Universal Ecclesia of One Christ.

2. Ordinary Members are incorporated with the Living Body of One Christ by two means: The Nature and Circumstance of Birth and secondly by the imprint and character of the most sacred Sacrament of Baptism, bestowed upon those not naturally borne into the Living Body of Christ:-

   Ordinary Members and the Living Body of One Christ

   (i) When a child is borne within the bounds of a professed and Sacred Christian or Jewish community, such a community is properly declared Sacred Circumscribed Space and those that service in medical and health and legal capacity as being capable to dispense certain key Sacraments as a function of community significance, such as the delivery of a new born baby. Therefore, the fact of a birth within a Sacred Circumscribed Space of One Christ is absolute proof recording of an Ordinary Member within the *Great Register* and Public Record of Heaven, held in temporal custody by the Universal Ecclesia of One Christ; and

   (ii) When a person not born within the bounds of a professed and Sacred Christian or Jewish community and not yet Baptised, chooses of their own volition to confirm their intention and will to be incorporated into the Living Body of One Christ, then the most sacred sacrament is both the confirmation and the act of incorporation.

3. An Ordinary Member may demonstrate their consent to being acknowledged as an Ordinary Member of the Universal Ecclesia of One Christ, through the Act of Redemption by redeeming and registering their Membership Number. Only Ordinary Members duly recorded as having redeemed their Membership Numbers may participate in voting within the Universal Ecclesia and in the use of certain services and benefits of the Universal Ecclesia.

   Redeemed Ordinary Member

4. Any man or woman domiciled within the bounds of the Universal Ecclesia of One Christ, whether or not they have previously redeemed their Member Number may at any point abjure, reject and revoke their Ordinary Membership.

   Abrogation or Revocation of Member

   When a man or woman, having demonstrated clearly their will and intent, without disability or incapacity to make such a decision, chooses to abjure, reject and revoke their Ordinary Membership, they become an exile and outcast to the Universal Ecclesia of One Christ and to all Christian and Jewish Societies and may not receive any aid, or support or sustenance or assistance whatsoever, upon their own choice and solemn act.

Furthermore, any and all property or Rights owned, derived, sourced and within the jurisdiction of the Universal Ecclesia of One Christ shall remain wholly within the Living Body of One Christ and such a man or woman who chooses to abjure or revoke their Ordinary Membership shall abjure, disclaim, disavow and revoke by the same act any claim or right to any and all such Property.

5. An Abjurer or Revoker may seek clemency from the Universal Ecclesia of One Christ in requesting reconciliation by only one of two means of Confession being either Remorse or Incompetence:- *Request of reconciliation by Abjurer or Revoker*

    (i)   A **"Confession of Remorse"** is when any Abjurer or Revoker seeking reconciliation and re-entry undertakes such a ceremony to withdraw and remove the blight of their previous abjuration and revocation. However, an Abjurer or Revoker may not receive any previous property otherwise disclaimed, surrendered, disavowed and rejected by their previous action; or

    (ii)   A **"Confession of Incompetence"** is when any Abjurer or Revoker seeking reconciliation and re-entry undertakes such a ceremony to withdraw and remove the blight of their previous abjuration and revocation by admitting such an act be evidence of temporary incompetence. As a result, upon any acceptance of re-entry and reconciliation, such property rights may be restored but temporarily held within the guardianship of the society until a proper determination is made that the Ordinary Member is no longer incapacitated by incompetence.

Article 58 – Association Member

1. **A**n Association is a Living Member as a body, or entity, or aggregate or partnership, duly validated and registered as an Association in the Association Rolls of Universal Ecclesia and incorporated into the Living Body of One Christ. *Association Member*

As a living being, an Association must having a definite birth date and a mandated date of death that does not exceed one hundred and twenty-eight (128) years, in accord with the conditions of the present sacred Covenant.

An Association Member possesses one Vote, while its own members may be recognised as Ordinary Members upon their proper registration in the Member Rolls of the Universal Ecclesia of One

Christ.

2. The character of an Association Member may be defined by five types being Religious, Secular, Devotional, Public or Personal:-

   (i) *Religious* means a Religious Association, living in a legitimately established house under the authority of a superior, duly designated according to the norm of Law; and

   (ii) *Secular* means a Secular Association where its members may live in the world and not be bound to the same house, nor religious robes; and

   (iii) *Devotional* means a Devotional or Charitable Association where its members may be laity that dedicate their lives in service of others; and

   (iv) *Public* means a Public Association where its members seek to serve the public good; and

   (v) *Personal* means a Personal Association where its members seek to serve the benefit of a single household or family or small community.

Characteristics of Association Member

3. An Association registration within the Association Rolls of the Universal Ecclesia of One Christ takes precedence over any and all registrations in inferior rolls, whether or not the date of registration within the Association Rolls of the Universal Ecclesia is at a later Sacred Space-Day-Time than the inferior registration of a lesser or foreign society.

Precedence of Association Member Registration

4. Notwithstanding the information required as part of any application registration, the essential criteria for acceptance of a valid Association Member is Permitted Registration, Unique Lawful Name, Legal Status, Association Borne Date, Association Death Date, Constitution and ByLaws:-

Essential Criteria for acceptance as Association Member

   (i) *Permitted Registration* is that the Founders or Directors are not banned from holding such office or registering an Association and that such an Association is not banned or forbidden from registration; and

   (ii) *Unique Lawful Name* is a valid and unique Association Name that does not infringe upon the rights, trademarks, patents or property of the Universal Ecclesia of One Christ or its organs, nor upon the pre-existing Association Members nor a name which is illegal and forbidden; and

   (iii) *Legal Status* being the clear identification of the type of

Association consistent with Law then reflected within its foundation documents; and

(iv) *Association Borne Date* being the clear date the founders of the Association first met in session and agreed to the founding principles and objects of the Association, as evidenced in its founding documents; and

(v) *Association Death Date* being the clear date of death when the Association shall cease to exist, consistent with the type and Legal Status of the Company in accord with Law; and

(vi) *Constitution* being the founding principles and objects of the Company consistent with Ucadia Law, identifying its Organs and Purposes for existence; and

(vii) *ByLaws* is any ByLaws of the Association consistent with Ucadia Law as permitted by its Constitution. If no ByLaws are provided, then the Codes of the Universal Ecclesia of One Christ shall take first precedence as the default ByLaws.

5. Notwithstanding the Code of Offences of the Universal Ecclesia of One Christ and other Laws, Statutes and Regulations, an Association shall be forbidden from being duly registered if it engages in, or seeks to engage in any of the following objects, activities or practices being Perfidious, Malevolent, Perverse and Repugnant:-

Banned or Forbidden Objects of Association

(i) *Perfidious* means any object, activity or practice which seeks to deliberately and intentionally cause harm to the Living Body of One Christ or any Ucadia Societies, or its laws and systems or to injure, steal, threaten, the property, rights, copyright, trademarks and uses of Ucadia and the Universal Ecclesia and any Ucadian Society; and

(ii) *Malevolent* means any object, activity or practice which seeks to deliberately and intentionally cause physical harm to others, particularly other members, or to promote hate-speech, or hostility, or venomous, or vicious, or vindictive, or vengeful behaviour against others, particularly upon racist, or bigotry based philosophies; and

(iii) *Perverse* means any object, activity or practice which seeks to deliberately and intentionally degrade, corrupt or deliberately obscure the accepted norms and bounds of decent moral behaviour within society, particularly in activities which target the young or vulnerable or seek to develop an unhealthy or negative dependence or negative self-image or addiction for then taking advantage of such artificially constructed dependence or self-image; and

(iv) *Repugnant* means any object, activity or practice which seeks to deliberately and intentionally promote repulsive, disgusting, offensive or averse information or activities in public.

6. The Universal Ecclesia of One Christ shall reserve the right to maintain a list of associations banned and forbidden from seeking registration based upon such entities being ill-suited and contrary in law to be recognised. The entry of such association must be based on justice and fair process, with any and all association having the right to appeal. Furthermore, no ban may be permanent beyond ten years and therefore every ban must be renewed and the basis of such forbiddance reinvestigated as to its efficacy.

Exclusion of Banned and Illegal Corporate Entities

Article 59 – Institute Member

1. An Institute is a **Living Member as a community or fraternity or order** duly validated and registered as an Institute in the Institute Rolls of the Universal Ecclesia and incorporated into the Living Body of One Christ.

Institute Member

As a living being, an Institute must have a definite birth date and a mandated date of death that does not exceed two hundred and sixty (260) years, in accord with the conditions of the present sacred Covenant. An Institute Member possesses one Vote, while its own members may be recognised as Ordinary Members upon their proper registration in the Member Rolls of the Universal Ecclesia.

2. The character of an Institute Member may be defined by five types being Religious, Secular, Fraternal, Educational or Scientific:-

Characteristics of Institute Member

(i) *Religious* means a Religious Institute of two or more communities, each living in a legitimately established house under the authority of a superior, duly designated according to the norm of Law; and

(ii) *Secular* means a Secular Institute where its members may live in the world and not be bound to the same house, nor religious robes; and

(iii) *Fraternal* means a Fraternal Institute where its members may be laity that dedicate their lives in service of others and pledge their loyalty to supporting one another and holding each other to account; and

(iv) *Educational* means an Educational Institution where its members seek to serve the public good through specific education objects and services; and

(v) *Scientific* means a Scientific Institution where its members seek to promote greater human knowledge and understanding, through scientific research, discovery and development.

3. An Institute registration within the Institute Rolls of the Universal Ecclesia of One Christ takes precedence over any and all registrations in inferior rolls, whether or not the date of registration within the Institute Rolls of the Universal Ecclesia is at a later Sacred Space-Day-Time than the inferior registration of a foreign or lesser society.

> Precedence of Institute Member Registration

4. Notwithstanding the information required as part of any application registration, the essential criteria for acceptance of a valid Institute Member is Permitted Registration, Unique Lawful Institute Name, Legal Status, Institute Borne Date, Institute Death Date, Constitution and ByLaws:-

> Essential Criteria for acceptance as Institute Member

(i) *Permitted Registration* is that the Founders or Directors are not banned from holding such office or registering an Institute and that such an Institute is not banned or forbidden from registration; and

(ii) *Unique Lawful Institute Name* is a valid and unique Institute Name that does not infringe upon the rights, trademarks, patents and property of the Universal Ecclesia of One Christ or its valid subsidiaries, nor upon the pre-existing Institute Members, nor a name which is illegal and forbidden; and

(iii) *Legal Status* being the clear identification of the type of Institute consistent with Ucadian Law then reflected within its foundation documents; and

(iv) *Institute Borne Date* being the clear date the founders of the Institute first met in session and agreed to the founding principles and objects of the Institute, as evidenced in its founding documents; and

(v) *Institute Death Date* being the clear date of death at which the Institute shall cease to exist, consistent with the type and Legal Status of the Institute in accord with Ucadian law; and

(vi) *Constitution* being the founding principles and objects of the Institute consistent with Ucadia Law, identifying its Organs and Purposes for existence; and

(vii) *ByLaws* is any ByLaws of the Institute consistent with Ucadia Law as permitted by its Constitution. If no ByLaws are provided, then the Codes of the Universal Ecclesia of One Christ shall take first precedence as the default ByLaws.

5. The Rights of Institute Members are those Rights of Use granted to valid registered Institute Members as defined by the present sacred Covenant including (but not limited to) Laws, Jurisdiction, Participation, Representation, Services and Finance:-

Rights of
Institute
Members

(i) *Laws* means an Institute Member is granted the right to use and apply the laws and systems of Ucadia in the governance of its own Members in accord with the conditions of such use as prescribed by the present sacred Covenant; and

(ii) *Jurisdiction* means an Institute Member is able to seek the benefit of the Jurisdiction and superior position of Ucadia societies and Ucadia law in comparison to inferior systems and those structures without proper Rule of Law; and

(iii) *Participation* means an Institute Member may participate in the voting and open, equal and fair process of seeking consent, direction, voting and governance of the Universal Ecclesia of One Christ; and

(iv) *Representation* means the elected leaders of an Institute Member, being granted status as Ordinary Members may participate in elections, even in the registration of political parties for representation in official capacity within the electoral framework of the Universal Ecclesia of One Christ; and

(v) *Services* means an Institute Member may utilise and enjoy those services provided to Institute Members and Members at large; and

(vi) *Finance* means an Institute Member may participate in the Ucadia Financial System, including (but not limited to) financial assistance and support to enable the Institute to achieve its objects and the objects of its members.

6. Notwithstanding the Criminal Code of the Universal Ecclesia of One Christ and other Laws, Statutes and Regulations, an Institute shall be forbidden from being duly registered if it engages in, or seeks to engage in any of the following objects, activities or practices being Perfidious, Malevolent, Perverse, Repugnant or Recalcitrant:-

Banned or
Forbidden
Objects of
Institute

(i) *Perfidious* means any object, activity or practice which seeks to

245

deliberately and intentionally cause harm to Ucadia, the Universal Ecclesia of One Christ or any Ucadia Societies, or its laws and systems or to injure, steal, threaten, the property, rights, copyright, trademarks and uses of Ucadia and the Universal Ecclesia and any Ucadian Institute; and

(ii) *Malevolent* means any object, activity or practice which seeks to deliberately and intentionally cause physical harm to others, particularly other members, or to promote hate-speech, or hostility, or venomous, or vicious, or vindictive, or vengeful behaviour against others, particularly upon racist, or bigotry based philosophies; and

(iii) *Perverse* means any object, activity or practice which seeks to deliberately and intentionally degrade, corrupt or deliberately obscure the accepted norms and bounds of decent moral behaviour within Institute, particularly in activities which target the young or vulnerable or seek to develop an unhealthy or negative dependence or negative self-image or addiction for then taking advantage of such artificially constructed dependence or self-image; and

(iv) *Repugnant* means any object, activity or practice which seeks to deliberately and intentionally promote repulsive, disgusting, offensive or averse information or activities in public; and

(v) *Recalcitrant* means any object, activity or practice which seeks to deliberately obstruct, delay, impede and defeat the principle obligations of Institute Membership (such as the provision of member details for dual membership or other reporting information prescribed by law) with legal or just cause.

7. No Institute Member once accepted as a full member of the Universal Ecclesia of One Christ shall be permitted to be expelled or excluded from the Universal Ecclesia, even when the leaders of the Institute openly defy the primary of clauses of the present Sacred Covenant, unless they are seen to actively participate in banned and forbidden objects, activities and purposes without recourse.

Institute Member Exclusion

Instead, the Supreme See shall have such rights and powers to restrict the membership rights and economic rights bestowed under the present Covenant until such time that the Institute who is in breach of its obligations has willingly agreed to restore proper law and function.

This clause is in recognition of the inherent respect and honour bestowed to all the peoples of the Universal Ecclesia of One Christ that while they may be sometimes ill-governed, it must never be an action of the Universal Ecclesia to exclude any member from their due rights to be recognised as part of the Universal Ecclesia.

Furthermore, in knowing that an Institute may in no way have its membership revoked by the present sacred Covenant, it compels both the Supreme See and the Institute in breach to seek some resolution beyond acts of extreme isolation and provocation.

Article 60 – Society Member

1. **A** **Society is a Living Member as a community or society or body politic**, duly validated and registered as a Society in the Society Rolls of the Universal Ecclesia and incorporated into the Living Body of One Christ.

   Society Member

   As a living being, a Society must have a definite birth date and a mandated date of death that does not exceed five hundred and forty years (540) years, in accord with the conditions of the present sacred Covenant.

   A Society Member possesses one Vote, while its own members may be recognised as Ordinary Members upon their proper registration in the Member Rolls of the Universal Ecclesia of One Christ.

   A Society Member is distinct from a State Member in that a Society is a recognised body wholly functioning within the bounds and laws of Ucadia and the present sacred Covenant.

2. The character of a Society Member may be defined by five types being *Traditional, Special, Indigenous, Monarchial or Political*:-

   Characteristics of Society Member

   (i) *Traditional* means a Traditional Religious Society, bound by a common and recognised Customary and Traditional Rite in accord with the present sacred Covenant; and

   (ii) *Special* means a Special Religious or Secular Society, defined and granted certain exclusive or unique rights and powers, honoured and recognised as having merit under the present sacred Covenant; and

   (iii) *Indigenous* means an Indigenous Society, defined by heritage, tradition and native custom consistent with *Authenticus Depositum Fidei*; and

   (iv) *Monarchial* means a Monarchial Society, defined by its tradition of honourable service of monarchs and royalty as leaders and protectors of a people; and

247

(v) *Political* means a Political Society, defined by its political constitution and unity.

3. A Society registration within the Society Rolls of the Universal Ecclesia of One Christ takes precedence over any and all registrations in inferior rolls, whether or not the date of registration within the Society Rolls of the Universal Ecclesia is at a later Sacred Space-Day-Time than the inferior registration of a foreign or lesser society.

Precedence of Society Member Registration

4. The Rights of Society Members are those Rights of Use granted to valid registered Society Members as defined by the present sacred Covenant including (but not limited to) Laws, Jurisdiction, Participation, Representation, Services and Finance:-

Rights of Society Members

   (i) *Laws* means a Society Member is granted the right to use and apply the laws and systems of Ucadia in the governance of its own Members in accord with the conditions of such use as prescribed by the present sacred Covenant; and

   (ii) *Jurisdiction* means a Society Member is able to seek the benefit of the Jurisdiction and superior position of Ucadia societies and Ucadia law in comparison to inferior systems and those structures without proper Rule of Law; and

   (iii) *Participation* means a Society Member may participate in the voting and open, equal and fair process of seeking consent, direction, voting and governance of the Universal Ecclesia of One Christ; and

   (iv) *Representation* means the elected leaders of a Society Member, being granted status as Ordinary Members may participate in elections, even in the registration of political parties for representation in official capacity within the electoral framework of the Universal Ecclesia of One Christ; and

   (v) *Services* means a Society Member may utilise and enjoy those services provided to Society Members and Members at large; and

   (vi) *Finance* means a Society Member may participate in the Ucadia Financial System, including (but not limited to) financial assistance and support to enable the society to achieve its objects and the objects of its members.

5. Notwithstanding the Criminal Code of the Universal Ecclesia of One Christ and other Laws, Statutes and Regulations, a Society shall be forbidden from being duly registered if it engages in, or seeks to engage in any of the following objects, activities or practices being

Banned or Forbidden Objects of Society

Perfidious, Malevolent, Perverse, Repugnant or Recalcitrant:-

(i)   *Perfidious* means any object, activity or practice which seeks to deliberately and intentionally cause harm to Ucadia, the Universal Ecclesia of One Christ or any Ucadia Societies, or its laws and systems or to injure, steal, threaten, the property, rights, copyright, trademarks and uses of Ucadia and the Universal Ecclesia and any Ucadian Society; and

(ii)   *Malevolent* means any object, activity or practice which seeks to deliberately and intentionally cause physical harm to others, particularly other members, or to promote hate-speech, or hostility, or venomous, or vicious, or vindictive, or vengeful behaviour against others, particularly upon racist, or bigotry based philosophies; and

(iii) *Perverse* means any object, activity or practice which seeks to deliberately and intentionally degrade, corrupt or deliberately obscure the accepted norms and bounds of decent moral behaviour within society, particularly in activities which target the young or vulnerable or seek to develop an unhealthy or negative dependence or negative self-image or addiction for then taking advantage of such artificially constructed dependence or self-image; and

(iv)   *Repugnant* means any object, activity or practice which seeks to deliberately and intentionally promote repulsive, disgusting, offensive or averse information or activities in public; and

(v)   *Recalcitrant* means any object, activity or practice which seeks to deliberately obstruct, delay, impede and defeat the principle obligations of Society Membership (such as the provision of member details for dual membership or other reporting information prescribed by law) without legal or just cause.

6.   No Society Member once accepted as a full member of the Universal Ecclesia of One Christ shall be permitted to be expelled or excluded from the Universal Ecclesia, even when the leaders of the Society openly defy the primary of clauses of the present Sacred Covenant, unless they are seen to actively participate in banned and forbidden objects, activities and purposes without recourse. Instead, the Supreme See shall have such rights and powers to restrict the membership rights and economic rights bestowed under the present Covenant until such time that the Society who is in breach of its obligations has willingly agreed to restore proper law and function.

Society Member Exclusion

This clause is in recognition of the inherent respect and honour bestowed to all the peoples of the Universal Ecclesia of One Christ that while they may be sometimes ill-governed, it must never be an action of the Universal Ecclesia to exclude any member from their due rights to be recognised as part of the Universal Ecclesia.

Furthermore, in knowing that an Society may in no way have its membership revoked by the present sacred Covenant, it compels both the Supreme See and the Society in breach to seek some resolution beyond acts of extreme isolation and provocation.

Article 61 – State Member

1. A State is a Living Member as an existing body politic, kingdom, dominion, country, territory or nation properly recognised by International Law as a sovereign body politic, country, territory or nation and duly validated and registered as a State in the State Rolls of the Universal Ecclesia and incorporated into the Living Body of One Christ.

   State Member

   As a living being, a State must have a definite birth date and a mandated date of death that does not exceed one thousand (1,000) years, in accord with the conditions of the present sacred Covenant.

   A State Member duly recognised and accepted assumes the permanent government and authority of either a Ucadia University and all subdivisions or a Ucadia Province and all subdivisions upon ratification.

   A State Member is distinct from a Society Member in that a State is a recognised body functioning primarily according to its own body of laws and customs and secondly within the bounds and laws of the Universal Ecclesia of One Christ and the most sacred Covenant *Pactum De Singularis Caelum* through amity, mutual recognition and treaty. A body not recognised as an existing body politic, country, territory or nation properly recognised by International Law may be registered as a State Member.

2. The Rights of State Members are those Rights of Use granted to valid registered State Members as defined by the present sacred Covenant including (but not limited to) Laws, Jurisdiction, Participation, Representation, Services and Finance:-

   State Member Rights and Privileges

   (i) *Laws* means a State Member is granted the right to use and apply the laws and systems of Ucadia in the governance of its own Members in accord with the conditions of such use as prescribed by the present sacred Covenant; and

(ii) *Jurisdiction* means a State Member is able to seek the benefit of the Jurisdiction and superior position of Ucadia societies and Ucadia law in comparison to inferior systems and those structures without proper Rule of Law; and

(iii) *Participation* means a State Member may participate in the voting and open, equal and fair process of seeking consent, direction, voting and governance of the Universal Ecclesia of One Christ; and

(iv) *Representation* means the elected leaders of a State Member, being granted status as Ordinary Members may be recognised as the leadership of a University or Province with its existing legislative and administrative subdivisions also being recognised as the valid Ucadian subdivisions of Provinces or Campuses respectively; and

(v) *Services* means a State Member may utilise and enjoy those services provided to State Members and Members at large; and

(vi) *Finance* means a State Member may participate in the Ucadia Financial System, including (but not limited to) financial assistance and support to enable the State to achieve its objects and the objects of its members and in particular access to the account established for the permanent Universities and Provinces of the Universal Ecclesia of One Christ.

3. A State registration within the State Rolls of the Universal Ecclesia of One Christ takes precedence over any and all registrations in inferior rolls, registers of foreign or lesser societies, whether or not the date of registration within the State Rolls of the Universal Ecclesia is at a later Sacred Space-Day-Time than the inferior registration of a foreign or lesser body, given the acceptance of a valid State Member is the acceptance of the permanent and valid government of a Ucadia University or Ucadia Province; and where such a state is already recognised as a sovereign and independent state of the same bounds by international law and a probational government is in place for the said Ucadia University or Ucadia Province. **Precedence of State Member Registration**

Where a permanent government for the Ucadia University or Ucadia Province exists, the ratification of the State Member shall see the requirement of elections to coincide with both bodies for their proper alignment as all members become dual members and therefore Ordinary Members of Ucadia.

4. No State Member once accepted as a full member of the Universal Ecclesia of One Christ shall be permitted to be expelled or excluded **State Member Exclusion**

251

from the Universal Ecclesia, even when the leaders of the State openly defy the primary of clauses of the present Sacred Covenant, unless they are seen to actively participate in banned and forbidden objects, activities and purposes without recourse.

Instead, the Supreme See shall have such rights and powers to restrict the membership rights and economic rights bestowed under the present Covenant until such time that the State that is in breach of its obligations has willingly agreed to restore proper law and function.

This clause is in recognition of the inherent respect and honour bestowed to all the peoples of the Universal Ecclesia of One Christ that while they may be sometimes ill-governed, it must never be an action of the Universal Ecclesia to exclude any member from their due rights to be recognised as part of the Universal Ecclesia.

Furthermore, in knowing that a State may in no way have its membership revoked by the present sacred Covenant, it compels both the Supreme See and the Institute in breach to seek some resolution beyond acts of extreme isolation and provocation.

5. While a State Member may not be expelled for any reason, a member state retains the absolute right to voluntarily resign from the Universal Ecclesia of One Christ, providing such action is lawful under its charter, that it is supported by two-thirds of the total eligible voting population, free from political intimidation and voting irregularities.

Separation from the Body of Christ

Where such conditions have been met, the Executive Government and all instrumentalities are instructed to undertake a comprehensive and clear process to disengage that member state from its obligations to the Universal Ecclesia of One Christ as well as withdraw all rights, title, property and privileges of membership according to the will of the free people of the State.

Where such conditions of voluntary resignation have not been met, then by the present sacred Covenant such unilateral acts of a national executive government to resign from the Universal Ecclesia of One Christ shall be considered an illegitimate and illegal act in contravention of the will of the people of the member state. Where such an action occurs, the Executive Government by this clause is obliged to notify the Executive Government of the member state that their request is denied.

TITLE IV - OFFICERS

Article 62 – Officer

1. An Officer is any legitimate and valid occupant or incumbent of an Office, lawfully invested into such an Office and commissioned by a superior power in accord with the most sacred Covenant *Pactum De Singularis Caelum* and the present sacred Covenant.

   As all rights and property are by definition sacred, all clerical and professional obligations and responsibilities in relation to the administration, transference and conveyance of any rights or property must be concluded in trust through a valid Office. All Officers are therefore Trustees and Fiduciaries.

   All valid official positions or "officers" of all legitimate governments of all societies within the jurisdiction of the present sacred Covenant therefore depend on the acknowledgement and recognition of the most sacred Covenant *Pactum De Singularis Caelum* as the highest law as the Covenant is nothing less than the perfect expression of Divine Will from the Divine Creator of all things in the Universe.

   Furthermore, as the very meaning and purpose of the word "authority" is ecclesiastical, all legitimate authority of all officials of all valid governments of all societies on planet Earth depends upon the acknowledgement and recognition that all authority is ultimately derived from the most sacred Covenant *Pactum De Singularis Caelum* as the highest source of authority being the perfect expression of Divine Law of the Divine Creator of all things in the Universe.

2. By definition, a properly invested Officer shall at all times be protected from unreasonable and unfair interference and claims of personal liability during the proper execution of their fiduciary obligations.

   Thus, an Officer should be unencumbered to perform their necessary duties with the highest integrity, consistent with the most sacred Covenant *Pactum De Singularis Caelum* and the present sacred Covenant.

3. While a properly invested Officer shall at all times be protected from unreasonable and unfair interference and claims of personal liability, no Officer may fairly or reasonably claim protection or immunity from investigation or prosecution or discipline in the event of a gross breach of trust and fiduciary capacity, or failure to properly execute and perform their duties.

   Any Officer that falsely and unreasonably claims immunity from investigation or prosecution or discipline in the event of a gross breach of trust and fiduciary capacity, or failure to properly execute and

Officer

Protection from Interference and Personal Liability

No Protection from Breach of Trust and Failure to Perform

253

perform their duties, is culpable of the worst transgression of impiety and a grave injury against Heaven and Earth.

Any juridic person or legislature that permits laws and enforcement of immunity for one or more Officials is also culpable of perfidy, tyranny and impiety, with such morally repugnant laws being null and void from the beginning, having no force or effect whatsoever.

4. An Office shall be declared vacant upon the death, removal or resignation of an Officer:- *Vacancy, Death or Resignation of Office*

    (i)   The death or removal or resignation of an Officer shall not necessarily dissolve an Office; and

    (ii)   If an Office be a Corporation Sole having a perpetual existence, then such an Office shall continue *Sedes Vacante* until a suitable candidate has been vested by sacred Oath and Vow into Office.

5. All Officers have the right to a hearing through Arbitrage of any dispute or controversy concerning their conduct of Office. However, conditions that may lead to the removal or temporary suspension of an Officer from Office includes, but is not limited to:- *Dispute or Controversy*

    (i)   If the Officer is currently facing any serious indictment or matter before any court where there is the possibility of a custodial sentence of two years or more; or

    (ii)   If the Officer is found to have wilfully and deliberately breached one or more of these Articles and after the opportunity to correct has chosen instead, to default to delinquency in their conduct.

6. The Living Body of One Christ reserves to itself its absolute right to investigate, indict, censure and discipline any and all Officials and Persons within the Jurisdiction of the Supreme See and to have such matters heard and resolved within the competent forums of the Universal Ecclesia of One Christ. *Right of Investigation, Indictment, Censure and Penalty*

A lesser or foreign body having received a complaint, or discovered evidence of an alleged breach of trust or failure of performance by one or more Officers of the Universal Ecclesia are duty bound to immediately report such a complaint or alleged offence to a superior Office of the Universal Ecclesia. Upon receipt of such a complaint, the superior Office that received the complaint is then duty bound to transmit the body of the complaint or alleged offence to the Supreme See within seven days.

Article 63 – Trustee

1. **A** Trustee is an Office formed by a valid Oath or Vow to the Terms of Trust to take possession of certain Rights and Property from a Trustor and perform certain Obligations. The manner and character of a Trustee may be described as a position of Trust which is equivalent to the term Fiduciary.

   Trustee

   The origin of the concept of Trustee and the fact that such an Office cannot exist except under sacred Oath and Vow is as old as the origin of civilised society and law itself and has been one of the most constant concepts of law throughout every age and era. It is founded on the most basic principle that a man or woman cannot legitimately possess the rights or property of others, unless they demonstrate the most exemplary and scrupulous character of good faith and good conscience.

   Therefore, any repudiation of these fundamental concepts is the repudiation of the Rule of Law and law itself. In the absence of a valid Oath and Vow, no Office may exist.

2. The Office of Trustee can only exist and be valid if all the following criteria exist:-

   Criteria for Valid Creation of Office of Trustee

   (i) The Trustor has the proper authority to grant, donate, assign or delegate the property for the proposed Trust; and

   (ii) Clear purpose, intent and terms for the proposed Trust exist; and

   (iii) Certainty of subject matter (the property) exists for the proposed Trust to exist; and

   (iv) The candidate for Trustee comes with good faith, good character and good conscience; and

   (v) The candidate for Trustee accepts the position with full knowledge of the terms and obligations; and

   (vi) The candidate makes a formal sacred oath to a higher Divine power upon a sacred object representing the form of law connected to such higher Divine power, before witnesses; and

   (vii) The event of making such a formal sacred oath is memorialised into some document, that itself is signed, sealed and executed.

3. When a person who claims to be a Trustee, but evidence exists of one or more of the following elements, then such a person is an imposter

   When No Office of Trust Exists

255

with no such Office or Trust existing:-

(i) Where a person belongs to a religion, religious rite, society, institute, entity or order that continues to perform any formal or sacred ritual to repudiate Oaths or Vows made in the past or into the future in direct contradiction to the present most sacred Covenant; or

(ii) Where a person belongs to a religion, religious rite, society, institute, entity or order that continues to require the making of one or more Oaths or Vows that are contradictory to the Golden Rule and Rule of Law, Justice and Due Process and the present most sacred Covenant; or

(iii) Where a person belongs to a religion, religious rite, society, institute, entity or order that continues to require the making of one or more Oaths or Vows that results in dishonest, perfidious, tyrannical or impious behaviour and the disregard of good faith, good character and good conscience in direct contradiction to the present most sacred Covenant; or

(iv) Where one or more of the criteria for the valid creation of the Office of Trustee does not exist.

4. No judge, magistrate or justice of the peace as a proper Jurist may adjudicate any matter of law within a competent forum of law or oratory unless they are presently a valid Trustee under Oath and secondly prepared to demonstrate under Oath the exemplary characteristics of a valid Trustee or valid Fiduciary:- *Jurists must act properly as Trustees*

(i) As a valid Oath is required to create and sustain the Office of judge, or magistrate or justice of the peace, the absence of a valid Oath of Office means such a person is the worst kind of imposter and without any legitimacy whatsoever; and

(ii) As any adjudication concerning rights or property requires exemplary character, any judge, magistrate or justice of the peace that is unwilling or refuses to be entrusted under Oath by all parties to perform in good faith, good character and good conscience is not a valid Fiduciary; and

(iii) The disregard to such fundamental principles may be properly construed as a formal and official admission of the absence of any proper Rule of Law, Justice or Due Process.

5. The eight standard characteristics of a Trustee as Fiduciary are Integrity, Frugality, Prudence, Humility, Faculty, Competence, *Standard Characteristics of Trustee*

Accountability and Capacity:-

(i)   *Integrity* is the characteristic of possessing a strict moral or ethical code as exemplified by the trinity of virtue (Good Faith, Good Character and Good Conscience); and

(ii)   *Frugality* is the characteristic of being economical and thrifty in the good use of those resources in one's own possession or custody. The opposite of waste; and

(iii)   *Prudence* is the characteristic of being practical, cautious, discrete, judicious and wise in the management of the affairs of the trust; and

(iv)   *Humility* is the characteristic of being modest, without pretension or loftiness; and

(v)   *Faculty* is the characteristic of possessing skill and ability in order to perform the obligations of trustee; and

(vi)   *Competence* is the characteristic of being fit, proper and qualified to produce and argue reason through knowledge and skill of Law, Logic and Rhetoric; and

(vii)   *Accountability* is the characteristic of being answerable and liable to faithfully render an account for all acts and transactions; and

(viii)   *Capacity* is the characteristic of possessing the legal and moral authority to hold such office, including demonstrating all the previous necessary characteristics.

6.   A valid Trustee may be responsible for some or all of the following thirty-three (33) Administrative Elements of Trust being *Rules, Standards, Forms, Procedures, Instruments, Transactions, Notices, Books, Registers, Rolls, Claims, Vouchers, Sureties, Assets, Liabilities, Credits, Debits, Accounts, Records, Manifests, Inventories, Memoranda, Journals, Ledgers, Summaries, Certificates, Audits, Transfers, Conveyances, Computations, Valuations, Derivations* and *Hypothecations*:-

Elements of Responsibility of Trustee

(i)   *Rules* are the ordinances, regulations or by-laws of the Trust as defined by its constituting Instrument; and

(ii)   *Standards* are the principles, means and measures of excellence used to compared the results of all activities and administrative duties; and

(iii)   *Forms* are the model of certain Instruments prescribed by law

257

or the constituting Instrument of the valid Trust, Estate or Fund and the manner by which they must be correctly completed, the method of their use and the matters to which they may apply; and

(iv) *Procedures* are ways and methods of performance of obligations and administrative duties, usually in association with one or more Forms; and

(v) *Instruments* are the legally formed documents received and issued by the Trust and held in Chancery; and

(vi) *Transactions* are all the communications, deals, exchanges, transfers, conveyances and proceedings of the Trust; and

(vii) *Notices* are both Instruments and service of process by which one or more Parties are made aware of any formal legal matter that may affect certain rights, obligations and duties; and

(viii) *Books* are traditionally stitched spine bound books used to create Registers, Accounts, Inventories, Memoranda, Journals and Ledgers; and

(ix) *Registers* are tables of one or more records of the receiving or granting or claiming of rights, privileges or property of a valid Trust or Estate or Fund in relation to one or more persons; and

(x) *Rolls* are types of tables and Register of one or more records being "legal persons" of the same condition or entered in the same engagement of obligations in relation to a valid Trust or Estate or Fund and created by their valid entry into the Roll; and

(xi) *Claims* are the oral or written assertion of a valid Right against another party regarding the possession or ownership of some property or thing withheld from the possession of the claimant; and

(xii) *Vouchers* are written or printed Instruments such as a note, or receipt, or bill of particulars, or acquittance, or release which shows on what account or by what authority a payment has been made and serving as evidence of payment or discharge of a debit, or to certify the correctness of accounts; and

(xiii) *Sureties* are written promises to pay or perform as a guarantee and therefore security against some other obligation or liability; and

(xiv) *Assets* are Valuations entered into the Accounts of a Trust, or

Estate, or Fund calculated at the time of an Inventory or by a special Valuation for each and every valid Record of Rights, Property and Title within the control of the Trust, or Estate, or Fund; and

(xv) *Liabilities* are Valuations entered into the Accounts of a Trust, or Estate, or Fund calculated at the time of an Inventory or by a special Valuation for each and every valid Record of an Obligation or Debit or within the performance and responsibility of the Trust, or Estate, or Fund; and

(xvi) *Credits* are Accounting computations of the addition of numbers to a particular type of Account within a Ledger associated with the posting of Journal entries and general practices of Accounting; and

(xvii) *Debits* are accounting computations of the deductions of numbers to a particular type of Account within a Ledger associated with the posting of Journal entries and general practices of Accounting; and

(xviii) *Accounts* are tabulations and summary arrangements of computations, valuations and derivations on the nature, value and disposition of objects, concepts and property of a valid Trust or Estate or Fund; and

(xix) *Records* are entries into Memoranda, Registers or Rolls; and

(xx) *Manifests* are evidential history of the provenance, possession and ownership of any property, rights, money and other interests now recorded as associated with the Trust or Estate or Fund; and

(xxi) *Inventories* are being a detailed survey of all property, assets and liabilities, debits or credits of a valid Trust, or Estate or Fund completed immediately after its creation and thereafter at an appointed day; and the stock of particular items and their location or business; and

(xxii) *Memoranda* are the Books of details of Records of all transactions associated with the Trust or Estate or Fund, including minutes, resolutions, letters, correspondence, decisions and procedural actions recorded in day and time order; and

(xxiii) *Journals* are Books derived as summary extracts of information from Memoranda and arranged in category order and then day/time order to produce a summary of facts, evidence, quantities and relations for the purpose of accounting and reckoning of the debits and credits of the Trust or Estate or Fund; and

(xxiv) *Ledgers* being Books that summarise information extracted from Journal entries to produce the most concise reckonings and balances of debits and credits, assets and liabilities of the Trust or Estate or Fund; and

(xxv) *Summaries* are extracts of a Ledger Balance or Simple Balance of Assets and Debits, or Concessions and Remittances or other elements to provide statements, reports or disclosures required in the operation of the Trust or Estate or Fund; and

(xxvi) *Certificates* are official, authorised and acknowledged extracts of Records of the Trust; and

(xxvii) *Audits* are annual surveys of the administrative elements of a Trust to determine if the Rules and Standards have been properly met; and

(xxviii)*Transfers* are the passing of possession and holding of certain rights, titles or objects of property; and

(xxix) *Conveyances* are the passing of ownership of certain rights, titles or objects of property; and

(xxx) *Computations* are the summarising, calculation and reckoning of arithmetic numbers and values associated with the Trust and Trust property; and

(xxxi) *Valuations* are estimations using some standard unit of measure and account, of the value or worth of an object or concept as property; and

(xxxii) *Derivations* are forms derived from another and possessing a value depending upon the underlying asset from which it was derived; and

(xxxiii) *Hypothecations* are pledges of an underlying asset associated with some Derivation of value as further surety to the Derivation, without delivering temporary possession or ownership of the pledged asset.

7. A valid Trustee may be appointed under the circumstances of Foundation, Death, Abandonment, Resignation, Refusal or Contestation:-   *Appointment of Trustee*

    (i) Foundation is when a new Trust is formed and a Trustee is appointed in accordance with the Instrument or Covenant for the first time; and

(ii) Death is when an existing Trustee dies and a vacancy is declared; and

(iii) Abandonment is when an existing Trustee is away from the domicile of the Trust for more than two years without word or adequate response and so a surrogate Trustee must be appointed; and

(iv) Resignation is when an existing Trustee applies for resignation of duties of Office, creating a Vacancy; and

(v) Refusal is when an existing Trustee refuses to act in the manner and characteristics required of such Office; and

(vi) Contestation is when the competency or legitimacy of a Trustee is challenged and upheld by a competent forum of Law before three Trustees, requiring the resignation of the Trustee.

8. A person is forbidden to act directly as Trustee in their own affairs and property or the affairs, property and estates of others under the following conditions:- *Forbiddance of appointment of Trustee*

(i) When the Trustee is presently a Newborn (under the age of 2); or

(ii) When the Trustee is presently a Child (under the age of 13); or

(iii) When a Trustee is presently a Youth (under the age of 21); or

(iv) When a person has been found culpable in accord with the present Canons and Rule of Law to be ethically and morally unfit to act in the capacity of a Trustee; or

(v) When a person has been found mentally incompetent and mentally incapable in accord with the present sacred Covenant to act in the capacity of a Trustee.

Article 64 – Fiduciary

1. Fiduciary be a person holding the character of a valid Trustee and the scrupulous good faith and honesty required for such Office. Thus, the term Fiduciary is equivalent to Trustee. *Fiduciary*

2. While the term Trustee typically denotes the position and powers established in Trust, the term Fiduciary by tradition emphasises the *Qualities of Fiduciary*

three essential criteria necessary in the capacity and character of a proper Fiduciary being good faith (*bona fides*), good character (*bona virtutes*) and good conscience (*bona conscientia*):-

(i)   *Good Faith*, also known as *bona fides* is the ancient custom that a man cannot be a Fiduciary except under proper Oath or Vow to a recognised Divinity upon some object or text representing a firm belief in the efficacy of some sacred and ethical standards of law existing in the same name as the Divinity; and

(ii)   *Good Character*, also known as *bona virtutes* is the ancient custom that a man cannot act as a Fiduciary except in accord with the highest virtues of honesty, impartiality, frugality and prudence, also sometimes known as "clean hands doctrine"; and

(iii)   *Good Conscience*, also known as *bona conscientia* is the ancient custom that a man or woman cannot act in the best interests of another, or fairly under the Rule of Law if they seek a contrary or negative outcome.

3. **"Fiduciary Capacity"** is when one receives money or contracts a debt or when the business which he transacts, or the money or property which he handles, is not his own or for his own benefit, but for the benefit of another person, as to whom he stands in a relation implying and necessitating the presence of good faith (*bona fides*), good character (*bona virtutes*) and good conscience (*bona conscientia*). Fiduciary Capacity

4. A **"Fiduciary Relation"** is a relation existing between two persons in regard to any implied or actual agreement concerning certain rights, or title or property associated with or derived from an estate whereby each party must therefore act in confidence and trust with the other in accord with good faith (*bona fides*), good character (*bona virtutes*) and good conscience (*bona conscientia*). Fiduciary Relation

Article 65 – Principal

1. **P**rincipal be a person holding the character of a valid **Trustee** and a term describing the powers of a Trustee to be a **Trustor** in delegating, granting or assigning certain Rights to Beneficiaries as Agents. A Principle therefore, is:- Principal

(i)   A type of Trustee that is given the powers by a Trustor through some Trust Instrument to delegate, assign, or grant certain Rights to others as Agents (Beneficiaries); and

(ii)   An Office that may appoint subordinates having certain powers of the same office as an extension of the authority of such Office.

2.   The definition of an Officer in terms of being a Trustee and a Principal may be defined by the Rules of Principal-Agent Relation, namely:-   *Rules of Principal – Agent Relation*

(i)   When a Trust instrument specifically names a person, or a Trustee who by their powers chooses to nominate a person as Beneficiary, this creates the Principal-Agent Relation; and

(ii)   It is only when the Beneficiary accepts the offer of the Benefit does such a Relation become a formal Principal-Agent Relation. Thus, any claim that a Principal can be secret or unknown as morally repugnant, absurd and void in law; and

(iii)   A Principal-Agent Relation does not exist in the case of an unnamed beneficiary. Instead, the relation when an unnamed Beneficiary relation is created is the Trustee as Debtor and the unnamed beneficiary as Creditor; and

(iv)   An Agent is by extension a representative of the Principal and is therefore obligated to perform in accord with the conditions of accepting the Benefit. The moment an Agent breaches their obligations, they become liable for their actions and lose any form of limited liability; and

(v)   As an Agent is an extension of the Office of Principal, a Principal is liable for the actions of his or her Agent(s). Thus Notice of an Agent is Notice to Principal and Notice to Principal is Notice to their Agent(s); and

(vi)   An Agent can never have the capacity or authority to form a sub-agent relation within the original Principal-Agent relation. Any relation formed then by the Agent with a third party must be as a Trustee of some stable right and authority.

Article 66 – Trustor

1.   **Trustor be the generic term for anyone possessing the proper authority to transfer any rights, title or property to another.** The other party upon acceptance of the Fiduciary obligations upon a valid oath and vow then formalises the valid Trust as Trustee. All persons that possess the proper authority to transfer any rights, title or property to another are by default "Trustors".   *Trustor*

263

2. There are only four (4) possible types of Trustor, depending upon the primary nature and intention associated with any conveyance of rights, title or property being Grantor, Donor, Assignor or Delegator:-

(i) A "**Grantor**" is a person who conveys or transfers complete possession and ownership of property for some financial consideration in return under one or more terms and conditions; and

(ii) A "**Donor**" is a person who conveys or transfers complete possession and ownership of property without any financial consideration under one or more terms and conditions; and

(iii) An "**Assignor**" is a person who temporarily conveys or transfers one or more benefits and rights of possession and use of some property for some financial consideration in return under one or more terms and conditions; and

(iv) A "**Delegator**" is a person who temporarily conveys or transfers one or more benefits and rights of possession and use of some property without any financial consideration under one or more terms and conditions.

3. A *Grantor* is a type of Trustor who conveys or transfers complete possession and ownership of property for some financial consideration in return under one or more conditions may be further defined as a Feoffor, Devisor, Testator, Settlor, Obligor, Addressor, Sender, Seller or Purchaser:

(i) A *Feoffor* is a type of Trustor and Grantor that grants any corporeal hereditament to another according to the custom of Fealty and ancient English and Feudal Law; and

(ii) A *Devisor* is a type of Trustor and Grantor (equivalent to a Testator) that grants lands or other property by Will and Testament; and

(iii) A *Testator* is a type of Trustor and Grantor (equivalent to a Devisor) that grants lands or other property to one or more beneficiaries by Will and Testament; and

(iv) A *Settlor* is a type of Trustor and Grantor that grants lands or property in trust for the benefit of one or more successors or filial descendants; and

(v) An *Obligor* is a type of Trustor and Grantor that grants a benefit to another party according to some binding agreement or promise; and

(vi)   An *Addressor* is a type of Trustor and Grantor as the person or organisation who authorises, addresses and grants any formal writing, instrument or notice to be sent or deposited in the mail or delivered for transmission by any other means of communication to an intended recipient or addressee; and

(vii)   A *Sender* is a type of Trustor and Grantor as the person or organisation who grants and delivers certain addressed mail or parcel or goods to an intended Receiver whom may or may not be the final and intended recipient or addressee; and

(viii)   A *Seller* is a type of Trustor and Grantor as one who agrees to grant and transfer the title and possession of an object of property in consideration of the payment or promise of payment of a certain price in money; and

(ix)   A *Purchaser* is a type of Trustor and Grantor as one who grants a certain price of money for the acquisition of title and possession of property.

4.   A *Donor* is a type of Trustor who conveys or transfers complete possession and ownership of property without any financial consideration under one or more terms and conditions may be further defined as a Giftor, Debtor, Guarantor, Indemnitor or Mortgagor:-

    Donor

(i)   A *Giftor* is a type of Trustor and Donor as one who voluntarily conveys and transfers land or goods, gratuitously and not upon any consideration of blood or money; and

(ii)   A *Debtor* is a type of Trustor and Donor as one who gives an unconditional written promise and certain property as surety in trust to repay a fixed sum of money known as the "debt sum" or debt to a Creditor in the event of any default and dishonour by the assured party; and

(iii)   A *Guarantor* is a type of Trustor and Donor as one who gives a promise as surety in trust to be answerable or liable for the repayment of a debt, or the performance of some duty in the event of a default and dishonour by the assured party; and

(iv)   An *Indemnitor* is a type of Trustor and Donor as one who agrees to be bound in trust by an indemnity agreement to insure, or assure or compensate another party in the event of any loss, injury or damage on the part of some third party resulting from some offence, omission or error of official duty or performance; and

(v)   A *Mortgagor* is a type of Trustor and Donor that pledges or surrenders certain property in trust as security for a debt for the benefit of a Mortagee.

5.   An *Assignor* is a type of Trustor who temporarily conveys or transfers one or more benefits and rights of possession and use of some property for some financial consideration in return under one or more terms and conditions may be further defined as a Consignor, Bailor, Depositor, Employer, Insurer, Hirer, Lessor, Lender, Creditor, Licensor, Lienor or Scrivener:-

        Assignor

(i)   A *Consignor* is a type of Trustor and Assignor as one who deposits goods intended to be sold into the custody of a carrier to be transmitted to the designated agent or party as the "consignee"; and

(ii)   A *Bailor* is a type of Trustor and Assignor as one who agrees to deliver goods or personal property in trust to another (Bailee) on the condition that the goods or personal property is redelivered by a certain time or under certain conditions (a process known as a bailment) and a reward paid; and

(iii)   A *Depositor* is a type of Trustor and Assignor as one who agrees to deliver goods or personal property in trust to another on the condition that the goods or personal property are preserved and redelivered by a certain time or under certain conditions (a process known as a bailment) but without reward; and

(iv)   An *Employer* is a type of Trustor and Assignor as the one who agrees to pay a wage or salary to a labourer or servant for possession and ownership of their works; and

(v)   An *Insurer* is a type of Trustor and Assigner who agrees to compensate another for loss on a specific subject by specific perils from an unknown or contingent event; and

(vi)   A *Hirer* is a type of Trustor and Assigner who agrees to temporarily take possession and use of a thing or for labour or services in trust in exchange for the payment of some reward or compensation; and

(vii)   A *Lessor* is a type of Trustor and Assignor who agrees to convey the right to use lands or tenements or other real property to a person for life, or for a term of years or at will under a lease agreement (in two parts being effectively a deed poll executed by the lessor as lease to lessee and a counterpart executed by lessee to lessor) in consideration of a return of rent or some other annual recompense; and

(viii) A *Lender* is a type of Trustor and Assignor as one who agrees to temporarily transfer some thing to another on the condition that the property is redelivered by a certain time or under certain conditions; and

(ix) A *Creditor* as one who agrees to lend a sum of money or goods of equivalent value to a Debtor for the payment of a debt, in exchange for the promissory note of the Debtor and the repayment of the debt in the event of a default by the assured party; and

(x) A *Licensor* is a type of Trustor and Assignor as one who issues a written and properly authorised permit or warrant to another, conferring the right(s) to do some act in relation to certain property held in trust which without such authorisation would be illegal, or considered a trespass or a tort; and

(xi) A *Lienor* is a type of Trustor and Assignor who licenses the temporary right of use, or holding, or seizure, or custody of certain real or personal property in trust, upon the Lienor possessing a claim of right to the temporary ownership or control of the property as security or charge against the performance of a debtor (in other words a Lien); and

(xii) A *Scrivener* is a type of Trustor and Assignor who agrees to create and temporarily assign original forms of instruments including (but not limited to) indulgences, charters, bills, bonds and mortgages for the purpose of lending them out at an interest payable to his principal and for a commission or bonus for himself.

6. A *Delegator* is a type of Trustor who temporarily conveys or transfers one or more benefits and rights of possession and use of some property without any financial consideration in return under one or more terms and conditions may be further defined as an Executor, Commissioner or Administrator:-

    Delegator

(i) An *Executor* is a type of Trustor and Delegator as one who delegates authority and franchise by charter, or deed or letters patent; and

(ii) A *Commissioner* is a type of Trustor and Delegator as one who delegates authority and agency by warrant, or deed or letters of marque; and

(iii) An *Administrator* is a type of Trustor and Delegator as a surrogate Executor, appointed under competent judicial authority as one who delegates authority by order.

7. In accord with the present sacred Covenant and the most sacred Covenant *Pactum De Singularis Caelum* and within the limits of certain Persons, associated Trusts and Rights:-

(i) A Divine Person as a valid Trustor is the only type of Trustor that may transfer Divine Rights; and

(ii) A True Person as a valid Trustor is the only type of Trustor that may transfer Natural Rights, excluding those rights that are Peremptory, Permanent, Immutable and Indefeasible; and

(iii) A Superior Ecclesiastical Person as a valid Trustor is the only type of Trustor that may transfer Ecclesiastical Rights, excluding those rights that are Peremptory, Permanent, Immutable and Indefeasible; and

(iv) A Superior Person or Inferior Person as a valid Trustor is the only type of Trustor that may transfer Positive Rights, excluding those rights that are Peremptory, Permanent, Immutable and Indefeasible.

Article 67 – Candidate

1. **C**andidate be a Person standing or making themselves eligible for Ecclesiastical or Public Office, in accord with the present sacred Covenant.

2. No Candidate may be appointed to an Office unless that Candidate is qualified for the position that they are to occupy in accordance with the present sacred Covenant. One person may hold more than one position as an Officer of the Universal Ecclesia of One Christ, providing such Office allows it.

3. A Member shall be ineligible to be a Candidate to Office:-

(i) If the Member does not qualify to be a Candidate for Office; or

(ii) If the Member refuses or fails to provide the necessary material to assess their suitability and qualifications to be a Candidate; and

(iii) If the Member provides false information, or withholds information to appear eligible as a Candidate; and

(iv) If the Member is currently facing any serious indictment or matter relating to fraud, dishonesty, sexual perversion or violent offences before any competent forum where there is the possibility of a custodial sentence of two years or more; and

(v)   If the Member has been previously convicted by any competent forum of law of a serious sexual offence or violent crime carrying a custodial sentence of two years or more; and

(vi)   If the Member has demonstrated a lack of good faith, or good conscience, or good character toward the integrity of the Universal Ecclesia of One Christ and there is strong likelihood that such behaviour may continue even if appointed or elected to Office.

Article 68 – Election

1.   An Election is a formal system, process and record of choosing and selecting by Vote one or more persons, candidates, things, courses or propositions from a greater number of the same type offered as genuine alternatives. As a valid and true Election is the expression of the individual intention and will of Members, as well as their collective intention and will, a valid and true Election shall always be free, equal, fair, without compulsion, threat, inducement or intimidation.

Election

All Candidates for Office shall be appointed upon an Election, whereby the appropriate Members of a fraternity, or association, or institute, or society, or order, or body express their will through casting a Vote, even if there is only one Candidate. A Candidate that does not receive the necessary votes for a particular Office cannot be installed into such Office.

2.   Where more than one Candidate is eligible to stand for the same Office, an Election Campaign, also known as a General Election may be called. Candidates are then permitted, according to the rules of the relevant body, fraternity, institute, association, society or state to campaign to persuade voters of their suitability to Office.

Election Campaign

3.   All valid registered Candidates must be entitled to receive Funding from a competent Electoral Commission to Fund their Election Campaigns and Election Materials; and all media associated with the Society are required to provide certain time and resources to Candidates to transmit their messages to Voters. The expense of providing individual funding to Candidates is recognised as a necessary and legitimate expense of Elections to protect the electoral process from corruption and external influence.

Election Campaigns always Publicly Funded

Political Donations to Candidates of any kind from any source, directly or indirectly; or in cash or in kind is absolutely forbidden and considered a serious offence, that may also result in the disqualification of one or more Candidates and the de-registration of a Political Party and the seizure of assets and funds.

Article 69 – Oath and Vows

1. **T**he Oath of Office is the particular type of oath a person must willingly make in forming the essential personality of Trustee and Fiduciary before assuming any Office of the Living Body of One Christ and performing any duties therein.

   Oath of Office

   The specific form and order of ceremony of Oaths of Office shall be in accord with the present sacred Covenant and the sacred *Missale Christus* of the Universal Ecclesia of One Christ.

   All Oaths of Office shall take three forms being Simple, Ordinary and Exemplary:-

   (i)   Simple, also known as Standard, is the form of an Oath for all Members pertaining to the particular Office, whether Lay or Religious; and

   (ii)   Ordinary, also known as Holy Orders, is the form of Oath for General Religious Dedication and usually accompanies Holy Vows of Humility, Frugality and Obedience; and

   (iii)   Exemplary, also known as Perfect Orders, is the form of Oath for Special Religious Dedication and usually accompanies Solemn Sacred Vows of Austerity, Chastity and Mercy.

2. All Candidates are expected to make a Simple Oath as part of their qualification and suitability for Office that there be no impediment and that everything that has been disclosed is true and correct.

   Oath of Candidacy

Article 70 – Discipline

1. **A**s the Universal Ecclesia of One Christ holds the absolute Officium of Heaven, the Supreme See holds the absolute Right to coerce, discipline and sanction any and all persons currently or previously holding an Office if found to have grossly breached their obligations, duties or performance.

   Discipline

Article 71 – Advocate

1.   **A**dvocate is a Sacred Office expressly ordained by Heaven for a person of suitable competence, humility, virtue, temperament and character to defend the Golden Rule of Law, Justice and Due Process by ensuring people of all races, ages, gender, status and religious beliefs are given the equal opportunity to be properly supported in matters of law and heard fairly within the appropriate competent forum.

Advocate

The Office of Advocate is one of the fourteen Superior Ecclesiastical Offices of the Four Hundred and Thirty Two (432) Great Offices of One Heaven.

Whenever one references, writes or speaks of a properly qualified, registered and competent attorney, or lawyer, or solicitor, or barrister, or counsel, or legal practitioner of any kind, it shall mean such a person is properly invested as an Advocate in accord with the most sacred Covenant *Pactum De Singularis Caelum* and the present most sacred Covenant and no other.

All Procedures including (but not limited to) the commission, obligations, authority, powers, function, standards, qualifications, honours, dignities, conduct, accountabilities, grades, benefits, legacies, term, investiture, enrolment, certification, review, audit, censure, sanction or cessation of the Office of Advocate shall be defined by the present Covenant and associated rules and covenants.

2.   Consistent with the absolute jurisdiction and authority of the Universal Ecclesia of One Christ as temporal custodian of the Great Register and Public Record of One Heaven, each and every University and Union ecclesiastical, sovereign, political and administrative unit of the Universal Ecclesia of One Christ shall prepare and manage exclusively a Sacred Roll of Advocates, making such records available to local, provincial, state and national civil authorities and competent forums as required, to ensure the validity and qualifications of persons engaged in matters of law.

Sacred Roll of Advocates

No one may claim to be a valid Advocate, unless a proper record exists within the Sacred Roll of Advocates. Therefore, no person who claims to be a properly qualified, registered and competent attorney, or lawyer, or solicitor, or barrister, or counsel, or legal practitioner of any kind may engage in matters of Law, or enter and participate in any competent forum of Law unless a proper record exists within the Sacred Roll of Advocates.

3. A unique Sacred Order of Advocates as a Secular and Laity Order shall be commissioned for each University of the Universal Ecclesia of Christ. The Sacred Order of Advocates shall then be permitted under their adopted rules to open and maintain Chapters at a Provincial Level and Branches at a Campus Level.

Sacred Order of Advocates

4. Upon the formal commissioning of a unique Sacred Order of Advocates for a particular University and then Chapters and Branches, all guilds, associations, fraternities and societies of law professionals must be suppressed and dissolved, with all remaining assets conveyed to the Sacred Order, or distributed to the appropriate civil and political governments of the same regions.

Suppression and Dissolution of Guilds, Associations and Societies of Law Professionals

Thereafter, it shall be reprobate, suppressed and forbidden to permit the formation, creation or reconstitution of law guilds, fraternities, associations or bodies other than the appropriate Sacred Order of Advocates.

5. The Oath of Advocate shall take precedence over any and all other lesser Oaths of fraternity, guild, association, society or body in Law. The effect of the Oath of Advocate shall be to expunge and dissolve any and all oaths, bonds, blood pledges, or obligations previously made, that if were still active would cause a person as an Advocate to breach their solemn Oath to protect the Golden Rule of Law, Justice and Fair Process for all.

Oath of Advocate and lesser Oaths

6. A person who is found to openly promote, support and lobby for the maintenance of any state sanctioned Death Penalty, ceases to be an Advocate upon receiving formal ecclesiastical notice of their transgression and then clear evidence is given of their deliberate and willing refusal to withdraw and recant their transgression against Heaven.

A person ceases to be Advocate if promotes Death Penalty

Article 72 – Jurist

1. **J**urist is a Sacred Office expressly ordained by Heaven for an Advocate of suitable jurisprudence experience, humility, virtue, temperament and character to physically embody the Oratorium and Judicial Plenary Authority of Heaven amongst the community, within competent forums of law. All Oratorium is dispensed from the ultimate temporal authority of the Supreme See and its highest physical embodiment within the most sacred Office of Supreme Patriarch and supported by the Prothonotary-General of Justice and Jurisprudence Systems of the Living Body of One Christ.

Jurist

The Office of Jurist is one of the twelve Original Offices of the Land of the Four Hundred and Thirty Two (432) Great Offices of One Heaven.

Whenever one references, writes or speaks of a properly qualified, registered and competent judge, justice, magistrate, registrar, jurist, proctor, prosecutor or arbitrator of any kind, it shall mean such a person is properly invested as a Jurist in accord with the most sacred Covenant *Pactum De Singularis Caelum* and the present most sacred Covenant and no other.

All Procedures including (but not limited to) the commission, obligations, authority, powers, function, standards, qualifications, honours, dignities, conduct, accountabilities, grades, benefits, legacies, term, investiture, enrolment, certification, review, audit, censure, sanction or cessation of the Office of Jurist shall be defined by the present Covenant and associated rules and covenants.

2. Consistent with the absolute jurisdiction and authority of the Universal Ecclesia of One Christ as temporal custodian of the Great Register and Public Record of One Heaven, each and every University and Union ecclesiastical, sovereign, political and administrative unit of the Universal Ecclesia of One Christ shall prepare and manage exclusively a Sacred Roll of Jurists, making such records available to local, provincial, state and national civil authorities and competent forums as required, to ensure the validity and qualifications of persons engaged as competent judges, or justices, or magistrates, or registrars, or jurists, or proctors, or prosecutors or arbitrators.

   Sacred Roll of Jurists

   No one may claim to be a valid Jurist, unless a proper record exists within the Sacred Roll of Jurists. Therefore, no person who claims to be a competent judge, justice, magistrate, registrar, jurist, proctor, prosecutor or arbitrator of any kind may engage in matters of Law, or enter and participate in any competent forum of Law unless a proper record exists within the Sacred Roll of Jurists.

3. A unique Sacred College of Jurists as a Secular and Laity Order shall be commissioned for each University of the Universal Ecclesia of Christ. The Sacred College of Jurists shall then be permitted under their adopted rules to open and maintain Chapters at a Provincial Level and Branches at a Campus Level.

   Sacred College of Jurists

4. Upon the formal commissioning of a unique Sacred College of Jurists for a particular University and then Chapters and Branches, all guilds, associations, fraternities and societies of judges, justices and magistrates must be suppressed and dissolved, with all remaining assets conveyed to the Sacred Order, or distributed to the appropriate civil and political governments of the same regions.

   Suppression and Dissolution of Guilds, Associations and Societies of Judges and Magistrates

Thereafter, it shall be reprobate, suppressed and forbidden to permit the formation, creation or reconstitution of law guilds, fraternities, associations or bodies other than the appropriate Sacred College of Jurists.

5. The Oath of Jurist shall take precedence over any and all other lesser Oaths of fraternity, guild, association, society or body in Law. The effect of the Oath of Jurist shall be to expunge and dissolve any and all oaths, bonds, blood pledges, or obligations previously made, that if were still active would cause a person as a Jurist to breach their solemn Oath to protect the Golden Rule of Law, Justice and Fair Process for all.

Oath of Jurist and lesser Oaths

6. A person who is found to openly promote, support and lobby for the maintenance of state sanctioned Death Penalty, ceases to be a Jurist upon receiving formal ecclesiastical notice of their transgression and then such deliberate and willing refusal to withdraw and recant their transgression against Heaven.

A person ceases to be Jurist if issues Death Penalty

Therefore, all state sanctioned sentences of the Death Penalty are an abomination, morally repugnant, profane and sacrilegious, with any person acting as an impostor and passing or endorsing such sentence fully and completely liable for their actions by the united forces of Heaven and Earth.

Article 73 – Tutor

1. **T**utor is a Sacred Office expressly ordained by Heaven for a person of suitable competence, humility, virtue, temperament and character to support the learning and teaching needs of the community, within competent teaching and education facilities.

Tutor

The Office of Tutor is one of the One Hundred and Thirty Six (136) Superior Offices of City of the Four Hundred and Thirty Two (432) Great Offices of One Heaven.

Whenever one references, writes or speaks of a properly qualified, registered and competent teacher, tutor, aid or trainer of any kind, it shall mean such a person is properly invested as a Tutor in accord with the most sacred Covenant *Pactum De Singularis Caelum* and the present most sacred Covenant and no other.

All Procedures including (but not limited to) the commission, obligations, authority, powers, function, standards, qualifications, honours, dignities, conduct, accountabilities, grades, benefits, legacies, term, investiture, enrolment, certification, review, audit, censure, sanction or cessation of the Office of Tutor shall be defined by the present Covenant and associated rules and covenants.

2. Consistent with the absolute jurisdiction and authority of the Universal Ecclesia of One Christ as temporal custodian of the Great Register and Public Record of One Heaven, each and every University and Union ecclesiastical, sovereign, political and administrative unit of the Universal Ecclesia of One Christ shall prepare and manage exclusively a Sacred Roll of Tutors, making such records available to local, provincial, state and national civil authorities and competent forums as required, to ensure the validity and qualifications of persons.

    Sacred Roll of Tutors

   No one may claim to be a valid Tutor, unless a proper record exists within the Sacred Roll of Tutors. Therefore, no person who claims to be a properly qualified, registered and competent teacher or tutor or educator of any kind may engage in matters of Education, or enter and participate in any competent education faculty or facility unless a proper record exists within the Sacred Roll of Tutors.

3. A unique Sacred Order of Tutors as a Secular and Laity Order shall be commissioned for each University of the Universal Ecclesia of Christ. The Sacred Order of Tutors shall then be permitted under their adopted rules to open and maintain Chapters at a Provincial Level and Branches at a Campus Level.

    Sacred Order of Tutors

4. Upon the formal commissioning of a unique Sacred Order of Tutors for a particular University and then Chapters and Branches, all guilds, associations, fraternities and societies of educators must be suppressed and dissolved, with all remaining assets conveyed to the Sacred Order, or distributed to the appropriate civil and political governments of the same regions.

    Suppression and Dissolution of Guilds, Associations and Societies of Educators

   Thereafter, it shall be reprobate, suppressed and forbidden to permit the formation, creation or reconstitution of education guilds, fraternities, associations or bodies other than the appropriate Sacred Order of Tutors.

Article 74 – Rector

1. **R**ector is a Sacred Office expressly ordained by Heaven for a Tutor of suitable educational experience, humility, virtue, temperament and character to physically embody the Magisterium and Teaching Authority of Heaven amongst the community, within competent teaching and education facilities. All Magisterium is dispensed from the ultimate temporal authority of the

    Rector

Supreme See and its highest physical embodiment within the most sacred Office of Supreme Patriarch and supported by the Rector-General of Doctrinal and Liturgical Systems and the Assistant-General of Knowledge Standards and Education Systems and the Custodian-General of Sacred Rites and Tradition Systems of the Living Body of One Christ.

The Office of Rector is one of the twelve Master Offices of the See of the Four Hundred and Thirty Two (432) Great Offices of One Heaven.

Whenever one references, writes or speaks of a properly qualified, registered and competent professor, headmaster or rector of any kind, it shall mean such a person is properly invested as a Rector in accord with the most sacred Covenant *Pactum De Singularis Caelum* and the present most sacred Covenant and no other.

All Procedures including (but not limited to) the commission, obligations, authority, powers, function, standards, qualifications, honours, dignities, conduct, accountabilities, grades, benefits, legacies, term, investiture, enrolment, certification, review, audit, censure, sanction or cessation of the Office of Rector shall be defined by the present Covenant and associated rules and covenants.

2. Consistent with the absolute jurisdiction and authority of the Universal Ecclesia of One Christ as temporal custodian of the Great Register and Public Record of One Heaven, each and every University and Union ecclesiastical, sovereign, political and administrative unit of the Universal Ecclesia of One Christ shall prepare and manage exclusively a Sacred Roll of Rectors, making such records available to local, provincial, state and national civil authorities and competent forums as required, to ensure the validity and qualifications of such persons. *Sacred Roll of Rectors*

   No one may claim to be a valid Rector, unless a proper record exists within the Sacred Roll of Rectors. Therefore, no person who claims to be a properly qualified, registered and competent principal, headmaster, leading teacher of any kind may engage in matters of education, or enter and participate in any competent education facility or faculty unless a proper record exists within the Sacred Roll of Rectors.

3. A unique Sacred College of Rectors as a Secular and Laity Order shall be commissioned for each University of the Universal Ecclesia of Christ. The Sacred Order of Rectors shall then be permitted under their adopted rules to open and maintain Chapters at a Provincial Level and Branches at a Campus Level. *Sacred College of Rectors*

4. Upon the formal commissioning of a unique Sacred College of Rectors *Suppression and*

for a particular University and then Chapters and Branches, all guilds, associations, fraternities and societies of law guilds must be suppressed and dissolved, with all remaining assets conveyed to the Sacred Order, or distributed to the appropriate civil and political governments of the same regions.

Dissolution of Guilds, Associations and Societies of leading educators

Thereafter, it shall be reprobate, suppressed and forbidden to permit the formation, creation or reconstitution of law guilds, fraternities, associations or bodies other than the appropriate Sacred College of Rectors.

Article 75 – Therapist

1. **Therapist is a Sacred Office expressly ordained by Heaven** for a person of suitable competence, humility, virtue, temperament and character to support excellence and compassion within competent therapeutic, health, medical, family and well-being facilities of the community.

Therapist

The Office of Therapist is one of the one hundred and two Superior Offices of Community of the Four Hundred and Thirty Two (432) Great Offices of One Heaven.

Whenever one references, writes or speaks of a properly qualified, registered and competent doctor, nurse, medical specialist, pharmacist, chemist, medical practitioner, medical registrar, paramedic or therapist of any kind, it shall mean such a person is properly invested as a Therapist in accord with the most sacred Covenant *Pactum De Singularis Caelum* and the present most sacred Covenant and no other.

All Procedures including (but not limited to) the commission, obligations, authority, powers, function, standards, qualifications, honours, dignities, conduct, accountabilities, grades, benefits, legacies, term, investiture, enrolment, certification, review, audit, censure, sanction or cessation of the Office of Therapist shall be defined by the present Covenant and associated rules and covenants.

2. Consistent with the absolute jurisdiction and authority of the Universal Ecclesia of One Christ as temporal custodian of the Great Register and Public Record of One Heaven, each and every University and Union ecclesiastical, sovereign, political and administrative unit of the Universal Ecclesia of One Christ shall prepare and manage exclusively a Sacred Roll of Therapists, making such records available to local, provincial, state and national civil authorities and competent forums as required, to ensure the validity and qualifications of such persons.

Sacred Roll of Therapists

No one may claim to be a valid Therapist, unless a proper record exists within the Sacred Roll of Therapists. Therefore, no person who claims to be a properly qualified, registered and competent doctor, nurse, medical specialist, pharmacist, chemist, medical practitioner, medical registrar, paramedic or therapist of any kind may engage in competent therapeutic, health, medical, family and well-being facilities of the community unless a proper record exists within the Sacred Roll of Therapists.

3. A unique Sacred Order of Therapists as a Secular and Laity Order shall be commissioned for each University of the Universal Ecclesia of Christ. The Sacred Order of Therapists shall then be permitted under their adopted rules to open and maintain Chapters at a Provincial Level and Branches at a Campus Level.

    Sacred Order of Therapists

4. Upon the formal commissioning of a unique Sacred Order of Therapists for a particular University and then Chapters and Branches, all guilds, associations, fraternities and societies of medical, pharmaceutical, health and therapeutic professionals must be suppressed and dissolved, with all remaining assets conveyed to the Sacred Order, or distributed to the appropriate civil and political governments of the same regions.

    Suppression and Dissolution of Guilds, Associations and Societies of Medical, Health & Therapeutic Professionals

    Thereafter, it shall be reprobate, suppressed and forbidden to permit the formation, creation or reconstitution of any such guilds, fraternities, associations or bodies other than the appropriate Sacred Order of Therapists.

5. A person who is found to openly promote, support and participate in the Abortion of a healthy unborn human being from the beginning of the 2nd trimester of a pregnancy of a healthy mother, ceases to be a Therapist upon receiving formal ecclesiastical notice of their transgression and then their subsequent deliberate and willing refusal to withdraw and recant their transgression against Heaven.

    A person ceases to be Therapist if engaged in Abortion

    Therefore, all deliberate acts of Abortion of a healthy unborn human being from the beginning of the 2nd trimester of a pregnancy of a healthy mother are an abomination, morally repugnant, profane and sacrilegious, with any person acting as an imposter and performing such procedure fully and completely liable to be held to account by the united forces of Heaven and Earth for their actions.

Article 76 – Physician

1. **Physician is a Sacred Office expressly ordained by Heaven** for a Physician of suitable health, therapeutic and medical experience, humility, virtue, temperament and character to physically embody the Sanitatum and Healing, Health and Well-Being Authority of Heaven amongst the community, within competent therapeutic, health, medical, family and well-being facilities. All Sanitatum is dispensed from the ultimate temporal authority of the Supreme See and its highest physical embodiment within the most sacred Office of Supreme Patriarch and supported by the Physician-General of Health and Therapeutic Systems and the Registrar-General of Families and Community Life Systems of the Living Body of One Christ.

   The Office of Physician is one of the one hundred and thirty six Superior Offices of the City of the Four Hundred and Thirty Two (432) Great Offices of One Heaven.

   Whenever one references, writes or speaks of a properly qualified, registered and competent medical specialist, or surgeon of any kind, it shall mean such a person is properly invested as a Physician in accord with the most sacred Covenant *Pactum De Singularis Caelum* and the present most sacred Covenant and no other.

   All Procedures including (but not limited to) the commission, obligations, authority, powers, function, standards, qualifications, honours, dignities, conduct, accountabilities, grades, benefits, legacies, term, investiture, enrolment, certification, review, audit, censure, sanction or cessation of the Office of Physician shall be defined by the present Covenant and associated rules and covenants.

   Physician

2. Consistent with the absolute jurisdiction and authority of the Universal Ecclesia of One Christ as temporal custodian of the Great Register and Public Record of One Heaven, each and every University and Union ecclesiastical, sovereign, political and administrative unit of the Universal Ecclesia of One Christ shall prepare and manage exclusively a Sacred Roll of Physicians, making such records available to local, provincial, state and national civil authorities and competent forums as required, to ensure the validity and qualifications of such persons.

   No one may claim to be a valid Physician, unless a proper record exists within the Sacred Roll of Physicians. Therefore, no person who claims to be a properly qualified, registered and competent doctor, nurse, medical specialist, pharmacist, chemist, medical practitioner, medical

   Sacred Roll of Physicians

registrar, paramedic, physician or therapist of any kind may engage in competent therapeutic, health, medical, family and well-being facilities of the community unless a proper record exists within the Sacred Roll of Physicians.

3. A unique Sacred College of Physicians as a Secular and Laity Order shall be commissioned for each University of the Universal Ecclesia of Christ. The Sacred College of Physicians shall then be permitted under their adopted rules to open and maintain Chapters at a Provincial Level and Branches at a Campus Level.

Sacred College of Physicians

4. Upon the formal commissioning of a unique Sacred College of Physicians for a particular University and then Chapters and Branches, all guilds, associations, fraternities and societies of leading medical specialists, physicians and surgeons must be suppressed and dissolved, with all remaining assets conveyed to the Sacred Order, or distributed to the appropriate civil and political governments of the same regions.

Suppression and Dissolution of Guilds, Associations and Societies of Physicians, Specialists and Medical Leaders

Thereafter, it shall be reprobate, suppressed and forbidden to permit the formation, creation or reconstitution of any such guilds, fraternities, associations or bodies other than the appropriate Sacred College of Physicians.

5. A person who is found to openly promote, support and participate in the Abortion of a healthy unborn human being from the beginning of the 2nd trimester of a pregnancy of a healthy mother, ceases to be a Physician upon receiving formal ecclesiastical notice of their transgression and then their subsequent deliberate and willing refusal to withdraw and recant their transgression against Heaven.

A person ceases to be Physician if engaged in Abortion

Therefore, all deliberate acts of Abortion of a healthy unborn human being from the beginning of the 2nd trimester of a pregnancy of a healthy mother are an abomination, morally repugnant, profane and sacrilegious, with any person acting as an imposter and performing such procedure fully liable to be held to account by the united forces of Heaven and Earth for their actions.

Article 77 – Scientist

1. Scientist is a Sacred Office expressly ordained by Heaven for a person of suitable competence, humility, virtue, temperament and character to support excellence, innovation and discovery within scientific, research and technology development facilities of the community.

Scientist

The Office of Scientist is one of the one hundred and thirty six Superior Offices of the City of the Four Hundred and Thirty Two (432) Great Offices of One Heaven.

Whenever one references, writes or speaks of a properly qualified, registered and competent scientist or scientific researcher of any kind, it shall mean such a person is properly invested as a Scientist in accord with the most sacred Covenant *Pactum De Singularis Caelum* and the present most sacred Covenant and no other.

All Procedures including (but not limited to) the commission, obligations, authority, powers, function, standards, qualifications, honours, dignities, conduct, accountabilities, grades, benefits, legacies, term, investiture, enrolment, certification, review, audit, censure, sanction or cessation of the Office of Scientist shall be defined by the present Covenant and associated rules and covenants.

2. Consistent with the absolute jurisdiction and authority of the Universal Ecclesia of One Christ as temporal custodian of the Great Register and Public Record of One Heaven, each and every University and Union ecclesiastical, sovereign, political and administrative unit of the Universal Ecclesia of One Christ shall prepare and manage exclusively a Sacred Roll of Scientists, making such records available to local, provincial, state and national civil authorities and competent forums as required, to ensure the validity and qualifications of such persons.
Sacred Roll of Scientists

No one may claim to be a valid Scientist, unless a proper record exists within the Sacred Roll of Scientists. Therefore, no person who claims to be a properly qualified, registered and competent scientist or scientific researcher of any kind may engage in scientific, research and technology development facilities of the community unless a proper record exists within the Sacred Roll of Scientists.

3. A unique Sacred Order of Scientists as a Secular and Laity Order shall be commissioned for each University of the Universal Ecclesia of Christ. The Sacred Order of Scientists shall then be permitted under their adopted rules to open and maintain Chapters at a Provincial Level and Branches at a Campus Level.
Sacred Order of Scientists

4. Upon the formal commissioning of a unique Sacred Order of Scientists for a particular University and then Chapters and Branches, all guilds, associations, fraternities and societies of scientists must be suppressed and dissolved, with all remaining assets conveyed to the Sacred Order, or distributed to the appropriate civil and political governments of the same regions.
Suppression and Dissolution of Guilds, Associations and Societies of Scientists

Thereafter, it shall be reprobate, suppressed and forbidden to permit the formation, creation or reconstitution of any such guilds, fraternities, associations or bodies other than the appropriate Sacred Order of Scientists.

Article 78 – Inventor

1. **I**nventor is a Sacred Office expressly ordained by Heaven for a Scientist of suitable scientific experience, humility, virtue, temperament and character to physically embody Instinctum and the Inspiration and Creative Manifesting Authority of Heaven amongst the community, within competent scientific, research and technology development facilities. All Instinctum is dispensed from the ultimate temporal authority of the Supreme See and its highest physical embodiment within the most sacred Office of Supreme Patriarch and supported by the Author-General of Technology & Scientific Systems of the Living Body of One Christ.

   Inventor

   The Office of Inventor is one of the one hundred and two Superior Offices of Community of the Four Hundred and Thirty Two (432) Great Offices of One Heaven.

   Whenever one references, writes or speaks of a properly qualified, registered and competent science professor, inventor or scientific theorist of any kind, it shall mean such a person is properly invested as an Inventor in accord with the most sacred Covenant *Pactum De Singularis Caelum* and the present most sacred Covenant and no other.

   All Procedures including (but not limited to) the commission, obligations, authority, powers, function, standards, qualifications, honours, dignities, conduct, accountabilities, grades, benefits, legacies, term, investiture, enrolment, certification, review, audit, censure, sanction or cessation of the Office of Inventor shall be defined by the present Covenant and associated rules and covenants.

2. Consistent with the absolute jurisdiction and authority of the Universal Ecclesia of One Christ as temporal custodian of the Great Register and Public Record of One Heaven, each and every University and Union ecclesiastical, sovereign, political and administrative unit of the Universal Ecclesia of One Christ shall prepare and manage exclusively a Sacred Roll of Inventors, making such records available to local, provincial, state and national civil authorities and competent forums as required, to ensure the validity and qualifications of such persons.

   Sacred Roll of Inventors

No one may claim to be a valid Inventor, unless a proper record exists within the Sacred Roll of Inventors. Therefore, no person who claims to be a properly qualified, registered and competent science professor, inventor or scientific theorist of any kind may engage in scientific, research and technology development facilities unless a proper record exists within the Sacred Roll of Inventors.

3. A unique Sacred College of Inventors as a Secular and Laity Order shall be commissioned for each University of the Universal Ecclesia of Christ. The Sacred College of Inventors shall then be permitted under their adopted rules to open and maintain Chapters at a Provincial Level and Branches at a Campus Level.

Sacred College of Inventors

4. Upon the formal commissioning of a unique Sacred College of Inventors for a particular University and then Chapters and Branches, all guilds, associations, fraternities and societies of inventors must be suppressed and dissolved, with all remaining assets conveyed to the Sacred Order, or distributed to the appropriate civil and political governments of the same regions.

Suppression and Dissolution of Guilds, Associations and Societies of Inventors

Thereafter, it shall be reprobate, suppressed and forbidden to permit the formation, creation or reconstitution of any such guilds, fraternities, associations or bodies other than the appropriate Sacred College of Inventors.

Article 79 – Academic

1. **A**cademic is a Sacred Office expressly ordained by **Heaven** for a person of suitable competence, humility, virtue, temperament and character to support academic excellence, research and development within academic, research and policy development facilities of the community.

Academic

The Office of Academic is one of the one hundred and thirty six Superior Offices of the City of the Four Hundred and Thirty Two (432) Great Offices of One Heaven.

Whenever one references, writes or speaks of a properly qualified, registered and competent academic of any kind, it shall mean such a person is properly invested as an Academic in accord with the most sacred Covenant *Pactum De Singularis Caelum* and the present most sacred Covenant and no other.

All Procedures including (but not limited to) the commission, obligations, authority, powers, function, standards, qualifications, honours, dignities, conduct, accountabilities, grades, benefits, legacies, term, investiture, enrolment, certification, review, audit, censure, sanction or cessation of the Office of Academic shall be defined by the present Covenant and associated rules and covenants.

2. Consistent with the absolute jurisdiction and authority of the Universal Ecclesia of One Christ as temporal custodian of the Great Register and Public Record of One Heaven, each and every University and Union ecclesiastical, sovereign, political and administrative unit of the Universal Ecclesia of One Christ shall prepare and manage exclusively a Sacred Roll of Academics, making such records available to local, provincial, state and national civil authorities and competent forums as required, to ensure the validity and qualifications of such persons.

Sacred Roll of Academics

No one may claim to be a valid Academic, unless a proper record exists within the Sacred Roll of Academics. Therefore, no person who claims to be a properly qualified, registered and competent academic of any kind may engage in academic, research and policy development facilities of the community unless a proper record exists within the Sacred Roll of Academics.

3. A unique Sacred Order of Academics as a Secular and Laity Order shall be commissioned for each University of the Universal Ecclesia of Christ. The Sacred Order of Academics shall then be permitted under their adopted rules to open and maintain Chapters at a Provincial Level and Branches at a Campus Level.

Sacred Order of Academics

4. Upon the formal commissioning of a unique Sacred Order of Academics for a particular University and then Chapters and Branches, all guilds, associations, fraternities and societies of academics must be suppressed and dissolved, with all remaining assets conveyed to the Sacred Order, or distributed to the appropriate civil and political governments of the same regions.

Suppression and Dissolution of Guilds, Associations and Societies of Academics

Thereafter, it shall be reprobate, suppressed and forbidden to permit the formation, creation or reconstitution of any such guilds, fraternities, associations or bodies other than the appropriate Sacred Order of Academics.

Article 80 – Philosopher

1. **P**hilosopher is a Sacred Office expressly ordained by **Heaven** for an Academic of suitable academic and philosophical experience, humility, virtue, temperament and character to physically embody Interpretum and the Visionary Wisdom and Prophetic Authority of Heaven amongst the community, within competent research and academic facilities. All Interpretum is

Philosopher

dispensed from the ultimate temporal authority of the Supreme See and its highest physical embodiment within the most sacred Office of Supreme Patriarch and supported by the Rector-General of Doctrinal and Liturgical Systems of the Living Body of One Christ..

The Office of Philosopher is one of the eleven Superior Offices of Life of the Four Hundred and Thirty Two (432) Great Offices of One Heaven.

Whenever one references, writes or speaks of a properly qualified, registered and competent tenured professor or recognised philosopher or esteemed author of any kind, it shall mean such a person is properly invested as a Philosopher in accord with the most sacred Covenant *Pactum De Singularis Caelum* and the present most sacred Covenant and no other.

All Procedures including (but not limited to) the commission, obligations, authority, powers, function, standards, qualifications, honours, dignities, conduct, accountabilities, grades, benefits, legacies, term, investiture, enrolment, certification, review, audit, censure, sanction or cessation of the Office of Philosopher shall be defined by the present Covenant and associated rules and covenants.

2. Consistent with the absolute jurisdiction and authority of the Universal Ecclesia of One Christ as temporal custodian of the Great Register and Public Record of One Heaven, each and every University and Union ecclesiastical, sovereign, political and administrative unit of the Universal Ecclesia of One Christ shall prepare and manage exclusively a Sacred Roll of Philosophers, making such records available to local, provincial, state and national civil authorities and competent forums as required, to ensure the validity and qualifications of such persons.

Sacred Roll of Philosophers

No one may claim to be a valid Philosopher, unless a proper record exists within the Sacred Roll of Philosophers. Therefore, no person who claims to be a properly qualified, registered and competent philosopher or leading academic of any kind may engage in research and academic facilities unless a proper record exists within the Sacred Roll of Philosophers.

3. A unique Sacred College of Philosophers as a Secular and Laity Order shall be commissioned for each University of the Universal Ecclesia of Christ. The Sacred College of Philosophers shall then be permitted under their adopted rules to open and maintain Chapters at a Provincial Level and Branches at a Campus Level.

Sacred College of Philosophers

4. Upon the formal commissioning of a unique Sacred College of Philosophers for a particular University and then Chapters and

Suppression and Dissolution of

Branches, all guilds, associations, fraternities and societies of philosophers and leading academics must be suppressed and dissolved, with all remaining assets conveyed to the Sacred Order, or distributed to the appropriate civil and political governments of the same regions.

Guilds, Associations and Societies of Philosophers and leading Academics

Thereafter, it shall be reprobate, suppressed and forbidden to permit the formation, creation or reconstitution of any such guilds, fraternities, associations or bodies other than the appropriate Sacred College of Philosophers.

Article 81 – Journalist

1. **Journalist is a Sacred Office expressly ordained by Heaven** for a person of suitable competence, humility, virtue, temperament and character to support independent and objective reporting, investigation and reporting to keep the community properly informed and empowered.

Journalist

   The Office of Journalist is one of the one hundred and two Superior Offices of the Community of the Four Hundred and Thirty Two (432) Great Offices of One Heaven.

   Whenever one references, writes or speaks of a properly qualified, registered and competent investigative writer, investigative reporter or journalist of any kind, it shall mean such a person is properly invested as a Journalist in accord with the most sacred Covenant *Pactum De Singularis Caelum* and the present most sacred Covenant and no other.

   All Procedures including (but not limited to) the commission, obligations, authority, powers, function, standards, qualifications, honours, dignities, conduct, accountabilities, grades, benefits, legacies, term, investiture, enrolment, certification, review, audit, censure, sanction or cessation of the Office of Journalist shall be defined by the present Covenant and associated rules and covenants.

2. Consistent with the absolute jurisdiction and authority of the Universal Ecclesia of One Christ as temporal custodian of the Great Register and Public Record of One Heaven, each and every University and Union ecclesiastical, sovereign, political and administrative unit of the Universal Ecclesia of One Christ shall prepare and manage exclusively a Sacred Roll of Journalists, making such records available to local, provincial, state and national civil authorities and competent forums as required, to ensure the validity and qualifications of such persons.

Sacred Roll of Journalists

No one may claim to be a valid Journalist, unless a proper record exists within the Sacred Roll of Journalists. Therefore, no person who claims to be a properly qualified, registered and competent journalist or reporter of any kind may engage in the community unless a proper record exists within the Sacred Roll of Journalists.

3. A unique Sacred Order of Journalists as a Secular and Laity Order shall be commissioned for each University of the Universal Ecclesia of Christ. The Sacred Order of Journalists shall then be permitted under their adopted rules to open and maintain Chapters at a Provincial Level and Branches at a Campus Level.

Sacred Order of Journalists

4. Upon the formal commissioning of a unique Sacred Order of Journalists for a particular University and then Chapters and Branches, all guilds, associations, fraternities and societies of journalists must be suppressed and dissolved, with all remaining assets conveyed to the Sacred Order, or distributed to the appropriate civil and political governments of the same regions.

Suppression and Dissolution of Guilds, Associations and Societies of Journalists

Thereafter, it shall be reprobate, suppressed and forbidden to permit the formation, creation or reconstitution of any such guilds, fraternities, associations or bodies other than the appropriate Sacred Order of Journalists.

Article 82 – Narrator

1. **N**arrator is a Sacred Office expressly ordained by Heaven for a Journalist of suitable media and communications experience, humility, virtue, temperament and character to physically embody Vocationem and the Summons, Speaking and Calling Authority of Heaven amongst the community, within competent media and communication facilities. All Vocationem is dispensed from the ultimate temporal authority of the Supreme See and its highest physical embodiment within the most sacred Office of Supreme Patriarch and supported by the Narrator-General of Media & Communications Systems of the Living Body of One Christ.

Narrator

The Office of Narrator is one of the twelve Great Offices of the Union of the Four Hundred and Thirty Two (432) Great Offices of One Heaven.

Whenever one references, writes or speaks of a properly qualified, registered and competent media commentator, media announcer, or spokesperson of any kind, it shall mean such a person is properly invested as a Narrator in accord with the most sacred Covenant *Pactum De Singularis Caelum* and the present most sacred Covenant and no other.

All Procedures including (but not limited to) the commission, obligations, authority, powers, function, standards, qualifications, honours, dignities, conduct, accountabilities, grades, benefits, legacies, term, investiture, enrolment, certification, review, audit, censure, sanction or cessation of the Office of Narrator shall be defined by the present Covenant and associated rules and covenants.

2. Consistent with the absolute jurisdiction and authority of the Universal Ecclesia of One Christ as temporal custodian of the Great Register and Public Record of One Heaven, each and every University and Union ecclesiastical, sovereign, political and administrative unit of the Universal Ecclesia of One Christ shall prepare and manage exclusively a Sacred Roll of Narrators, making such records available to local, provincial, state and national civil authorities and competent forums as required, to ensure the validity and qualifications of such persons. *Sacred Roll of Narrators*

No one may claim to be a valid Narrator, unless a proper record exists within the Sacred Roll of Narrators. Therefore, no person who claims to be a properly qualified, registered and competent media spokesperson or media owner or leader of any kind may engage in the community unless a proper record exists within the Sacred Roll of Narrators.

3. A unique Sacred College of Narrators as a Secular and Laity Order shall be commissioned for each University of the Universal Ecclesia of Christ. The Sacred College of Narrators shall then be permitted under their adopted rules to open and maintain Chapters at a Provincial Level and Branches at a Campus Level. *Sacred College of Narrators*

4. Upon the formal commissioning of a unique Sacred College of Narrators for a particular University and then Chapters and Branches, all guilds, associations, fraternities and societies of leading media owners and professionals must be suppressed and dissolved, with all remaining assets conveyed to the Sacred Order, or distributed to the appropriate civil and political governments of the same regions. *Suppression and Dissolution of Guilds, Associations and Societies of Media Professionals and Leaders*

Thereafter, it shall be reprobate, suppressed and forbidden to permit the formation, creation or reconstitution of any such guilds, fraternities, associations or bodies other than the appropriate Sacred College of Narrators.

Article 83 – Producer

1. **Producer is a Sacred Office expressly ordained by Heaven** for a person of suitable competence, humility, virtue, temperament and character to produce the necessary food, nourishment, beverages, materials and goods for the community.

The Office of Producer is one of the one hundred and thirty six Superior Offices of the City of the Four Hundred and Thirty Two (432) Great Offices of One Heaven.

Whenever one references, writes or speaks of a properly qualified, registered and competent farmer, manufacturer, grower, creator, builder, maker or producer of any kind, it shall mean such a person is properly invested as a Producer in accord with the most sacred Covenant *Pactum De Singularis Caelum* and the present most sacred Covenant and no other.

All Procedures including (but not limited to) the commission, obligations, authority, powers, function, standards, qualifications, honours, dignities, conduct, accountabilities, grades, benefits, legacies, term, investiture, enrolment, certification, review, audit, censure, sanction or cessation of the Office of Producer shall be defined by the present Covenant and associated rules and covenants.

2. Consistent with the absolute jurisdiction and authority of the Universal Ecclesia of One Christ as temporal custodian of the Great Register and Public Record of One Heaven, each and every University and Union ecclesiastical, sovereign, political and administrative unit of the Universal Ecclesia of One Christ shall prepare and manage exclusively a Sacred Roll of Producers, making such records available to local, provincial, state and national civil authorities and competent forums as required, to ensure the validity and qualifications of such persons.

No one may claim to be a valid Producer, unless a proper record exists within the Sacred Roll of Producers. Therefore, no person who claims to be a properly qualified, registered and competent farmer, manufacturer, grower, creator, builder, maker or producer of any kind may engage in community matters unless a proper record exists within the Sacred Roll of Producers.

3. A unique Sacred Order of Producers as a Secular and Laity Order shall be commissioned for each University of the Universal Ecclesia of Christ. The Sacred Order of Producers shall then be permitted under their adopted rules to open and maintain Chapters at a Provincial

Producer

Sacred Roll of Producers

Sacred Order of Producers

Level and Branches at a Campus Level.

4. Upon the formal commissioning of a unique Sacred Order of Producers for a particular University and then Chapters and Branches, all guilds, associations, fraternities and societies of producers, manufacturers, makers and growers must be suppressed and dissolved, with all remaining assets conveyed to the Sacred Order, or distributed to the appropriate civil and political governments of the same regions.

Suppression and Dissolution of Guilds, Associations and Societies of Producers, Manufacturers and Makers

Thereafter, it shall be reprobate, suppressed and forbidden to permit the formation, creation or reconstitution of any such guilds, fraternities, associations or bodies other than the appropriate Sacred Order of Producers.

Article 84 – Distributor

1. **Distributor is a Sacred Office expressly ordained by Heaven** for a Producer of suitable producing and distribution experience, humility, virtue, temperament and character to physically embody Alumentum and the Food, Nourishment, Sustenance and Domicile Authority of Heaven amongst the competent producers, manufacturers, builders and distributors of the community. All Alumentum is dispensed from the ultimate temporal authority of the Supreme See and its highest physical embodiment within the most sacred Office of Supreme Patriarch and supported by the Distributor-General of Ethical Agriculture, Food & Organic Systems of the Living Body of One Christ.

Distributor

The Office of Distributor is one of the one hundred and two Superior Offices of Community of the Four Hundred and Thirty Two (432) Great Offices of One Heaven.

Whenever one references, writes or speaks of a properly qualified, registered and competent distributor of any kind, it shall mean such a person is properly invested as a Distributor in accord with the most sacred Covenant *Pactum De Singularis Caelum* and the present most sacred Covenant and no other.

All Procedures including (but not limited to) the commission, obligations, authority, powers, function, standards, qualifications, honours, dignities, conduct, accountabilities, grades, benefits, legacies, term, investiture, enrolment, certification, review, audit, censure, sanction or cessation of the Office of Distributor shall be defined by the present Covenant and associated rules and covenants.

2. Consistent with the absolute jurisdiction and authority of the

Sacred Roll of

Universal Ecclesia of One Christ as temporal custodian of the Great Register and Public Record of One Heaven, each and every University and Union ecclesiastical, sovereign, political and administrative unit of the Universal Ecclesia of One Christ shall prepare and manage exclusively a Sacred Roll of Distributors, making such records available to local, provincial, state and national civil authorities and competent forums as required, to ensure the validity and qualifications of such persons.

Distributors

No one may claim to be a valid Distributor, unless a proper record exists within the Sacred Roll of Distributors. Therefore, no person who claims to be a properly qualified, registered and competent producer, manufacturer, builder or distributor of goods within the community unless a proper record exists within the Sacred Roll of Distributors.

3. A unique Sacred College of Distributors as a Secular and Laity Order shall be commissioned for each University of the Universal Ecclesia of Christ. The Sacred College of Distributors shall then be permitted under their adopted rules to open and maintain Chapters at a Provincial Level and Branches at a Campus Level.

Sacred College of Distributors

4. Upon the formal commissioning of a unique Sacred College of Distributors for a particular University and then Chapters and Branches, all guilds, associations, fraternities and societies of distribution professionals must be suppressed and dissolved, with all remaining assets conveyed to the Sacred Order, or distributed to the appropriate civil and political governments of the same regions.

Suppression and Dissolution of Guilds, Associations and Societies of Distributors

Thereafter, it shall be reprobate, suppressed and forbidden to permit the formation, creation or reconstitution of any such guilds, fraternities, associations or bodies other than the appropriate Sacred College of Distributors.

Article 85 – Merchant

1. **Merchant is a Sacred Office expressly ordained by Heaven** for a person of suitable competence, humility, virtue, temperament and character to support useful, productive and dignified work through business, merchant, market and commercial facilities in the community.

Merchant

The Office of Merchant is one of the one hundred and thirty six Superior Offices of the City of the Four Hundred and Thirty Two (432) Great Offices of One Heaven.

Whenever one references, writes or speaks of a properly qualified, registered and competent business person or merchant of any kind, it shall mean such a person is properly invested as a Merchant in accord with the most sacred Covenant *Pactum De Singularis Caelum* and the present most sacred Covenant and no other.

All Procedures including (but not limited to) the commission, obligations, authority, powers, function, standards, qualifications, honours, dignities, conduct, accountabilities, grades, benefits, legacies, term, investiture, enrolment, certification, review, audit, censure, sanction or cessation of the Office of Merchant shall be defined by the present Covenant and associated rules and covenants.

2. Consistent with the absolute jurisdiction and authority of the Universal Ecclesia of One Christ as temporal custodian of the Great Register and Public Record of One Heaven, each and every University and Union ecclesiastical, sovereign, political and administrative unit of the Universal Ecclesia of One Christ shall prepare and manage exclusively a Sacred Roll of Merchants, making such records available to local, provincial, state and national civil authorities and competent forums as required, to ensure the validity and qualifications of such persons.

Sacred Roll of Merchants

No one may claim to be a valid Merchant, unless a proper record exists within the Sacred Roll of Merchants. Therefore, no person who claims to be a properly qualified, registered and competent business person or merchant of any kind may engage in the community unless a proper record exists within the Sacred Roll of Merchants.

3. A unique Sacred Order of Merchants as a Secular and Laity Order shall be commissioned for each University of the Universal Ecclesia of Christ. The Sacred Order of Merchants shall then be permitted under their adopted rules to open and maintain Chapters at a Provincial Level and Branches at a Campus Level.

Sacred Order of Merchants

4. Upon the formal commissioning of a unique Sacred Order of Merchants for a particular University and then Chapters and Branches, all guilds, associations, fraternities and societies of merchants must be suppressed and dissolved, with all remaining assets conveyed to the Sacred Order, or distributed to the appropriate civil and political governments of the same regions.

Suppression and Dissolution of Guilds, Associations and Societies of Merchants

Thereafter, it shall be reprobate, suppressed and forbidden to permit the formation, creation or reconstitution of any such guilds, fraternities, associations or bodies other than the appropriate Sacred Order of Merchants.

Article 86 – Master

1. **M**aster is a Sacred Office expressly ordained by Heaven for a Merchant of suitable business experience, humility, virtue, temperament and character to physically embody Commercium and the Possession and Trade of Goods with Authority of Heaven amongst the community, within competent business, merchant, market and commercial facilities. All Commercium is dispensed from the ultimate temporal authority of the Supreme See and its highest physical embodiment within the most sacred Office of Supreme Patriarch and supported by the Chancellor-General of Member Services & Charitable Systems and Director-General of Facilities, Constructions & Preservation Systems and Distributor-General of Ethical Agriculture, Food & Organic Systems of the Living Body of One Christ.

   The Office of Master is one of the twelve Master Offices of the See of the Four Hundred and Thirty Two (432) Great Offices of One Heaven.

   Whenever one references, writes or speaks of a properly qualified, registered and competent leader of business or marketing or merchandising of any kind, it shall mean such a person is properly invested as a Master in accord with the most sacred Covenant *Pactum De Singularis Caelum* and the present most sacred Covenant and no other.

   All Procedures including (but not limited to) the commission, obligations, authority, powers, function, standards, qualifications, honours, dignities, conduct, accountabilities, grades, benefits, legacies, term, investiture, enrolment, certification, review, audit, censure, sanction or cessation of the Office of Master shall be defined by the present Covenant and associated rules and covenants.

2. Consistent with the absolute jurisdiction and authority of the Universal Ecclesia of One Christ as temporal custodian of the Great Register and Public Record of One Heaven, each and every University and Union ecclesiastical, sovereign, political and administrative unit of the Universal Ecclesia of One Christ shall prepare and manage exclusively a Sacred Roll of Masters, making such records available to local, provincial, state and national civil authorities and competent forums as required, to ensure the validity and qualifications of such persons.

   No one may claim to be a valid Master, unless a proper record exists within the Sacred Roll of Masters. Therefore, no person who claims to be a properly qualified, registered and competent leader of business or

Master

Sacred Roll of Masters

marketing or merchandising of any kind may engage in the community unless a proper record exists within the Sacred Roll of Masters.

3. A unique Sacred College of Masters as a Secular and Laity Order shall be commissioned for each University of the Universal Ecclesia of Christ. The Sacred College of Masters shall then be permitted under their adopted rules to open and maintain Chapters at a Provincial Level and Branches at a Campus Level.

Sacred College of Masters

4. Upon the formal commissioning of a unique Sacred College of Masters for a particular University and then Chapters and Branches, all guilds, associations, fraternities and societies of leading business owners and directors must be suppressed and dissolved, with all remaining assets conveyed to the Sacred Order, or distributed to the appropriate civil and political governments of the same regions.

Suppression and Dissolution of Guilds, Associations and Societies of Masters and Business Leaders and Directors

Thereafter, it shall be reprobate, suppressed and forbidden to permit the formation, creation or reconstitution of any such guilds, fraternities, associations or bodies other than the appropriate Sacred College of Masters.

Article 87 – Banker

1. **B**anker is a Sacred Office expressly ordained by **Heaven** for a person of suitable competence, humility, virtue, temperament and character to support competent banking, finance, monetary and accounting facilities in the community.

Banker

The Office of Banker is one of the one hundred and two Superior Offices of Community of the Four Hundred and Thirty Two (432) Great Offices of One Heaven.

Whenever one references, writes or speaks of a properly qualified, registered and competent accountant, financial agent, attorney-in-fact or banker of any kind, it shall mean such a person is properly invested as a Banker in accord with the most sacred Covenant *Pactum De Singularis Caelum* and the present most sacred Covenant and no other.

All Procedures including (but not limited to) the commission, obligations, authority, powers, function, standards, qualifications, honours, dignities, conduct, accountabilities, grades, benefits, legacies, term, investiture, enrolment, certification, review, audit, censure, sanction or cessation of the Office of Banker shall be defined by the present Covenant and associated rules and covenants.

2. Consistent with the absolute jurisdiction and authority of the Universal Ecclesia of One Christ as temporal custodian of the Great Register and Public Record of One Heaven, each and every University and Union ecclesiastical, sovereign, political and administrative unit of the Universal Ecclesia of One Christ shall prepare and manage exclusively a Sacred Roll of Bankers, making such records available to local, provincial, state and national civil authorities and competent forums as required, to ensure the validity and qualifications of such persons.

Sacred Roll of Bankers

No one may claim to be a valid Banker, unless a proper record exists within the Sacred Roll of Bankers. Therefore, no person who claims to be a properly qualified, registered and competent accountant, financial agent, attorney-in-fact or banker of any kind may engage in the community unless a proper record exists within the Sacred Roll of Bankers.

3. A unique Sacred Order of Bankers as a Secular and Laity Order shall be commissioned for each University of the Universal Ecclesia of Christ. The Sacred Order of Bankers shall then be permitted under their adopted rules to open and maintain Chapters at a Provincial Level and Branches at a Campus Level.

Sacred Order of Bankers

4. Upon the formal commissioning of a unique Sacred Order of Bankers for a particular University and then Chapters and Branches, all guilds, associations, fraternities and societies of bankers must be suppressed and dissolved, with all remaining assets conveyed to the Sacred Order, or distributed to the appropriate civil and political governments of the same regions.

Suppression and Dissolution of Guilds, Associations and Societies of Bankers

Thereafter, it shall be reprobate, suppressed and forbidden to permit the formation, creation or reconstitution of any such guilds, fraternities, associations or bodies other than the appropriate Sacred Order of Bankers.

Article 88 – Bursar

1. **B**ursar is a Sacred Office expressly ordained by Heaven for a Banker of suitable fiduciary experience, humility, virtue, temperament and character to physically embody Creditum and the Credit, Trust and Absolute Financial Authority of Heaven amongst the community, within competent banking, finance, monetary and accounting facilities. All Creditum is dispensed from the ultimate temporal authority of the Supreme See and its highest physical embodiment within the most sacred Office of Supreme Patriarch and supported by the Bursar-General of Banking, Finance &

Bursar

Economic Systems of the Living Body of One Christ.

The Office of Bursar is one of the one hundred and thirty six Superior Offices of the City of the Four Hundred and Thirty Two (432) Great Offices of One Heaven.

Whenever one references, writes or speaks of a properly qualified, registered and competent fiduciary, treasurer or bursar of any kind, it shall mean such a person is properly invested as a Bursar in accord with the most sacred Covenant *Pactum De Singularis Caelum* and the present most sacred Covenant and no other.

All Procedures including (but not limited to) the commission, obligations, authority, powers, function, standards, qualifications, honours, dignities, conduct, accountabilities, grades, benefits, legacies, term, investiture, enrolment, certification, review, audit, censure, sanction or cessation of the Office of Bursar shall be defined by the present Covenant and associated rules and covenants.

2. Consistent with the absolute jurisdiction and authority of the Universal Ecclesia of One Christ as temporal custodian of the Great Register and Public Record of One Heaven, each and every University and Union ecclesiastical, sovereign, political and administrative unit of the Universal Ecclesia of One Christ shall prepare and manage exclusively a Sacred Roll of Bursars, making such records available to local, provincial, state and national civil authorities and competent forums as required, to ensure the validity and qualifications of such persons.

   Sacred Roll of Bursars

   No one may claim to be a valid Bursar, unless a proper record exists within the Sacred Roll of Bursars. Therefore, no person who claims to be a properly qualified, registered and competent bursar or treasurer of any kind may engage in the community unless a proper record exists within the Sacred Roll of Bursars.

3. A unique Sacred College of Bursars as a Secular and Laity Order shall be commissioned for each University of the Universal Ecclesia of Christ. The Sacred Order of Bursars shall then be permitted under their adopted rules to open and maintain Chapters at a Provincial Level and Branches at a Campus Level.

   Sacred College of Bursars

4. Upon the formal commissioning of a unique Sacred College of Bursars for a particular University and then Chapters and Branches, all guilds, associations, fraternities and societies of leading financiers, treasurers and bursars must be suppressed and dissolved, with all remaining assets conveyed to the Sacred Order, or distributed to the appropriate civil and political governments of the same regions.

   Suppression and Dissolution of Guilds, Associations and Societies of Bursars and Financial Leaders

Thereafter, it shall be reprobate, suppressed and forbidden to permit the formation, creation or reconstitution of any such guilds, fraternities, associations or bodies other than the appropriate Sacred College of Bursars.

Article 89 – Soldier

1. **S**oldier is a Sacred Office expressly ordained by Heaven for a person of suitable competence, humility, courage, virtue, temperament and character to defend a community and support action against forces that would otherwise seek to damage or destroy communities and civilisation.

    Soldier

    The Office of Soldier is one of the one hundred and thirty six Superior Offices of the City of the Four Hundred and Thirty Two (432) Great Offices of One Heaven.

    Whenever one references, writes or speaks of a properly qualified, registered and competent soldier of any kind, it shall mean such a person is properly invested as a Soldier in accord with the most sacred Covenant *Pactum De Singularis Caelum* and the present most sacred Covenant and no other.

    All Procedures including (but not limited to) the commission, obligations, authority, powers, function, standards, qualifications, honours, dignities, conduct, accountabilities, grades, benefits, legacies, term, investiture, enrolment, certification, review, audit, censure, sanction or cessation of the Office of Soldier shall be defined by the present Covenant and associated rules and covenants.

2. Consistent with the absolute jurisdiction and authority of the Universal Ecclesia of One Christ as temporal custodian of the Great Register and Public Record of One Heaven, each and every University and Union ecclesiastical, sovereign, political and administrative unit of the Universal Ecclesia of One Christ shall prepare and manage exclusively a Sacred Roll of Soldiers, making such records available to local, provincial, state and national civil authorities and competent forums as required, to ensure the validity and qualifications of such persons.

    Sacred Roll of Soldiers

    No one may claim to be a valid Soldier, unless a proper record exists within the Sacred Roll of Soldiers. Therefore, no person who claims to be a professional soldier of any kind may engage in any military unit or order unless a proper record exists within the Sacred Roll of Soldiers.

3. A unique Sacred Order of Soldiers as a Secular and Laity Order shall

    Sacred Order of

be commissioned for each University of the Universal Ecclesia of Christ. The Sacred Order of Soldiers shall then be permitted under their adopted rules to open and maintain Chapters at a Provincial Level and Branches at a Campus Level.

Soldiers

4. Upon the formal commissioning of a unique Sacred Order of Soldiers for a particular University and then Chapters and Branches, all guilds, associations, fraternities and societies of military professionals and soldiers must be suppressed and dissolved, with all remaining assets conveyed to the Sacred Order, or distributed to the appropriate civil and political governments of the same regions.

Suppression and Dissolution of Guilds, Associations and Societies of Soldiers

Thereafter, it shall be reprobate, suppressed and forbidden to permit the formation, creation or reconstitution of any such guilds, fraternities, associations or bodies other than the appropriate Sacred Order of Soldiers.

Article 90 – Knight

1. Knight is a Sacred Office expressly ordained by Heaven for a Soldier of suitable military and command experience, humility, virtue, temperament and character to physically embody Imperium and the Military Command and Strategic Authority of Heaven amongst all military and paramilitary services and branches. All Imperium is dispensed from the ultimate temporal authority of the Supreme See and its highest physical embodiment within the most sacred Office of Supreme Patriarch and supported by the Marshal-General of Military & Security Systems of the Living Body of One Christ.

Knight

The Office of Knight is one of the fourteen Superior Ecclesiastical Offices of the Four Hundred and Thirty Two (432) Great Offices of One Heaven.

Whenever one references, writes or speaks of a properly qualified, registered and competent Knight of any kind, it shall mean such a person is properly invested as a Knight in accord with the most sacred Covenant *Pactum De Singularis Caelum* and the present most sacred Covenant and no other.

All Procedures including (but not limited to) the commission, obligations, authority, powers, function, standards, qualifications, honours, dignities, conduct, accountabilities, grades, benefits, legacies, term, investiture, enrolment, certification, review, audit, censure, sanction or cessation of the Office of Knight shall be defined by the present Covenant and associated rules and covenants.

2. Consistent with the absolute jurisdiction and authority of the Universal Ecclesia of One Christ as temporal custodian of the Great Register and Public Record of One Heaven, each and every University and Union ecclesiastical, sovereign, political and administrative unit of the Universal Ecclesia of One Christ shall prepare and manage exclusively a Sacred Roll of Knights, making such records available to local, provincial, state and national civil authorities and competent forums as required, to ensure the validity and qualifications of such persons.

Sacred Roll of Knights

No one may claim to be a valid Knight, unless a proper record exists within the Sacred Roll of Knights. Therefore, no person who claims to be a properly qualified, registered and competent fraternal member or Knight of any kind may engage in an order or fraternity claiming spiritual or sovereign authority unless a proper record exists within the Sacred Roll of Knights.

3. A unique Sacred College of Knights as a Secular and Laity Order shall be commissioned for each University of the Universal Ecclesia of Christ. The Sacred College of Knights shall then be permitted under their adopted rules to open and maintain Chapters at a Provincial Level and Branches at a Campus Level.

Sacred College of Knights

4. Upon the formal commissioning of a unique Sacred College of Knights for a particular University and then Chapters and Branches, all guilds, associations, fraternities and societies of Knights must be suppressed and dissolved, with all remaining assets conveyed to the Sacred Order, or distributed to the appropriate civil and political governments of the same regions, excluding those Sovereign or Military or Religious Orders recognised under Customary and Traditional Rites.

Suppression and Dissolution of Guilds, Orders, Associations and Societies of Knights

Thereafter, it shall be reprobate, suppressed and forbidden to permit the formation, creation or reconstitution of any such guilds, fraternities, associations or bodies other than the appropriate Sacred College of Knights.

Article 91 – Constable

1. Constable is a Sacred Office expressly ordained by Heaven for a person of suitable competence, humility, courage, virtue, temperament and character to defend and protect the community, reduce the incidence of injury and offences, enforce the codes and policies of the community and ensure the safety and well being of officials and the community.

Constable

The Office of Constable is one of the twelve Great Offices of the State of the Four Hundred and Thirty Two (432) Great Offices of One Heaven.

Whenever one references, writes or speaks of a properly qualified, registered and competent police, or peace officers or constables of any kind, it shall mean such a person is properly invested as a Constable in accord with the most sacred Covenant *Pactum De Singularis Caelum* and the present most sacred Covenant and no other.

All Procedures including (but not limited to) the commission, obligations, authority, powers, function, standards, qualifications, honours, dignities, conduct, accountabilities, grades, benefits, legacies, term, investiture, enrolment, certification, review, audit, censure, sanction or cessation of the Office of Constable shall be defined by the present Covenant and associated rules and covenants.

2. Consistent with the absolute jurisdiction and authority of the Universal Ecclesia of One Christ as temporal custodian of the Great Register and Public Record of One Heaven, each and every University and Union ecclesiastical, sovereign, political and administrative unit of the Universal Ecclesia of One Christ shall prepare and manage exclusively a Sacred Roll of Constables, making such records available to local, provincial, state and national civil authorities and competent forums as required, to ensure the validity and qualifications of such persons.

Sacred Roll of Constable

No one may claim to be a valid Constable, unless a proper record exists within the Sacred Roll of Constables. Therefore, no person who claims to be a properly qualified, registered and competent police officer or security officer or sheriff or deputy of any kind may engage in the community unless a proper record exists within the Sacred Roll of Constables.

3. A unique Sacred Order of Constables as a Secular and Laity Order shall be commissioned for each University of the Universal Ecclesia of Christ. The Sacred Order of Constables shall then be permitted under their adopted rules to open and maintain Chapters at a Provincial Level and Branches at a Campus Level.

Sacred Order of Constables

4. Upon the formal commissioning of a unique Sacred Order of Constables for a particular University and then Chapters and Branches, all guilds, associations, fraternities and societies of Police and Security Professionals must be suppressed and dissolved, with all remaining assets conveyed to the Sacred Order, or distributed to the appropriate civil and political governments of the same regions.

Suppression and Dissolution of Guilds, Associations and Societies of Police and Security Professionals

Thereafter, it shall be reprobate, suppressed and forbidden to permit the formation, creation or reconstitution of any such guilds, fraternities, associations or bodies other than the appropriate Sacred Order of Constables.

Article 92 – Marshal

1. **M**arshal is a Sacred Office expressly ordained by Heaven for a Constable of suitable jurisprudence experience, humility, virtue, temperament and character to physically embody Virtus and the Protective Courage, Virtue and Excellence of Character with Authority of Heaven amongst all police, sheriff, paramilitary and security services tasked with the safety and well being of officials and the community. All Virtus is dispensed from the ultimate temporal authority of the Supreme See and its highest physical embodiment within the most sacred Office of Supreme Patriarch and supported by the Marshal-General of Military and Security Systems of the Living Body of One Christ.

   The Office of Marshal is one of the twelve Great Offices of the State of the Four Hundred and Thirty Two (432) Great Offices of One Heaven.

   Whenever one references, writes or speaks of a properly qualified, registered and competent marshal or military commander of any kind, it shall mean such a person is properly invested as a Marshal in accord with the most sacred Covenant *Pactum De Singularis Caelum* and the present most sacred Covenant and no other.

   All Procedures including (but not limited to) the commission, obligations, authority, powers, function, standards, qualifications, honours, dignities, conduct, accountabilities, grades, benefits, legacies, term, investiture, enrolment, certification, review, audit, censure, sanction or cessation of the Office of Marshal shall be defined by the present Covenant and associated rules and covenants.

2. Consistent with the absolute jurisdiction and authority of the Universal Ecclesia of One Christ as temporal custodian of the Great Register and Public Record of One Heaven, each and every University and Union ecclesiastical, sovereign, political and administrative unit of the Universal Ecclesia of One Christ shall prepare and manage exclusively a Sacred Roll of Marshals, making such records available to local, provincial, state and national civil authorities and competent forums as required, to ensure the validity and qualifications of such persons.

   No one may claim to be a valid Marshal, unless a proper record exists within the Sacred Roll of Marshals. Therefore, no person who claims

Marshal

Sacred Roll of Marshals

to be a properly qualified, registered and competent police commissioner or leader of security services of any kind may engage in matters of Law, or enter and participate in the community unless a proper record exists within the Sacred Roll of Marshals.

3. A unique Sacred College of Marshals as a Secular and Laity Order shall be commissioned for each University of the Universal Ecclesia of Christ. The Sacred College of Marshals shall then be permitted under their adopted rules to open and maintain Chapters at a Provincial Level and Branches at a Campus Level.

Sacred College of Marshals

4. Upon the formal commissioning of a unique Sacred College of Marshals for a particular University and then Chapters and Branches, all guilds, associations, fraternities and societies of Police Commissioners, Sheriffs and leaders of Law Enforcement must be suppressed and dissolved, with all remaining assets conveyed to the Sacred Order, or distributed to the appropriate civil and political governments of the same regions.

Suppression and Dissolution of Guilds, Associations and Societies of Police Commissioners and Sheriffs

Thereafter, it shall be reprobate, suppressed and forbidden to permit the formation, creation or reconstitution of any such guilds, fraternities, associations or bodies other than the appropriate Sacred College of Marshals.

TITLE V - MINISTERS

Article 93 – Minister

1. **M**inister be one authorised by delegation under the most sacred Covenant *Pactum De Singularis Caelum* and the present sacred Covenant, to perform certain functions and acts. A Minister is therefore an Agent and a named Beneficiary, with an Ecclesiastical Agency being identified as a Benefice.

   The Office of Minister is one of the fourteen Superior Ecclesiastical Offices of the Four Hundred and Thirty Two (432) Great Offices of One Heaven.

   All Procedures including (but not limited to) the commission, obligations, authority, powers, function, standards, qualifications, honours, dignities, conduct, accountabilities, grades, benefits, legacies, term, investiture, enrolment, certification, review, audit, censure, sanction or cessation of the Office of Minister shall be defined by the most sacred Covenant *Pactum De Singularis Caelum* and the present sacred Covenant.

2. The primary mission of a Minister is to exemplify and personify the highest virtues of good character, good conscience and good trust as leader of community spirit and dignified life. The main purposes of a Minister are:-

   (i) Evangelise as true and competent witnesses to the message of forgiveness, redemption and the restoration of the Golden Rule of Law as expressed throughout the canonical scriptures of the twenty two collections known as *Maxima Textibus Sacris*; and

   (ii) Restore integrity and trust to the prudent, transparent and diligent management of rights, trusts, property, estates and funds entrusted to be properly managed under the Golden Rule of Law, true Justice and fair Process; and

   (iii) Educate others to become competent in the knowledge of the application of the Golden Rule of Law through the laws of Ucadia to deliver true Justice and fair Process to all; and

   (iv) Counsel and assist members of the community in their matters in complete confidence and trust; and

   (v) Personify the living law as the highest jurist in legal forums and places absent of competence, or honour or any valid form of law; and

   (vi) Officiate rituals associated with the dispensation of one or more

303

of the thirty three sacred sacraments of *Summa Sacramenta*; and

(vii) Dispense the appropriate sacraments in solemnity, respect according to the liturgy and instruction associated with the *Summa Sacramenta*.

Article 94 – Agent

1. **A**gent be one authorised by delegation in trust to act for or in place of a Principal. The Authority of an Agent is always in Trust, as the Trust itself is called an Agency and exists so long as the prescribed time, or the proper performance of the Agent. A Minister therefore may be described as an Agent. An Agent binds not himself but the Principal with the agreements made.

Agent

Article 95 – Beneficiary

1. **B**eneficiary be one who consents to receive a good in trust from a Benefactor and to perform the obligations that such a "benefit" entails. A Benefit must always relate to a good of some tangible thing of value and may entail Ecclesiastical Goods, or Public Goods or Personal Goods, or some combination.

Beneficiary

A Benefit is a Trust, just as a Benefice is an Ecclesiastical Trust. Therefore, a Beneficial relation cannot and does not exist unless the prospective person is aware of the proposal and tacitly agrees and acknowledges the conditions and obligations of it. A Minister therefore may be described as a Beneficiary.

TITLE VI - CLERICS

Article 96 – Cleric

1. Cleric is a competent and capable Member of the Universal Ecclesia of One Christ, properly consecrated and ordained into the full Ministry of Christ, themselves becoming the physical and spiritual embodiment of the Living Body of One Christ in the conduct of the sacramentals of the thirty three most sacred Sacraments and in the pastoral care and duties of such Divine Commission.

   Cleric

   A Cleric of the Universal Ecclesia of One Christ is therefore a Member of a fraternity of equals in the eye of God and the Divine Creator of all Heaven and Earth. A Cleric is also an equal servant to the People of God and the Divine Creator of all Heaven and Earth, called through their Holy Orders to be an exemplary to all.

   The Office of Cleric is one of the fourteen Superior Ecclesiastical Offices of the Four Hundred and Thirty Two (432) Great Offices of One Heaven.

   All skilled, competent and capable persons of ordained formal religious services shall be firstly known as Clerics, consistent with the present sacred Covenant, before any other title of honour of particular religious doctrine. Only Clerics may obtain Offices whereby the exercise of religious orders or ecclesiastical governance is required.

   Every member of the Traditions of Christianity or Abraham, united as One Christ, receiving the Cardinal Sacrament of Consecration (*Ritus Sacramentum Consecratio*), shall be known as a Cleric. No person may administer or dispense any Sacraments in the ordinary manner and name of the Ecclesia of One Christ, without first the Consecrated Character of Cleric. No person may function in a delegated or ordinary position, without first the Consecrated Character of Cleric.

   All Procedures including (but not limited to) the commission, obligations, authority, powers, function, standards, qualifications, honours, dignities, conduct, accountabilities, grades, benefits, legacies, term, investiture, enrolment, certification, review, audit, censure, sanction or cessation of the Office of Cleric shall be defined by the most sacred Covenant *Pactum De Singularis Caelum* and the present sacred Covenant.

2. A Cleric is first and foremost called to a Divine Commission, exemplified through their Holy Orders and confirmed through the Cardinal Sacrament of Consecration (*Ritus Sacramentum Consecratio*). The primary mission of the Office of Cleric is to exemplify and personify the highest virtues of good character, good

   Mission of Cleric

conscience and good trust in support of community spirit and dignified life. The main purposes of the Office of Cleric are:-

(i) Evangelise as true and competent witnesses to the message of forgiveness, redemption and the restoration of the Golden Rule of Law as expressed throughout the canonical scriptures of the twenty two collections known as *Maxima Textibus Sacris*; and

(ii) Restore and maintain integrity and trust to the prudent, transparent and diligent management of rights, trusts, property, estates and funds entrusted to be properly managed under the Golden Rule of Law, true Justice and fair Process; and

(iii) Educate others to become competent in the knowledge of the application of the Golden Rule of Law through the laws of Ucadia to deliver true Justice and fair Process to all; and

(iv) Counsel and assist members of the community in their matters in complete confidence and trust; and

(v) Personify the living law as the highest jurist in legal forums and places absent of competence, or honour or any valid form of law; and

(vi) Officiate rituals associated with the dispensation of one or more of the thirty three sacred sacraments of *Summa Sacramenta*; and

(vii) Dispense the appropriate sacraments in solemnity and respect according to the liturgy and instruction associated with the *Summa Sacramenta*.

3. Whilst a member of equals, a Cleric may be characterised by their sacramental authority and pastoral duties as an Acolyte, Presbyter, Deacon, Bishop and Patriarch:-

Characteristics of Cleric

(i) *Acolyte* is a Cleric consecrated and ordained in the Key Sacraments; and

(ii) *Presbyter* is a Cleric consecrated and ordained in the Key Sacraments, the Apostolic Life Sacraments and the Cardinal Sacraments of the Eucharist, Matrimony, Union, Penance and Mercy; and

(iii) *Deacon* is a Cleric consecrated and ordained in the Key Sacraments, the Apostolic Life Sacraments and the Cardinal Sacraments of the Eucharist, Matrimony, Union, Penance,

Mercy, Record, Oath and Vow; and

(iv)   *Bishop* is a Cleric fully consecrated and ordained in the Key
Sacraments, the Apostolic Life Sacraments and the Cardinal
Sacraments having Pastoral Care of a Diocese or Community of
a Customary and Traditional Rite; and

(v)   *Patriarch* is a Cleric fully consecrated and ordained in the Key
Sacraments, the Apostolic Life Sacraments and the Cardinal
Sacraments having Pastoral Care of a University and
Patriarchal See or the See of a Customary and Traditional Rite.

4.   All Clerics shall be Members of a recognised and accepted Religious or
Secular Association, or Institute or Society.

Cleric as Member

5.   Without dispute, the calling to witness the Revelation of God and the
Divine Creator of Heaven and Earth through the Holy Spirit is open
equally to men and women, regardless of race or economic status or
faith. The Universal Ecclesia of One Christ is bestowed a supreme and
unique position, yet is not qualified nor permitted to judge a calling to
Consecrated Life as more or less worthy based upon gender alone.

Gender and Clerical Life

In accord with the most sacred Covenant *Pactum De Singularis
Caelum*, the present sacred Covenant recognises those customary and
traditional rites that hold to the historic roles of men and women
consecrated and ordained to religious life. Those that choose to
celebrate and worship through those sacred customary and traditional
rites are acknowledged as having a Divine Mandate to honour such
distinctions.

Furthermore, the Supreme See is empowered to makes rules and
define certain Clerical Roles as unique to gender, where in the interest
of transition and unity of the Living Body of One Christ, it is
considered appropriate. However, without prejudice to those
acknowledged Customary and Traditional Rites, the Universal Ecclesia
of One Christ is compelled to full equality of gender during its sacred
lifetime.

6.   Celibacy is a state of voluntary abstinence from any form of sexual
relations, stimulation or activity. Celibacy is enacted as one of the
Three Sacred Vows of an Exemplary Consecrated Life and is one of the
greatest demonstrations of universal love, self sacrifice and objective
service to humanity in maintaining the union of the Covenant uniting
Heaven and Earth as one.

Celibacy and Clerical Life

So precious, important and profound is the sacred vow of Celibacy and
dedication to a Celibate Life, that such a vow cannot be imposed or

demanded without grossly damaging its sacredness and integrity. Furthermore, implied universal requirements of permanent Celibacy has the consequence of not only completely negating the effectiveness and holiness of such sacred Vows, but cleaving the true Spirit from the body of Christ.

Therefore, universal demands for Celibacy across all Clerics or sections of community prior to the sacrament of Matrimony are an abomination, profane, sacrilegious, reprobate and to be suppressed and never revived.

Instead, the most sacred vow of Celibacy shall be reserved for those consecrated and ordained Clerics of suitable temperament and competence to strengthen and guide the Living Body of One Christ.

Presbyters, Deacons and Bishops living within the general community and entrusted with the pastoral care of a community of faithful to One Christ, shall be free to enter into and maintain Matrimonial vows through the sacrament of Matrimony, without impediment to their See. Furthermore, Clerics living a full and secular life in the fulfilment of their Holy Orders and Commission shall be free to enter into and maintain Matrimonial vows through the sacrament of Matrimony.

However, Bishops fulfilling Cardinalate obligations and Patriarchs are expected to have taken the sacred vow of Celibacy for the duration of their encumbancy.

In respect of religious communities of consecrated life seeking to live an exemplary and holy existence, it is expected that all members of such a fraternity take the sacred vow of Celibacy.

Furthermore, in respect of secular communities of consecrated life, possessing the Divine Commission of sovereign or military orders, the sacred vow of Celibacy is regarded as a condition of such a high sacred calling.

7. Sexuality is the capacity, predilection and orientation of a man or woman in respect of another member of the species, or some other life form regarding sexual relations, stimulation or sexual activity.

Sexuality and Clerical Life

The Universal Ecclesia of One Christ is firm and resolute in condemning depraved, injurious and criminal acts of sexual abuse of minors, or perverted sexual acts with other forms of life. However, the Universal Ecclesia of One Christ does not and cannot condemn men and women purely for homosexual or heterosexual predilections and orientation.

Thus, a Supplicant for Clerical life cannot be ruled ineligible purely upon their sexual orientation of heterosexuality or homosexuality. Instead, the suitability of a Supplicant shall be based upon their complete aptitude and competence for the type of Cleric life they seek.

A Cleric with homosexual orientation is unsuited for a community and pastoral commission, whereby the Living Body of One Christ places and protects the heterosexual family unit as the foundation stone of civilised life. However, such a Cleric may be suited for life within a Religious Community under the sacred vow of Celibacy.

The Universal Ecclesia of One Christ cannot condone, nor tolerate active homosexual relations amongst its Clerics and the community at large and shall do everything in its power to suppress, remove and extinguish such activity.

Article 97 – Clerical Obligation

1.   **S**ince all Clerics devote their lives for the same purpose, namely, the nourishment, well-being and strength of the Living Body of One Christ, they are to be united among themselves by a bond of fraternity and mutual respect and are to strive for cooperation among themselves according to the prescripts of particular law.

Clerical
Obligation

The calling of a true Cleric of the Living Body of One Christ is unique and not without self-sacrifice and challenge. It is a path reserved for those specially touched by the Holy Spirit to enter into the service of their community and all of humanity; and to devote their lives to the fulfilment of the propositions of the Universal Ecclesia of One Christ.

In leading their lives, Clerics are bound in a special way to pursue holiness since, having been consecrated to God and the Divine Creator of all Heaven and Earth by a new title in the reception of orders, they are dispensers of Divine Mercy and Redemption through the most Holy Sacraments.

Just as it is the primary obligation of Clerics to tend to the needs of the Members and People of God and the Divine Creator of all Heaven and Earth, so it is a primary obligation of the Universal Ecclesia to ensure the education, sustenance, well-being and strength of its Clergy.

2.   Clerics are bound absolute by special obligation to reverence and obedience to the Supreme Patriarch of the Universal Ecclesia of One Christ through their pastoral and organisation superiors.

Clerical
Obedience

Clerics bound by their sacred Oath and Vows to an Association, or Institute or Society being an accepted Customary and Traditional Rite are also bound to reverence and obedience to their Patriarch through their pastoral and organisation superiors.

Unless a legitimate impediment excuses them, Clerics are bound to undertake and fulfil faithfully those tasks and functions the Supreme Patriarch and their pastoral and organisation superior have entrusted to them.

3. Religious Clerics are expected to wear suitable and modest ecclesiastical garb according to the norms issued by their Association or Institute or Society and according to any associated Customary and Traditional Rite.

Clerical Dress

4. Clerics are to behave with due prudence towards persons whose company can endanger their obligation to observe continence or give rise to scandal among the faithful.

Clerical Relations

Clerics are to refrain completely from all those things which are unbecoming to their state, according to the prescripts of particular law.

Secular Clerics have the right to associate with others to pursue purposes in keeping with the clerical state. Secular Clerics are to hold in esteem especially those associations which, having statutes recognised by competent authority, foster their holiness in the exercise of the ministry through a suitable and properly approved rule of life and through fraternal assistance and which promote the unity of clerics among themselves and with their own bishop.

5. Without the permission of their superior, Clerics are not to take on the management of goods belonging to lay persons or secular offices that entail an obligation of rendering accounts.

Temporal Goods and Personal Wealth

Clerics are strictly prohibited from giving surety even with their own goods without consultation with their proper superior. Clerics also are to refrain from signing promissory notes or other instruments, unless such activity is specifically approved in relation to one or more approved funds of the Universal Ecclesia.

Clerics are prohibited from conducting business or trade personally or through others, for their own advantage or that of others, except with the permission of legitimate ecclesiastical authority.

6. In faithfully and obediently fulfilling those tasks and functions the Supreme Patriarch and their pastoral and organisation superior have entrusted to Clerics, the convening and recording of official meetings are to be recorded according to the norms of the Association, or Institute or Society; and with due care to greater community

Official and Pastoral Clerical Meetings

obligations.

7. Consistent care is to be given to all personal meetings by Clerics and non-religious Members, in particular the young and the vulnerable. In such cases of personal clerical meetings with those possessing particular issues of mental and physical vulnerability, such personal and non-official visits should be conducted in the presence of competent witnesses.

Personal Clerical Meetings

8. In accord with the approved Rules or Constitutions of Religious or Secular Associations, Institutes or Societies, Clerics are to be unencumbered with their Divine and Pastoral Missions to participate in non-religious associations and non-violent political bodies, even if such activity cannot be reconciled with the obligations proper to the clerical state.

Clerical Secular and Public Activities

Unless the approved Rules or Constitutions of Religious or Secular Associations, Institutes or Societies permit, Clerics are to refrain from establishing or participating in associations whose purpose or activity cannot be reconciled with the obligations proper to the clerical state or can prevent the diligent fulfilment of the function entrusted to them by competent ecclesiastical authority.

Upon approval of the appropriate Patriarch, subject to the Rules or Constitution of the particular Institute, or Association or Society, Clerics may assume public offices that entail a participation in the exercise of civil power.

Clerics are not to have an active part in political parties and in governing labour unions unless, in the judgement of competent ecclesiastical authority, the protection of the rights of the Universal Ecclesia or the promotion of the common good requires it.

Clerics are to use exemptions from exercising functions and public civil offices foreign to the clerical state that laws and agreements or customs grant in their favour unless their proper superior has decided otherwise in particular cases.

9. Clerics are obligated by their acceptance of Holy Orders to consider their lives as a devotion to continuous study and learning. Therefore, even after ordination, Clerics are expected to pursue further and continual studies, not only in sacred doctrine, sacred scripture and works of historical religious significance, but in the acquisition of knowledge of other sciences, especially of those which are connected with the sacred sciences, particularly insofar as such knowledge contributes to the exercise of pastoral ministry.

Continuing Clerical Studies

According to the Divine and Pastoral Missions of Clerics as defined within the approved Rules or Constitution of their respective Religious or Secular Association, or Institute or Society, Clerics are expected to attend pastoral lectures; and attend other lectures, theological meetings, and conferences offering the opportunity to acquire a fuller knowledge of the sacred sciences and pastoral methods.

10. Every Cleric of the Living Body of Christ is expected at least once in their life to pilgrimage to those most sacred places and cities central to the tradition and life journey of the united faith of God and the Divine Creator of Heaven and Earth.

Clerical Pilgrimages

Whilst time and circumstances may not allow several pilgrimages, every Cleric is expected to make at least one earnest pilgrimage during their life, where such an event entails a level of austerity, humility, faith and separation from the distractions of technology and artificial comforts of modern society.

Such an experience of deep reflection and honest contemplation should therefore be a touchstone for each and every Cleric as to the absolute necessity for the health and well-being of pastoral spirit first, in order to serve, support and assist the spirit of a community.

11. Even if Clerics do not have a residential office, they nevertheless are not to be absent from their diocese for a notable period of time, to be determined by particular law, without at least the presumed permission of their proper ordinary. However, every Cleric is entitled to a fitting and sufficient time of vacation each year as determined by universal or particular law.

Clerical Vacations and Sabbaticals

Every man and woman endeavouring to better serve God and the Divine Creator of Heaven and Earth and humanity shall inevitably face times of exhaustion, doubt and loss of spirit. It is therefore encumbered upon the superiors of all Clerics to ensure that every man and woman courageous enough to seek to live in holiness is given a reasonable amount of physical and spiritual rest at least once every ten years.

Such periods of simple and sanctified reflection or "sabbaticals" may be an opportunity for pilgrimage, or further study or an activity other than pastoral duties as time and considerations allow.

Some practice of common life is highly recommended to clerics during such a time; where it exists, it must be preserved as far as possible.

12. Since Clerics dedicate themselves to ecclesiastical ministry, they deserve remuneration that is consistent with their condition, taking

Clerical Remuneration

into account the nature of their function and the conditions of places and times, and whereby they can provide for the necessities of their life as well as for the equitable payment of those whose services they need.

Provision must also be made so that they possess that social assistance which provides for their needs suitably if they suffer from illness, incapacity, or old age.

Married Clerics who devote themselves completely to ecclesiastical ministry deserve remuneration whereby they are able to provide for the support of themselves and their families. Those who receive remuneration by reason of a civil profession which they exercise or have exercised, however, are to take care of the needs of themselves and their families from the income derived from it.

Clerics are to foster simplicity of life and are to refrain from all things that have a semblance of vanity.

Article 98 – Formation of Cleric

1. **T**he **Living Body of One Christ** has the solemn obligation and exclusive right to form the character of those who are properly designated to become consecrated and ordained Clerics.

   Formation of Cleric

   The obligation of fostering vocations rests with the entire united Christian and Jewish community so that the needs of the sacred ministry in the Universal Ecclesia of One Christ are provided for sufficiently.

   This obligation especially binds Christian families, educators, and, in a special way, priests, particularly pastors. Diocesan bishops, who most especially are to be concerned for promoting vocations, are to teach the people entrusted to them of the importance of the sacred ministry and of the need for ministers in the Universal Ecclesia and are to encourage and support endeavours to foster authentic vocations.

2. A male or female of age eighteen years or older, in seeking to enter the Consecrated Life of the Living Body of One Christ shall be called at first a Supplicant, in reflection of their outward and inward sincere and genuine humility and prayerful yearning to such a life.

   Supplicant and Novice

   Whilst not seeking to dampen the heartfelt and earnest actions of a Supplicant that sincerely feels a calling to Consecrated Life, the Universal Ecclesia of One Christ must first be a wise and objective guide and counsel to its most fervent Members, before seeking to regard the passion of a Supplicant as ground alone to be accepted as a Novice.

Thus, all Supplicants must be interviewed over a period of not less than nine months, to discern their competency in seven core qualities being:-

(i)   Scholastic Respect, means that the Supplicant has completed higher studies or is committed to completing higher studies upon being accepted to a Novitiate; and

(ii)   Emotional Honesty, means that the Supplicant has undergone thorough psychological and emotional interview to gauge their emotional maturity and suitability for the form of consecrated life they seek; and

(iii)   Courageous Commitment, means the Supplicant demonstrates a willingness and ability to remain focused and disciplined and to restore their dedication in the event of challenges or doubts; and

(iv)   Heartfelt Enthusiasm, means the Supplicant is passionate and enthusiastic as to their request and sense of calling; and

(v)   Authentic Compassion, means the Supplicant possesses and demonstrates authentic compassion, mercy and care towards others as an outward focus of their calling, beyond any inward calling for a scholastic or meditative form of consecrated life; and

(vi)   Humble Cheerfulness, means the Supplicant possesses a joyous and happy disposition and is not grossly affected by senses of ego, or pride; and

(vii)   Objective Discernment, means the Supplicant demonstrates an objective discernment of themselves, the Universal Ecclesia and the world around them.

3.   By Religious Profession, members assume the observance of the Doctrines and Rules of the Universal Ecclesia of One Christ by public Oath and Vows; and are therefore consecrated to God and the Divine Creator of Heaven and Earth through the ministry of the Universal Ecclesia; and are incorporated into their Association, Institute or Society with the rights and duties defined by law. *Religious Profession*

Upon acceptance, a new Cleric makes a Temporary Profession for a period defined in proper law; it is not to be less than three years nor longer than six. For the validity of temporary profession it is required that:-

(i) The person who is to make it has completed at least eighteen years of age; and

(ii) The novitiate has been validly completed; and

(iii) Admission has been given freely by the competent superior with the vote of the council according to the norm of law; and

(iv) The profession is expressed and made without force, grave fear, or malice; and

(v) The profession is received by a legitimate superior personally or through another.

4. When the period that profession was made has elapsed, a religious who freely petitions and is judged suitable is to be admitted to renewal of profession or to perpetual profession; otherwise, the religious is to depart.

Renewal of Profession

If it seems opportune, however, the competent superior can extend the period of temporary profession according to proper law, but in such a way that the total period in which the member is bound by temporary vows does not exceed nine years.

Article 99 – Presbyter

1. **P**resbyter is a Cleric consecrated and ordained in the Key Sacraments, the Apostolic Life Sacraments and the Cardinal Sacraments of the Eucharist, Matrimony, Union, Penance and Mercy.

Presbyter

2. Presbyters may be defined according to seven primary characteristic being Fraternal, Parochial, Chaplain, Rector, Rabbi, Secular and Missionary:-

Characteristics of Presbyter

(i) Presbyter-Fraternal, or simply Friar, is a Presbyter cloistered in a Religious Community and Fraternity according to the norms of law of a particular Religious Association, Institute or Society; and

(ii) Presbyter-Parochial, or simply Pastor, is a Presbyter to whom is entrusted in a stable manner the pastoral care of a parish and community; and

(iii) Presbyter-Chaplain, or simply Chaplain, is a Presbyter to whom is entrusted in a stable manner the pastoral care, at least in part, of some community or particular group of the Living Body of Christ; and

(iv)   Presbyter-Rector, or simply Rector, is a Presbyter to whom is committed the care of some church which is neither parochial nor capitular nor connected to a house of a religious community or society of apostolic life that may also celebrate services in the same sanctuary; and

(v)   Presbyter-Rabbi, or simply Rabbi, is a Presbyter of a Jewish Customary and Traditional Rite to whom is entrusted in a stable manner the pastoral care, at least in part, of some community or particular group of the Living Body of Christ; and

(vi)   Presbyter-Secular, or simply a Priest, is a Presbyter being a member of a Secular Association, Institute or Society that permits Presbyters to live in the world and outside religious houses; and

(vii)   Presbyter-Missionary, or simply Missionary is a Presbyter granted a specific holy commission beyond their Association, Institute or Society to perform a specific function over a certain period of time.

Article 100 – Deacon

1.   **D**eacon is a Cleric consecrated and ordained in the Key Sacraments, the Apostolic Life Sacraments and the Cardinal Sacraments of the Eucharist, Matrimony, Union, Penance, Mercy, Record, Oath and Vow.

Deacon

2.   Deacons may be defined according to seven primary characteristic being Abbot, Diocesan, Chief, Dean, Canon, Vicar and Prelate:-

Characteristics of Deacon

(i)   Deacon-Abbot, or simply Abbot (or Abbess for a religious house for Nuns), is a Deacon cloistered in a Religious Community and Fraternity according to the norms of law of a particular Religious Association, Institute or Society; and

(ii)   Deacon-Diocesan, or simply Diocesan, is a Deacon to whom is entrusted in a stable manner by the Diocesan Bishop the assistance and support of two or more Presbyter-Parochial or parishes within the bounds of the Diocese; and

(iii)   Deacon-Chief, or simply Chief Rabbi, is a Deacon of a Jewish Customary and Traditional Rite to whom is entrusted in a stable manner the pastoral care or at least two or more Rabbi and their communities in communion with the Living Body of Christ; and

(iv)   Deacon-Dean, or simply Dean, is a Deacon to whom is committed the care of some churches that are neither parochial nor capitular nor connected to houses of religious communities or societies of apostolic life that may also celebrate services in the same churches; and

(v)   Deacon-Canon, or simply Canon, is a Deacon to whom is committed the care and function of a cathedral or major church for their Bishop; and

(vi)   Deacon-Vicar, or simply Vicar, is a Deacon to whom is committed the care of some churches that are neither parochial nor capitular nor connected to houses of religious communities or societies of apostolic life that may also celebrate services in the same churches; and

(vii) Deacon-Prelate, or simply Prelate, is a Deacon to whom is committed a personal or territorial Prelature.

Article 101 – Bishop

1.   **B**ishop is a Cleric fully consecrated and ordained in the Key Sacraments, the Apostolic Life Sacraments and the Cardinal Sacraments having Pastoral Care of a Diocese or Community of a Customary and Traditional Rite.

Bishop

Bishops, who by divine institution succeed to the place of the Apostles through the Holy Spirit who has been given to them, are constituted pastors in the Church, so that they are teachers of doctrine, priests of sacred worship, and ministers of governance.

Through episcopal consecration itself, bishops receive with the function of sanctifying also the functions of teaching and governing; by their nature, however, these can only be exercised in hierarchical communion with the head and members of the college.

Article 102 – Patriarch

1.   **P**atriarch is a Cleric fully consecrated and ordained in the Key Sacraments, the Apostolic Life Sacraments and the Cardinal Sacraments having Pastoral Care of a University and Patriarchal See or the See of a Customary and Traditional Rite.

Patriarch

317

Article 103 – Directorium Ecclesiam Christus

1. **A**ll living Persons possessing the valid character and impression of Consecrated and Holy Orders shall be listed within the Directory of Ecclesiastical Persons of Christ, also known as *Directorium Ecclesiam Christus*.

   The Directory shall be published annually in print and maintained electronically and made available, subject to terms and conditions of use.

   Directory of Ecclesiastical Persons of Christ

2. All men and women possessing a valid Clerical State shall be required to be properly registered and listed within the Directorium Ecclesiam Christus.

   Requirement of Directory Registration

3. A living man or woman not being properly listed within the Directorium Ecclesiam Christus shall not have the authority to act as Cleric or Celebrant of religious ceremony.

   All Sacred Gifts and Rites dispensed at the time by an unregistered man or woman shall have no force or effect spiritually, morally, lawfully and legally.

   No Authority

Article 104 – Loss of Clerical State

1. **O**nce sacred ordination is validly received and imprinted upon the character of a man or woman, via the sacrament of Consecration, it can never be withdrawn or made invalid. However, a Cleric, nevertheless, may lose the clerical state:-

   Loss of Clerical State

   (i) By issue of a judicial sentence or administrative decree as an Interdict effectively declaring the man or woman without a valid Association or Institute or Society, nor a valid superior and effectively an outcast; or

   (ii) By rescript of the Supreme See, binding the man to an austere cloistered contemplative religious house for a period of penance, prayer and reflection.

2. In the event a Cleric or Sacred Office is commanded by Holy Writ, in accord with the strict conditions defined by the present sacred Covenant, to defend and protect the Living Body of One Christ, then such a sacred instrument authorised from Heaven therefore absolves the Cleric or Sacred Office from certain transgressions that might otherwise be considered offences against the Universal Ecclesia and Civil Powers.

   Absolution of Clerical and Sacred Function

3. In the event a Cleric is accused and found culpable of gross offences of breach of trust, or sexual depravity, or abuse of minors or violence against the innocent, then the superior shall be duty bound to offer the Cleric up to the Civil authorities in determining the just sentence.

    However, if such Civil Powers refuse to acknowledge the barbarity of Capital Punishment and the culpable religious is in jeopardy, then the superior and the Bishop and Patriarch are duty bound to protect the religious against the vengeance of Civil Powers.

Offences against Civil Powers

Article 105 – Restoration of Clerical State

1. **J**ust as Divine Mercy and Divine Forgiveness washes away the blood and transgressions of all people, so too the Universal Ecclesia of One Christ cannot abandon nor condemn a religious that has fallen, no matter how grave the transgression.

    Therefore, so as the Clerical State can be removed, it can and must be considered restored in the right, just and correct circumstances.

Restoration of Clerical State

2. The Conditions for restoration of the Clerical State begin with the circumstances and behaviour of the religious from the beginning that such offences become revealed:-

Conditions for Restoration of the Clerical State

    (i)   A religious that honestly and openly confesses to their transgressions to their superior, without relapse during investigation, is deserving of mercy; and

    (ii)   A religious that genuinely and earnestly engages in rigorous and thorough contemplation and reflection, without relapse or further signs of gross transgression is deserving of mercy; and

    (iii)   A religious that experiences genuine spiritual and mental suffering and physical austerity as part of their penance, without relapse is deserving of mercy.

3. It is a sad possibility for the Universal Ecclesia that a religious found culpable of gross transgressions, may demonstrate no signs of remorse, nor the courage or will to bind themselves to dignified self-control and humility to never relapse.

Conditions preventing Restoration

    Therefore, it is a fundamental prerequisite of any investigation on any offence against a religious, that their mental state and potential for recidivity is properly assessed. At the conclusion of such a report, it must be provided immediately to the Supreme See.

TITLE VII - UNIVERSAL ORGANS

Article 106 – Universal Organs of One Christ

1. The Universal Body of Christ shall be divided and defined by distinct structural units or Organs, representing its vital parts. The existence of the Body Corporate as a Body shall depend upon twenty Organs being:-

Universal Organs

(i)   Sol Ecclesia; and

(ii)   Authentic Living Body of One Christ; and

(iii)   One Holy Apostolic Universal Ecclesia; and

(iv)   Supreme Patriarch; and

(v)   Holy See; and

(vi)   Customary & Traditional Rites; and

(vii)   General Counsel; and

(viii) Apostolic College; and

(ix)   Ecumenical Council; and

(x)   Divina Templum (Treasury of Heaven); and

(xi)   Apostolic Penitentiary; and

(xii)   Supreme Chancery; and

(xiii) Sacred Camera; and

(xiv)   Holy Curia; and

(xv)   Sacred Congregations; and

(xvi)   Sacred Citadel; and

(xvii) Supreme Tribunal; and

(xviii) Supreme Vestry; and

(xix)   Sacred Conservatory; and

(xx)   International Cities and Sanctuaries.

Article 107 – Sol Ecclesia

1. **T**he Universal Ecclesia of One Christ as the Sol Ecclesia is a Supernatural and Spiritual entity registered and recognised in accord with the Great Ledger and Public Record of One Heaven as a Divine Person and Divine Trust possessing certain Divine Rights of Use and Purpose.

Sol Ecclesia symbolises the eternal forgiveness, mercy and redemption of all Christians and Jews that have physically departed; and the truth and fulfilment of the Divine Promise that the faithfully departed continue to live on in true spirit in the presence of the Divine Creator of all existence and the glory and joy of One Heaven.

As a Divine Person and Divine Trust, the Universal Ecclesia of One Christ as the Sol Ecclesia signifies the permanent and perfect presence of the Holy Spirit bound in sacred matrimony to the Universal Ecclesia. Thus, the permanent, perfect and irrevocable presence of the Holy Spirit personified as the Sol Ecclesia of the Universal Ecclesia signifies an eternal and complete communion between the Universal Ecclesia of One Christ and with God and the Divine Creator of all Existence and all Heaven and Earth.

Sol Ecclesia

Article 108 – Living Body of One Christ

1. **T**he Universal Ecclesia of One Christ as the Authentic Living Body of Christ is a Living and Universal entity registered and recognised in accord with the Great Ledger and Public Record of One Heaven as a True Person and Universal True Trust possessing certain Natural Rights of Use and Purpose.

The Authentic Living Body of Christ symbolises all Living Members as being incorporated into the true Living Body of Christ as one united family; and the fulfilment of Sacred Scripture in the return and permanent presence of Christ Redeemed.

As a Universal True Trust, the Universal Ecclesia of One Christ possesses a True Personality based upon its Divine Personality guided by its True Mind and Intent being the Covenant of One Christ. The Society of One Christ shall have mortal life for one (1) complete Era of three thousand two hundred ten (3210) years until its physical death.

Upon its physical death, the people of the Earth may choose for the Society to be reborn for another Era, or for a new named Society to be created in accord with the canons and laws of One Heaven.

Authentic Living Body of One Christ

Article 109 – One Holy Apostolic Universal Ecclesia

1. The Universal Ecclesia of One Christ as One Holy Apostolic Universal Ecclesia is a Supreme Body and See registered and recognised in accord with its own Ledgers, Rolls, Records and Bylaws as a Superior Person and Superior Trust as the one, true and authentic Kingdom of Heaven upon the Earth, possessing certain Ecclesiastical and Sovereign Rights.

   One Holy Apostolic Universal Ecclesia

   As a Superior Trust, the Universal Ecclesia of One Christ possesses a Superior Personality based upon its True Personality guided by the present most sacred Covenant of One Christ.

Article 110 – Supreme Patriarch and See

1. The Pope as the Supreme Patriarch, in whom continues the Apostolic Traditions of Sacred Office of the Universal Ecclesia of all in One Christ, is the head of the college of bishops, the Vicar of Christ and the pastor of the Universal Ecclesia on earth. By virtue of his office he possesses supreme, full, immediate, and universal ordinary power within the community of the Church.

   Supreme Patriarch

   All Procedures concerning the function of the office of Pope as Supreme Patriarch, the execution of duty, the inauguration into office, events relating to the vacancy of office and the death of current and previous office holders shall be defined by the present Covenant according to the associated rules of the most sacred Covenant *Pactum De Singularis Caelum*.

2. The Supreme See of the Universal Ecclesia of One Christ, also known as the Holy See, shall be the seat of the Pope as Supreme Patriarch, the first church and diocese. The Supreme See of the Ecclesia shall be sovereign absolute, possessing complete control and authority over the land, buildings, space and environment within its established boundaries. In recognition of the Golden Rule of Law governing all proper international law, the Supreme See makes itself a legal entity, recognisable under international law in the exercising of its sovereign, legislative, executive and judicial functions.

   Supreme See

   For the first term of the most sacred Divina, and the period of one hundred and twenty eight years, the Supreme See shall be Rome as Nova Roma representing Rome redeemed, reborn and renewed. Thereafter upon the conclusion of the second Great Conclave and for the second term of the most sacred Divina of Heaven, and the period of one hundred and twenty eight years, the Supreme See shall be seated at Paris, in honour of the Carolingians and the founding of the Catholicus Ecclesia. Thereafter upon the conclusion of the third Great Conclave and for the third term of the most sacred Divina of Heaven, and the period of one hundred and twenty eight years, the Supreme See shall be seated at Constantinople, also known at the founding of Christianity as Antioch. Thereafter, all future seats of the Supreme See shall be decided by a vote at the preceding Great Conclave.

Article 111 – Customary & Traditional Rites

1. **All Christian communities that honour tradition and custom**, respecting Sacred Scripture and who have been incorporated into the True Living Body of One Christ are recognised as essential Universal Organs in their own Customary and Traditional Rite, headed by a Patriarch, who is then an honoured member of the Apostolic College of Patriarchs.

Customary & Traditional Rites

The Systems, Service and Support to the family of customary and traditional rites shall be embodied in the Great Office of Custodian-General of Sacred Rites & Tradition Systems.

Article 112 – General Counsel

1. **The General Counsel** is the supreme and universal advisory organ of the Living Body of One Christ, constituted by the Generals of the Systems of the Universal Ecclesia of One Christ.

General Counsel

The Chairperson of the Counsel shall always be the Supreme Patriarch or their nominated legate. The other permanent members of the Counsel shall be:-

(i) Society-General of Religious Associations, Institutes and Societies Systems; and

(ii) Secretary-General of Ecclesiastical Unions, Universities & Diplomatic Systems; and

(iii) Regional-General of Ecclesiastical Province & Campus Systems; and

(iv) Vicar-General of Vocational & Clerical Systems; and

(v) Minister-General of Evangelical, Devotional & Veneration Systems; and

(vi) Rector-General of Doctrinal & Liturgical Systems; and

(vii)   Custodian-General of Sacred Rites & Tradition Systems; and

(viii)   Prefect-General of Ecumenical & Collegial Systems; and

(ix)   Registrar-General of Families and Community Life Systems; and

(x)   Chancellor-General of Member Services & Charitable Systems; and

(xi)   Assistant-General of Knowledge Standards and Education Systems; and

(xii)   Prothonotary-General of Justice and Jurisprudence Systems; and

(xiii)   Physician-General of Health and Therapeutic Systems; and

(xiv)   Author-General of Technology & Scientific Systems; and

(xv)   Bursar-General of Banking, Finance & Economic Systems; and

(xvi)   Steward-General of Environmental Protection & Preservation Systems; and

(xvii)   Distributor-General of Ethical Agriculture, Food & Organic Systems; and

(xviii)   Marshal-General of Military & Security Systems; and

(xix)   Narrator-General of Media & Communications Systems; and

(xx)   Director-General of Facilities, Constructions & Preservation Systems; and

(xxi)   Conservator-General of Heritage, Arts & Cultural Systems; and

(xxii)   Administrator-General of Administrative & Logical Systems.

Article 113 – Apostolic College

1.   The **Apostolic College of Patriarchs** is the primary Executive Organ of the Universal Ecclesia of One Christ, embodied and personified through the Great Office of Prefect-General of Ecumenical & Collegial Systems.

Apostolic College of Patriarchs of One Christ

Article 114 – Ecumenical Council

1. **The Ecumenical Council** is the primary Legislative and Doctrinal Organ of the Universal Ecclesia of One Christ, embodied and personified through the Great Office of Prefect-General of Ecumenical & Collegial Systems.

   The Ecumenical Council shall comprise of all Patriarchs, Bishops and Deacons once every ten years as equal delegates.

Ecumenical Council of One Christ

Article 115 – Templum Divina

1. **The Divine Temple** is the primary Treasury Organ of the Universal Ecclesia of One Christ, embodied and personified through the Great Office of Bursar-General of Banking, Finance & Economic Systems.

Divine Temple Treasury

Article 116 – Supreme Chancery

1. **The Supreme Chancery** is the primary administrative Organ of rights, trusts, estates, lands and guardians of the Universal Ecclesia of One Christ, embodied and personified through the Great Office of Chancellor-General of Member Services & Charitable Systems.

Supreme Chancery

Article 117 – Sacred Camera

1. **The Sacred Camera** is the primary administrative Organ of taxes, revenues, funds and securities of the Universal Ecclesia of One Christ, embodied and personified through the Great Office of Administrator-General of Administrative & Logical Systems.

Sacred Camera

Article 118 – Curia

1. **The Curia** is the primary diplomatic, communication and inter-departmental services of the Universal Ecclesia of One Christ, embodied and personified through the Great Office of Secretary-General of Ecclesiastical Unions, Universities & Diplomatic Systems. The Curia is also the administrative and legal systems of the Holy See.

Curia

Article 119 – Sacred Congregations

1. The embodiment of the Sacred Congregations of the Ecumenical Council shall be through the Great Office of Rector-General of Doctrinal & Liturgical Systems.

Sacred Congregations

Article 120 – Sacred Citadel

1. The Sacred Citadel is the primary military and security Organ of the Universal Ecclesia of One Christ, embodied and personified through the Great Office of Marshal-General of Military & Security Systems.

Sacred Citadel

Article 121 – Supreme Tribunal

1. The Supreme Tribunal is the primary judicial appeal Organ of the Universal Ecclesia of One Christ, embodied and personified through the Great Office of Prothonotary-General of Justice and Jurisprudence Systems.

Supreme Tribunal

Article 122 – Supreme Vestry

1. The Supreme Vestry is the primary administrative Organ of vital and sacred records, births, deaths, matrimony, events, covenants, treaties, titles and contracts of the Universal Ecclesia of One Christ, embodied and personified through the Rector-General of Doctrinal & Liturgical Systems.

Supreme Vestry

Article 123 – Sacred Conservatory

1. The Sacred Conservatory is the primary Organ of the Universal Ecclesia of One Christ, embodied and personified through the Great Office of Conservator-General of Heritage, Arts & Cultural Systems.

Sacred Conservatory

TITLE VIII - UNION ORGANS

Article 124 – Union Organs

1. **U**nion is the name used to describe the second largest spiritual, ecclesiastical, sovereign and operational division of the Body of Christ. A Union corresponds in boundary and name to one of the six Unions of planet Earth being the Africans Union, Arabian Union, Americas Union, Asia Union, Euro Union and Oceanic Union.

   Union

2. The foundation structures and properties of each Union represent those organs and bodies defined by the Constitutional Charter of the particular Ucadia Union for the effective management and operations of government by the will and intent of all Members in accordance with the laws of One Heaven and Ucadia.

   Union Organs

   These Union Organs and bodies include, but are not limited to:-

   (i)   **"Synod"** is the supreme legislative body of the Union, comprised of members known as **"Archons"**; and

   (ii)   **"Mediator"** is a corporation sole and ex-officio head of the Synod; and

   (iii)   **"Academy"** is the supreme administrative body of the Union; and

   (iv)   **"Alexander"** is a corporation sole and ex-officio head of the Academy; and

   (v)   **"Basilica"** is the supreme juridical, plenary and appellate forum of law in all matters concerning the Union; and

   (vi)   **"Basileus"** is a corporation sole and ex-officio head of the Basilica; and

   (vii)   **"Econos"** is the supreme treasury for all revenue, banking and finances concerning the Union; and

   (viii)   **"Economos"** is a corporation sole and ex-officio head of the Econos; and

   (ix)   **"Stratos"** is the supreme military command and resources concerning the Union; and

   (x)   **"Stratagos"** is a corporation sole and ex-officio head of the Stratos; and

   (xi)   **"Energeia"** is the supreme business and trade body of the Union; and

(xii) **"Kephalos"** is a corporation sole and ex-officio head of the Energeia; and

(xiii) **"Psyches"** is the supreme spiritual and ecclesial body of the Union; and

(xiv) **"Mentor"** is a corporation sole and ex-officio head of the Psyches; and

(xv) **"Sunedrion"** is the supreme governing body of the Union; and

(xvi) A number of Subsidiaries, Funds, Trusts and other Bodies, whether incorporated or unincorporated.

Article 125 – Union Psyches

1. The executive Power of the Union in respect of the Universal Ecclesia of shall be vested in an executive body comprising those representatives of the Universal Ecclesia of One Christ elected to the Ucadia Union Psyches being the supreme spiritual and ecclesial body of the Union.

Union Psyches

Article 126 – Union Agora

1. All legislative Powers of the Union shall be vested in an Agora. The Agora shall be made up of all Patriarchs, Bishops and Deacons of the Union. The Agora shall then convene at least once every five years.

Union Agora

TITLE IX - UNIVERSITY ORGANS

Article 127 – University Organs

1. **U**niversity is the name used to describe second largest administrative division of government and administration of a Union of the Supreme See. A University is an ecclesiastical, sovereign, official, lawful, legal and administratively constituted subdivision of the Union and is equivalent to the term "absolute sovereign domain" and the traditional terms including but not limited to "politea", "sovereign state", "dominion" and "independent sovereign nation".

   In accord with Article 103 (*Ucadia Universities, Provinces & Campuses*) of the most sacred Covenant *Pactum De Singularis Caelum* a valid University is a Spiritual and Supernatural Body, recognised as a true and apostolic Ecclesiastical Patriarchal See (Metropolitan Sedos) and Politia of supreme temporal authority of the Society of One Heaven.

2. There are established as the principal Organs of a University:-

   (i)   A Patriarch and (Patriachal) See; and

   (ii)   Supreme Legate (Apostolic Nuncio); and

   (iii)   Conference of Bishops; and

   (iv)   Plenary Council.

University

Ecclesiastical Organs of University

Article 128 – Patriarch and See

1. **T**he Patriarch is the head of the Universal Ecclesia of One Christ for a University region, also known as a nation or country or state.

2. A Patriarchal See is the official jurisdiction of a Patriarch of a Politeia (State), or University, or recognised head of a Traditional and Customary Rite. In accord with the most sacred Covenant *Pactum De Singularis Caelum* and associated sacred Covenants, Canons and Rules, a Patriarchal See may encompass the full spiritual, ecclesiastical, temporal, territorial, topographic and political bounds of a State (Politeia), otherwise known as a sovereign nation, or may encompass the whole planet Earth, yet only applying to those sacred places and people recognised within their Jurisdiction. To distinguish between the differences, a Patriarch appointed for a Politeia (State) is also known as a Metropolitan Patriarch and a Patriarch recognised as ultimate head of a Traditional and Customary Rite is also known as an

Patriarch and Patriarchal See

Patriarchal See

Apostolic Patriarch.

A Metropolitan Patriarch is so named as the Episcopal Bishop of the capital or "metropolitan" of a particular Politeia (State).

An Apostolic Patriarch as head of an accepted Traditional and Customary Rite is so named and honoured in recognition of the long standing historical ties and connections that many Christian Churches and Bodies possess and that one of the greatest historic divisions between Christian fraternities over centuries was the claim of Apostolic authenticity. Furthermore, an Apostolic Patriarch of an accepted Traditional and Customary Rite also retains the right to their Traditional and Customary Titles.

A Patriarch must always be a Bishop accepted into the full dispensing of the most sacred Sacraments of One Christ and therefore recognised also in title as Cardinal in reference to the full authority and power to dispense all Cardinal Sacraments of Summa Sacramenta.

Article 129 – Supreme Legate (Papal Nuncio)

1. A Supreme Legate, also known as an Apostolic Nuncio is an official envoy or permanent diplomatic representative of the Supreme See and the Holy See to a State or supranational body.

   Supreme Legate (Apostolic Nuncio)

   The Apostolic Nuncio is head of the diplomatic mission, or Apostolic Nunciature endowed with the full respect, dignity and powers of an embassy.

Article 130 – Conference of Bishops

1. A Conference of Bishops, also known as an Episcopal Conference or national Conference of Bishops, is an official assembly of all the Bishops of all Rites of a given State, territory or nation. Each Conference of Bishops shall convene at least one session each year.

   Conference of Bishops

Article 131 – Plenary Council

1. A Plenary Council, also known as an Ecclesiastical Synod is a convention of all Bishops, Deacons and Presbyters of a given State, nation or territory. A Plenary Council should be held at least once every year.

   Plenary Council

TITLE X - PROVINCE ORGANS

Article 132 – Province Organs

1. In accord with Article 129 of the most sacred Covenant *Pactum De Singularis Caelum*, a Ucadia Province is the second smallest primary unit of ecclesiastical and ordinary power of all Heaven and Earth, all sanctuaries and clergy and all bodies and persons claiming any form of ecclesiastical authority, office, power or right within the bounds of a Ucadia Province. A Consulate holds plenary authority as the one holy universal and apostolic Diokesia (Diocese) and Episcopal See. — Province

2. A Provincial See is the official jurisdiction of an Archbishop of a Province and Bishop of the Provincial Capital. In accord with the most sacred Covenant *Pactum De Singularis Caelum* and associated sacred Covenants, Canons and Rules, a Provincial See may encompass the full spiritual, ecclesiastical, temporal, territorial, topographic and political bounds of a Province. — Provincial See

   An Archbishop of a Provincial See may (or may not) be a Bishop accepted into the full dispensing of the most sacred Sacraments of One Christ. If acceptance is the case, the Archbishop shall also be recognised by the Title of Cardinal in reference to the full authority and power to dispense all Cardinal Sacraments of *Summa Sacramenta*.

Article 133 – College of Deacons

1. A College of Deacons shall be formed in each and every Province of all Deacons. The College shall convene at least once every six months, in assisting the Archbishop of the Province. — College of Deacons

TITLE XI - CAMPUS ORGANS

Article 134 – Campus

1. In accord with Article 103 (*Ucadia Universities, Provinces & Campuses*) of the most sacred Covenant *Pactum De Singularis Caelum*, a Campus, also known as a Mission is the smallest primary unit of ecclesiastical and ordinary power of all Heaven and Earth, where all sanctuaries and clergy and all bodies and persons claiming any form of ecclesiastical authority, office, power or right within the bounds of a Ucadia Campus. When a Campus holds plenary authority embodied in the person of a Bishop, it shall also be known as a Diocese.

   Campus Organs

2. An Episcopal See, also known as a Diocese, is the ecclesiastical jurisdiction of a Bishop. To distinguish between the differences, a Bishop appointed for a Diocese is also known as a Diocesan Bishop; and a Bishop recognised as a leader of a Traditional and Customary Rite is also known as an Apostolic Bishop.

   Episcopal See

3. A Diocesan Curia of the Bishop and his Deacons shall be formed for the good administration of the Diocese.

   Diocesan Curia

Article 135 – Diocesan Synod

1. A Diocesan Synod shall be formed of all Deacons and Presbyters and senior Laity of the Diocese. The Diocesan Synod shall meet at least once every ninety days.

   Diocesan Synod

TITLE XII - SYSTEMS

Article 136 – Systems of One Christ

1. **A**ll ecclesiastical, sovereign and administrative support, services, skills and resources of the Universal Ecclesia of One Christ at each and every level of jurisdiction and administration is divided into permanent and standard Systems, in accord with the present most sacred Covenant.

   Systems of One Christ

2. The Twenty Two Systems of the Body of One Christ shall be:-

   Twenty Two Systems of One Christ

   (i)   Religious Associations, Institutes and Societies Systems; and

   (ii)   Ecclesiastical Unions, Universities & Diplomatic Systems; and

   (iii)   Ecclesiastical Province & Campus Systems; and

   (iv)   Vocational & Clerical Systems; and

   (v)   Evangelical, Devotional & Veneration Systems; and

   (vi)   Doctrinal & Liturgical Systems; and

   (vii)   Sacred Rites & Tradition Systems; and

   (viii)   Ecumenical & Collegial Systems; and

   (ix)   Families and Community Life Systems; and

   (x)   Member Assistance & Charitable Systems; and

   (xi)   Knowledge and Education Systems; and

   (xii)   Justice and Jurisprudence Systems; and

   (xiii)   Health and Therapeutic Systems; and

   (xiv)   Technology & Scientific Systems; and

   (xv)   Banking, Finance & Economic Systems; and

   (xvi)   Environmental Protection & Preservation Systems; and

   (xvii)   Ethical Agriculture, Food & Organic Systems; and

   (xviii) Military & Security Systems; and

   (xix)   Media & Communications Systems; and

   (xx)   Facilities, Constructions & Preservation Systems; and

   (xxi)   Heritage, Arts & Cultural Systems; and

   (xxii)   Administrative & Logistical Systems.

3. Each and every System of the Universal Ecclesia of One Christ shall be represented by a suitably qualified, competent and dedicated Bishop as its Head. The Head of a System shall also be known as a General, having full Cardinal Sacramental Powers and consecrated into a proper Cardinalate.

Head of System

4. The General Powers of a Head shall be those powers and authorities defined and granted in accord with the present sacred Covenant, notwithstanding any and all additional responsibilities granted in writing by the Supreme Patriarch or as prescribed by Law. The powers and authorities are:-

General Powers of System Head

   (i)   Oversight and responsibility for the planning, budgeting, efficiency and operation of the Systems, Divisions and the Departments under its control; and

   (ii)   Notwithstanding Ecclesiastical and Legal considerations, the general identification of suitable talented personnel and the interview and recruitment of personnel to the System and Divisions; and

   (iii)   The day-to-day tasks, activities and productivity of personnel assigned to the System and Divisions; and

   (iv)   The immediate behaviour, culture and discipline of members of the Division and all its Departments.

5. Excluding Secretariats, all Systems of the Universal Ecclesia of One Christ shall follow the same rules of Organisational Structure in defining subdivisions within itself:-

Standard Structure of Systems

   (i)   *Unit* shall be the term used to describe a subdivision of a Section whereby ten or more people, to a maximum of one hundred and twenty people function according to some technical function and mandate; and

   (ii)   *Section* shall be the term used to describe a subdivision of a Department whereby twenty or more people, to a maximum of three hundred and sixty people function according to some technical function and mandate; and

   (iii)   *Department* shall be the term used to describe a subdivision of a Division whereby thirty or more people, to a maximum of two thousand people function according to some general division of services; and

   (iv)   *Division* shall be the term used to describe the largest organ of the twenty-two primary Systems of the Universal Ecclesia of

One Christ.

6.   A Department is a subdivision of a Division of the Universal Ecclesia **Departments**
of One Christ, whereby thirty or more people, to a maximum of two
thousand people function according to some general division of
services. All Departments are constructed from Sections of between
twenty to three hundred and sixty people; and all Sections are
constructed from Units of between ten to one hundred and twenty
people.

There are primarily two types of Departments of Divisions of the
Universal Ecclesia of One Christ, being Internal and External:-

(i)   An *Internal* Department is when a particular Department
provides services and functions only to the Division that it
belongs. Therefore the primary direction of service of the
Department are other Departments of other Divisions of the
Universal Ecclesia; and

(ii)   An *External* Department is when a particular Department
provides services or goods or functions to Members or non-
Members.

7.   There are nine key types of Internal Departments, notwithstanding **Standard Types**
other Internal Departments that may be approved from time to time:- **of Departments**

(i)   Secretariat is the Office in support of the Divisional Head in
terms of compliance, official meetings, reporting, accountability
and oversight. A Secretariat cannot be introduced as a
dedicated Internal Department to a Division of the Universal
Ecclesia of One Christ until at least one other External
Department of the Division is established and the total count of
Officers, Agents and Contractors employed is forty (40) or
greater; and

(ii)   Contact & Help Department is an Internal Department
providing front-line inbound and outbound call centre
management, online help requests, live chat, sms, email and
other first line inquiries. The Department shall be part of the
Administrative Support & Electoral Systems Division first and
then the particular Division as a managed service; and

(iii)   Issue & Resolution Department is an Internal Department
providing complaints management and dispute resolution
services. The Department formally belongs to the Legal Support
& Justice Systems Division first and then the particular Division
as a managed service; and

(iv)   Accounts & Finance Department is an Internal Department providing accounts and finance compliance, entry, reconciliation and transactions. The Department formally belongs to the Finance & Revenue Systems Division first and then the particular Division as a managed service; and

(v)   Records & Archives Department is an Internal Department providing records management and archival services. The Department formally belongs to the Administrative Support & Electoral Systems Division first and then the particular Division as a managed service; and

(vi)   Vocation & Training Department is an Internal Department providing recruitment, job description, team member development, personnel administration, payroll, skills development and periodic performance reviews. The Department formally belongs to the Vocational Support & Skills Development Systems Division first and then the particular Division as a managed service; and

(vii)   Technology & Equipment Department is an Internal Department providing systems administration, computer and technology support, software and configuration support and IT security. The Department formally belongs to the Technology Support & Development Systems Division first and then the particular Division as a managed service; and

(viii)   Facilities & Maintenance Department is an Internal Department providing facilities management, facilities fit out and facilities asset management. The Department formally belongs to the Facilities Management & Construction Systems Division first and then the particular Division as a managed service; and

(ix)   Integrity & Security Department is an Internal Department providing internal security and fraud detection, threat assessments and enforcement. The Department formally belongs to the Security & Emergency Systems Division first and then the particular Division as a managed service.

8. All Secretariats operating within any Division of the Universal Ecclesia of One Christ or any part thereof shall identify all Officers, Agents and Contractors according to the following three levels of Desk, Station and Chapter:- *(Standard Structure of Secretariats)*

(i)   Desk shall be the term used to describe a subdivision of a Station whereby one or more persons, to a maximum of thirty people function according to some defined task; and

(ii)   Station shall be the term used to describe a subdivision of a Chapter whereby three or more people, to a maximum of one hundred and twenty people function according to some technical function and mandate; and

(iii)   Chapter shall be the term used to describe the primary divisions of a Secretariat of Officers, Agents and Contractors employed within the structure.

9. All planning, budgeting, approval and allocation of resources, personnel and services within the Divisions of the Universal Ecclesia of One Christ shall be in accord with the following principles:-

Divisional Resource Allocation

(i)   Minimal Vertical Duplication shall mean that levels of duplication of function within a vertical service delivery chain must be minimal and full service duplication across vertical levels of a service delivery chain is forbidden; and

(ii)   Front-Line Service Priority shall mean that the priority of resourcing in any service chain shall always begin with the actual front-line service being the first priority and support, management and logistics always having second priority; and

(iii)   Local Service Priority shall mean that where duplication of function and services exist, the lower and more local functions and services shall take priority over the higher vertical functions and services, unless the service and function pertains primarily to policy, planning or standards whereby the duplication will resolve in favour of higher vertical administration; and

(iv)   Services as Public Asset shall mean that the services delivered shall remain a public asset and service, because of this, services cannot be subject to any sell off to private corporations or private-public ventures or downscaling or outsourcing to private interests; and

(v)   Limits on Consultants shall mean that the management of such systems are forbidden to recruit, hire, engage or contract private or external consulting firms where such services, skills, abilities or knowledge provided already exists within the public services of the Society.

Article 137 – Religious Associations, Institutes & Societies

1. The One True Holy Apostolic Universal Ecclesia of One Christ is a body duly formed by Sacred Covenant for the Cure and Care of Souls and for the fulfilment of the Primary and Ancillary Propositions as described within these sacred Articles.

   The existence of Sacred Land and Places, duly consecrated Religious Institutes, Associations and Societies shall be at the very core of the purpose of existence of the Universal Ecclesia.

   Religious Associations, Institutes and Societies

2. The System of the Body of One Christ known as Religious Associations, Institutes & Society Systems shall be the primary Division authorised, empowered and responsible for the management of all Religious Associations, Institutes and Societies within the Jurisdiction of One Christ.

   Religious Associations, Institutes and Society Systems

3. The Head of Religious Associations, Institutes and Societies Systems shall be known as the Society-General; and shall be a Bishop consecrated into the Cardinalate, possessing the prerequisite skills, experience, aptitude and energy required to execute such Great Office.

   Head of Religious Associations, Institutes and Society Systems

4. Excluding the Divisional Secretariat and any Internal Services Departments, the core Departments of the Division shall include (but not be limited to): Clerical Services, Ministerial Services, Liturgical Services and Religious Institutes.

   Departments

5. The Society-General of Religious Associations, Institutes and Societies Systems shall be responsible for the conduct and operation of Congregation for Religious Associations, Institutes and Societies.

   Congregation for Religious Associations, Institutes and Societies

Article 138 – Ecclesiastical Unions, Universities & Diplomatic Systems

1. The formation and maintenance of harmonious and amicable diplomatic relations with ecclesiastical, political, foreign and lesser bodies, societies and entities is essential to the fulfilment of the Primary and Ancillary Propositions of the Universal Ecclesia as defined by the present sacred Covenant.

   Ecclesiastical Unions, Universities & Diplomacy

2. The System of the Body of One Christ known as Ecclesiastical Unions, Universities & Diplomatic Systems shall be the primary Division authorised, empowered and responsible for the management of all Ucadian Union Administration Establishment, Ucadia Union Entity Establishment, Foreign Diplomatic Agreements and Treaties, Foreign

   Ecclesiastical Unions, Universities & Diplomatic Systems

Diplomatic Relations within the Jurisdiction of One Christ.

3. The Head of Ecclesiastical Unions, Universities & Diplomatic Systems shall be known as the Secretary-General; and shall be a Bishop consecrated into the Cardinalate, possessing the prerequisite skills, experience, aptitude and energy required to execute such Great Office.

Head of Ecclesiastical Unions, Universities & Diplomatic Systems

4. The Secretary-General of Ecclesiastical Unions, Universities & Diplomatic Systems shall also be the Secretary of State for the Holy See.

Secretariat of State of Holy See

Article 139 – Ecclesiastical Province & Campus Systems

1. The establishment, management and support of stable Ecclesiastical Provinces and Campuses within the bounds and jurisdiction of the Supreme See, whereby the community of Christ is properly united is a fundamental purpose of the Universal Ecclesia for One Christ.

Ecclesiastical Provinces & Campuses

2. The System of the Body of One Christ known as Ecclesiastical Province & Campus Systems shall be the primary Division authorised, empowered and responsible for the management of all Ucadia Province Establishment, Ucadia Campus Establishment, Ucadia Province Administration Relations, Ucadia Campus Administration Relations and Ucadia Province and Campus Standards and Development within the Jurisdiction of One Christ.

Ecclesiastical Province & Campus Systems

3. The Head of Ecclesiastical Province & Campus Systems shall be known as the Regional-General; and shall be a Bishop consecrated into the Cardinalate, possessing the prerequisite skills, experience, aptitude and energy required to execute such Great Office.

Head of Ecclesiastical Province & Campus Systems

Article 140 – Vocational & Clerical Systems

1. It is a fundamental tenet of the Divine Revelation of Divine Mercy and Forgiveness embodied within the present sacred Covenant, that each and every man and woman possesses value and purpose; and furthermore that one of the noblest ideals is for a man or woman to seek to learn, to develop new and existing skills and become more self aware of themselves as well as the needs, wants and wisdom of their family, community, the planet and the universe.

Vocations and Consecrated Life

For the effective and optimum function of the Universal Ecclesia of One Christ, it shall be vital that comprehensive vocational support systems exist and that people find the roles that best suit their skills, abilities and aptitude when choosing a consecrated life; and that the best people are selected for the appropriate roles throughout the Living Body of One Christ.

2. The System of the Body of One Christ known as Vocational & Clerical Systems shall be the primary Division authorised, empowered and responsible for the management of all Vocation Classification, Enterprise Purpose Hierarchy (EPH), Payments and Best Practice, Skills Classification and Accreditation, Skills Training, Performance and Productivity Assessments within the Jurisdiction of One Christ.

Vocational & Clerical Systems

3. The Head of Vocational & Clerical Systems shall be known as the Vicar-General; and shall be a Bishop consecrated into the Cardinalate, possessing the prerequisite skills, experience, aptitude and energy required to execute such Great Office.

Head of Vocational & Clerical Systems

4. The Vicar-General of Vocational & Clerical Systems shall be responsible for the good conduct and function of the Sacred Congregation for Vocations and Consecrated Life.

Congregation for Vocations and Consecrated Life

Article 141 – Evangelical, Devotional & Veneration Systems

1. The investigation and veneration of the Saints and the beloved that have passed into the sanctity and Divine Gift of a united Heaven, is an authentic act of piety and humility before God and the Divine Creator of all Heaven and Earth.

Evangelicalism, Devotion and Veneration

The celebration of the Holy Sacraments and major feasts and events of Liturgical and Ecclesiastical Life requires special care and sobriety to ensure the preservation of sanctity at all times and the deepest respect to all living and deceased Members of the united Body of One Christ.

2. The System of the Body of One Christ known as Evangelical, Devotional & Veneration Systems shall be the primary Division authorised, empowered and responsible for the management of all Religious Celebrations, Holy Days, Venerations and Devotions within the Jurisdiction of One Christ.

Evangelical, Devotional & Veneration Systems

3. The Head of Evangelical, Devotional & Veneration Systems shall be known as the Minister-General; and shall be a Bishop consecrated into the Cardinalate, possessing the prerequisite skills, experience, aptitude and energy required to execute such Great Office.

Head of Evangelical, Devotional & Veneration Systems

4. The Minister-General of Evangelical, Devotional & Veneration Systems shall be responsible for the conduct and function of the Sacred Congregation for Evangelicalism, Devotion & Veneration.

Congregation for Evangelicalism, Devotion and Veneration

Article 142 – Doctrinal & Liturgical Systems

1. The System of the Body of One Christ known as Doctrinal & Liturgical Systems shall be the primary Division authorised, empowered and responsible for the management of all sacred texts, doctrines and liturgical instructions within the Jurisdiction of One Christ.

   Sacred Doctrine and Liturgy

2. The System of the Body of One Christ known as Doctrinal & Liturgical Systems shall be the primary Division authorised, empowered and responsible for the management of all Religious Doctrine and Liturgical Systems within the Jurisdiction of One Christ.

   Doctrinal & Liturgical Systems

3. The Head of Doctrinal & Liturgical Systems shall be known as the Rector-General; and shall be a Bishop consecrated into the Cardinalate, possessing the prerequisite skills, experience, aptitude and energy required to execute such Great Office.

   Head of Doctrinal & Liturgical Systems

4. The Rector-General of Doctrinal & Liturgical System shall be responsible for the conduct and function of the Sacred Congregation for Sacred Doctrine and Liturgy.

   Congregation for Sacred Doctrine and Liturgy

Article 143 – Sacred Rites & Tradition Systems

1. The System of the Body of One Christ known as Sacred Rites & Tradition Systems shall be the primary Division authorised, empowered and responsible for the management, liaison and support of all Customary and Traditional Rites, particularly in seeking and ensuring Liturgical unity at major feasts and celebrations of the Universal Ecclesia.

   Sacred Rites & Tradition

2. The System of the Body of One Christ known as Sacred Rites & Tradition Systems shall be the primary System and Divisions authorised, empowered and responsible for the management of all Sacred Rites and Traditional Systems within the Jurisdiction of the Universal Ecclesia of One Christ.

   Sacred Rites & Tradition Systems

3. The Head of Sacred Rites & Tradition Systems shall be known as the Custodian-General; and shall be a Bishop consecrated into the Cardinalate, possessing the prerequisite skills, experience, aptitude and energy required to execute such Great Office.

   Character of Summa Sacramenta

4. The Custodian-General of Sacred Rites & Tradition Systems shall be responsible for the function and conduct of the Sacred Congregation for Sacred Rites & Tradition.

   Congregation for Sacred Rites & Tradition

Article 144 – Ecumenical & Collegial Systems

1. As a Living Body, the One True Holy Apostolic Universal Ecclesia of One Christ must empower all Clergy united in truth to bear witness to Divine Revelation of the Holy Spirit and ensure a stable and responsible transition, guidance and support of the united community of God and the Divine Creator of all Heaven and Earth.

   Ecumenical Councils and Colleges

   The Ecumenical Council to be convened once every ten years shall be both the catalyst and the doorway, that the Living Body and Spirit of One Christ must walk in order to fulfil its earthly and apostolic mission as expressed within the Primary and Ancillary Propositions of the present sacred Covenant.

2. The System of the Body of One Christ known as Ecumenical & Collegial Systems shall be the primary Division authorised, empowered and responsible for the management of all Ecumenical and Collegial Systems within the Jurisdiction of One Christ.

   Ecumenical & Collegial Systems

3. The Head of Ecumenical & Collegial Systems shall be known as the Prefect-General; and shall be a Bishop consecrated into the Cardinalate, possessing the prerequisite skills, experience, aptitude and energy required to execute such Great Office.

   Head of Ecumenical and Collegial Systems

Article 145 – Families and Community Life Systems

1. The sanctification, protection and nurturing of the Family and Community is essential to the future of the Universal Ecclesia of One Christ and to human civilisation. The future of humanity rests in strengthening the primacy of the family as the building block of all stable and sustainable society.

   Families and Community Life

2. The System of the Body of One Christ known as Families and Community Life Systems shall be the primary Division authorised, empowered and responsible for the management of all Family Life and Community Life Systems within the Jurisdiction of One Christ.

   Families and Community Life Systems

3. The Head of Families and Community Life Systems shall be known as the Registrar-General; and shall be a Bishop consecrated into the Cardinalate, possessing the prerequisite skills, experience, aptitude and energy required to execute such Great Office.

   Head of Families and Community Life Systems

4. The Registrar-General of Families and Community Life Systems shall be responsible for the conduct and function of the Sacred Congregation for Families and Community Life.

   Congregation for Families and Community Life

Article 146 – Member Assistance & Charitable Systems

1. **Through the Guaranteed and Authorised Capital Funds** of the Universal Ecclesia of One Christ, based upon the purified Divine Credit of Christ, the Universal Ecclesia is obliged to give account for the talents of ecclesiastical money bestowed unto it by Divine Mercy and Forgiveness and to put such valuable talents to good use and not to bury them, nor hide them in the fulfilment of the Primary and Ancillary Propositions of the present sacred Covenant.

   Member Assistance & Charity

2. The System of the Body of One Christ known as Member Assistance & Charitable Systems shall be the primary Division authorised, empowered and responsible for the management of all member relations, member support, member services and charitable assistance within the Jurisdiction of One Christ.

   Member Assistance & Charitable Systems

3. The Head of Member Services & Charitable Systems shall be known as the Chancellor-General; and shall be a Bishop consecrated into the Cardinalate, possessing the prerequisite skills, experience, aptitude and energy required to execute such Great Office.

   Head of Member Assistance & Charitable Systems

Article 147 – Knowledge and Education Systems

1. **Knowledge is by definition information with relation and meaning.** The Ucadia Model itself is a complex and comprehensive set of systems of knowledge.

   Knowledge and Education

   The establishment, development, maintenance and training of knowledge standards, classification systems shall be essential to the proper organisation and operation of the Universal Ecclesia of One Christ.

2. The System of the Body of One Christ known as Knowledge and Education Systems shall be the primary Division authorised, empowered and responsible for the management of all Ucadia Sacred Texts & Liturgy, Ucadia Canons & Codes, Education Classification Systems, Curriculum Systems, Pre-School Education, Primary Education, Secondary Education, Poly-Tech Education, Tertiary Education, Advanced Post-Graduate, Teaching Models and Methods, Academic Assessments and Academic Accreditations within the Jurisdiction of One Christ.

   Knowledge and Education Systems

3. The Head of Knowledge Standards and Education Systems shall be known as the Assistant-General; and shall be a Bishop consecrated into the Cardinalate, possessing the prerequisite skills, experience, aptitude and energy required to execute such Great Office.

Head of Knowledge and Education Systems

Article 148 – Justice and Jurisprudence Systems

1. **The restoration of the Golden Rule of Law**, of true justice and fair processes are fundamental to the purpose and existence of the Universal Ecclesia of One Christ. Furthermore, many foreign bodies and societies seeking to improve internal issues, need trustworthy services capable of assisting in their own legal retraining issues.

   The legal support of members and the provision of useful, relevant legal systems shall be a core responsibility of the Universal Ecclesia.

Justice and Jurisprudence

2. The System of the Body of One Christ known as Justice and Jurisprudence Systems shall be the primary Division authorised, empowered and responsible for the management of all Civil Standards, Criminal Law Standards, Professional Accreditation and Standards, Oversight and Complaints, Prosecutions, Judge Training and College, Court Systems and Administration, Appeals, Prisoner Classification and Correctional Facility Administration within the Jurisdiction of One Christ.

Justice and Jurisprudence Systems

3. The Head of Justice and Jurisprudence Systems shall be known as the Prothonotary-General; and shall be a Bishop consecrated into the Cardinalate, possessing the prerequisite skills, experience, aptitude and energy required to execute such Great Office.

Head of Justice and Jurisprudence Systems

Article 149 – Health and Therapeutic Systems

1. **The health and ethical well being** of all Members of the Living Body of One Christ shall be a primary concern of the Universal Ecclesia of One Christ.

Health and Ethical Well-being

2. The System of the Body of One Christ known as Health and Therapeutic Systems shall be the primary Division authorised, empowered and responsible for the management of all Health Knowledge, Standards and Principles, Health and Fitness Education, Professional Accreditation, Certification and Review, General Medical Clinics, General Dental Clinics, Community Medical Centres, Intensive Care Centres, Recovery and Rehabilitation Centres, Specialist Medical Centres, Medical Research Institutes, Mobile Medical Clinics and Health and Fitness Administration within the Jurisdiction of One

Health and Therapeutic Systems

Christ.

3. The Head of Health and Therapeutic Systems shall be known as the Physician-General; and shall be a Bishop consecrated into the Cardinalate, possessing the prerequisite skills, experience, aptitude and energy required to execute such Great Office.

Head of Health and Therapeutic Systems

Article 150 – Technology & Scientific Systems

1. **The development of efficient, reliable, ethical and responsible technology** remains one of the most important areas for improving the productivity of a society and the quality of life of all Members. The success of the Universal Ecclesia of One Christ in fulfilling its Objects relies in part upon systems of technology that are consistent, standard, ethical and efficient.

Technology & Science

2. The System of the Body of One Christ known as Technology & Scientific Systems shall be the primary Division authorised, empowered and responsible for the management of all Technology and Scientific Systems within the Jurisdiction of One Christ.

Technology & Scientific Systems

3. The Head of Technology & Scientific Systems shall be known as the Author-General; and shall be a Bishop consecrated into the Cardinalate, possessing the prerequisite skills, experience, aptitude and energy required to execute such Great Office.

Head of Technology & Scientific Systems

Article 151 – Banking, Finance & Economic Systems

1. **Through the Eternal Grace and Supreme Majesty of the Divine Creator of all Existence** and in the name of all Heaven and Earth, the Living Body of Christ is gifted all the Capital it requires to fully discharge its mission, obligation and functions.

Banking, Finance & Economics

It shall be encumbered upon the Supreme See of the Universal Ecclesia of One Christ to ensure the proper administration of the Authorised and Guaranteed Capital Stock of the Universal Ecclesia.

2. The System of the Body of One Christ known as Finance & Economic Systems shall be the primary Division authorised, empowered and responsible for the management of all Banking, Finance, Asset Management and Economic Systems within the Jurisdiction of One Christ.

Banking, Finance & Economic Systems

3. The Head of Banking, Finance & Economic Systems shall be known as the Bursar-General; and shall be a Bishop consecrated into the Cardinalate, possessing the prerequisite skills, experience, aptitude

Head of Banking, Finance & Economic

and energy required to execute such Great Office.   Systems

Article 152 – Environmental Protection & Preservation Systems

1. The wilderness and natural areas of planet Earth are   Environmental
    assets to be protected and nurtured especially the native   Protection &
    animals of the planet. It shall remain a primary objective of the   Preservation
    Universal Ecclesia to ensure the proper protection and expansion of
    the natural environment so that land is reclaimed as specific
    wilderness as well as the regeneration of natural wilderness areas for
    the habitat of species.

2. The System of the Body of One Christ known as Environmental   Environmental
    Protection & Preservation Systems shall be the primary Division Protection &
    authorised, empowered and responsible for the management of all   Preservation
    protection, support and recognition of the environment within the   Systems
    Jurisdiction of One Christ.

3. The Head of Environmental Protection & Preservation Systems shall Head of
    be known as the Steward-General; and shall be a Bishop consecrated   Environmental
    into the Cardinalate, possessing the prerequisite skills, experience,   Protection &
    aptitude and energy required to execute such Great Office.   Preservation
                                                                       Systems

Article 153 – Ethical Agriculture, Food & Organic Systems

1. Agriculture as knowledge, land, waters, animals, food   Ethical
    and technology of a society represent its most fundamental   Agriculture,
    groups of assets. Without agriculture, there would be no food   Food & Organic
    and people would go hungry. Food security, water security and bio   Systems
    security through sustainable and effective Agriculture represents a
    critical element of the quality of life for current and future generations
    of all men and women of planet Earth.

    It shall be a primary objective of the Universal Ecclesia of One Christ
    to ensure the proper standards of ethical agriculture, technology and
    systems exist so that sufficient food and diversity is grown to enable
    every man and woman on planet Earth to receive sufficient nutrition
    to be free from hunger and disease.

    Furthermore, access to ethical, safe and low cost quality food,
    beverages and therapeutic goods is a critical need for all Members of
    the Universal Ecclesia of One Christ. Access to appropriate, ethically
    and safely produced food and therapeutic goods shall be a
    fundamental requirement to the health and well being of every
    community of Members.

2.   The System of the Body of One Christ known as Ethical Agriculture, Food & Organic Systems shall be the primary Division authorised, empowered and responsible for the management of all Agriculture and Farm Related Services, Plant Biological Integrity, Sustainability, Health and Safety, Animal Biological Integrity, Health and Safety, Water and Environment Management and Education, Agriculture Research, Development and Funding, Bio-security, Sustainable and Optimum Plant/Crop Development, Food and Drugs Classification Standards, Natural Food Sources and End Products, Synthetic Food Sources and End Products, Therapeutic Drug Sources and End Products, Food Production Standards, Animal Food Production Standards, Food Services and Therapeutic Product Services within the Jurisdiction of One Christ.

Ethical Agriculture, Food & Organic Systems

The Systems of the Universal Ecclesia of One Christ known as Ethical Food & Therapeutic Systems shall be responsible for the defence, adherence and promotion of the highest bio-ethical standards, consistent with the bio-ethical laws of Ucadia. No food product or therapeutic system that is derived or manufactured in a method or process that contravenes the bio-ethical laws of Ucadia is permitted to be promoted, endorsed, sold, or marketed by the Universal Ecclesia and its Members.

3.   The Head of Ethical Agriculture, Food & Organic Systems shall be known as the Distributor-General; and shall be a Bishop consecrated into the Cardinalate, possessing the prerequisite skills, experience, aptitude and energy required to execute such Great Office.

Head of Ethical Agriculture, Food & Organic Systems

Article 154 – Military & Security Systems

1.   The security of the Universal Ecclesia of One Christ and its assets from both external threats and internal threats is a vital objective. Furthermore, it is a core responsibility of the Universal Ecclesia to ensure it possesses the necessary capacity to assist all forms and types of Members in times of potential emergency and crisis.

Military & Security

It shall be a primary objective of the Universal Ecclesia to ensure the proper security of its borders, assets and Members from both internal and external threats and potential dangers.

2.   The System of the Body of One Christ known as Military & Security Systems shall be the primary Division authorised, empowered and responsible for the management of all Threat Assessment, Protection and Facility Security, Police Investigation and Operational Standards, Police Services, Veterans and Care and Emergency Administration

Military & Security Systems

351

within the Jurisdiction of One Christ.

3. The Head of Military & Security Systems shall be known as the Marshal-General or Superior-General; and shall be the superior of the religious military order and Society of Jesus.

Head of Military & Security Systems

Article 155 – Media & Communications Systems

1. **C**ommunications and Information Networks represent fundamental infrastructure to the Universal Ecclesia of One Christ. The development and production of Media content is an essential service and demand of Members, particularly in bearing witness to the truth of the Christ Risen and the fulfilment of Divine Scripture. Furthermore, the existence of an open, transparent and accountable Media shall be essential to safeguard the freedoms and rights of Members.

Media & Communications

2. The System of the Body of One Christ known as Media & Communications Systems shall be the primary Division authorised, empowered and responsible for the management of all Universal Number Indexing Systems (UNIS), Digital Communications Networks, Digital Communications Devices, Print Communications Networks, Postal Communications Networks, Communications Content Services, Media Production and Media Publishing within the Jurisdiction of One Christ.

Media & Communications Systems

3. The Head of Media & Communications Systems shall be known as the Narrator-General; and shall be a Bishop consecrated into the Cardinalate, possessing the prerequisite skills, experience, aptitude and energy required to execute such Great Office.

Head of Media & Communications Systems

Article 156 – Facilities, Constructions & Preservation Systems

1. **T**he buildings and fixed assets represent a critical element of the quality of life for current and future generations of all Members. Over time, the Universal Ecclesia of One Christ shall acquire, develop and build a wide variety of facilities, buildings and assets that shall require construction as well as maintenance and management.

Facilities, Constructions & Preservation

Facilities Management and Construction shall be critical areas of service for the Universal Ecclesia to Members as well as departments and units of the Universal Ecclesia itself.

2. The System of the Body of One Christ known as Facilities, Constructions & Preservation Systems shall be the primary Division

Facilities, Constructions & Preservation

authorised, empowered and responsible for the management of all Building and Occupancy Standards and Principles, Surface Building Standards, Subterranean Building Standards, Accreditation and Competencies, Architecture, Continuity and Standards Compliance, Site Environmental Impact Modelling and Authorisation, Construction, Materials Testing and Certification, Building Fit-out and Maintenance, Facility Life-cycle and Accreditations within the Jurisdiction of One Christ.

Systems

3. The Head of Facilities, Constructions & Preservation Systems shall be known as the Director-General; and shall be a Bishop consecrated into the Cardinalate, possessing the prerequisite skills, experience, aptitude and energy required to execute such Great Office.

Head of Facilities, Constructions & Preservation Systems

Article 157 – Heritage, Arts & Cultural Systems

1. **T**he Universal Ecclesia of One Christ is the humble custodian of significant heritage, art and culture of human civilisation by virtue of its long traditions and the blessings of the faithful.

Heritage, Arts & Culture

By such Divine Commission as expressed and to be enforced through the present most sacred Covenant, the Universal Ecclesia of One Christ must be the very best custodians and conservators of human knowledge, art, heritage and culture for present and future generations.

2. The System of the Body of One Christ known as Heritage, Arts & Cultural Systems shall be the primary Division authorised, empowered and responsible for the management of all Heritage Buildings and Sites, Historic and Precious Art Collections and Cultural Systems within the Jurisdiction of One Christ.

Heritage, Arts & Cultural Systems

3. The Head of Heritage, Arts & Cultural Systems shall be known as the Conservator-General; and shall be a Bishop consecrated into the Cardinalate, possessing the prerequisite skills, experience, aptitude and energy required to execute such Great Office.

Head of Heritage, Arts & Cultural Systems

Article 158 – Administrative & Logistical Systems

1. **M**anagement of free, fair and open elections is essential to the preservation of the rights and ideals of the Universal Ecclesia of One Christ. Furthermore, the efficient and productive operation of the Executive, Legislatures and Public Service in general demands a strong and transparent Administrative

Administrative & Logistical

The transport of people and property across the planet is critical for the healthy economic well being of each and every community. Transport and logistics is a critical factor in enabling Members to produce and receive key goods and services. Therefore, it shall remain a primary objective of the Universal Ecclesia of One Christ to ensure the best possible transport and logistics systems are in place.

2. The System of the Body of One Christ known as Administrative & Logistical Systems shall be the primary Division authorised, empowered and responsible for the management of all Contact and Help Management, Records and Archives and the conduct of free and fair Elections and Polls, Transport & Travel Classification, Transport Traffic Rules, Road Transport Vehicles Certification, Travel Warrants, Mass Transit System Vehicles Certification, Aircraft Development and Design, Land Vehicle Development and Design, Water-craft Development and Design within the Jurisdiction of One Christ.

Administrative & Logistical Systems

3. The Head of Administrative & Logical System shall be known as the Administrator-General; and shall be a Bishop consecrated into the Cardinalate, possessing the prerequisite skills, experience, aptitude and energy required to execute such Great Office.

Head of Administrative & Logistical Systems

TITLE XIII – SACRAMENTS & EXTRA-SACRAMENTAL RITES & RUBRICS

Article 159 - Sacramental & Extra-Sacramental Rites & Rubrics

1. **S**acramental **Rites and Rubrics of Heaven** shall be the customary rules, standards and procedures whereby the Thirty-Three (33) Sacraments are properly administered and dispensed by qualified and authorised persons, in accord with the most sacred Covenant *Pactum De Singularis Caelum* and the present sacred Covenant.

   Sacramental & Extra-Sacramental Rites and Rubrics

   "**Extra-Sacramental Rites**" and Rubrics of Heaven shall be the customary rules, standards and procedures of rites and rituals beyond the Thirty-Three (33) Sacraments as defined by the most sacred Covenant *Pactum De Singularis Caelum*; and whereby such Extra-Sacramental Rites and Rubrics are properly administered and dispensed by qualified and authorised persons.

   Just as all valid, legitimate and proper sacraments are derived from Heaven and the Divine Grace and Mercy of the Divine Creator, in accord with the most sacred Covenant *Pactum De Singularis Caelum*, all rules, customs, traditions, standards and procedures for their administration and ministration are ultimately derived from the same most sacred Covenant *Pactum De Singularis Caelum*.

   No rule, custom, tradition, standard or procedure in relation to Sacramental or Extra-Sacramental Rites and Rubrics shall be valid, legitimate or permitted, unless it firmly adheres to the present sacred Covenant.

2. The following forms of Extra-Sacramental Rites and Rubrics are recognised and subject to the most sacred Covenant *Pactum De Singularis Caelum* and the present sacred Covenant, including (but not limited to):-

   Recognised Forms of Extra-Sacramental Rites and Rubrics

   (i)   *Dedication* being a form of Extra-Sacramental Rite for the consecration of places, buildings, monuments and structures; and

   (ii)   *Restoration* being a form of Extra-Sacramental Rite for the reconsecration and bringing a place, building, moment or structure to its original state; and

   (iii)   *Reformation* being a form of Extra-Sacramental Rite for the restoring of a cleric state of office to a sacred state; and

   (iv)   *Blessing* being a form of Extra-Sacramental Rite giving for invoking Divine assistance, favour, approval or protection; and

(v)   *Expulsion* being a form of Extra-Sacramental Rite for the driving out of a particular spirit or presence from Sacred Circumscribed Space; and

(vi)   *Nullification* being a form of Extra-Sacramental Rite for making legally and lawfully invalid a previous agreement or right; and

(vii)   *Deconsecration* being a form of Extra-Sacramental Rite for the removal of the consecrated and sacred state and function of a place, building, moment or structure; and

(viii)   *Secularisation* being a form of Extra-Sacramental Rite for the removal of the clerical authority of a person previously ordained; and

(ix)   *Exorcism* being a form of Extra-Sacramental Rite for the enforced removal, arrest or custody of one or more spirits in breach of the rules governing Sacred Circumscribed Space and the laws of Divine Trust, Mind and Spirit; and

(x)   *Inquisition* being a form of Extra-Sacramental Rite for the formal investigation into the truth and efficacy of some matter; and

(xi)   *Dispensation* being a form of Extra-Sacramental Rite for the granting of permission to do or perform an act otherwise permitted, or to omit doing something otherwise enjoined; an exemption; and

(xii)   *Abrogation* being a form of Extra-Sacramental Rite for the repealing by authority some legislative act; and

(xiii)   *Ordination* being a form of Extra-Sacramental Rite for the consecration of a qualified candidate for the clerical state; and

(xiv)   *Inauguration* being a form of Extra-Sacramental Rite for the inducting into office with solemnity a person elected to high civil office; and

(xv)   *Sanction* being a form of Extra-Sacramental Rite for the enforced censuring, restriction or punishment of a person holding or occupying an office, in response to a demonstrated and proven act of maladministration or malfeasance; and

(xvi)   *Unction* being a form of Extra-Sacramental Rite for the anointing of a person in time of ill-health, trauma; and

(xvii) *Coronation* being a form of Extra-Sacramental Rite for the solemn sacred ceremonial investiture of a person into sovereign office and the formation of a new sacred sovereign trust between the people and the new sovereign; and

(xviii) *Investiture* being a form of Extra-Sacramental Rite for the solemn sacred acceptance of a person into office that involves the formation of a new trust involving the transfer and vesting of one or more Ecclesiastical or Sovereign or Official Rights; and

(xix) *Hours* being a form of Extra-Sacramental Rite for the recitation of prayers and forms of invocation, in relation to significant days, times and seasons, often involving chants or singing.

Article 160 – Sacrament of Recognition

1. **R**ecognition (***Ritus Sacramentum Recognosco***) is the first of the seven (7) Key Sacraments, also known as the Keys of Heaven. The Sacrament of Recognition is the Key that unlocks the Living Virtue of Respect. It is present in all fourteen (14) of the Cardinal Sacraments.

    The Sacrament of Recognition may also be granted and conferred on its own in accordance with the most sacred Covenant *Pactum De Singularis Caelum*, the present sacred Covenant, the *Missale Christus* and associated approved liturgy.

    [margin: Sacrament of Recognition (Ritus Sacramentum Recognosco)]

2. The Divine Purpose of the Sacrament of Recognition is to assist persons in establishing a firm and clear respect of both their inner thoughts and mind and of the outer world around them. Thus, the Sacrament of Recognition is the formal observance and respect of a person, object or concept through its proper classification and estimation.

    Recognition (and therefore Respect), is seen as the foundation Living Virtue as all other virtues depend first upon the firm foundation of respect. Without self-respect, there can be no respect of others. Without respect of the world, there can be no self-respect.

    [margin: Divine Purpose of the Sacrament of Recognition]

3. There are only two (2) valid and licit forms for the Sacrament of Recognition as defined by the most sacred *Missale Christus* and associated approved liturgy being General and Ordinary:-

    (i)   "**General Recognition**" is when the Sacrament of

    [margin: Forms of the Sacrament of Recognition]

Recognition is bestowed automatically as part of the proper performance of duties by a person entrusted to act as a fiduciary or agent; and

(ii) **"Ordinary Recognition"** is when the Sacrament of Recognition is bestowed automatically as an element of a formal sacramental ritual performed by properly consecrated and ordained clergy.

Article 161 – Sacrament of Purification

1. Purification (*Ritus Sacramentum Purificatio*) is the second of the seven (7) Key Sacraments, also known as the Keys of Heaven. The Sacrament of Purification is the Key that unlocks the Living Virtue of Honesty (and Truth). It is present in all fourteen (14) of the Cardinal Sacraments.

   Sacrament of Purification (Ritus Sacramentum Purificatio)

   The Sacrament of Purification may also be granted and conferred on its own in accordance with the most sacred Covenant *Pactum De Singularis Caelum*, the present sacred Covenant, the *Missale Christus* and associated approved liturgy.

2. The Divine Purpose of the Sacrament of Purification is firstly to aid to clear and cleanse the mind from the temporary presence of negative, confusing or distracting thoughts, in order to help better focus attention and intention toward some sacred purpose. Secondly, Purification exists to prepare physical objects and bodies to receive other sacraments by dissolving any negative bonds, previous uses or intentions, or applications. Thus Purification is a necessary action in the preparing of sacramentals and the body of a priest before the ceremony of Mass.

   Divine Purpose of the Sacrament of Purification

   Purification does not exist as a form of "antidote" to an opposing construct known as impurities or impure thoughts. Such mental constructs give a wide margin for subjective interpretation and promote obsessive negative critique on temporary states of behaviour, in direct contradistinction to the purpose of Purification.

3. There are only two (2) valid and licit forms for the Sacrament of Purification as defined by the most sacred *Missale Christus* and associated approved liturgy being General and Ordinary:-

   Forms of the Sacrament of Purification

   (i) **"General Purification"** is when the Sacrament of Purification is bestowed automatically as part of the proper performance of duties by a person entrusted to act as a fiduciary or agent; and

(ii) **"Ordinary Purification"** is when the Sacrament of Purification is bestowed automatically as an element of a formal sacramental ritual performed by properly consecrated and ordained clergy.

Article 162 – Sacrament of Invocation

1. Invocation (*Ritus Sacramentum Invocatio*) is the third of the seven (7) Key Sacraments, also known as the Keys of Heaven. The Sacrament of Invocation shall be granted and conferred in accordance with the most sacred Covenant *Pactum De Singularis Caelum*, the present sacred Covenant, the *Missale Christus* and associated approved liturgy.

   Sacrament of Invocation (Ritus Sacramentum Invocatio)

2. Invocation by its very definition means "to vocalise some call for assistance; or the presence; or manifestation of one or more divine beings". Thus the positive vocal expression of such a call or entreaty or prayer is fundamental to the operative function of any proper Invocation. When it is not vocalised, an Invocation is properly defined as a Meditation.

   Invocation

   All communication to the *Angelorum Systemata* (Angelic Systems) of Angels, Saints and Beloved of Heaven by living Members of One Heaven shall be by Invocation in accord with the most sacred Covenant *Pactum De Singularis Caelum*. The methods, rules and standards of proper Invocation are defined by the most sacred Covenant *Pactum De Singularis Caelum* and associated covenants and no other. All properly conferred Invocation shall be received, recorded and acknowledged by the *Angelorum Systemata* (Angelic Systems) of One Heaven.

   An Invocation may be memorialised in writing as witness to the event. However, any such memorandum or certificate is always dependent upon the action of the said Invocation first being spoken.

   A proper Invocation may stand alone, or may represent part of a more complex series of ritual or events. When an Invocation is made from the use of some formula of words in prose, or sung or spoken, then it shall be known more formally as an Incantation. However, when a proper Invocation stands alone and involves the use of free form and self selection of words by the one making the Invocation, then it shall be known simply as an Invocation.

3. In accord with the most sacred Covenant *Pactum De Singularis Caelum*, an Invocation shall be reprobate, profane, repugnant and therefore invalid and improper and rejected by the Angels, Saints and Beloved of the *Angelorum Systemata* (Angelic Systems) of Heaven:-

   Reprobate, Profane and Repugnant forms of

Invocation

(i)   If it is deliberately harmful, negative or malevolent in its intent, design or inference; or

(ii)   If it is deliberately dishonest, deceptive or perfidious in its intent, design or inference; or

(iii)   If it is frivolous, or profane or disrespectful in its intent, or tone, or design or inference; or

(iv)   If it is irrational, or unreasonable or illogical in its intent, or tone, or design or inference; or

(v)   If it motivated or driven by hate, greed, jealously, anger or lust; or

(vi)   If it motivated or driven by an attempt to shift blame or avoid accepting self-responsibility; or

(vii)   If it motivated or driven by a desire, or wish, or worship of money or abundant material wealth.

4.   While the genuine Intention of a proper Invocation or Meditation (non-vocalised Invocation) is in itself the most important element of a valid Invocation, the following elements are recognised as the optimum structure for a valid Invocation being Identity, Petition and Affirmation:-

The fundamental elements of valid Invocation

(i)   Identity is the identity of the person or group in whose name the Invocation is directed; and

(ii)   Petition is the body of the Invocation itself; and

(iii)   Affirmation is the offering and affirmation of the one who makes the Invocation as their commitment to the positivity of Intention and the truth of Petition.

5.   Seven types of Invocation or Meditation (non-vocalised Invocation) are recognised being *Adoration, Blessing, Intervention, Intercession, Confession, Lamentation* and *Thanksgiving*:-

Characteristics of Invocation

(i)   **"Adoration"** is recognised as the type of Invocation or Meditation used for giving honour and praise to a higher spiritual presence; and

(ii)   **"Blessing"** is recognised as the type of Invocation or Meditation used to summons an authentic spiritual presence to another, often consonant with the act of consecration and the ritual of anointing; and

(iii)   **"Intervention"** is recognised as the type of Invocation or

Meditation used for directly summonsing the presence of spirits or asking something for one's self; and

(iv) **"Intercession"** is recognised as the type of Invocation or Meditation used for asking something for others; and

(v) **"Confession"** is recognised as the type of Invocation or Meditation used for the atonement and repentance of wrongdoing and the asking of forgiveness; and

(vi) **"Lamentation"** is recognised as the type of Invocation or Meditation used for crying in distress and asking for vindication; and

(vii) **"Thanksgiving"** is recognised as the type of Invocation or Meditation used for offering gratitude.

Article 163 – Sacrament of Obligation

1. Obligation (*Ritus Sacramentum Obligatio*) is the fourth of the seven (7) Key Sacraments, also known as the Keys of Heaven. The Sacrament of Obligation is the Key that unlocks the Living Virtue of Commitment and Fortitude. It is present in all fourteen (14) of the Cardinal Sacraments.

   Sacrament of Obligation (Ritus Sacramentum Obligatio)

   The Sacrament of Obligation may also be granted and conferred on its own in accordance with the most sacred Covenant *Pactum De Singularis Caelum*, the present sacred Covenant, the *Missale Christus* and associated approved liturgy.

2. The purpose of the sacrament of Obligation is the formal recognition and celebration of entrusting to the Divine Creator through a solemn consensual covenant certain promises which one or more persons bind themselves to honour and uphold.

   Divine Purpose of the Sacrament of Obligation

3. There are only two (2) valid and licit forms for the Sacrament of Obligation as defined by the most sacred *Missale Christus* and associated approved liturgy being General and Ordinary:-

   Forms of the Sacrament of Obligation

   (i) **"General Obligation"** is when the Sacrament of Obligation is bestowed automatically as part of the proper formation of a Binding relation in association with a promise, or pledge, or agreement or security, or surety or bond; and

   (ii) **"Ordinary Obligation"** is when the Sacrament of Obligation is bestowed automatically as an element of a formal sacramental ritual performed by properly consecrated and ordained clergy.

Article 164 – Sacrament of Delegation

1. **D**elegation (*Ritus Sacramentum Delegatio*) is the fifth of the seven (7) Key Sacraments, also known as the Keys of Heaven. The Sacrament of Delegation is the Key that unlocks the Living Virtue of Trust and Faith. It is present in all fourteen (14) of the Cardinal Sacraments.

    The Sacrament of Delegation may also be granted and conferred on its own in accordance with the most sacred Covenant *Pactum De Singularis Caelum*, the present sacred Covenant, the *Missale Christus* and associated approved liturgy.

    Sacrament of Delegation (Ritus Sacramentum Delegatio)

2. The purpose of the Sacrament of Delegation is the formal recognition and blessing of a relationship and agreement whereby certain Form, Rights and Obligations are lawfully delegated to the control of one or more Persons as fiduciaries for the benefit of one or more other Persons.

    Divine Purpose of the Sacrament of Delegation

3. There are only two (2) valid and licit forms for the Sacrament of Delegation as defined by the most sacred *Missale Christus* and associated approved liturgy being General and Ordinary:-

    Forms of the Sacrament of Delegation

    (i) **"General Delegation"** is when the Sacrament of Delegation is bestowed automatically as part of the proper formation of a Trust relation in the making of a true Oath and one or more Vows and then accepting such Oath to form the positions of Trustor and Trustee in relation; and

    (ii) **"Ordinary Delegation"** is when the Sacrament of Delegation is bestowed automatically as an element of a formal sacramental ritual performed by properly consecrated and ordained clergy.

Article 165 – Sacrament of Satisfaction

1. **S**atisfaction (*Ritus Sacramentum Satisfactio*) is the sixth of the seven (7) Key Sacraments, also known as the Keys of Heaven. It is present in all fourteen (14) of the Cardinal Sacraments.

    The Sacrament of Satisfaction may also be granted and conferred on its own in accordance with the most sacred Covenant *Pactum De Singularis Caelum*, the present sacred Covenant, the *Missale Christus*

    Sacrament of Satisfaction (Ritus Sacramentum Satisfactio)

and associated approved liturgy.

2. The purpose of the sacrament of Satisfaction is the formal recognition of the fulfilment and completion of any outstanding conditions and terms of an agreement recognised as possessing sacred value and importance.

Divine Purpose of the Sacrament of Satisfaction

3. There are only two (2) valid and licit forms for the Sacrament of Satisfaction as defined by the most sacred *Missale Christus* and associated approved liturgy being General and Ordinary:-

Forms of the Sacrament of Satisfaction

  (i)   "**General Satisfaction**" is when the Sacrament of Satisfaction is bestowed automatically as part of the noble and pious forgiveness of debts, the proper settlement and closure of accounts, the zeroing of balances and the provision of proper proof of such fiduciary obligations; and

  (ii) "**Ordinary Satisfaction**" is when the Sacrament of Satisfaction is bestowed automatically as an element of a formal sacramental ritual performed by properly consecrated and ordained clergy.

Article 166 – Sacrament of Resolution

1. Resolution (*Ritus Sacramentum Resolutio*) is the seventh of the seven (7) Key Sacraments, also known as the Keys of Heaven. It is present in all fourteen (14) of the Cardinal Sacraments.

Sacrament of Resolution (Ritus Sacramentum Resolutio)

   The Sacrament of Resolution may also be granted and conferred on its own in accordance with the most sacred Covenant *Pactum De Singularis Caelum*, the present sacred Covenant, the *Missale Christus* and associated approved liturgy.

2. The purpose of the Sacrament of Resolution is the formal recognition of agreed decisions, determinations and solutions as both a conclusion as well as progression of events.

Divine Purpose of the Sacrament of Resolution

3. There are only two (2) valid and licit forms for the Sacrament of Resolution as defined by the most sacred *Missale Christus* and associated approved liturgy being General and Ordinary:-

Forms of the Sacrament of Resolution

  (i)   "**General Resolution**" is when the Sacrament of Resolution is bestowed automatically as part of the proper conduct and intention of two or more persons in respect of a formal proposal of solution; and

(ii) **"Ordinary Resolution"** is when the Sacrament of Resolution is bestowed automatically as an element of a formal sacramental ritual performed by properly consecrated and ordained clergy.

Article 167 – Sacrament of Sanctification & Rite of Consecration

1.   **S**anctification (*Ritus Sacramentum Sanctificatio*) and Rite of Consecration is the first of the fourteen (14) Cardinal Sacraments, also known as the Ways of Heaven.

Sacrament of Sanctification (Ritus Sacramentum Sanctificatio) & Rite of Consecration

The Sacrament of Sanctification and Rite of Consecration may also be granted and conferred on its own in accordance with the most sacred Covenant *Pactum De Singularis Caelum*, the present sacred Covenant, the *Missale Christus* and associated approved liturgy.

2. The purpose of the Sacrament of Sanctification and Rite of Consecration is the solemn dedication to Divine purpose and service a particular person, place, object or thing, thus the formation of Sacred Circumscribed Space. Only the Rite of Consecration properly conferred creates Sacred Circumscribed Space.

Divine Purpose of the Sacrament of Consecration

3. There are only four (4) valid and licit forms for the Rite of Consecration as defined by the most sacred *Missale Christus* and associated approved liturgy being General, Dedicatory, Ordinary and Extraordinary:-

Forms of the Rite of Consecration

(i) **"General Consecration Rite"** is when the Sacrament of Sanctification is imparted through the authority and character of Holy Orders of one who is properly ordained, to then solemnly dedicate to Divine purpose and service a particular person, place, object or thing and the formation of Sacred Circumscribed Space. For example, General Consecration is the implicit form of the sacrament as an element of all Apostolic Life Sacraments; and

(ii) **"Dedicatory Consecration Rite"** is when the Sacrament of Sanctification is imparted through the authority and character of Holy Orders of one who is propertly ordained, to then solemnly dedicate a place, object or thing, already generally consecrated (already created as Sacred Circumscribed Space) and set it apart for religious purposes; and

(iii) **"Ordinary Consecration Rite"**, also known as Holy Orders, is when the Sacrament of Sanctification is permanently imprinted upon the character of willing, qualified and competent candidates, to be set apart as Clergy and dedicated in life and service to the Evangelisation of the Paschal Mystery of Christ; and the Sacred Scripture; and the most sacred unity and fulfilment of the Good News; and the pastoral care of the people through the continual performance of heroic acts of virtue; and the gift of the religious rites and ceremonies of the Living Body of Christ; and

(iv) **"Extraordinary Consecration Rite"**, also known as Holy Writ, is when the Sacrament of Sanctification is bestowed by and through the authority of the Supreme Patriarch; or through the authorised and licit actions of specifically commissioned and competent clergy to perform certain solemn rites and actions of Invocation, Incantation, Officium, Testification, Dispensation, Veneration, Sanction and Unction.

4. Consecration is an implicit sacrament and element of all Life Sacraments and may not be conducted as a replacement or alternate sacrament to an established Sacrament identified as possessing the quality of consecration.

Relations of the Sacrament of Consecration

5. There exists four (4) degrees of the form of Ordinary Consecration, corresponding to the four (4) forms that may be permanently and irrevocable imprinted upon the character of a willing, qualified and competent candidate, being:-

Degrees of the form of Ordinary Consecration

(i) **"Presbyterial Ordinary Consecration"** is the conferral of a particular Holy Degree of Sanctification upon a suitably willing, qualified and competent candidate for a Presbyterate; and

(ii) **"Diaconal Ordinary Consecration"** is the conferral of a particular Holy Degree of Sanctification upon a suitably willing, qualified and competent Presbyterial candidate for Diaconate; and

(iii) **"Episcopal Ordinary Consecration"** is the conferral of a particular Holy Degree of Sanctification upon a suitably willing, qualified and competent Diaconal candidate for Episcopate; and

(iv) **"Patriarchal Ordinary Consecration"** is the conferral of a particular Holy Degree of Sanctification upon a suitably willing, qualified and competent Episcopal candidate for Patriarchate.

Article 168 – Sacrament of Sustentation & Rite of Eucharist

1. **S**ustentation (*Ritus Sacramentum Sustentatio*) and Rite of Eucharist is the second of the fourteen (14) Cardinal Sacraments, also known as the Ways of Heaven.

   The Sacrament of Sustentation and Rite of Eucharist is the embodiment of the Spirit of the Paschal Mystery of Christ Risen, whereby God and the Divine Creator of all Existence personified as Christ chooses willingly to be the instrument of Divine Mercy, Forgiveness and Joy for all who have lived and all who will ever live, now and into the future forever.

   The Sacrament is granted and conferred in accordance with the most sacred Covenant *Pactum De Singularis Caelum*, the present sacred Covenant, the *Missale Christus* and associated approved liturgy.

   Sacrament of Sustentation (Ritus Sacramentum Sustentatio) & Rite of Eucharist

2. The celebration of the most Holy Eucharist is rightly central to the Christian and Jewish experience as a plenary union in Christ in the form of the one true Holy Apostolic Universal Ecclesia and therefore is fundamental to the human experience of all Christians and Jews.

   Divine Purpose of the Sacrament of Sustentation and Rite of Eucharist

   In the celebration of the most sacred Sacrament of the Eucharist, the united members of the Living Body of Christ remember not only the consent and acceptance of the Holy Spirit to be made flesh and blood, but to then suffer the uncertainties and doubt and emotions of human experience, and furthermore to freely sacrifice himself as the Testament of the Lamb, as the one true Christ Risen, so that all men and women and his church are freed from sin, from condemnation and are forever redeemed and saved.

   While Customary and Traditional Rites are free to honour the Eucharist from the perspective of the ritual of bread and blood representing the embodiment of the self-sacrifice of Christ through the Cross and the sign of spiritual nourishment, it is also necessary to express the entirety of the Paschal teaching and not merely its beginning, middle or end.

   The celebration of the Eucharist in simple and visible signs of unleavened bread, water and wine, is as much the wedding feast in celebration of the matrimony of Christ with his Church and the perpetual presence of the Holy Spirit, as it is a symbol of self-sacrifice and a symbol of renewal.

   Great care and diligence must be taken therefore in the formation of Eucharistic Celebration in the form of Mass, that the entirety of the

Eucharist is properly respected.

3. There exists only one form of the Sacrament of Sustentation and Rite of Eucharist being the Supernatural and Divine Eucharist.

Form of the Sacrament of Sustentation

4. No higher order life form including but not limited to any Homo Sapien, animal or non-hydro carbon higher order life form may be harmed or injured in any way by any celebration of the sacrament of Eucharist. For the proper and sacred celebration of the most holy Eucharist is in honouring the self-sacrifice of Christ and the votive offering of those willing to dedicate an element of Self-Sacrifice through self discipline, mercy, frugality, simplicity for the benefit of others.

Forbiddance of any harm associated with Rite of Eucharist

Any form of sacrifice of animals or any form of higher order life is an abomination against all united Heaven and Earth; and a profound sacrilege and act of contempt against God and the Divine Creator of all Existence, Christ and the Holy Spirit; and a disgrace against the name of every Angel, Saint, Spirit and Demon.

Article 169 – Sacrament of Unification & Rite of Matrimony

1. Unification (*Ritus Sacramentum Unificatio*) and Rite of Matrimony is the third of the fourteen (14) Cardinal Sacraments, also known as the Ways of Heaven.

Sacrament of Unification (Ritus Sacramentum Unificatio) & Rite of Matrimony

The Sacrament of Unification and Rite of Matrimony is granted and conferred in accordance with the most sacred Covenant *Pactum De Singularis Caelum*, the present sacred Covenant, the *Missale Christus* and associated approved liturgy.

2. The Sacrament of Unification and Rite of Matrimony is granted and administered when a man and a woman upon reaching majority choose and consent of their own free will to sanctify their union through a registered divine matrimonial covenant in accordance with the present sacred Covenant and associated approved liturgy. The Sacrament of Unification and Rite of Matrimony may only be bestowed once.

Divine Purpose of the Sacrament of Unification

3. There exists only one form of the Sacrament of Unification and Rite of Matrimony being Sacred and Irrevocable Unification. Therefore, as the Sacrament is a Sacred and Irrevocable Event, producing a Supreme Sacred Record in Heaven and upon the Earth, no properly conferred Sacrament of Unification can be withdrawn, or annulled or dissolved.

Form of the Sacrament of Unification and Rite of Matrimony

However, upon such circumstances of separation or death, one who has been bestowed the Sacrament of Unification is permitted to formalise a new Union through the Sacrament of Amaglamation and Rite of Union. Thus, the act of Divorce only applies to civil unions and the Sacrament of Amaglamation and never to Unification.

Furthermore, the transgression of Adultery only applies to both perpetrators equally culpable of acts of sexual extramarital affairs whilst one or the other or both are still publicly and legally being bound to another through the Sacrament of Unification or Sacrament of Amaglamation. The application of unequal punishment based on gender, or capital punishment in any form for the delict of Adultery is morally repugnant, profane, sacrilegious, forbidden, reprobate and to be suppressed now and forever.

Article 170 – Sacrament of Amalgamation & Rite of Union

1. Amalgamation (*Ritus Sacramentum Amalgamatio*) and Rite of Union is the fourth of the fourteen (14) Cardinal Sacraments, also known as the Ways of Heaven.

   Sacrament of Amalgamation (Ritus Sacramentum Amalgamatio) & Rite of Union

   The Sacrament of Amalgamation and Rite of Union is granted and conferred in accordance with the most sacred Covenant *Pactum De Singularis Caelum*, the present sacred Covenant, the *Missale Christus* and associated approved liturgy.

2. Amalgamation is granted and administered when two (2) or more parties come together of their own free will and competence and agree to form a new body in mutual union.

   Divine Purpose of the Sacrament of Amalgamation

3. There are only six (6) valid and licit forms for the Sacrament of Amalgamation as defined by the most sacred *Missale Christus* and associated approved liturgy being Sovereign, Political, Commercial, Corporate, Civil and Mutual:-

   Forms of the Sacrament of Amalgamation

   (i) **"Sovereign Union"** is when the Sacrament of Amalgamation is imparted through the Act of Coronation of an elected Monarch; and

   (ii) **"Political Union"** is when the Sacrament of Amalgamation is imparted through the Act of Inauguration of a democratically elected Leader; and

   (iii) **"Commercial Union"** is when the Sacrament of Amalgamation is imparted through the Act of Ratification of a Treaty between political or corporate bodies; and

(iv)   **"Corporate Union"** is when the Sacrament of Amalgamation is imparted through the Act of Incorporation of an Association; and

(v)   **"Civil Union"** is when the Sacrament of Amalgamation is imparted through the Act of Recordation to two (2) consenting adults; and

(vi)   **"Mutual Union"** is when the Sacrament of Amalgamation is imparted through the Registration of a mutual agreement between two (2) or more parties.

4.   Civil Union is granted and administered when a couple of the same gender or a man and woman upon reaching majority choose and consent of their own free will to validate their union through a registration and covenant of trust in accordance with the present sacred Covenant and associated approved liturgy. While a man or a woman may enter into more than one Union consecutively and never concurrently, a man and a woman may only be bestowed the sacrament of Holy Matrimony once.

Form of the Sacrament of Amalgamation & Civil Union

When the Sacrament of Amalgamation is approved to be bestowed upon a same sex couple, in recognition of their right to civil equality, the ceremony is forbidden to be performed within the main body of a Sacred Place of Worship. However, such a ceremony is permitted to be performed in a Side Chapel, providing the Eucharist is not celebrated in such space for that day.

The reason the Sacrament of Amalgamation is absolutely forbidden to be performed in the main body of a Sacred Place of Worship for a same sex couple, is not to prejudice, condemn or exclude such persons from the unity of the Living Body of Christ, but to protect with the utmost sanctity the exclusive and most holy sacrament of Unification.

Any civil or lesser body that seeks to attack, undermine, denigrate the absolute moral authority of the Universal Ecclesia of One Christ in such matters, or to contort words and phrases to imply a delinquency of duty and obligation to protect the Sacraments and Civil Equality is culpable of the most grievous transgressions.

Article 171 – Sacrament of Authentication & Rite of Record

1.   Authentication (*Ritus Sacramentum Authentico*) is the fifth of the fourteen (14) Cardinal Sacraments, also known as the Ways of Heaven.

Sacrament of Authentication (Ritus Sacramentum

The Sacrament of Authentication and Rite of Record may also be granted and conferred on its own in accordance with the most sacred Covenant *Pactum De Singularis Caelum*, the present sacred Covenant, the *Missale Christus* and associated approved liturgy.

2. Authentication is granted and administered upon the formal recording of the name and details of a particular object or concept in the Great Register and Public Record of One Heaven or associated Great Registers under Oath and evidence in accordance with the present sacred Covenant and associated approved liturgy.

3. There are only three (3) valid and licit forms for the Sacrament of Authentication as defined by the most sacred *Missale Christus* and associated approved liturgy being Ecclesiastical, Vital and Public:-

   (i)   **"Ecclesiastical Record"** is when the Sacrament of Authentication is bestowed automatically as part of the proper formation of an Ecclesiastical Record in accord with the most sacred Covenant *Pactum De Singularis Caelum* and the present sacred Covenant; and

   (ii)   **"Vital Record"** is when the Sacrament of Authentication is bestowed automatically as part of the proper formation of a Vital Record relating to Members, in accord with the most sacred Covenant *Pactum De Singularis Caelum* and the present sacred Covenant; and

   (iii) **"Public Record"** is when the Sacrament of Authentication is bestowed automatically as part of the proper formation of a Public Record in accord with the most sacred Covenant *Pactum De Singularis Caelum* and the present sacred Covenant.

Article 172 – Sacrament of Absolution & Rite of Confession

1.   Absolution (*Ritus Sacramentum Absolutio*) and Rite of Confession is the sixth of the fourteen (14) Cardinal Sacraments, also known as the Ways of Heaven.

The Sacrament of Absolution and Rite of Confession is granted and conferred in accordance with the most sacred Covenant *Pactum De Singularis Caelum*, the present sacred Covenant, the *Missale Christus* and associated approved liturgy.

2. Whilst Divine Forgiveness is absolute, immediate and irrevocable to all who have transgressed, the full effect of the Divine Sacrament of Absolution can only be received upon the genuine act of Contrition

Margin notes:
Authentico) & Rite of Record

Divine Purpose of the Sacrament of Authentication

Form of the Sacrament of Authentication & Rite of Record

Sacrament of Absolution (Ritus Sacramentum Absolutio) & Rite of Confession

Divine Purpose of the Sacrament of Absolution & Rite of

through the proper conferral of the Rite of Confession, also known as the Act of Reconciliation.

In the Rite of Confession, a Member who confesses their offences to a legitimate minister; and is authentically contrite and remorseful for such actions; and truly intends to reform themselves; and accepts without duress the necessary ecclesiastical or civil penalties, thereby removes any impediment to full reconciliation with God and the Divine Creator of all Heaven and Earth; and the full receipt of the absolute unconditional Divine Grace of Divine Mercy, Divine Forgiveness and Divine Love.

Thus, the proper and pious Cardinal Sacrament of Absolution, also known as the Act of Reconciliation itself does not presume to be the mechanism of conferring Divine Mercy, Divine Forgiveness and Divine Love, nor to presume to place conditions upon God and the Divine Creator of all Heaven and Earth and Christ and the Holy Spirit as to whether one is worthy or not worthy of Divine Salvation. Instead, the Sacrament of Absolution recognises the free will and choice of the penitent in openly reconciling with God and the Divine Creator of all Existence; and thus removing any impediment to the full receipt of Divine Grace.

Most importantly, within and through the authentic Sacrament of Absolution, the competent minister becomes the living embodiment of Christ the Witness and Messenger of the Good News of the Divine Mercy, Divine Forgiveness and Eternal Love of God and the Divine Creator of all Existence to each and every higher order life form and life itself.

3. There is only one form of the Sacrament of Absolution being Ordinary as defined by the most sacred *Missale Christus* and associated approved liturgy.

Form of the Sacrament of Absolution

4. Whilst it is a grievous error to consider that men or women or any church may interpret a holy position of trust into the presumption of adjudicating for Heaven the merits of a candidate for Divine Mercy, it is also a gross error to presume a man or woman is free to receive the full Grace of Divine Mercy and Divine Forgiveness without first being authentic, contrite, remorseful and pious in seeking reconciliation through the Rite of Confession.

Rite of Confession, Penance and the removal of any impediment to Divine Grace

The impediment is self inflicted and self sustaining, so long as the transgressor chooses to separate themselves from the truth of their actions and such consequences. Thus, the belligerent suffers the double ignominy of being estranged from the Grace and Divine Love of God and the Divine Creator as well as accepting by default the full

Confession

371

spiritual liability of their actions in placing themselves as opposite to the laws of Heaven. Thus, it is the belligerent transgressor and not the Universal Ecclesia, that chooses to put themselves in such danger and suffering.

5. The competent minister is not bound to impart the Sacrament of Absolution, unless the following conditions are clearly met by the person seeking to partake in the Rite of Confession:-

Conditions for Sacrament of Absolution

    (i)   That the person has been baptised and christened into the Living Body of Christ; and

    (ii)   That the person is of sufficient age of reason; and is sober and lucid, without mental impediment that might otherwise hinder their ability to recall to the best of their ability, what is fact compared to what might be speculation or imagination; and

    (iii)   That the person genuinely and authentically seeks to be reconciled with God and the Divine Creator of all Existence and remove any impediment in receiving the full Divine Grace of Divine Mercy and Divine Forgiveness; and

    (iv)   That the person acknowledges and agrees without duress that in the event they are culpable of acts without cause of Holy Writ or lawful excuse, and such acts are considered civilly criminal as well as immoral, then such penalty may also entail the necessary confession of such acts to civil authorities.

6. The Proper Seal of Confession, once formed through the bond of an authentically contrite, remorseful and pious Penitent and the competent, compassionate and discerning Confessor is absolute, permanent and irrevocable. In accord with the most sacred Covenant *Pactum De Singularis Caelum*, no force within Heaven or upon the Earth is permitted to break such a properly formed Seal.

Seal of Confession

However, an incomplete or tainted Act of Contrition, particularly when a Penitent is found not to be genuinely contrite, or remorseful or pious by their lack of subsequent penance or actions, fully dissolves any bond or constraints upon the Confessor and instead impels him under the Laws of Heaven to remedy the injury of the false Penitent in giving notice of the facts pertaining to such Act:-

    (i)   There can be no proper Seal of Confession or completed Act of Reconciliation where a Penitent continues to be culpable of sexual abuse or molestation against minors, unless such a person agrees to make a full and frank confession to the relevant ecclesiastical authorities and civil authorities within seven days of such admission under Confession; and

(ii) There can be no proper Seal of Confession or completed Act of Reconciliation where the Penitent is culpable of murder or terror without justifiable cause, unless such a person agrees to make a full and frank confession to the relevant ecclesiastical authorities and civil authorities within seven days of such admission under Confession.

Article 173 – Sacrament of Volition & Rite of Oath

1. **V**olition (*Ritus Sacramentum Volitio*) and Rite of Oath is the seventh of the fourteen (14) Cardinal Sacraments, also known as the Ways of Heaven.

   Sacrament of Volition (Ritus Sacramentum Volitio) & Rite of Oath

   The Sacrament of Volition and Rite of Oath is granted and conferred in accordance with the most sacred Covenant *Pactum De Singularis Caelum*, the present sacred Covenant, the *Missale Christus* and associated approved liturgy.

2. The Sacrament of Holy Oath is a recognition of a binding of obligation and performance duly recorded in the Great Register and Divine Records of Heaven and the temporal records on Earth and the Solar System.

   Divine Purpose of the Sacrament of Volition

   The Sacrament of Holy Oath is granted and conveyed upon the pronouncement of a valid oath in accordance with the present sacred Covenant and associated approved liturgy.

3. There are only four (4) valid and licit forms for the Sacrament of Volition as defined by the most sacred *Missale Christus* and associated approved liturgy being Personal, Public, Ordinary and Extraordinary:-

   Form of the Sacrament of Volition

   (i) **"Personal Oath"** is when the Sacrament of Volition is bestowed automatically as part of the proper formation of a Solemn and Binding Personal Oath performed and witnessed by at least one other person;and

   (ii) **"Public Oath"** is when the Sacrament of Volition is bestowed automatically as part of the proper formation of a Solemn and Binding Public Oath; and

   (iii) **"Ordinary Oath"** is when the Sacrament of Volition is bestowed automatically as part of the proper formation of a Solemn and Binding Sacred Oath by properly consecrated and ordained clergy; and

(iv) **"Extraordinary Oath"** is when the Sacrament of Volition is bestowed automatically as part of the proper formation of a Solemn and Binding Pious Oath by properly consecrated and ordained clergy choosing to live a heroic and virtuous life of austerity in the same manner of Christ.

Article 174 – Sacrament of Vocation & Rite of Vow

1. Vocation (*Ritus Sacramentum Vocatio*) and Rite of Vow is the eighth of the fourteen (14) Cardinal Sacraments, also known as the Ways of Heaven.

   The Sacrament of Vocation and Rite of Vow is granted and conferred in accordance with the most sacred Covenant *Pactum De Singularis Caelum*, the present sacred Covenant, the *Missale Christus* and associated approved liturgy.

   Sacrament of Vocation (Ritus Sacramentum Vocatio) & Rite of Vow

2. The purpose of the sacrament of Vocation is the formal recognition and endorsement of a person pledging themselves as assurance and security for the obligations of another in accordance with the present sacred Covenant and associated approved liturgy.

   Divine Purpose of the Sacrament of Vocation

3. There are only four (4) valid and licit forms for the Sacrament of Vocation (Sacramentum) as defined by the most sacred *Missale Christus* and associated approved liturgy being Personal, Public, Ordinary and Extraordinary:-

   Form of the Sacrament of Vocation

   (i) **"Personal Vow"** is when the Sacrament of Vocation is bestowed automatically as part of the proper formation of a Solemn and Binding Personal Vow; and

   (ii) **"Public Vow"** is when the Sacrament of Vocation is bestowed automatically as part of the proper formation of a Solemn and Binding Public Vow; and

   (iii) **"Ordinary Vow"** is when the Sacrament of Vocation is bestowed automatically as part of the proper formation of a Solemn and Binding Sacred Vow by properly consecrated and ordained clergy; and

   (iv) **"Extraordinary Vow"** is when the Sacrament of Vocation is bestowed automatically as part of the proper formation of a Solemn and Binding Pious Vow by properly consecrated and ordained clergy choosing to live a heroic and virtuous life of austerity in the same manner of Christ.

Article 175 – Sacrament of Testification & Rite of Testimony

1. **T**estification (*Ritus Sacramentum Testificatio*) and the Rite of Testimony is the ninth of the fourteen (14) Cardinal Sacraments, also known as the Ways of Heaven.

   The Sacrament of Testification and Rite of Testimony may also be granted and conferred on its own in accordance with the most sacred Covenant *Pactum De Singularis Caelum*, the present sacred Covenant, the *Missale Christus* and associated approved liturgy.

   Sacrament of Testification (Ritus Sacramentum Testificatio) & Rite of Testimony

2. Testification is by definition the act of vocalising and giving testimony or evidence; being a vocalised act involving not only at least one Invocation, but at least one promise and obligation in relation to the performance of a valid office. All valid offices are based upon truth and trust and so no office can be formed without a proper Testification.

   Nature of Testification

   All communication to the *Officium Systemata* (Offices Systems) of Heaven by living Members of One Heaven shall be by Testification of an Oath and at least one Vow in accord with the most sacred Covenant *Pactum De Singularis Caelum*. The methods, rules and standards of proper Testification shall be defined by the most sacred Covenant *Pactum De Singularis Caelum* and associated covenants and no other. All properly conferred Testification shall be received, recorded and acknowledged by the Officium Systemata (Offices Systems) of One Heaven.

3. There is only one form of the Sacrament of Testification in recognition of the fact that all Testimony is predicated on the solemn attestation of the truth, without embellishment.

   Form of the Sacrament of Testification

Article 176 – Sacrament of Compassion & Rite of Mercy

1. **C**ompassion (*Ritus Sacramentum Compassio*) and the Rite of Mercy is the tenth of the fourteen (14) Cardinal Sacraments, also known as the Ways of Heaven.

   The Sacrament of Compassion and Rite of Mercy may also be granted and conferred on its own in accordance with the most sacred Covenant

   Sacrament of Compassion (Ritus Sacramentum Compassio) & Rite of Mercy

Pactum De Singularis Caelum, the present sacred Covenant, the *Missale Christus* and associated approved liturgy.

2. The purpose of the Sacrament of Compassion and Rite of Mercy is the formal blessing of charity and benevolence to those in need; and the formal remittance and discharge of part or all of an offence as well as any prescribed punishment, in accordance with the present sacred Covenant and associated approved liturgy.

Divine Purpose of the Sacrament of Mercy

3. There are only four (4) valid and licit corporeal forms for the Sacrament of Compassion as defined by the most sacred *Missale Christus* and associated approved liturgy being Personal, Public, Ordinary and Extraordinary:-

Form of the Sacrament of Mercy

   (i)   **"Personal Mercy"** is when the Sacrament of Compassion is bestowed automatically as part of a formal forgiveness of some grievance between parties; or the benevolent assistance or selfless act of one to another; and

   (ii)   **"Public Mercy"** is when the Sacrament of Compassion is bestowed automatically as part of a formal public decree of clemency and mercy in light of some sentence; or as part of some organised charitable and benevolent support to the less fortunate; and

   (iii) **"Ordinary Mercy"** is when the Sacrament of Compassion is bestowed automatically as an element of a formal sacramental ritual performed by properly consecrated and ordained clergy; and

   (iv)   **"Extraordinary Mercy"** is when the Sacrament of Compassion is bestowed automatically as an element of a formal sacramental ritual performed by the Supreme Patriarch.

Article 177 – Sacrament of Conscription & Rite of Binding

1. Conscription (*Ritus Sacramentum Conscripto*) is the eleventh of the fourteen (14) Cardinal Sacraments, also known as the Ways of Heaven.

Sacrament of Conscription (Ritus Sacramentum Conscripto) & Rite of Binding

   The Sacrament of Conscription and Rite of Binding may also be granted and conferred on its own in accordance with the most sacred Covenant *Pactum De Singularis Caelum*, the present sacred Covenant, the *Missale Christus* and associated approved liturgy.

2. Binding is a fundamental concept of society as it permits people to

Divine Purpose of the Sacrament

engage in trusted relations of significant trust. The purpose of the sacrament of Binding is the formal recognition and acknowledgement of the Divine Authority given to the Universal Ecclesia of One Christ whereby what is bound on Earth shall be bound in Heaven and what is loosed upon the Earth shall likewise be loosened in Heaven.

of Conscription

3. There are only four (4) valid and licit corporeal forms for the Sacrament of Conscription as defined by the most sacred *Missale Christus* and associated approved liturgy being Personal, Public, Ordinary and Extraordinary:-

Form of the Sacrament of Conscription

   (i)   **"Personal Binding"** is when the Sacrament of Conscription is bestowed automatically as part the acceptance of a promise, or bond or surety of some written form between parties; and

   (ii)   **"Public Binding"** is when the Sacrament of Conscription is bestowed automatically as part of the formal public acceptance and registration of securities, sureties, promises associated with one or more rights and property; and

   (iii)   **"Ordinary Binding"** is when the Sacrament of Conscription is bestowed automatically as an element of a formal sacramental ritual performed by properly consecrated and ordained clergy, associated with a binding obligation accepted by a party, such as the penalty and duties associated with the Sacrament of Penance; and

   (iv)   **"Extraordinary Binding"** is when the Sacrament of Conscription is bestowed automatically as an element of a formal sacramental ritual performed by the Supreme Patriarch or his agents, such as the ritual of Exorcism.

Article 178 – Sacrament of Convocation

1. Convocation (*Ritus Sacramentum Convocatio*) is the twelfth of the fourteen (14) Cardinal Sacraments, also known as the Ways of Heaven.

Sacrament of Convocation (Ritus Sacramentum Convocatio)

The Sacrament of Convocation may also be granted and conferred on its own in accordance with the most sacred Covenant *Pactum De Singularis Caelum*, the present sacred Covenant, the *Missale Christus* and associated approved liturgy.

2. The purpose of the sacrament of Convocation is the formal summons to attendance with the members of a sacred body in accordance with the present sacred Covenant and associated approved liturgy. The meaning of Convocation is derived from the Latin word *convoco*

Divine Purpose of the Sacrament of Convocation

meaning "to call meeting of".

3. There are only three (3) valid and licit forms for the Sacrament of Convocation as defined by the most sacred *Missale Christus* and associated approved liturgy being General, Ordinary and Extraordinary:-

Form of the Sacrament of Convocation

   (i) **"General Convocation"** is when the Sacrament of Convocation is bestowed automatically as part of the proper formation of a meeting in trust, such as attendance to a competent forum of law; and

   (ii) **"Ordinary Convocation"** is when the Sacrament of Convocation is bestowed automatically as an element of a formal sacramental ritual performed by properly consecrated and ordained clergy; and

   (iii) **"Extraordinary Convocation"** is when the Sacrament of Convocation is bestowed automatically as part of an Ecumenical Council, or Conclave or Great Conclave.

Article 179 – Sacrament of Authorisation

1. Authorisation (*Ritus Sacramentum Auctoriso*) **is the thirteenth of the fourteen (14) Cardinal Sacraments,** also known as the Ways of Heaven.

Sacrament of Authorisation (Ritus Sacramentum Auctoriso)

   The Sacrament of Authorisation may also be granted and conferred on its own in accordance with the most sacred Covenant *Pactum De Singularis Caelum*, the present sacred Covenant, the *Missale Christus* and associated approved liturgy.

2. The purpose of the sacrament of Authorisation is the formal blessing of a decree or judgement issued by a valid minister or one possessing the proper level of authority in accordance with the present sacred Covenant and associated approved liturgy.

Divine Purpose of the Sacrament of Authorisation

3. There are only three (3) valid and licit forms for the Sacrament of Authorisation as defined by the most sacred *Missale Christus* and associated approved liturgy being Official, Ordinary and Extraordinary:-

Form of the Sacrament of Authorisation

   (i) **"Official Authorisation"** is when the Sacrament of Authorisation is bestowed automatically as part of the proper formation of an instrument of direction, command or order associated with the authority of the relevant position; and

   (ii) **"Ordinary Authorisation"** is when the Sacrament of

378

Authorisation is bestowed automatically as part of the proper formation of an instrument of direction, command or order associated with the authority of properly consecrated and ordained clergy; and

(iii) **"Extraordinary Authorisation"** is when the Sacrament of Authorisation is bestowed automatically as part of the proper formation of an instrument of direction, command or order associated with the authority of the Supreme Patriarch.

Article 180 – Sacrament of Elucidation

1. Elucidation (*Ritus Sacramentum Elucidato*) is the fourteenth of the fourteen (14) Cardinal Sacraments, also known as the Ways of Heaven.

   Sacrament of Elucidation (Ritus Sacramentum Elucidato)

   The Sacrament of Elucidation may also be granted and conferred on its own in accordance with the most sacred Covenant *Pactum De Singularis Caelum*, the present sacred Covenant, the *Missale Christus* and associated approved liturgy.

2. The purpose of the sacrament of Elucidation is opinion, answer or judgement promulgated by an Official Person, subject to the limits of their authority, in accordance with associated approved liturgy and the procedures of their Office.

   Divine Purpose of the Sacrament of Elucidation

3. There are only three (3) valid and licit forms for the Sacrament of Elucidation as defined by the most sacred *Missale Christus* and associated approved liturgy being Official, Ordinary and Extraordinary:-

   Form of the Sacrament of Elucidation

   (i) **"Official Elucidation"** is when the Sacrament of Elucidation is bestowed automatically as part of the proper formation of an instrument of direction, command or order associated with the authority of the relevant position; and

   (ii) **"Ordinary Elucidation"** is when the Sacrament of Elucidation is bestowed automatically as part of the proper formation of an instrument of direction, command or order associated with the authority of properly consecrated and ordained clergy; and

   (iii) **"Extraordinary Elucidation"** is when the Sacrament of Elucidation is bestowed automatically as part of the proper formation of an instrument of direction, command or order associated with the authority of the Supreme Patriarch.

Article 181 – Sacrament of Inspiration & Rite of Annunciation

1. Inspiration (*Ritus Sacramentum Inspiratio*) and Rite of Annunciation is the first of the twelve (12) Apostolic Life Sacraments, also known as "The Twelve", "The Twelve Apostles" and "The Means".

   The Sacrament of Inspiration and Rite of Annunciation is granted and conferred exclusively to an expectant mother and her living unborne child according to most sacred Covenant *Pactum De Singularis Caelum*, the present sacred Covenant, the *Missale Christus* and associated approved liturgy.

   Sacrament of Inspiration (Ritus Sacramentum Inspiratio) & Rite of Annunciation

2. All life is sacred and human life is especially sacred. Thus, the journey of conception to gestation and finally birth is an extraordinary journey and gift. The purpose of the Sacrament of Inspiration and Rite of Annunciation is the recognition of the ancient custom and tradition of celebrating the certainty of pregnancy and the arrival of the Holy Spirit into the unborne child from the fiftieth day.

   Divine Purpose of the Sacrament of Annunciation

   It is the Holy Spirit that helps form the very beginnings of the human mind and consciousness and this Divine Contribution appears the moment that the fetus is unmistakably and unquestionably of the higher order life form of Homo Sapien from the end of the first trimester.

3. It is a gross error to presume the Spirit is fully present in Human Form from the precise moment of Conception. Laws and Canons that are enacted according to this error are profane against God and the Divine Creator of all Life.

   Errors of Presumption concerning Spirit and Conception

   The reason the Spirit is not fully present in Human Form within the foetus until the end of the first trimester is threefold:-

   (i) The new life must first experience and overcome each and every form and era of history of evolution of life upon planet Earth over more than two (2) billion years in a matter of fifty (50) to sixty (60) days. Thus, to be human is to first experience what it is to be all other forms of lesser complex life; and

(ii)   The Holy Spirit must be invited into the new unborne life by the Spirit of the mother, even if the lower consciousness of the mother is unaware of such status of the pregnancy or may even be against the idea of pregnancy. If the Holy Spirit were not invited, but simply imposed itself upon the mother, then the arrival of the Spirit would be a fundamental breach of all the Laws of Heaven; and

(iii)   The body of the mother must reach the state of no longer reacting to the pregnancy as if it were an infection and instead must demonstrate at this miraculous moment a metamorphosis whereby the body of the mother ceases to fight for the death of the new life form and instead normally begins to change in order to support by every means the successful nurturing of the unborne infant to full term.

Therefore, any teachings or laws that seek to impose the denial of the rights of the mother prior to this key event, over an unborne life form, not yet enjoined with the Holy Spirit is morally repugnant, profane, sacrilegious, illogical and is forbidden and to be suppressed.

However, any teachings or laws that deny this momentous event and ignore the rights of the unborne child from this moment at the end of the first trimester, in favour of the mother having extended rights to destroy a life beyond the first trimester are also morally repugnant, profane, sacrilegious, illogical and is forbidden and to be suppressed.

4.   There are only three (3) valid and licit forms for the Sacrament of Inspiration and Rite of Annunciation as defined by the most sacred *Missale Christus* and associated approved liturgy being General, Ordinary and Extraordinary:

Form of the Sacrament of Inspiration

(i)   **"General Annunciation"** is when the Sacrament of Inspiration is bestowed automatically as part of the proper medical announcements of a Therapist or Physician of an Order or College in conformity with the Universal Ecclesia; and

(ii)   **"Ordinary Annunciation"** is when the Sacrament of Inspiration is bestowed automatically as part of the proper formation of pastoral announcements at the main Sunday mass by properly consecrated and ordained clergy; and

(iii)   **"Extraordinary Annunciation"** is when the Sacrament of Inspiration is bestowed automatically as part of the proper formation of special Patriarchal instrument of blessing from the

Patriarchal Registry.

5. Upon the estimated fiftieth day of pregnancy and before the one hundredth day, the expectant mother, or nominated guardian shall appoint a Herald by extraordinary condition to formally make known the news of the pregnancy to friends, family and the community. The promulgation of the news represents the Heraldic Prayer which represents the moment of conferral of the sacrament and the appointment of a Divine Guardian Angel to watch over the unborne child and the safety of the mother until birth.

Dispensing the Sacrament of Inspiration and Rite of Annunciation

Should no Herald be appointed by the mother or nominated guardian and the Heraldic Prayer not be instanced, then by ordinary condition a Divine Guardian Angel shall be automatically appointed by the powers of Heaven to watch over her unborne child and her safety not later than one hundred and fifty days since the beginning of the pregnancy.

In the instance that the unborne baby was not successfully delivered to full term, the Sacrament of Resurrection (Rite of Baptism) may be conferred upon all who have received the sacrament of Inspiration not earlier than two (2) hundred days after the Sacrament of Inspiration.

Article 182 – Sacrament of Resurrection & Rite of Baptism

1. Resurrection (*Ritus Sacramentum Resurrectio*) and Rite of Baptism is the second of the twelve (12) Apostolic Life Sacraments, also known as "The Twelve", "The Twelve Apostles" and "The Means".

Sacrament of Resurrection (Ritus Sacramentum Resurrectio) & Rite of Baptism

The Sacrament of Resurrection and Rite of Baptism is granted and conferred to a new borne Homo Sapien child at the final stage of birth or within 90 days of being borne in accordance with the most sacred Covenant *Pactum De Singularis Caelum*, the present sacred Covenant, the *Missale Christus* and associated approved liturgy.

2. The purpose of the Sacrament of Resurrection and Rite of Baptism is the formal bestowal or presentation of a possessory or prescriptive right of Office to an incumbent including taking possession of the insignia of Office.

Divine Purpose of the Sacrament of Resurrection

The birth of a child into flesh also represents the birth of a True Trust through the conveyance of divinity, also known as Divine right of use from the Divine Personality of the spirit of the child with the flesh of the child the eventual rightful trustee of the True Trust upon age of majority. Until such time, the Divine Person of the child grants temporary guardian powers to the parent or parents, or those properly designated as immediate carer.

3. There are only three (3) valid and licit forms for the Sacrament of Resurrection and Rite of Baptism as defined by the most sacred *Missale Christus* and associated approved liturgy being General, Ordinary and Extraordinary:-

    (i)   "**General Baptism**" is conferred by the delivery, by a Therapist or Physician of an Order or College in conformity with the Universal Ecclesia, of a child without the presence of an ordained minister and through the witness of the birth by two (2) or more people apart from the mother; and

    (ii)   "**Ordinary Baptism**" is conferred by the delivery of a child in the presence of an ordained minister; and

    (iii) "**Extraordinary Baptism**" is conferred by an ordained minister in the presence of the body of a still borne infant, or in formal dedication of the spirit of the still borne infant at the next celebration of the Eucharist and then such record entered into the Rolls to the fact of such sacred act.

4. In accordance with Divine Law and the most sacred Covenant *Pactum De Singularis Caelum*, if a foetus having received the sacrament of Inspiration dies before being borne, then this unique Divine Immortal Spirit shall be fully entitled to receive the sacrament of Resurrection and Rite of Baptism within 90 days of what otherwise would have been its borne day and all Life Sacraments thereafter at their appointed time.

    In accordance with Divine Law and the most sacred Covenant *Pactum De Singularis Caelum*, the mother or father or next of living kin of any foetus that failed to be borne, yet was not previously granted the Sacrament of Resurrection and Rite of Baptism may apply for the special ceremony of Life Sacraments where all sacraments are granted beginning with Annunciation to the sacrament representing the same age as if the foetus had been borne and lived to the present day.

5. All fraudulent and inferior sacraments of Baptism are forbidden and shall have no lawful effect. No documents, oral promises or any other inferred agreement by the parents of a new borne baby to the hospital, or competent civil authority or by implication to any Religion or Cult can in anyway diminish the rights of the parents as Guardians unless by willing and deliberate behaviour they have been legally proven through a formal hearing to be incompetent as trustees and guardians

Form of the Sacrament of Resurrection

Form of the Sacrament of Extraordinary Resurrection and Rite of Baptism

False and Profane Rituals of claimed Baptism

of their new borne child.

The Sacrament of Resurrection and Rite of Baptism negates the presumptions, validity and existence of any claimed *Cestui Que Vie* Trusts or any other curses, spells and unlawful conveyances by any Religion, Cult or their agents.

Article 183 – Sacrament of Incarnation & Rite of Christening

1. Incarnation (*Ritus Sacramentum Incarnatio*) and Rite of Christening is the third of the twelve (12) Apostolic Life Sacraments, also known as "The Twelve", "The Twelve Apostles" and "The Means".

   The Sacrament of Incarnation and Rite of Christening shall be granted and administered by the second (2nd) birthday of a child that has received the Sacrament of Resurrection and Rite of Baptism in accordance with the most sacred Covenant *Pactum De Singularis Caelum*, the present sacred Covenant, the *Missale Christus* and associated approved liturgy.

2. The purpose of the Sacrament of Incarnation and Rite of Christening is to officially recognise the transition of a baby to a child and their commencement of valid organised learning systems of the community. The child is now welcomed into the tribe and protection is given in exchange for the child understanding that it is time to learn.

3. There are only two (2) valid and licit forms for the Sacrament of Incarnation and Rite of Christening as defined by the most sacred *Missale Christus* and associated approved liturgy being Ordinary and Extraordinary:-

   (i) **"Ordinary Christening"** is conferred by a competent minister upon a child having reached the age of two (2) years; and

   (ii) **"Extraordinary Christening"** is conferred by a competent minister in formal dedication to the spirit of a still-borne infant, or deceased child upon the calculation of what would have been their second birthday. Such a ceremony may be conducted as a Special Mass, with such records then entered into the rolls to the fact of such sacred act.

4. In accordance with Divine Law and the most sacred Covenant *Pactum*

Sacrament of Incarnation (Ritus Sacramentum Incarnatio) & Rite of Christening

Divine Purpose of the Sacrament of Incarnation and Rite of Christening

Form of the Sacrament of Incarnation

Extraordinary

De Singularis Caelum, if a child having received the Sacrament of Resurrection and Rite of Baptism dies at or prior to the age of two (2), then this unique Divine Immortal Spirit shall be fully entitled to receive the Sacrament of Incarnation and Rite of Christening two (2) years since being borne and all Life Sacraments thereafter at their appointed time.

Form of the Sacrament of Incarnation

In accordance with Divine Law and the most sacred Covenant *Pactum De Singularis Caelum*, the mother or father or next of living kin of any child that died at or prior to the age of two (2) yet was not previously granted the Sacrament of Resurrection and Rite of Baptism may apply for the special ceremony of Life Sacraments where all sacraments are granted beginning with Sacrament of Inspiration and Rite of Annunciation to the sacrament representing the same age as if the child had lived and grown up to the present day.

Article 184 – Sacrament of Confirmation & Rite of First Communion

1. Confirmation (*Ritus Sacramentum Confirmatio*) and Rite of First Communion is the fourth of the twelve (12) Apostolic Life Sacraments, also known as "The Twelve", "The Twelve Apostles" and "The Means".

Sacrament of Confirmation (Ritus Sacramentum Confirmatio) & Rite of First Communion

The Sacrament of Confirmation and Rite of First Communion shall be granted and administered by the twelfth (12th) birthday of a child that has received the Sacrament of Incarnation and Rite of Christening in accordance with the most sacred Covenant *Pactum De Singularis Caelum*, the present sacred Covenant, the *Missale Christus* and associated approved liturgy.

2. The Divine purpose of the Sacrament of Confirmation and Rite of First Communion is to celebrate the admittance of a child into the rights of possessions and responsibility of their respective community through the formal celebration and bestowal of certain Ecclesiastical and Public rights to the child as a member of the community. Upon a child demonstrating their ability to distinguish right from wrong; and the basic competence of logic, reason and discernment; and an essential understanding of morals and consequences, a child is permitted to own property in their own name and to participate in the Holy Eucharist. A child having received Holy Communion is also expected to acknowledge their responsibilities and duties to their family and community.

Divine Purpose of the Sacrament of Confirmation and Rite of First Communion

3. There are only two (2) valid and licit forms for the Sacrament of Confirmation and Rite of First Communion as defined by the most

Form of the Sacrament of

sacred *Missale Christus* and associated approved liturgy being Ordinary and Extraordinary:

(i) **"Ordinary Communion"** is conferred by a competent minister upon a child having reached the age of twelve (12) years; and

(ii) **"Extraordinary Communion"** is conferred by a competent minister in formal dedication to the spirit of a still-borne infant, or deceased child upon the calculation of what would have been their twelfth birthday. Such a ceremony may be conducted as a Special Mass, with such records then entered into the rolls to the fact of such sacred act.

4. The Ordinary Form of the Sacrament of Confirmation and Rite of First Communion cannot be conferred unless the child is clearly prepared and able to become a productive and exemplary member of their community. Thus, the priority of education and preparation must pertain to skills of reason, logic, discernment, morality, ethics and the consequences of actions before any detailed knowledge of the laws of the Universal Ecclesia of One Christ are then necessary.

A child that is able to recite scripture and the catechises of the Universal Ecclesia, yet is unable to apply reason, logic and virtue to their decisions is not competent for First Communion and those that failed to adequately prepare such a child are not competent to teach, until they acknowledge such failings.

This is because, to be a Christian or Jew united as the Living Body of Christ is to be an ambassador of Christ; and an exemplary to the world. First Communion is a sacred ceremony that heralds such a moment. Therefore an absence of proper preparation is a grave offence against the child and the present sacred Covenant itself.

5. In accordance with Divine Law and the most sacred Covenant *Pactum De Singularis Caelum*, if a child having received the Sacrament of Confirmation and Rite of First Communion dies before being the age of twelve (12), then this unique Divine Immortal Spirit shall be fully entitled to receive the Sacrament of Confirmation and Rite of First Communion within sixty (60) days of twelve (12) years since being borne.

In accordance with Divine Law and the most sacred Covenant *Pactum De Singularis Caelum*, the mother or father or next of living kin of any child that died prior to the age of twelve (12) yet was not previously granted the Sacrament of Confirmation and Rite of First Communion may apply for the special ceremony of Life Sacraments where all sacraments are granted beginning with Sacrament of Inspiration and Rite of Annunciation to the sacrament representing the same age as if the child had lived and grown up to the present day.

Article 185 – Sacrament of Illumination & Rite of Majority

1. **I**llumination (*Ritus Sacramentum Illuminatio*) is the fifth of the twelve (12) Apostolic Life Sacraments, also known as "The Twelve", "The Twelve Apostles" and "The Means".

    The Sacrament of Illumination and Rite of Majority shall be granted and administered by the twenty-first (21st) birthday of a young adult in accordance with the most sacred Covenant *Pactum De Singularis Caelum*, the present sacred Covenant, the *Missale Christus* and associated approved liturgy.

    Sacrament of Illumination (Ritus Sacramentum Illuminatio) & Rite of Majority

2. Every enlightened and civilised culture of history has recognised the significance of the moment of welcoming a new member of the community as an adult, whatever age was prescribed for such tradition. Since then, the age of adulthood has progressively increased to eighteen in some societies to the age of twenty one in others.

    Divine Purpose of the Sacrament of Illumination

    The purpose of the Sacrament of Illumination and Rite of Majority is to formalise the welcoming of new adults into the community at an age whereby most should have successfully finished some learning and qualification of useful skills.

    Most importantly, the Sacrament of Illumination and Rite of Majority is essential to the Christian and Jewish community of the Living Body of Christ to ensure all new Adult Members are fully competent in their moral, spiritual and behavioural obligations, particularly in the forming and supporting of their own families. Thus the Sacrament of Illumination and Rite of Majority is a necessary element to stable and fruitful Matrimonial relations throughout a healthy, productive and joyous society.

3. There are only two (2) valid and licit forms for the Sacrament of Illumination and Rite of Majority as defined by the most sacred *Missale Christus* and associated approved liturgy being Ordinary and

    Form of the Sacrament of Illumination & Rite of Majority

Extraordinary:-

(i) **"Ordinary Majority Rite"** is conferred by a competent minister upon a youth having reached the age of twenty one years; and

(ii) **"Extraordinary Majority Rite"** is conferred by a competent minister in formal dedication to the spirit of a still-borne infant, or deceased child or youth upon the calculation of what would have been their twenty first birthday. Such a ceremony may be conducted as a Special Mass, with such records then entered into the rolls to the fact of such sacred act.

4. A condition of Sacrament of Illumination and Rite of Majority is that the youth knowingly and willingly consents to dedicating their life to continuous self improvement and virtue and to contributing to the benefit and improvement of their community and society.

Conditions of the Sacrament of Illumination

5. In accordance with Divine Law and the most sacred Covenant *Pactum De Singularis Caelum*, if a teenager having received the Sacrament of Confirmation and Rite of First Communion dies before being the age of twenty-one (21), then this unique Divine Immortal Spirit shall be fully entitled to receive the Sacrament of Illumination and Rite of Majority within thirty (30) days of twenty-one (21) years since being borne and all Life Sacraments thereafter at their appointed time.

Extraordinary Form of the Sacrament of Illumination

In accordance with Divine Law and the most sacred Covenant *Pactum De Singularis Caelum*, the mother or father or next of living kin of any child that died prior to the age of twenty-one (21) yet was not previously granted the Sacrament of Confirmation and Rite of First Communion may apply for the special ceremony of Life Sacraments where all sacraments including Sacrament of Illumination and Rite of Majority are granted beginning with Sacrament of Inspiration and Rite of Annunciation to the sacrament representing the same age as if the child had lived and grown up to the present day.

Article 186 – Sacrament of Exultation & Rite of Maturity

1. Exultation (*Ritus Sacramentum Exultatio*) is the sixth of the twelve (12) Apostolic Life Sacraments, also known as "The Twelve", "The Twelve Apostles" and "The Means".

Sacrament of Exultation (Ritus Sacramentum Exultatio) & Rite of Maturity

The Sacrament of Exultation and Rite of Maturity shall be granted and administered by the thirty-third (33rd) birthday of an adult in accordance with the most sacred Covenant *Pactum De Singularis Caelum*, the present sacred Covenant, the *Missale Christus* and associated approved liturgy.

2. The Sacrament of Exultation and Rite of Maturity is the celebration of the point of transition from being a Young Adult to a fully mature Adult.

Divine Purpose of the Sacrament of Exultation Rite of Maturity

3. There are only two (2) valid and licit forms for the Sacrament of Exultation and Rite of Maturity as defined by the most sacred *Missale Christus* and associated approved liturgy being Ordinary and Extraordinary:

Form of the Sacrament of Exultation Rite of Maturity

    (i) **"Ordinary Maturity"** is conferred by a competent minister upon an adult having reached the age of thirty-three (33) years; and

    (ii) **"Extraordinary Maturity"** is conferred by a competent minister in formal dedication to the spirit of a still-borne infant, or deceased child or youth or adult upon the calculation of what would have been their thirty-third birthday. Such a ceremony may be conducted as a Special Mass, with such records then entered into the rolls to the fact of such sacred act.

Article 187 – Sacrament of Glorification & Rite of Seniority

1. Glorification (*Ritus Sacramentum Glorificatio*) is the seventh of the twelve (12) Apostolic Life Sacraments, also known as "The Twelve", "The Twelve Apostles" and "The Means".

Sacrament of Glorification (Ritus Sacramentum Glorificatio) & Rite of Seniority

The Sacrament of Glorification and Rite of Seniority shall be granted and administered by the fifty-fifth (55th) birthday of an adult in accordance with the most sacred Covenant *Pactum De Singularis Caelum*, the present sacred Covenant, the *Missale Christus* and associated approved liturgy.

2. The Sacrament of Glorification and Rite of Seniority is the celebration of the point of transition from Maturity to Seniority. It recognises the experience and contribution of older adults while they are still active members of their society.

Divine Purpose of the Sacrament of Glorification

3. There are only two (2) valid and licit forms for the the Sacrament of Glorification and Rite of Seniority as defined by the most sacred *Missale Christus* and associated approved liturgy being Ordinary and

Form of the Sacrament of Glorification

Extraordinary:-

(i) **"Ordinary Seniority"** is conferred by a competent minister upon an adult having reached the age of fifty-five (55) years; and

(i) **"Extraordinary Seniority"** is conferred by a competent minister in formal dedication to the spirit of a still-borne infant, or deceased child or youth or adult upon the calculation of what would have been their fifty-fifth birthday with such records then entered into the rolls to the fact of such sacred act.

Article 188 – Sacrament of Divination & Rite of Elders

1. **D**ivination (*Ritus Sacramentum Divinatio*) is the eighth of the twelve (12) Apostolic Life Sacraments, also known as "The Twelve", "The Twelve Apostles" and "The Means".

   The Sacrament of Divination and Rite of Elders shall be granted and administered by the seventy-seventh (77th) birthday of a senior in accordance with the most sacred Covenant *Pactum De Singularis Caelum*, the present sacred Covenant, the *Missale Christus* and associated approved liturgy.

   Sacrament of Divination (Ritus Sacramentum Divinatio) & Rite of Elders

2. An enlightened society venerates its elders, protects them and seeks their counsel and wisdom. The Sacrament of Divination and Rite of Elders is the celebration of the point of transition from Seniority to Elderhood. It is the celebration of becoming an elder.

   Divine Purpose of the Sacrament of Divination

3. There are only two (2) valid and licit forms for the Sacrament of Divination and Rite of Elders as defined by the most sacred *Missale Christus* and associated approved liturgy being Ordinary and Extraordinary:-

   Form of the Sacrament of Divination

   (i) **"Ordinary Elder"** is conferred by a competent minister upon an adult having reached the age of seventy-seven (77) years; and

   (ii) **"Extraordinary Elder"** is conferred by a competent minister in formal dedication to the spirit of a still-borne infant, or deceased child or youth or adult upon the calculation of what would have been their seventy-seventh birthday. Such a ceremony may be conducted as a Special Mass, with such records then entered into the rolls to the fact of such sacred act.

Article 189 – Sacrament of Visitation

1. Visiation (*Ritus Sacramentum Visitatio*) is the ninth of the twelve (12) Apostolic Life Sacraments, also known as "The Twelve", "The Twelve Apostles" and "The Means".

   Sacrament of Visitation (Ritus Sacramentum Visitatio)

   The Sacrament of Visitation shall be granted and administered within months of most certain death in accordance with the most sacred Covenant *Pactum De Singularis Caelum*, the present sacred Covenant, the *Missale Christus* and associated approved liturgy.

2. It is the natural order of life and the universe that we are borne, we live and our bodies age and become less reliable until the day that we must leave our bodies behind and return to our eternal Heavenly Home.

   Divine Purpose of the Sacrament of Visitation

   Thus, it is not the natural order, but profoundly unnatural, profane and supremely arrogant to consider that such natural order should be suspended and that Homo Sapiens live according to an undetermined lifespan. For while it is perfectly reasonable to aspire to a world without debilitating and painful disease, it is encumbered upon all men and women with heroic virtue to protect the boundaries of life of our species, so that we do not become consumed as other species in other parts of the universe did become in past ages, and assume themselves to be equals to the Universal Divine Creator.

   The Holy Spirit reveals through the Risen Christ the true nature of God and the Divine Creator of all Existence and all Heaven and Earth to be Divine Mercy, Divine Forgiveness and Divine Love. Thus, it is not the nature or wish of the Father, nor Christ or the Holy Spirit that any man or woman suffer the indignity of a slow, agonising and wasteful death.

   Therefore, when a man or woman approaches such a trial as a slow and debilitating terminal illness and death, the Universal Ecclesia of One Christ has an ecclesiastical and moral obligation as the true Disciples of Christ to do everything within its power to support the dignity of the dying and help them find peace.

   Dying with dignity is a fundamental determination of an enlightened society under God and the Divine Creator. Visitation is a celebration that enables those people who have some time before the point of death to seek resolution and peace before death; and before a loss of consciousness deprives the person of the full appreciation of the sacrament.

3. There is only one form of the Sacrament of Visitation as defined by the most sacred *Missale Christus* and associated approved liturgy.

   Form of the Sacrament of

Visitation

Article 190 – Sacrament of Salvation & Last Rites

1. **S**alvation (*Ritus Sacramentum Salvatio*) and Last Rites is the tenth of the twelve (12) Apostolic Life Sacraments, also known as "The Twelve", "The Twelve Apostles" and "The Means".

   The Sacrament of Salvation and Last Rites shall be granted and administered within days of imminent death in accordance with the most sacred Covenant *Pactum De Singularis Caelum*, the present sacred Covenant, the *Missale Christus* and associated approved liturgy.

2. The purpose of the Sacrament of Salvation and Last Rites is the formal final (last) rites of bestowal or presentation of a possessory or prescriptive right to an incumbent in accordance with the present sacred Covenant and associated approved liturgy.

   The Sacrament of Salvation and Last Rites is the special celebration of blessing and cleansing to help an individual in the final stages of death to find a point of peace and resolution to their life in the hope of evoking the care of other minds already crossed to help guide the person safely.

3. There is only one form of the Sacrament of Salvation and Last Rites as defined by the most sacred *Missale Christus* and associated approved liturgy.

Sacrament of Salvation (Ritus Sacramentum Salvatio) & Last Rites

Divine Purpose of the Sacrament of Salvation and Last Rites

Form of the Sacrament of Salvation and Last Rites

Article 191 – Sacrament of Emancipation & Funerary Rites

1. **E**mancipation (*Ritus Sacramentum Emancipatio*) and Funerary Rites is the eleventh of the twelve (12) Apostolic Life Sacraments, also known as "The Twelve", "The Twelve Apostles" and "The Means".

   The Sacrament of Emancipation and Funerary Rites shall be granted and administered after death and prior to the sacrament of Veneration and the burial or disposal of the body in accordance with the most sacred Covenant *Pactum De Singularis Caelum*, the present sacred Covenant, the *Missale Christus* and associated approved liturgy.

2. The purpose of the Sacrament of Emancipation and Funerary Rites is the formal funeral rites to an incumbent in accordance with the

Sacrament of Emancipation (Ritus Sacramentum Emancipatio) & Funerary Rites

Divine Purpose of the Sacrament of Emancipation

present sacred Covenant and associated approved liturgy.

The Sacrament of Emancipation and Funerary Rites is both the sacrament and ceremony that remembers the deceased, their life and provides an opportunity for those in attendance to speak, celebrate and honour the memory of the departed.

3. There are only four (4) valid and licit forms for the Sacrament of Emancipation as defined by the most sacred *Missale Christus* and associated approved liturgy being Ordinary, Public, Sovereign and Extraordinary:-

   (i)   **"Ordinary Funerary Rites"** is conferred by at least one competent minister; and

   (ii)   **"Public Funerary Rites"** is conferred by at least three (3) competent ministers as a public act of honour and respect upon the death of a notable person; and

   (iii)   **"Sovereign Funerary Rites"** is conferred by a Patriarch and at least twelve (12) competent ministers assisting upon the death of a sovereign; and

   (iv)   **"Extraordinary Funerary Rites"** is conferred by at least three (3) Patriarchs and all the Bishops and Clergy upon the death of a Patriarch, or the College of Patriarchs and Synod of Bishops upon the death of the Supreme Patriarch.

Article 192 – Sacrament of Veneration

1. Veneration (*Ritus Sacramentum Veneratio*) is the twelfth of the twelve (12) Apostolic Life Sacraments, also known as "The Twelve", "The Twelve Apostles" and "The Means".

The Sacrament of Veneration shall be granted and administered by a valid Minister following death and the sacrament of Remembrance in accordance with the most sacred Covenant *Pactum De Singularis Caelum*, the present sacred Covenant, the *Missale Christus* and associated approved liturgy.

2. The purpose of the sacrament of Veneration is a formal rite of blessing and remembrance in favour of the formal recognition, honour and trust of an incumbent in Heaven in accordance with the present sacred Covenant and associated approved liturgy.

3. There are only four (4) valid and licit forms for the Sacrament of Veneration as defined by the most sacred *Missale Christus* and

associated approved liturgy being Exemplary, Heroic, Blessed and Beatific:- Veneration

(i) **"Exemplary Veneration"** is when the title and sacramental grace of Exemplar is conferred upon the memory, name and relics of a deceased person; and

(ii) **"Heroic Veneration"** is when the title and sacramental grace of Venerable is conferred upon the memory, name and relics of a deceased person; and

(iii) **"Blessed Veneration"** is when the title and sacramental grace of Blessed is conferred upon the memory, name and relics of a deceased person; and

(iv) **"Beatific Veneration"** is when the title and sacramental grace of Beatification is conferred upon the memory, name and relics of a deceased person.

Article 193 – Rite of Dedication

1. **Dedication, also known as the Rite of Dedicatory Consecration** shall be when the Sacrament of Sanctification is imparted through the authority and character of Holy Orders of one who is properly ordained, to then solemnly dedicate a place, object or thing, already generally consecrated (already created as Sacred Circumscribed Space) and set it apart for religious purposes; and Rite of Dedication

The Rite of Dedication (Dedicatory Consecration) shall be granted and conferred in accordance with the most sacred Covenant *Pactum De Singularis Caelum*, the present sacred Covenant, the *Missale Christus* and associated approved liturgy.

2. A place, object or thing worthy and suitable to be set apart for dedicated religious service, function or use, requires the formation of a special and significant form of Sacred Circumscribed Space, wherein the full effect of such intention and ceremony may be protected, preserved and respected. This is the purpose and function of the Rite of Dedication. Divine Purpose of the Rite of Dedication

The Rite of Dedication does not create the original Sacred Circumscribed Space of a place, object or thing. Such space is either automatically defined and recognised by its customary presence and existence or is recognised during the time of its construction or near completion.

3. There are only two (2) valid and licit forms for the Rite of Dedication as defined by the most sacred *Missale Christus* and associated approved liturgy being Ordinary and Extraordinary:-

    (i)   **"Ordinary Dedication"** is when the Rite of Dedication is imparted through the authority and character of Holy Orders of one who is properly ordained, to then solemnly suppress the Clerical character and authority of a previously Ordained person; and

    (i)   **"Extraordinary Dedication"** is when the Rite of Dedication is bestowed by and through the authority of the Supreme Recurrence; or through the authorised and licit actions of specifically commissioned and competent clergy to suppress the Clerical character, service or function or any person, object, place or thing previously consecrated and set aside for dedicated religious service or duties.

Form of the Rite of Dedication

Article 194 – Rite of Deconsecration

1. **D**econsecration shall be when a person, place, object or thing set aside for religious purposes through a form of the Sacrament of Sanctification and Rite of Consecration is formally removed from such service or purpose and ecclesiastical status. The Rite for deconsecration of persons of the ecclesial state is the Rite of Secularisation.

Rite of Deconsecration

    The Rite of Deconsecration shall be granted and conferred in accordance with the most sacred Covenant *Pactum De Singularis Caelum*, the present sacred Covenant, the *Missale Christus* and associated approved liturgy.

2. Only the Rite of Consecration properly conferred creates Sacred Circumscribed Space. Once the Sacrament of Sanctification and Rite of Consecration forms certain Sacred Circumscribed Space, such space cannot be dissolved or destroyed, only set aside.

Divine Purpose of the Rite of Deconsecration

    Thus the Rite of Deconsecration is the temporary suppression of Sacred Circumscribed Space dedicated to Divine purpose or service. The Rite itself does not create any new character, nor does it taint, defile or diminish the original Sacrament of Sanctification and Rite of Consecration.

    A person, place, object or thing properly deconsecrated has its ecclesiastical character, purpose and service temporarily suppressed, thus constricting its ability to perform or be used for certain licit ecclesiastical acts.

Deconsecration does not create, nor infer the formation of "unholy" space, as such a notion is an abomination and a defiance of the logic and articles of the most sacred Covenant *Pactum De Singularis Caelum* and the present sacred Covenant.

3. There are only three (3) valid and licit forms for the Rite of Deconsecration as defined by the most sacred *Missale Christus* and associated approved liturgy being General, Ordinary and Extraordinary:- Forms of the Rite of Deconsecration

    (i) **"General Deconsecration Rite"** is when the Rite of Deconsecration is imparted through the authority and character of Holy Orders of one who is properly ordained, to then solemnly order the suppression of use of Sacred Circumscribed Space for a dedicated ecclesiastical purpose, service or use; and

    (ii) **"Ordinary Deconsecration Rite"** is when the Rite of Deconsecration is imparted through the authority and character of Holy Orders of one who is properly ordained, to then solemnly suppress the Ecclesial character and authority of a previously consecrated place, object or thing; and

    (iii) **"Extraordinary Deconsecration Rite"** is when the Rite of Deconsecration is bestowed by and through the authority of the Supreme Patriarch; or through the authorised and licit actions of specifically commissioned and competent clergy to suppress the ecclesiastical character, service or function of any object, place or thing previously consecrated and set aside for dedicated religious service or duties.

Article 195 – Rite of Restoration

1. **R**estoration shall be when a place, object or thing previously Deconsecrated has its original character restored through the lifting of any previous suppression. The proper Rite to restore the Ecclesial state of Deconsecrated of clergy or officials is the Rite of Reformation. Rite of Restoration

    The Rite of Restoration shall be granted and conferred in accordance with the most sacred Covenant *Pactum De Singularis Caelum*, the present sacred Covenant, the *Missale Christus* and associated approved liturgy.

2. There are only two (2) valid and licit forms for the Rite of Restoration as defined by the most sacred *Missale Christus* and associated Forms of the Rite of

approved liturgy being General and Extraordinary:-

(i) **"General Restoration Rite"** is when the Rite of Restoration is imparted through the authority and character of Holy Orders of one who is properly ordained, to then solemnly remove the suppression of use of Sacred Circumscribed Space for a dedicated ecclesiastical purpose, service or use; and

(ii) **"Extraordinary Restoration Rite"** is when the Rite of Restoration is bestowed by and through the authority of the Supreme Patriarch; or through the authorised and licit actions of specifically commissioned and competent clergy to remove the suppression of the ecclesiastical character, service or function or any object, place or thing previously consecrated and set aside for dedicated religious service or duties.

Article 196 – Rite of Ordination

1. By divine institution, the Rite of Ordinary Consecration, also known as Holy Orders shall establish a distinct and unique form of Sacred Circumscribed Space possessing an indelible sacred and religious character, through the Sacrament of Sanctification and Rite of Consecration. The formation of the unique Sacred Circumscribed Space shall also be known as the Clerical State.

The Rite of Ordination shall be granted and conferred in accordance with the most sacred Covenant *Pactum De Singularis Caelum*, the present sacred Covenant, the *Missale Christus* and associated approved liturgy.

2. The minister of sacred Rite of Ordination shall be a consecrated bishop. Ordination, through the Sacred Rite of Ordinary Consecration is ideally to be celebrated within the solemnities of the Mass on a Sunday or holy day of obligation. Ordination generally is to be celebrated in the cathedral church, with Clerics and other members of the Christian faithful invited to the Ordination so that as large an assembly as possible is present at the celebration:-

(i) For the celebration of a *Presbyterial Ordinary Consecration*, the minister of sacred ordination is a consecrated bishop; and

(ii) For the celebration of a *Diaconal Ordinary Consecration*, the ministers of sacred ordination is a consecrated bishop and at least two (2) Deacons; and

(iii) For the celebration of an *Episcopal Ordinary Consecration*, the ministers of sacred ordination is a consecrated patriarch and at least two (2) bishops; and

(iv) For the celebration of a *Patriarchal Ordinary Consecration*, the ministers of sacred ordination is the Supreme Patriarch and at least two (2) other patriarchs.

Article 197 – Rite of Secularisation

1. **S**ecularisation shall be when the Clerical State (Sacred Circumscribed Space) person set aside for religious purposes through a form of the Sacrament of Sanctification and Rite of Consecration is formally removed from such service or purpose and ecclesiastical status. The Rite for deconsecration of persons of the ecclesial state is the Rite of Secularisation.

   Rite of Secularisation

   The Rite of Secularisation shall be granted and conferred in accordance with the most sacred Covenant *Pactum De Singularis Caelum*, the present sacred Covenant, the *Missale Christus* and associated approved liturgy.

2. Only the Rite of Ordination properly conferred creates the Cleric State through Ordinary Consecration. Once the Sacrament of Sanctification and Rite of Consecration forms certain Sacred Circumscribed Space as the Clerical State, such space cannot be dissolved or destroyed, only set aside.

   Divine Purpose of the Rite of Secularisation

   Thus the Rite of Secularisation is the temporary suppression of Sacred Circumscribed Space dedicated to the Clerical State. The Rite itself does not create any new character, nor does it taint, defile or diminish the original Sacrament of Sanctification and Rite of Consecration.

   The person deprived of their character does not have to be present during the Rite. However, a person called upon to be present who then refuses a formal summons, may not in the future be considered nor granted the Rite of Reformation as a restoration of Clerical State.

   A person deconsecrated has their ecclesiastical character, purpose and service temporarily suppressed, by depriving them of their authorised Sacred Circumscribed Space or Clerical State, thus constricting their ability to perform certain licit ecclesiastical acts.

   Secularisation does not create, nor infer the formation of "unholy" space, as such a notion is an abomination and a defiance of the logic and articles of the most sacred Covenant *Pactum De Singularis*

Caelum and the present sacred Covenant.

3. There are only four (4) valid and licit forms for the Rite of Secularisation as defined by the most sacred *Missale Christus* and associated approved liturgy being Presbyterial, Diaconal, Episcopal and Patriarchal:-

    Form of the Rite of Secularisation

    (i)   For the issuance of a *Presbyterial Secularisation*, the minister of the Rite of Securalisation shall be a consecrated bishop; and

    (ii)   For the issuance of a *Diaconal Secularisation*, the ministers of the Rite of Securalisation shall be a consecrated bishop and at least two (2) Deacons; and

    (iii) For the issuance of an *Episcopal Secularisation*, the ministers of the Rite of Securalisation shall be a consecrated patriarch and at least two (2) bishops; and

    (iv)   For the issuance of a *Patriarchal Secularisation*, the ministers of the Rite of Securalisation shall be the Supreme Patriarch and at least two (2) other patriarchs.

Article 198 – Rite of Reformation

1. **R**eformation shall be when a person previously deprived of their Clerical State (Sacred Circumscribed Space) has their original character restored through the lifting of any previous suppression. The proper Rite to restore the Ecclesiastical state of Deconsecrated persons is the Rite of Reformation.

    Rite of Reformation

    The Rite of Reformation shall be granted and conferred in accordance with the most sacred Covenant *Pactum De Singularis Caelum*, the present sacred Covenant, the *Missale Christus* and associated approved liturgy.

2. The loss of Clerical State (Sacred Circumscribed Space) is an extreme sanction of the Universal Ecclesia. Thus, the grounds for its restoration through the Rite of Reformation must be equally compelling.

    Divine Purpose of the Rite of Reformation

    Unlike places, objects and things, human beings that have undergone the significant life changing events of the loss of Clerical State; and through authentic remorse, prayer and deep personal discernment, with continual acts of penance and charity, a person may merit in their lifetime a restoration of such a state.

    Under clear and unmistakable circumstances of remorse, reform and redemption, the term "reformation" more appropriately describes the accumulative lessons of such a soul being more than simply a "restoration", but an enlarging of experience as to the eternal presence of Divine Mercy and Forgiveness.

However, a person who previously refused to acknowledge their culpability; and refused to attend on summons the Rite of Secularisation shall be forbidden from receiving the Rite of Reformation by their own actions. Such a person may still seek restoration through a posthumous Reformation following their death.

3. There are only four (4) valid and licit forms for the Rite of Reformation as defined by the most sacred *Missale Christus* and associated approved liturgy being Presbyterial, Diaconal, Episcopal and Patriarchal:-

    Form of the Rite of Secularisation

    (i)   For the issuance of a *Presbyterial Reformation*, the minister of the Rite of Reformation shall be a consecrated bishop; and

    (ii)   For the issuance of a *Diaconal Reformation*, the ministers of the Rite of Reformation shall be a consecrated bishop and at least two (2) Deacons; and

    (iii)   For the issuance of an *Episcopal Reformation*, the ministers of the Rite of Reformation shall be a consecrated patriarch and at least two (2) bishops; and

    (iv)   For the issuance of a *Patriarchal Reformation*, the ministers of the Rite of Reformation shall be the Supreme Patriarch and at least two (2) other patriarchs.

Article 199 – Rite of Blessing

1. **B**lessing is an Incantation and formula of words and specific actions to consecrate a person, or object or place or thing; or to summons an authentic spiritual presence; or to anoint a person and dedicated them to God and the Divine Creator of all Heaven and Earth; or to bestow the expectation and experience of divine favour. Thus, Blessing may refer to a formal procedure of Consecration, or Invocation or Anointing or Dispensation.

    Rite of Blessing

Blessing is a fundamental set of formal rituals and acts of the Living Body of Christ, with holy water replacing blood as to the origin of the word and rituals. The conduct of any form of ritual in blood is hereby profane, sacrilegious, reprobate, forbidden and to be suppressed now and forever, in honour of the sacred Covenant *Pactum De Singularis Caelum* and the present most sacred Covenant.

All formula and actions of Blessing are subject to the liturgical norms of the Universal Ecclesia of One Christ in accord with the most sacred *Missale Christus* and associated approved liturgical texts.

Article 200 – Rite of Exorcism

1. **E**xorcism is an extraordinary rite reserved exclusively for competent Clergy to bind any and every form of malevolent spirit, elemental or ghost under a Holy Writ; and thus removed, by any and every coercive plenary authority in Heaven and upon the Earth, from a place, or person, or animal, or object or thing.

   Rite of Exorcism

   A fundamental and immutable Law of the Universe, as sealed permanently and irrevocable through the most sacred Covenant *Pactum De Singularis Caelum*, that every spirit and mind entrusted with a physical body is entitled to its use and enjoyment without malevolent and vexatious interference or haunting or possession by some disembodied spirit or ghost. Therefore, such a malevolent and vexatious spirit, form or ghost is a trespasser, and in contempt of the laws of Heaven and Earth.

   Through the most sacred Covenant *Pactum De Singularis Caelum* and the present sacred Covenant, the Universal Ecclesia of One Christ is entrusted to protect the Living Members from any and all forms of spirits, elementals and ghosts that refuse to accept the Rule of Law, Decency and the Law of Sanctity of Spirit. The rite of Exorcism is therefore a most potent and dreadful action of last resort; and not to be administered unless the conditions and form is followed in accord with the most sacred *Missale Christus* and associated approved liturgical texts.

2. Exorcism properly conducted in accord with the most sacred *Missale Christus* and associated approved liturgical texts, is a visible and immediate exhibition of the defeat of Evil.

   Exorcism and the visible defeat of Evil

   However, care must be made not to perpetuate gross error or ignorance in presuming all cases for the need for Exorcism involves demonic possession, or the presence of the Evil One. Indeed, such ignorance itself, negates the authority and power of Exorcism itself by applying presumptions that may be completely false.

Of all possible instances and examples of malevolent haunting, infestations or possessions, the greatest majority are a result of ghosts and not demons. Indeed, there are ample examples whereby malevolent ghosts will assume the stereotypical role of pretending to be demons, in mimic to inferior rites of Exorcism, producing an entirely unsatisfactory spiral of ignorance.

In truth, all such malevolent spirits and ghosts, regardless of their primary form are in direct and deliberate violation of the law of Heaven and the Universe that no unwanted consciousness in spirit has the right to impose itself upon another in physical form to the detriment, debilitation and injury of the living person. Therefore, all such spiritual entities are properly defined as Evil in character by such wilful action of ignorance and contempt, rather than traditional terms of demonic.

3. Of all the elements essential to the successful conduct of the rite of Exorcism, wise discernment in the form of Intelligent Research is essential – both in terms of the state of mind, experience and events that may have affected the candidate for Exorcism, as well as the domicile, friends, family and activities.

Intelligence as a key weapon to defeat Evil

Every element in detailed research into the past events, circumstances and people is essential, particularly as the vast majority of malevolent experiences are due to ghosts of people previously known to the family, or place or the victim.

Without Intelligence and knowledge of the precise context, the Rite of Exorcism is defective and in error, even if performed in accord with sacred liturgy. Evil as wilful ignorance and arrogance, cannot be defeated by the same demonstration of such wilful ignorance and prejudice. Thus, all clergy are forbidden to perform the rite of Exorcism, except in clear and unmistakable signs of supernatural malevolence and the immediate and dire threat against the life of the victim.

4. Contrary to ignorant presumptions, the greatest power of the competent Exorcist is their ability to manifest intelligent and authentic compassion not only for the victim, but the malevolent spirits and ghosts in breach of the Laws of Heaven.

Manifest Compassion as a key weapon to defeat Evil

It is only in this ability to confidently name the ghost, through proper research or spirit, through careful reading and review and then demonstrate the qualities of Mercy, Love and Forgiveness does the Exorcist become the embodiment of the Spirit of Christ and a beacon of the purest light that none in spirit can hide.

When the heart of the Exorcist is truly open, they create the doorway necessary to effect the proper binding of the malevolent spirit or ghost through the full and complete spiritual forces of Heaven as the final weapon to defeat evil.

Article 201 – Rite of Inquisition

1. **I**nquisition shall be an ecclesiastical authority conferred by Rite for the proper investigation of any matter of thing within the Jurisdiction of the Universal Ecclesia, in accordance with the most sacred Covenant *Pactum De Singularis Caelum* and the present sacred Covenant.

    The Rite of Inquisition shall be granted and conferred in accordance with the most sacred Covenant *Pactum De Singularis Caelum*, the present sacred Covenant, the *Missale Christus* and associated approved liturgy.

2. There exists only one form of the Rite of Inquisition.

Rite of Inquisition

Form of the Rite of Inquisition

Article 202 – Rite of Dispensation

1. **D**ispensation, also known as Indulgence, shall be the mode of proper publication, or distribution of certain rights, usually memorialised in document form. Therefore, Dispensation is usually a derivative of some other sacred act occurring first. Thus, the first forms of instruments of value were the forms of indulgences and instruments themselves called "dispensations".

    As all rights come from Divine Rights, all documents and instruments of value must by definition be Dispensations properly conferred and issued in accord with the most sacred Covenant *Pactum De Singularis Caelum* and the present sacred Covenant.

2. A Dispensation shall be reprobate, profane, repugnant and therefore invalid and improper and rejected:-

    (i)   That a personal payment or payment of profit is made to the maker or issuer body, beyond the legitimate recovery of costs; or

    (ii)   That the issuance contains such exclusive or restrictive rights that contradict the most sacred Covenant *Pactum De Singularis*

Rite of Dispensation

Reprobate, Profane and Repugnant forms of Dispensation

Caelum or the present sacred Covenant; or

(iii)   That the issuance contains language of promises or benefits contrary to the most sacred Covenant *Pactum De Singularis Caelum* or the present sacred Covenant; or

(iv)   If it motivated or driven by an attempt to shift blame or avoid accepting self-responsibility; or

(v)   If it motivated or driven by a desire, or wish, or worship of money or abundant material wealth.

Article 203 – Rite of Abrogation

1.   **A**brogation shall be the formal repeal by Rite and authority of a previously issued edict, act, regulation or instrument. All and any edicts, acts, regulations or instruments found to be contrary to the articles of the most sacred Covenant *Pactum De Singularis Caelum* or the present sacred Covenant shall be automatically suppressed, having no force or effect from the date of first publication.

Rite of Abrogation

The Rite of Abrogation shall be granted and conferred in accordance with the most sacred Covenant *Pactum De Singularis Caelum*, the present sacred Covenant, the *Missale Christus* and associated approved liturgy.

2.   There exists only one form of the Rite of Abrogation.

Form of the Rite of Abrogation

Article 204 – Rite of Nullification

1.   **N**ullification shall be the formal striking and removal of any record, page, leaf, or document or instrument found to be contrary to the articles of the most sacred Covenant *Pactum De Singularis Caelum* and the present sacred Covenant shall be automatically suppressed, having no force or effect from the date of first publication.

Rite of Nullification

The Rite of Nullification shall be granted and conferred in accordance with the most sacred Covenant *Pactum De Singularis Caelum*, the present sacred Covenant, the *Missale Christus* and associated approved liturgy.

2.   There exists only one form of the Rite of Nullification.

Form of the Rite of Nullification

Article 205 – Rite of Inauguration

1. **I**nauguration shall be the formal Rite and ceremony for the induction and investiture of a proper and eligible candidate into high secular office.

   The Rite of Inauguration shall be granted and conferred in accordance with the most sacred Covenant *Pactum De Singularis Caelum*, the present sacred Covenant, the *Missale Christus* and associated approved liturgy.

   Rite of Inauguration

2. There exists only one form of the Rite of Inauguration.

   Form of the Rite of Inauguration

3. By definition, the Rite of Inauguration is unique compared to the Rite of Investiture in that a proper candidate duly inaugurated, assumes occupancy of an existing office, without the reconstitution of the trust or property of such Office.

   Inauguration and Office

   The Oath of Office creates unique Sacred Circumscribed Space and Trust that is firmly bound to the character and existing person as occupant of that Office; and remains attached to the person even after leaving office.

4. As a solemn Oath of Office is mandatory and fundamental to the proper formation of the Trust of Office, any failure to repair a defect or failure to properly execute such an Oath shall render such occupancy of Office null and voice, having no legitimacy or validity whatsoever.

   Inauguration and Oath of Office

Article 206 – Rites of Investiture

1. **I**nvestiture shall be the formal Rite and ceremony for the induction and investiture of a suitable and proper candidate into high fiduciary office.

   The Rite of Investiture shall be granted and conferred in accordance with the most sacred Covenant *Pactum De Singularis Caelum*, the present sacred Covenant, the *Missale Christus* and associated approved liturgy.

   Rite of Investiture

2. There exists only one form of the Rite of Investiture.

   Form of the Rite of Investiture

3. By definition, the Rite of Investiture is unique compared to the Rite of Inauguration in that a proper candidate duly invested, assumes occupancy of an existing office, but through the reconstitution of the trust and property of such Office, by their Oath.

   Investiture and Office

   The Oath of Office creates unique Sacred Circumscribed Space and Trust that is firmly bound to the character and existing Office; and dissolves upon gross breach of trust or in leaving such office.

4. As a solemn Oath of Office is mandatory and fundamental to the proper formation of the Trust of Office, any failure to repair a defect or failure to properly execute such an Oath shall render such occupancy of Office null and voice, having no legitimacy or validity whatsoever.

Investiture and Oath of Office

Article 207 – Rite of Coronation

1. Coronation shall be the formal Rite and ceremony for the investiture of a proper royal candidate into the sacred office of sovereign.

Rite of Coronation

The Rite of Coronation shall be granted and conferred in accordance with the most sacred Covenant *Pactum De Singularis Caelum*, the present sacred Covenant, the *Missale Christus* and associated approved liturgy.

2. There exists only one form of the Rite of Coronation.

Form of the Rite of Coronation

3. By definition, the Rite of Coronation is unique compared to the Rite of Inauguration and Investiture in that a proper candidate duly invested, assumes occupancy of an existing office, but through the reconstitution of the trust and property of the Dominion, including all the laws of the Dominion, by their solemn Sacred Oath.

Coronation and Office

The Sacred Oath of Sovereign Office creates unique Sacred Circumscribed Space and Trust that is firmly bound to the character and existing Office of Sovereign; and dissolves only upon death or abdication.

4. As a solemn Oath of Office is mandatory and fundamental to the proper formation of the Trust of Office, any failure to repair a defect or failure to properly execute such an Oath shall render such occupancy of Office null and void, having no legitimacy or validity whatsoever.

Coronation and Oath of Office

TITLE XIV – STANDARDS & PROCEDURES

Article 208 – Confirmation and Amendment

1. **T**he present most sacred Covenant shall be Confirmed seven (7) times, by Revelation, Ratification, Sanctification, Testification, Exemplification, Legislation and Consummation upon or within seven (7) years of its formation:-

Covenant
Confirmation

(i) By *Revelation*, the present most sacred Covenant is the self-evident manifestation of Divine Truth and fulfilment of the most sacred and revered scripture from MARS E8:Y3208:A48:S4:M25:D3, also known as [Saturday, 15 August 2009]; and

(ii) By *Ratification*, the present most sacred Covenant being ratified upon GAIA E8:Y3209:A1:S1:M6:D1, also known as [Monday, 21 Dec 2009], as the first and highest law of Heaven by the properly constituted government of One Heaven being the one hundred forty four (144) united as the Unique Collective Awareness of Divine Mind, also known as the "Divina"; and

(iii) By *Sanctification*, the present most sacred Covenant is fulfilled, finished and perfected by one borne of Holly (Holy) Blood from VENUS E8:Y3210:A0:S1:M27:D6, also known as [Wednesday, 21 December 2011]; and

(iv) By *Testification*, the present most sacred Covenant sources its power, legitimacy and authority from each and every signed, sealed and executed Voluntatem Et Testamentum (Will and Testament) in the proper prescribed form of Level 6 Higher Order life forms bearing witness to their Divinity and the validity of the present Covenant from GAIA E1:Y1:A1:S1:M9:D1, also known as [Friday, 21 December 2012]; and

(v) By *Exemplification*, the present most sacred Covenant is signed, sealed and delivered by one possessing the absolute authority by the most sacred and revered scripture to do so from JOVIUS E1:Y1:A17:S2:M4:D4, also known as [Thursday, 14 March 2013]; and

(vi) By *Legislation*, the present most sacred Covenant shall be the first statute as law enacted within each and every Ucadia community from SOL E1:Y3:A0:S1:M11:D5, also known as [Monday, 21 December 2015]; and

(vii) By *Consummation*, the present most sacred Covenant fulfilment, finished and made perfect from MARS

407

E1:Y4:A48:S4:M14:D3, also known as [Monday, 15 August 2016].

2. The present most sacred Covenant shall be permitted to be amended from time to time, in accord with the strict interpretation of the present Article, according to Technical and Special:-

Covenant Amendment

    (i)   A *Technical Amendment* is where a specific clause contained within the present Covenant is approved for a minor amendment either through the complete replacement of all the words contained within the clause, or minor word alteration, due to an error of presentation, or translation, or grammar by a properly constituted and authorised Ecumenical Council; and

    (ii)   A *Special Amendment* is where a new clause or enhanced meaning to a clause is proposed and added to the Covenant at a properly constituted and authorised Ecumenical Council.

3. A *Technical Amendment* is where a specific clause contained within the present Covenant is approved for a minor amendment either through the complete replacement of all the words contained within the clause, or minor word alteration. A Technical Amendment is permitted to occur providing the approval of the highest bodies of temporary or permanent presence on Earth, under one or more of the following conditions:-

Technical Amendment

    (i)   That the clause contains a style, typographical or simple grammatical error which will be corrected through the proposed amendment; or

    (ii)   That the clause contains a significant grammatical or semantic error that renders any true intention of the clause impossible and that the proposed amendment will correct this error to the original intent; or

    (iii)   That the clause contains a significant error contradicting one or more other clauses of the Covenant and that the proposed amendment will correct this error to the original intent.

4. A *Special Amendment* is where a new clause or enhanced meaning to a clause is proposed and added to the Covenant other than in relation to a Technical Amendment.

Special Amendment

A proposed Special Amendment may not in any way contradict a major tenet or principle of the present Covenant. Any proposed Special Amendment that introduces a deliberate contradiction or abrogation of a major tenet or principle of the present Covenant is automatically null and void having no force or effect *ab initio* (from the beginning).

A Special Amendment shall only be permitted after Consummation where such proposal is made at a Great Conclave where a vote is taken for its approval, framed as a free and fair vote to the delegates. For an amendment to be valid and enacted requires a two thirds (2/3) of the total votes cast by the total delegates to an Ecumenical Council.

Article 209 – Words, Punctuation and Reference

1. In the present most sacred Covenant of the One Holy Apostolic Universal Ecclesia of One Christ, unless the context requires otherwise:-

Words, Punctuation and Reference

(i) Capitalised Words (other than words capitalised by convention at the beginning of a sentence or phrase) defined within these Articles have the same meaning as described within the present Articles; or if not defined within the the present Articles, then in accord with the *Divine Collection of Maxims of Law*; or if not defined within the the *Divine Collection of Maxims of Law*, then in accord with the *Ucadia Lexicon of Language*; and

(ii) Words importing the singular include the plural and vice versa; and

(iii) Words that are gender neutral or gender specific include each gender; and

(iv) An expression of Words importing a Person includes an Association, Institute, Company, Partnership, Joint Venture, Association, Corporation, Society, Agency or other body corporate; and

(v) The coupling of Words together demonstrates that such Words are to be understood in the same sense, unless the grammar used permits otherwise; and

(vi) Other parts of speech and grammatical forms of a Word or phrase defined in these Articles have a corresponding meaning; and

(vii) The departure from the signification and meaning of Words is not permitted unless it is evident through these Articles that such signification and meaning of Words are not conformable to the intent of the whole; and

(viii) The misspelling of a Word shall have no material impact on the validity, legitimacy or effect of a clause of these Articles to the extent that the intended meaning and spelling is evident or able to be reasonably deduced; and

(ix) Subsequent Words, added for the purpose of clarity only, must be isolated by a consistent form of open and closed square brackets. When interpreting the whole, a Form of Words isolated by open and closed square brackets is to be taken as not existing on the page.

2. In the present most sacred Covenant, unless the context requires otherwise:

Punctuation and Style

(i) A Full Stop shall signify the end of a sentence, or occasionally the deliberate shortening of a Word into an identifiable abbreviation; and

(ii) A Colon shall signify a mark of relationship and sequence; and

(iii) A Semicolon shall signify a separation of distinct clauses, or listed clauses linked to a continued theme; and

(iv) Parentheses shall signify the enclosure of a brief definition, or comment, or clarification within the context of a broader clause; and

(v) Hyphen shall signify either the combination of Words to form a new word or phrase, or as means of separating clause or expression within a broader clause; and

(vi) Square Brackets shall signify interpolations or insertions made, or to be made by someone other than the author, such as the user of a particular model of Form and Instrument; and

(vii) Headings are for convenience only and do not affect the interpretation of these Articles; and

(viii) The use of any style of font, font size, bolding, italics, underline or any other style are for cosmetic purpose only and do not affect the interpretation of these Articles.

3. In the present most sacred Covenant, unless the context requires otherwise:

Citation and Reference

(i) Reference to a thing includes a part of that thing; and

(ii) A reference to a clause, party, schedule or attachment is a reference to a clause of these Articles, and a party, schedule or attachment to these Articles; and

(iii) A reference to a law includes a constitutional provision, treaty, decree, convention, statute, regulation, ordinance, by-law judgement, rule of common law or equity or a rule of a competent juridic person and is a reference to that law as amended, consolidated or replaced; and

(iv)   A reference to a document includes all amendments or supplements to that document, or replacements or novation of it; and

(v)   A reference to a party to a document includes that party's successors and permitted assigns; and

(vi)   An Agreement on the part of two or more persons binds them severally; and

(vii)   A reference to an Agreement, other than the present Covenant, includes an undertaking, Covenant, Agreement or legally enforceable arrangement or understanding, whether or not in writing.

Article 210 – Summa Dogma (Greatest Principle)

1.   **W**hen the Oratorium, also known as the One Supreme Court, also known as the Supreme Court of One Heaven is in Supreme Session within the Organs of the Living Body of One Christ possessing the proper authority of *Imperium*, then such an organ of the Universal Ecclesia may use its Powers of Original Jurisdiction to make absolute and final rulings in accord with Divine Canon Law by Final Irrevocable Judgement. These absolute and final rulings shall be called "**Summa Dogma**" in accord with Article 131 (*Greatest Principles*) of the most sacred Covenant *Pactum De Singularis Caelum*.

Summa Dogma (Greatest Principle)

2.   God and the Divine Creator of all Existence and all Heaven and Earth, through Christ and the Holy Spirit have entrusted the Universal Ecclesia of One Christ to be the highest trustees and fiduciaries, for the good care of planet Earth and the Solar System; and the health and well-being of all Living Members, in accord with the most sacred Covenant *Pactum De Singularis Caelum* and the present sacred Covenant.

Imperium Authority and Summa Dogma

There exists only five (5) general states of Imperium being Supremum, Universalem, Ordinarium, Publicum and Administrationis:-

(i)   "**Imperium Supremum**" or Supreme Imperium is the absolute Right of Imperium entrusted to the Universal Ecclesia of One Christ through the Right of *Ius Ecclesiae Imperium* and

411

embodied within the person of Supreme Patriarch in session with a Tribunal, or College of Patriarchs, or Synod of Bishops or Ecumenical Council. No other temporal body possesses the same right of Imperium, except the faiths of One Islam and One Spirit if not impeded; and

(ii) **"Imperium Universalem"** or Universal Imperium is the Right of Imperium through *Ius Ecclesiae Imperium* entrusted to a Patriarch or Bishop in communion with the Living Body of Christ and in session with a Synod or Tribunal; and

(iii) **"Imperium Ordinarium"** or Ordinary Imperium is the Right of Imperium through *Ius Regnum Imperium* entrusted to a Sovereign or Deacon and in session with a Tribunal or Council as inherited from *Ius Ecclesiae Imperium*; and

(iv) **"Imperium Publicum"** or Public Imperium is the Right of Imperium through *Ius Publicum Imperium* entrusted to a Public Minister or Jurist or elected Executive Government, as inherited from *Ius Regnum Imperium*; and

(v) **"Imperium Administration"** or Administrative Imperium is the Right of Imperium through *Ius Administrationis Imperium* entrusted to the military, police, law enforcement officials and public servants, as the Official Right of Command, Occupation and Enforcement, as inherited from *Ius Publicum Imperium*.

3. A Summa Dogma under Supreme Imperium or Universal Imperium is *ipso facto* (as a matter of fact) original law and primary law and the highest possible final and irrevocable tenet, principle and edict from a validly constituted forum of law of any and all societies, aggregates, associations, persons, entities and higher order spirits, living and deceased having universal and absolute, divine and temporal jurisdiction:- *Summa Dogma as Absolute and Final Law*

(i) Providing the Summa Dogma adheres to the Criteria of valid Summa Dogma as prescribed by the present Article; and

(ii) The officer or body issuing the Summa Dogma has the power and authority to do so in accord with the present sacred Covenant; and

(iii) That the Summa Dogma does not seek to define or create a new Right, or new Property, or seek to grant, give, devise, convey, alienate, surrender, seize, disqualify, enclose, capture, arrest, securitise, suppress, forfeit or annul any existing Rights unless such an action has already been acknowledged and defined as permitted within the present sacred Covenant or associated Covenants and Charters; and

(iv) That the Summa Dogma does not contradict the most sacred present Covenant or the body of canons known as *Astrum Iuris Divini Canonum*; and

(v) The new Summa Dogma does not contradict any previous Summa Dogma.

4. A valid Summa Dogma adheres to the following essential criteria:-   *Criteria for valid Summa Dogma*

(i) The Oratorium as the Supreme Court of One Heaven is in Session through the competent and authorised organ of the Universal Ecclesia and capable of properly rendering a Summa Dogma; and

(ii) That a properly constituted body is the highest and most competent forum of the Universal Ecclesia as defined by the present Covenant; and

(iii) A petition and memorandum is received by the competent forum in the prescribed form, duly lodged, recorded and gazetted for a Summa Dogma to be rendered; and

(iv) That the specific subject matter of the petition and memorandum is within the Powers of Original Jurisdiction of the Oratorium as the Supreme Court of One Heaven temporarily embodied and personified within the supreme body and organ of the Living Body of One Christ; and

(v) That the core questions outlined within the Petition to be answered have not previously been specifically addressed in a previous Summa Dogma.

5. Sacred and Historic Decrees, Pronouncements, Bulls, Edicts of Customary and Traditional Rights are permitted to be endorsed through a properly convened Ecumenical Council of the Universal Ecclesia as Summa Dogma, on the strict conditions:-   *Declaratory Promulgation of historic instruments as valid Summa Dogma*

(i) That such instruments and their contents do not diminish the authority, power or rights of the present sacred Covenant, nor associated Covenants, Canons and Codes; and

(ii) That such instruments and their contents are not morally repugnant, perfidious, sacrilegious or contradictory to the most sacred Covenant *Pactum De Singularis Caelum*; and

(iii)   Until such endorsement or repudiation, all Sacred and Historic Decrees, Pronouncements, Bulls, Edicts of Customary and Traditional Rights are concluded in the affirmative, unless specifically forbidden, reprobate and to be suppressed by one more clauses of the most sacred Covenant *Pactum De Singularis Caelum* and the present most sacred Covenant and associated Covenants, Canons and Instruments.

Article 211 – Summa Doctrina

1. **W**hen the Oratorium, also known as the One Supreme Court, also known as the Supreme Court of One Heaven is in Supreme Session through temporal embodiment and personification within an authorised body in accord with the present sacred Covenant, the relevant body possessing the proper authority of Magisterium, may use its Powers of Appellate Jurisdiction to make absolute and final rulings in accord with Divine Canon Law and Doctrines by Teaching and Adjudication, providing a sacred writ has been duly issued. These absolute and final rulings of teaching and adjudication shall be called "**Summa Doctrina**" in accord with Article 132 (*Greatest Teachings*) of the most sacred Covenant *Pactum De Singularis Caelum*.

    Summa Doctrina (Greatest Teaching)

2. Just as God and the Divine Creator of all Heaven and Earth through Christ and the Holy Spirit have entrusted the most sacred teachings, scriptures and covenants as embodied within the *Authenticus Depositum Fidei* to the Living Body of Christ, it is to the Universal Ecclesia of One Christ that the power and responsibility of Magisterium is entrusted through the most sacred Covenant *Pactum De Singularis Caelum* and the present sacred Covenant.

    Magisterium Authority and Summa Doctrina

    There exists only three (3) states of Magisterium as inherited from *Ius Ecclesiae Magisterium* as the Ecclesiastical Right to Teach, Instruct and Interpret Divine Will, being Supremum, Universalem and Ordinarium:-

    (i)   "**Magisterium Supremum**" or Supreme Magisterium is the absolute Right of Magisterium entrusted to the Universal Ecclesia of One Christ through the Right of *Ius Ecclesiae Magisterium* and embodied within the person of Supreme Patriarch. No other temporal body possesses the same right of Magisterium, except the faiths of One Islam and One Spirit if not impeded; and

    (ii)   "**Magisterium Universalem**" or Universal Magisterium is the Right of Imperium through *Ius Ecclesiae Magisterium*

414

entrusted to a Patriarch or Bishop in communion with the Living Body of Christ; and

(iii) **"Magisterium Ordinarium"** or Ordinary Magisterium is the Right of Imperium through *Ius Ecclesiae Magisterium* entrusted to a Deacon.

3. Summa Doctrina under Supreme or Universal Magisterium is *ipso facto* (as a matter of fact) the absolute highest possible and final appeal and judgement, edict, teaching instrument and legal instruction from a validly constituted forum of law of any and all societies, aggregates, associations, persons, entities and higher order spirits, living and deceased having universal and absolute, divine and temporal jurisdiction:-

> Summa Doctrina as Absolute and Final Appeal and Judgement

(i) Providing the Summa Doctrina adheres to the Criteria of a valid Summa Doctrina as prescribed by the present Article; and

(ii) The officer or body issuing the Summa Doctrina has the power and authority to do so in accord with the present sacred Covenant; and

(iii) That the Summa Doctrina does not contradict the most sacred present Covenant or the body of canons known as *Astrum Iuris Divini Canonum.*

4. A valid Summa Doctrina adheres to the following essential criteria:-

> Criteria for valid Summa Doctrina

(i) The Oratorium as the Supreme Court of One Heaven is in Session and capable of properly rendering a Summa Doctrina; and

(ii) That a properly constituted and highest and most competent forum of Living Members as Justices as defined by the present Covenant and associated Covenants exists as the union of the three (3) Supreme Courts of the Three Faiths, or if the three (3) faiths are not yet in proper operation then the Globe Union Forum, or if the Globe Union Forum is not yet in proper operation, then a Union Basilica; and

(iii) That the Justices and officials and parties of the competent temporal forum have been duly invoked to evoke a Special Hearing for a Summa Doctrina; and

(iv) A petition and memorandum is received by the competent forum in the prescribed form, duly lodged, recorded and gazetted for a Summa Doctrina to be rendered; and

(v) That the specific subject matter of the petition and

memorandum is within the Powers of Appellate Jurisdiction of the Oratorium as the Supreme Court of One Heaven; and

(vi) That the core questions outlined within the Petition to be answered have not previously been specifically addressed in a previous Summa Doctrina.

5. Sacred and Historic Decrees, Pronouncements, Bulls, Edicts of Customary and Traditional Rights are permitted to be endorsed through a properly convened Ecumenical Council of the Universal Ecclesia as Summa Doctrina, on the strict conditions:-

Declaratory Promulgation of historic instruments as valid Summa Doctrina

(i) That such instruments and their contents do not diminish the authority, power or rights of the present sacred Covenant, nor associated Covenants, Canons and Codes; and

(ii) That such instruments and their contents are not morally repugnant, perfidious, sacrilegious or contradictory to the most sacred Covenant *Pactum De Singularis Caelum*; and

(iii) Until such endorsement or repudiation, all Sacred and Historic Decrees, Pronouncements, Bulls, Edicts of Customary and Traditional Rights are concluded in the affirmative, unless specifically forbidden, reprobate and to be suppressed by one more clauses of the most sacred Covenant *Pactum De Singularis Caelum* and the present most sacred Covenant and associated Covenants and Instruments.

Article 212 – Veneration and Causes

1. **V**eneration is a formal rite of blessing, Sacred Gift and remembrance in favour of the formal recognition, honour and trust of an incumbent Spirit Member in Heaven in accordance with the present sacred Covenant and the most sacred Covenant *Pactum De Singularis Caelum*.

Veneration

Historically, anyone recognised with certainty as being a Spirit Member of Heaven was honoured by the title of "saint". However, this led to the confusion and gross error by implication that anyone not honoured as a saint was not then present in Heaven.

This is now corrected by ensuring that the Sacrament of Veneration is to dignify the title and memory of exemplary, heroic, blessed and saintly Members of One Christ; and that the title of "saint" is strictly to honour those recognised by the fourth degree of Veneration through Beatification.

2. By custom and tradition, a martyr to the cause of Heaven, demonstrating chivalrous and heroic virtue midst the trial of persecution and danger, shall automatically be considered Venerable, not withstanding any claimed

Martyrdom and Veneration

impediment.

A person culpable of the death of innocent men, women or children in connection to their ultimate death, is never permitted to be called a martyr by any faith of Heaven, but an impostor.

3. A person culpable of acts of terror and murder of innocent men, women and children in the name of God and the Divine Creator of all Heaven and Earth is forbidden to ever be called a martyr, or be honoured in death in any manner as a martyr. Instead such people must be recorded as the condemned, who bind their spirit in spiritual sanction and custody for one hundred years for every death they caused of an innocent.

Exclusion from Honour or Veneration

Article 213 – Ecclesiastical Registers

1. The Ecclesiastical Register is the Public Record of the Universal Ecclesia of One Christ, also known as the Great Ledger, also known as the Great Register, also known as the Supreme Roll, also known as the Great Register of Title and Rights; and also known as the Public Record.

Ecclesiastical Registers

When referring to the highest Public Record, Roll(s), Register(s), Title(s) and Certificates of Title above any Society or Body Politic or Corporation or Person within the bounds of the Universal Ecclesia of One Christ, it shall mean the Great Register and Public Record of Universal Ecclesia and no other.

2. A Valid Register Entry is the minimum required information recorded into the Great Register after a Form has been accepted. A Valid Register Entry includes a Unique Ledger Key as well as associated information. The minimum required information for a Valid Register Entry, includes (but is not limited to):-

Valid Register Entry

   (i)   A Unique Identifying Number also called the Unique Register Number (URN); and

   (ii)   A Name for the Register Entry; and

   (iii) The Day of entry into the Register; and

   (iv) The Member that petitioned for the entry of the Record; and

   (v)   The Capacity (Office) of the Member as Petitioner; and

   (vi) The Registrar that approved the entry.

3. The Unique Register Number (URN) represents a Unique Ledger Key that is created from the unique combination of eight (8) Unique Ledger Numbers, each comprising a combination of eighteen (18) digits so that the total number, excluding spaces or dashes is equal to

Unique Register Number

the number one hundred and forty-four (144). A "Short Form" Unique Register Number represents the first eighteen (18) digits of an existing Unique Ledger Key of the Public Record. The "Standard Form" order of Unique Ledger Numbers to form a Valid Unique Register Number of 144 digits is:-

(i)   Unique Ledger Number; and

(ii)   Unique Society Number; and

(iii)   Unique Member Number; and

(iv)   Unique Office Number; and

(v)   Unique Category Number; and

(vi)   Unique Space-Day-Time Number; and

(vii)   Unique Notice Number; and

(viii) Unique Registrar Number.

4. The Universal Form Code (UFC) is a standard for the naming, construction, recording and management of standard forms, completed forms and the information contained within. The UFC Identifier is an eighteen (18) digit number that uniquely identifies each and every valid form received and accepted by all Ucadian Societies. No two forms will ever have the same UFC Identifier. The Universal Form Code is based on (1) An Alpha Prefix of two characters, then (2) four numbers representing category and standard form, then (3) twelve characters representing the unique society and number of the form.

Universal Form Code

5. Only Permitted and Valid Forms shall be entered into the Public Register and Public Record. A Permitted Form is when:-

Permitted Form

(i)   An Instrument is identified as an Approved Form as defined by the present sacred Covenant, or associated Rules and Procedures of the Universal Ecclesia of One Christ to be entered; and

(ii)   The Instrument possesses the minimum information required for a Valid Register Entry; and

(iii)   The Instrument does not require material correction, alteration or addition; and

(iv)   The Member as Petitioner is not precluded from requesting such an entry, or otherwise temporarily banned from such services; and

(v)   The Instrument does not contradict any of the provisions of the present sacred Covenant.

6.   Members of the Universal Ecclesia of One Christ, not otherwise suspended or banned from such services, possess the Right of Petition for an entry in the Public Register, not a Right of Entry. The approval to record and publish in the Public Register of the Universal Ecclesia shall always be a determination of the appropriate Officials of the Universal Ecclesia, subject to the present sacred Covenant and therefore a privilege to Members.

Petition not a Right of Entry

7.   In respect of the Public Register:-

Publication and Promulgation of Register

(i)   The Registrar shall protect and keep the Great Register in a reliable medium and ensure that its entire contents are published and promulgated in a printed form, with updated publication of new entries available upon the day of approved entry; and

(ii)   The Registrar shall also produce a daily or weekly publication promulgated in an electronic and printed form of all new entries for that week known as the Gazette; and

(iii)   The Registrar shall also provide public access to the full contents of the Public Register from the widest possible range of mediums, including internet, computer, microfilm, paper and other mediums; and

(iv)   The Registrar may charge minimal fees for the processing of applications and requests for entry into the Public Register where such entries involve a degree of complexity and audit; and

(v)   While the Registrar may charge a minimal service fee for any costs associated with the requested research projects, print requests and publications, all online and simple electronic Register search services are to be provided free of charge.

8.   All Persons and Members are forbidden to make demands or threats for entry of one or more Instruments into the Public Register. Only when proper requests as petitions are made by following the instructions as per the present sacred Covenant and additional information provided from time to time, shall any Instrument be considered on its merits. The persistent demands and/or threats of a Member for one or more Instruments to be entered into the Public Register, contrary to the present sacred Covenant shall be a serious

Demand of Entry an Offence

offence, punishable by temporary suspension of some or all services given to them.

Article 214 – Ecclesiastical Notices and Gazette

1. **N**otice is the term used to describe the type of notice and service of process whereby a party is made aware of any formal legal matter that may affect certain Rights, obligations or Duties as well as the form of Document used to transmit such facts.

Ecclesiastical Notices and Gazette

The seven (7) primary types of notice used by the Universal Ecclesia of One Christ are: *Physical, Posted, Direct, Indirect, Public (legal), Implied* and *Constructive*:-

(i) *Physical Notice* or Actual Notice is a type of notice and service of process whereby the specific information concerning a formal legal matter is listed in a Document and then physically handed to a party or their representative, with proof, attestation or acknowledgment of such service recorded as evidence; and

(ii) *Posted Notice* or Mail Notice is a type of notice and service of process whereby specific information concerning the formal legal matter is personally addressed to the party and sent through a certified or registered mail delivery system recognised by the International Postal Union; and

(iii) *Direct Notice* is a type of notice and service of process whereby specific information concerning the formal legal matter is personally addressed to the party and sent via email, fax, sms or other recorded and verifiable transmission medium; and

(iv) *Indirect Notice* is a type of notice and service of process whereby specific information concerning the formal ecclesiastical, sovereign, legal or administrative matter is published in any broadcast medium such as media releases, stories, advertorial content and advertising and likely to be viewed by one or more parties; and

(v) *Public Notice* is a type of notice and service of process whereby specific information concerning the formal legal matter is published in a company, local, regional, national or international publication possessing status as a gazette and therefore an official newspaper of record or physically posted at a site reasonably expected to be visible to the Person; and

(vi) *Implied Notice* is a type of notice inferred from facts that a

Person had means of knowing and would have caused a reasonable Person to take action to gain further information concerning a formal legal matter. It is a notice inferred or imputed to a party by reason of his/her knowledge collateral to the main fact; and

(vii) *Constructive Notice* is a type of notice inferred from facts that a Person unable to be served with Actual Notice may be reasonably inferred or imputed to have received notice, if Actual Notice was restricted or not possible and a minimum number of attempts of Physical, Posted, Direct or Public Notice were concluded.

2. Excluding matters subject to legal dispute, the Universal Ecclesia of One Christ shall use Diplomatic Courier, Posted and Direct Notice as the preferred medium for communicating matters of a confidential, privileged or private nature between the Universal Ecclesia and its Delegates, Members, Officers, Agents, Employees or other parties. In matters that are not of a confidential, privileged or private nature, the Universal Ecclesia may also use Indirect Notice.

General Services of Notices

3. A Gazette is a public journal and authorised newspaper of Record. The most authoritative and highest temporal Gazette is the Ucadia Gazette, published by Divine Authority in accordance with the present sacred Covenant and the sacred Covenant *Pactum De Singularis Caelum* and is the Official Newspaper of Record for UCADIA and a modern, efficient way to disseminate and record official, regulatory and lawful information in print, online and electronic forms.

Gazette

4. Any lesser publication known as a Gazette that repudiates the absolute supremacy of the Gazette of the Supreme See is without validity, or legitimacy as a publication of record, with all records contained within it, false, determined, null and void.

All Gazettes source Authority from Gazette of Supreme See

5. All publications within the Gazette of the Universal Ecclesia of One Christ shall be by virtue of the approval of entry of at least one Instrument into the Public Record and Public Register.

Publication in Gazette via approved Register Entry

6. The publishing of any Proclamation, Order, Regulation or Notice within the Ucadia Gazette shall be *Prima Facie* Evidence of such Fact and Truth; and that all Courts, Judges, Justices, Masters, Magistrates or Commissioners judicially acting, and all other judicial Officers shall take judicial Notice of such *Prima Facie* Evidence in all legal proceedings whatsoever.

Gazette Notices as Prima Facie Evidence

7. In any matter pertaining to change in the position of rights or reporting of the Universal Ecclesia of One Christ in relation to

Service of Notices to

Members, Posted Notice is required to be given by the Universal Ecclesia to any Member, or in the case of joint holders to the Member whose name stands first in the Register, regardless of whether Direct Notice or any other form of Notice is also used. All Posted Notices sent by prepaid post to persons whose registered address is not in the same Jurisdiction as the Registered Office of the Universal Ecclesia are to be sent by airmail.

8. Notice shall be deemed to have been properly and duly served, when:-

    (i)   Any Physical Notice served personally or left at the registered address by a servicing agent is deemed to have been served when delivered and such fact is attested by a certificate of service signed by the agent who executed the service; and

    (ii)   Any Notice sent by Post is deemed to have been served at the expiration of forty-eight (48) hours after the envelope containing the Notice is posted and, in proving service, it is sufficient to prove that the envelope containing the Notice was properly addressed and posted; and

    (iii)   Any Direct Notice served on a party by courier is deemed to have been served on receipt by the Universal Ecclesia of One Christ when the courier confirmation has been received. Any notice served on a party by facsimile transmission is deemed to have been served when the transmission is sent. Any notice served on a party by email or sms or any other form of direct electronic messaging is deemed to have been served after twenty-four (24) hours and no error message or failed transmission notice is received; and

    (iv)   Any Indirect Notice is deemed to have been served three (3) days after receipt or proof of the publication of such notice; and

    (v)   Any Public Notice is deemed to have been served three (3) days after receipt or proof of the publication in a gazette and official publication of record of such Notice; and

    (vi)   Any Implied Notice is deemed to have been served fourteen (14) days after receipt or proof of publication of at least two (2) forms of Indirect Notice or Public Notice; and

    (vii)   Any Constructive Notice is deemed to have been served fourteen (14) days after receipt or proof of at least one attempted Physical Notice or two (2) Posted Notices and at least two (2) forms of Indirect Notice or Public Notice.

9. Where a Member does not have a registered address or where the

Members

When Notice is Deemed to be Served

Member not

Universal Ecclesia of One Christ has a reason in good faith to believe that a Member is not known at the Member's registered address, a Notice is deemed to be given to the Member if the Notice is exhibited by Indirect Notice in the Office for a period of forty-eight (48) hours (and is deemed to be duly served at the commencement of that period) unless and until the Member informs the Universal Ecclesia of a registered place of address.

known at Registered Address

10. The signature to any Notice to be given by the Universal Ecclesia of One Christ may be written or printed. The formatting of the name of an Officer of the Universal Ecclesia in capitals as the signature line upon a Notice shall be deemed a valid legal signature.

Signature to Notice

11. Where a Notice gives of a certain number of days, or the limit of time is mandated for some proper form of Notice, the days of service are not to be reckoned in the number of days, until the actual date of proof of service, thereby limiting the possibility of an unfair or unreasonable service.

Reckoning of Period of Notice

Article 215 – Sacred Places and Times

1. **S**acred Places are those designated for divine worship, by dedication through the liturgical and sacramental rituals provided in accord with the most sacred covenant *Pactum De Singularis Caelum*.

Sacred Places and Times

Sacred Places are recognised, established maintained and protected in character through the receiving and written memorial of the Cardinal Sacrament of Consecratio (Consecration) forming Sacred Circumscribed Space.

Only those things that serve the exercise or promotion of worship, piety or religion are permitted in a Sacred Place. Therefore, anything that is not consonant with the holiness of the place is forbidden, unless in individual cases the relevant Bishop permits another use that is not contrary to the holiness of the Sacred Place.

Sacred Places temporarily lose their dedication or blessing if they have been destroyed in large part, or have been turned over permanently to profane use. The Clergy are not permitted to decree, nor endorse the profane or sordid use of Sacred Places and instead must use all its resources and abilities to prevent such injury.

Sacred Places are violated by gravely injurious actions done in them with scandal to the faithful, or by actions considered so grave and contrary to the holiness of the place that it is not permitted to carry on worship in them until the damage is repaired by a penitential rite according to the most sacred Missale Christus and associated approved liturgical books.

The Universal Ecclesia of One Christ shall acquire, retain and manage such Land and Places suitable as locations for worship, both within established urban environments, in rural and agricultural regions of planet Earth.

The Universal Ecclesia of One Christ shall acquire such Land and Places suitable as locations for spiritual retreat, education and healing within areas of preserved and pristine wilderness and majestic beauty within the bounds and jurisdiction of each University and shall ensure its presence within each and every major community.

2. A Religious Place of Worship is a sacred building designated and duly consecrated for divine worship whereby Members of the Living Body of One Christ possess the right of entry for the exercise of such divine worship.

   The Universal Ecclesia of One Christ shall acquire, build and modify suitably consecrated buildings as Religious Institutes for Divine Worship, Sacramental Rites and Sacred Education. However, no Religious Place of Worship is to be built or designated and consecrated without the express written consent of the appropriate Apostolic Bishop of a Customary and Traditional Rite or Diocesan Bishop.

   Religious Places of Worship

3. An Oratory is a Sacred Place for divine worship designated by permission of the relevant Diocesan Bishop or Apostolic Bishop for the benefit of some community or group of the faithful who gather in it and to which other members can also come with the consent of the competent superior.

   Oratories

   The relevant Diocesan Bishop or Apostolic Bishop is not to grant the permission required to establish an oratory unless he has first visited the place destined for the oratory personally or through another and has found it properly prepared.

   After permission has been given, however, an oratory cannot be converted to profane use without the authority of the same ordinary.

   All sacred celebrations can be performed in legitimately established oratories except those which the law or a prescript of the local ordinary excludes or the liturgical norms prohibit.

   It is fitting for oratories to be blessed according to the rite prescribed in the liturgical books. They must, however, be reserved for divine worship alone and free from all domestic uses.

4. A Personal Chapel is a Sacred Place for divine worship designated by

   Personal

permission of the relevant Diocesan Bishop or Apostolic Bishop for the benefit of one or more physical persons holding Offices. All forms and concepts of private chapels is hereby morally repugnant, reprobate, forbidden and to be suppressed.

Chapels

Bishops can establish a Personal Chapel for themselves that possesses the same rights as an oratory. However, the permission of the relevant Diocesan Bishop or Apostolic Bishop is required for Mass or other sacred celebrations to take place in any private chapel.

It is fitting for Personal Chapels to be blessed according to the rite prescribed in the liturgical books. They must, however, be reserved for divine worship alone and free from all domestic uses.

5. A Shrine is a Sacred and Holy Place dedicated and consecrated to Heaven and to one or more venerated deities, ancestors, heroes, martyrs, saints or spirits, where Living Ordinary Members make pilgrimage as a mark of respect and piety.

Shrines

A Shrine may exist in a number of forms including (but not limited to) a sanctuary, or preserved location, or holy city, or temple, or church or altar. In all cases, a Shrine must be respected as a place of great sanity and free from approved profane or sordid behaviours. Above all, a Shrine is a spiritual portal between Heaven and Earth, given to all people as a means of sustaining and edifying their faith and enlarging and strengthening their trust and knowledge in God and the Divine Creator of all Existence.

All Shrines may be defined by six characters being: Supreme, Traditional, National, Historical, Communal or Familial, whereby a particular Shrine may qualify according to one or more characteristics:-

(i)   *Supreme Shrine* is a Sacred and Holy Place ordained by Heaven in unity and perpetual remembrance of the present sacred Covenant. There are eleven Sacred Cities and Sanctuaries representing supreme sacredness across all six Unions (Africa, Americas, Arabia, Asia, Europe and Oceania) being the Holy See, the Holy City of Jerusalem, the Holy City of Mecca, the Holy City of Istanbul (Constantinople), the Holy City of Bodh Gaya, the Holy City of Varanasi, the Holy City of Tunis (Carthage), the Holy City of London, the Holy City of Washington, the Holy City of Melbourne and the Holy Sovereign Sanctuary of One Ireland.

(ii) *Traditional Shrine* is a Sacred and Holy Place ordained and worshipped by one or more Customary and Traditional Rites as a Sacred Place of the utmost significance; and

(iii) *National Shrine* is a Sacred and Holy Place ordained by approval of the Supreme See and the Bishops and Patriarch of the relevant University and nation; and

(iv) *Historical Shrine* is a Sacred and Holy Place approved by the Patriarch and Bishops of a University and Nation as a place of sanctity and importance, deserving of preservation and reverence; and

(v) *Communal Shrine* is a Sacred and Holy Place approved by the relevant Diocesan Bishop or Apostolic Bishop for a community; and

(vi) *Familial Shrine* is a Sacred and Holy Place within a building occupied by one or more households, approved by the relevant Diocesan Bishop or Apostolic Bishop for votive offerings and celebrations.

6. An Altar is any fixed or movable structure dedicated for the purpose of votive, or penitential or sacramental offerings. The most sacred ceremony upon a properly sanctified and dedicated altar is sacrament of Holy Eucharist.

Altars

Fixed altars must be dedicated, and movable altars must be dedicated or blessed, according to the rites prescribed in the liturgical books. An altar, whether fixed or movable, must be reserved for divine worship alone, to the absolute exclusion of any profane use. However, Altars, whether fixed or movable, do not lose their dedication or blessing if the church or other sacred place is relegated to profane uses.

The Customary and Traditional Rite of placing relics of martyrs or other saints under a fixed Altar is permitted to be preserved within those Customary and Traditional Rites that deem such ancient tradition as absolutely necessary. However, in all other instances, no bones or relics or bodies are to be buried within or beneath Altars.

7. A proper designated character of a Cemetery or Crematorium is by definition a sacred circumscribed space in accord with the norms of the liturgical books. There exists no spiritual impediment whether a deceased or their family chooses burial or cremation.

Cemeteries and Crematoriums

Furthermore, there exists no spiritual impediment if a deceased is buried or cremated in a sacred circumscribed space that is not dedicated to the faith of One Christ. However, where possible and for the dignity of its Members, the Church is to have its own cemeteries or at least areas in civil cemeteries that are designated for the deceased members of the faithful and properly blessed.

Parishes and religious institutes may have their own cemetery. Other juridic persons or families may also have a special cemetery or tomb, to be blessed according to the judgement of the local Diocesan or Apostolic Bishop.

In respect to church burial, bodies are not to be buried or entombed within churches unless it is a matter of dignity of position to certain offices of clergy, or in relation to the dedication of a church also as a Shrine to a beloved and saintly life.

8. Clerics and Ministers holding such sacred office (such as one of the Great Offices of State), must live in legitimately established Religious Houses, designated according to the norm of law of Ucadia and the Universal Ecclesia of One Christ. The erection of such Religious Houses shall take place with consideration for their advantage and proximity to Religious Institutes of the Universal Ecclesia of One Christ.

Religious Houses

No Religious House is to be erected or acquired or modified unless it can be judged prudent to the needs of the Members and that such buildings honour the religious duties, standing, honour and purpose of those that live in them.

The Universal Ecclesia of One Christ shall make early provision to contribute to the acquisition, or building, or development of a Religious House befitting for the standing, office and sanctity of the Visitor. As Superior to the House, the Visitor may designate who may live within it, providing such will and intention is made in writing.

9. It is only for the supreme ecclesiastical authority to establish, transfer, and suppress feast days and days of penance common to the Universal Ecclesia of One Christ.

Sacred Times

Diocesan or Apostolic Bishops can decree special feast days or days of penance for their dioceses or places, but only in individual instances.

Without prejudice to the right of Diocesan or Apostolic Bishops, for a just cause and according to the prescripts of law, a pastor can grant in individual cases a dispensation from the obligation of observing a feast day or a day of penance or can grant a commutation of the obligation into other pious works. A superior of a religious institute or society of apostolic life, if they are clerical, can also do this in regard to his own subjects and others living in the house day and night.

10. Sunday is and continues by apostolic tradition to be the primordial holy day of obligation in the remembrance of the original paschal

Sacred Feasts

mystery, the confirmation of the most sacred covenant of One Heaven and celebration of the Universal Ecclesia of One Christ as the one, true and only Living Body of Christ.

Customary and Traditional Rites that celebrate Saturday or Friday evening in a similar manner are granted special and exclusive dispensation in accord with the present sacred Covenant, that such celebrations may be preserved and treated the same.

The following days must also be observed: the Divine Conception, the Nativity of Christ, the Epiphany, the Beatitudes, the Paschal Sacrifice, the Resurrection, the Ascension, the Pentecost, the Apostles and All Saints.

On Sundays and other holy days of obligation, Ordinary Members are obliged to participate in the Mass. Moreover, they are to abstain from those works that hinder the worship to be rendered to God, the joy proper to the Lord's day, or the suitable relaxation of mind and body.

11. Divine Law binds all the Christian and Jewish faithful to do penance each in his or her own way. In order for all to be united among themselves by some common observance of penance, however, penitential days are prescribed whereby the Christian and Jewish faithful devote themselves in a special way to prayer, perform works of piety and charity, and austerity. Days of Penance

The penitential days and times in the universal Church are every Friday of the whole year and the season of Lent.

Abstinence from meat, or from some other food as determined by the Episcopal Conference, is to be observed on all Fridays, unless a solemnity should fall on a Friday. Abstinence and fasting are to be observed on Ash Wednesday and Good Friday.

The law of abstinence binds those who have completed their fourteenth year. The law of fasting binds those who have attained their majority, until the beginning of their sixtieth year. Pastors of souls and parents are to ensure that even those who by reason of their age are not bound by the law of fasting and abstinence, are taught the true meaning of penance.

The conference of bishops can determine more precisely the observance of fast and abstinence as well as substitute other forms of penance, especially works of charity and exercises of piety, in whole or in part, for abstinence and fast.

Article 216 – Epistle

1. An Epistle is a personal or intimate letter of instruction directed or sent to a person or group of people by a Patriarch or the Supreme Patriarch. Only the Supreme Patriarch or lesser Patriarchs may issue an Epistle.

   Epistle

   As a personal or intimate letter of instruction, an Epistle when first written cannot be considered Summa Dogma or Summa Doctrina. However, unlike an Encyclical, an Epistle is considered suspended in Magisterium, whereby the Epistle may be tested by a properly constituted body such as an Ecumenical Council at a later date, to determine if such writing was so inspired and exemplary, that it may be accepted into the *Maxima Textibus Sacris* of the Universal Ecclesia of One Christ.

2. A properly formed Epistle by the Supreme Patriarch or lesser Patriarch is an embodiment of Pastoral Care and the function of such holy positions of trust as true Disciples of Christ. The personal and intimate nature is a recall to the very beginnings of the Church and scripture and the use of Epistles to comfort, assist and teach the earliest communities.

   Purpose and Limits of an Epistle

   As a general rule, a Supreme Patriarch is expected to provide such pastoral care and the promulgation of at least one Epistle to each Union during the life of their office. As it is a matter of free will and choice, a Supreme Patriarch may choose how frequently and to whom they direct such Epistles.

Article 217 – Encyclical

1. An Encyclical is a formal letter, usually on one particular subject, promulgated by the Supreme Patriarch, or a Patriarch under authority, to all Christian and Jewish Members of the Universal Ecclesia of One Christ.

   Encyclical

   Only the Supreme Patriarch or lesser Patriarchs may issue Encyclicals.

   The term comes from the Greek *enkyklios* meaning "circular", in reference to the manner of its distribution, beginning with all the Patriarchs and Cardinals, then all Clergy and Customary and Traditional Rites and then through the Clergy to all Christian and Jewish Members of the Living Body of Christ.

   An Encyclical issued by the Supreme Patriarch shall be honoured with the title of a Papal Encyclical and those issued by lesser Patriarchs shall be known as a Patriarchal Encyclical.

2. The purpose and function of an Encyclical is to provide guidance, or encourage discussion and reflection, or consolidation or exhortation on a particular subject area concerning the doctrines or established customs of the Universal Ecclesia of One Christ, without necessarily the formality of an instrument of Summa Doctrina or Summa Dogma.

Purpose and Limits of Encyclical

Given the rich and broad history of the Customary and Traditional Rites of the Living Body of Christ, properly authorised Encyclicals provide a purposeful and real assistance in comprehension, unity and competence.

Generally, Encyclicals should be limited to periods distinct and separate from significant periods of debate, discussion and reflection surrounding Ecumenical Councils and other major ecclesiastical assemblies.

Article 218 – Rules and Regulations

1. **Rules and regulations** of all organs and bodies of the Universal Ecclesia of One Christ shall be subject to the most sacred Covenant *Pactum De Singularis Caelum* and the present sacred Covenant.

Rules and Regulations

All organs and bodies of the Universal Ecclesia of One Christ shall be firmly bound to the original, first and primary jurisdiction of the One Holy Apostolic Universal Ecclesia.

Organs and bodies formed in accord with the present sacred Covenant shall be permitted to define their Rules and Regulations subject to the present sacred Covenant and conditions of the present Article.

2. The Rules and Regulations of any and all Universal, Union and University Organs and bodies shall be required to first be approved by the Supreme Patriarch and Supreme See, before such rules may be effected or enforced.

Approval and Review of Rules subject to Supreme Patriarch and Supreme See

No Universal, Union and University organ or body shall be permitted to operate under any rules or regulations not approved by Universal, Union and University. All other lesser rules and regulations shall be subject to the appropriate Patriarch.

Article 219 – Sanctions and Penalties

1. **S**anction is by definition the approval, consent and validation of one or more acts such as penalties, or some other coercive measure, intended to ensure compliance, as defined by law, contract, treaty or other agreement; or its enaction in accord with the terms of such instruments. Therefore, the existence of proper Sanctions is essential both in terms of moral and lawful enforcement, in the fair administration of justice.

   Sanction

   All communication to the *Obligationum Systemata* (Enforcement Systems) of Heaven by living Members of One Heaven of Obligations, Penalties or Condemnations shall be by Sanction in accord with the present sacred Covenant.

   All properly conferred Sanction shall be received, recorded and acknowledged by the *Obligationum Systemata* (Enforcement Systems) of One Heaven.

2. While it is the authority of the Universal Ecclesia of One Christ to administer all forms of temporal Sanctions such as Ecclesiastical Sanctions and all lesser Sanctions, it is forbidden for the Universal Ecclesia or any clergy to issue or imply one or more Supernatural or Divine Sanctions against a person, or family, or group or wider community or nation.

   Forbidden to issue Divine Sanctions against Living Members

   Therefore, the concept of Anathema is forbidden, reprobate and to be suppressed in all its forms concerning any form of sanction against Living Members of humanity.

   Such statements as "God's Will" in the face of natural and predictable disasters, or to judge the loss of life in war, or terror, or illness as the willing judgement of God and the Divine Creator is an act of profound moral repugnancy, apostasy and sacrilege against the Teachings of the Crucified and Risen Christ, against the present most Sacred Covenant and against the Universal Ecclesia itself. Any clergy culpable of encouraging, or promoting such false, profane and erroneous views as to imply the true Divine Nature of God and the Divine Creator of all Heaven and Earth as now being a vengeful or capricious being that endorses the murder of women and children is such an abomination that such clergy must be prevented at all costs from further sacrilege and injury.

3. The right to sanction Spirit Members is a necessary plenary authority in support of the fact that united Heaven functions as a society according to certain rules. In order to properly function, every society

   Right to issue Divine Sanctions against Spirit Members

must possess the right to impose certain sanctions against those members culpable of breaching the rules of the society, or refusing to remedy such breaches.

All sanctions against Spirit Members shall be temporary and none shall include any notion of exclusion or exile. Instead, any sanctions issued against Spirit Members shall be firmly constrained within the rites of Exorcism and the sacrament or Orthodoxos (Binding).

4. By authority of the present sacred Covenant, the Universal Ecclesia of One Christ possesses full, immediate and perfect coercive powers of enforcement to compel any and all Living Members to comply with all reasonable penalties including, (but not limited to): prevention, protection, restitution, restoration, seizure, search, sanction, arrest, custody or satisfaction.

By definition, a valid Default or Delinquency must be proven before a Penalty may be imposed by a duly authorised person

Penalties

5. Properly formed Excommunication is a medicinal penalty that temporarily deprives a Living Member from full participation in the blessings and sacraments of the ecclesiastical society of the Living Body of Christ.

Just as all societies possess the right to issue penalties upon proof of default or delinquency or perfidy, so the Universal Ecclesia of One Christ possesses the exclusive right to Excommunicate Living Members as an act of last resort in a manner to cause a shift in their conscience toward a genuine reconciliation.

Any and all forms of interpretation of Excommunication as permanent is forbidden.

Right of Excommunication

6. There are three types of alleged offender in respect of Penance being Penitent, Resistant and Belligerent:-

Identity of Offender in nature to Penalty

   (i)   A Penitent is one who voluntarily confesses through an act of contrition as to their culpability and seeks to make amends and restore their honour through the acceptance of those prescribed Penalties; and

   (ii)   A Resistant is one who does not disavow the existence of an original agreement and therefore a binding, but resists making a voluntary confession and instead relies upon the strength and will of others to prove their culpability and impose the fair prescribed Penalties; and

   (iii)   A Belligerent is one who disavows any previous agreement and instead declares themselves hostile to any act to restore honour, or honour the Rule of Law and justice in the application of Penalties, instead relying on the power of others to bring them into custody and impose the fair prescribed Penalties upon valid proof.

Article 220 – Sacred Rights and Writs of Action

1. **T**he eleven most sacred Ecclesiastical Writs of Right *(Recto Ecclesiae Iurium)* are the highest possible valid temporal forms of Coercive Powers, Enforcement, Right of Remedy, Right of Original Entry and Original Action of all Reality and Existence of Society and Rule of Law, in accord with the present Covenant and Article 41 (*Superior Rights*) of the most sacred Covenant *Pactum De Singularis Caelum.*

Rights and Writs of Action

Evidence of a valid record within the Great Register and Divine Records of Heaven through the Ucadia Gazette shall be prima facie proof of a duly promulgated Ecclesiastical Writ of Right.

By their nature, the Ecclesiastical Writs of Right (Recto Ecclesiae Iurium) shall be known individually as a "**Holy Writ**" and thus no force on Earth has the right to reject it or dishonour it.

The following valid eleven (11) Ecclesiastical Writs of Rights (Recto Ecclesiae Iurium) are recognised in accord with the present Covenant as being *Holy Writs*:-

(i)   *Recto Ecclesiae Petitionis* as the Ecclesiastical Writ of Claim of Right, as inherited from *Recto Divinum Petitionis*; and

(ii)   *Recto Ecclesiae Originalis* as the Ecclesiastical Original Writ (of Right), as inherited from *Recto Divinum Originalis*; and

(iii)   *Recto Ecclesiae Apocalypsis* as the Ecclesiastical Writ of Right of Revelation, as inherited from *Recto Divinum Apocalypsis*; and

(iv)   *Recto Ecclesiae Investigationis* as the Ecclesiastical Writ of Inquiry and Search, as inherited from *Recto Divinum Investigationis*; and

(v)   *Recto Ecclesiae Capionis* as the Ecclesiastical Writ of Seizure and Return, as inherited from *Recto Divinum Capionis*; and

(vi)   *Recto Ecclesiae Custodiae* as the Ecclesiastical Writ of Arrest and Custody, as inherited from Recto Divinum Custodiae; and

(vii)   *Recto Ecclesiae Documentis* as the Ecclesiastical Writ of correcting Records of Proof, as inherited from *Recto Divinum Documentis*; and

(viii)   *Recto Ecclesiae Expungo* as the Ecclesiastical Writ of expunging Records of Proof, as inherited from *Recto Divinum Expungo*; and

(ix)   *Recto Ecclesiae Abrogationis* as the Ecclesiastical Writ of Annulment of Previous Laws and Instruments, as inherited from *Recto Divinum Abrogationis*; and

(x)   *Recto Ecclesiae Interdico* as the Ecclesiastical Writ of Prohibition and Imposition, as inherited from *Recto Divinum Interdico*; and

(xi) *Recto Ecclesiae Restitutio* as the Ecclesiastical Writ of Compensation and Restoration, as inherited from *Recto Divinum Restitutio*.

Article 221 – Temporal and Spiritual Penitential Custody

1.   **All coercive power and force of confinement, containment, reflection, penitence and reform** is the Right of *Ius Divinum Penitentiaria* in accord with Article 65 (*Penitentiaria*) of the most sacred Covenant *Pactum De Singularis Caelum*. The method of bestowing the authority of Penitentiaria is reserved to those official bodies duly authorised under the Oratorium, such as the competent forums of the Universal Ecclesia of One Christ.

Temporal and Spiritual Penitential Custody

2.   In accord with Article 65 (*Penitentiaria*) of the most sacred Covenant *Pactum De Singularis Caelum*, when any spirit or living Member openly, willingly and defiantly disobeys the most sacred Laws of Heaven, the enforcement systems of Heaven and Earth may be properly granted the Right of Penitentiaria to enforce the confinement of such a belligerent spirit and mind, until such time as through genuine penitence and knowledge, they recognise the wisdom of the Law and respect:-

Forced Confinement and Penitence

(i)   *Malevolent Ghosts* are immediately subject to Penitentiaria if upon the exercise of proper prayer and invocation of Living Members, such deceased minds refuse to cease and desist from further damaging acts of influence and harm; and

(ii)   *Belligerent Spirits* are immediately subject to Penitentiaria if upon the exercise of the proper Sacred Gifts and Rites they refuse to vacate sacred space or places as required by Law; and

(iii) Wicked and Damaging Beings are immediately subject to Penitentiaria if upon the exercise of the Rite of Exorcism, they belligerently and malevolently refuse to obey and depart from active possession of living bodies, things or places as required by Law.

3.   Any and all forced confinement as Penitentiaria shall be temporary; and no spirit or living being may be condemned under any eternal curse or sentence to such confinement, nor may such confinement be

All Forced Confinement Temporary

434

construed or corrupted to imply cruel and barbaric torture, but the opportunity for the confined mind to reflect, to grow and to heal.

4. In recognition to the end and suppression of the concept and notion of Hell, all sentences of condemnation of deceased and spiritual beings shall be by proper execution of the Right of Penitentiaria through the competent forums of Law of One Christ and none other.

Sentences of Spiritual Custody

The issuance of a sentence of condemnation to Penitentiaria of a deceased and spiritual being shall use the same essential principles as if the person was a living member, subject to the rule of law, justice and fair process.

All sentences of Penitentiaria shall be subject to appeal and clemency and any sentence of Penitentiaria seeking permanent, eternal or unspecified limit of custody shall be morally repugnant, profane, abhorrent and null and void from the time of issuance, having no force or effect.

Article 222 – Great Seal of Divine Mercy and Redemption

1. **J**ust as the Holy Spirit reveals that God and the Divine Creator of all Existence and all Heaven and Earth are united and resolved in absolute Love and Mercy to redeem every single soul, all ecclesiastical churches, orders, bodies, associations, fraternities, institutes, colleges and societies are also absolutely forgiven for past transgressions and errors, upon their absolute acceptance and solemn acknowledgement of the present most sacred Covenant, sealed and bound by their submission to the unity of the Living Body of One Christ. However, any Christian or Jewish church, or order, or body, or association, or fraternity, or institute or college or society that refuses to acknowledge the primacy of the present most sacred Covenant and submit to their redemption, not only accepts full liability but the consequences of their actions are ripened to then be reaped, but by the injury, perfidy and impiety of their actions they call upon all the forces of Heaven and Earth to hold and enforce them to account.

Great Seal of Divine Mercy and Redemption

Any forum of law that disavows the bestowing of Divine Mercy and Divine Forgiveness unto a Christian or Jewish church, or order, or body, or association, or fraternity, or institute or college or society that has submitted itself in solemn and sacred oath and vow to the most sacred Covenant *Pactum De Singularis Caelum* and the present most sacred Covenant, is therefore a forum without jurisdiction or authority.

2. Rejoice! For Christ is Risen! Rejoice! For the Holy Spirit is eternally

Proclamation of the Good News

present within the One True Apostolic Universal Ecclesia of One Christ as the Living Body of Christ! Rejoice! For the Covenant of One Christ is made manifest and through the Kingdom of Heaven upon the Earth now and forever more! Amen.

of such Divine Love

Made in the USA
San Bernardino, CA
10 July 2020